Mark Twain and the Spiritual Crisis of His Age

Studies in American Literary Realism and Naturalism

Mark Twain and the Spiritual Crisis of His Age

Harold K. Bush Jr.

The University of Alabama Press
Tuscaloosa

Typeface: Minion

∞

The paper on which this book is printed
meets the minimum requirements of
American National Standard
for Information Sciences-Permanence of Paper
for Printed Library Materials,
ANSI Z39.48–1984.

Library of Congress Cataloging-in-Publication Data

Bush, Harold K. (Harold Karl), 1956–
Mark Twain and the spiritual crisis of his age / Harold K. Bush, Jr.
Includes bibliographical references and index.
ISBN-13: 978-0-8173-1538-2 (alk. paper)
ISBN-10: 0-8173-1538-1 (alk. paper)
1. Twain, Mark, 1835–1910—Religion. 2. Christianity and literature—United States—History—19th century. I. Title. II. Series.
PS1342.R4B87 2006
818′.409—dc22

2006013112

This book is dedicated to Daniel Harrison Mitsunobu Bush

原　光信

1993–99

"We do not want you to be uninformed, brethren, about those who are asleep."

I Thessalonians 4:13

Contents

Illustrations

Mark Twain and the Spiritual Crisis of His Age

Introduction

A few years after he married, while summering in Elmira, New York, Mark Twain rapidly read and digested W. E. H. Lecky's *History of European Morals from Augustus to Charlemagne* (1869). He wrote a summary of his reactions in the book's margins: "If I have understood this book aright, it proves two things beyond shadow or question: 1: That Christianity is the very invention of Hell itself; 2 & that Christianity is the most precious and elevating and ennobling boon ever vouchsafed to the world."[1] The first half of this inscription constitutes by far the most popular critical approach to Twain's treatment of religion: he mocked and ridiculed it and considered belief to be the root cause of a lot of pain in the world. This much is well known about Twain's views toward religion. Much less, however, has been said about Twain's attraction to and veneration for what Jenny Franchot has called the "invisible domain" of faith, as signified by the second half of the inscription.[2] This attraction is evident throughout Twain's life, from his highly religious courting letters to his future bride, Olivia, to his close friendships with clergymen (especially the Reverend Joseph H. Twichell), his regular attendance at and charitable giving to Twichell's Asylum Hill Congregational Church in Hartford, and more generally to his lifelong championing of moral causes and his cagey deployment of Christian rhetoric. Oddly, however, many biographers overlook Twain's obvious attractions to faith. For example, they regularly omit discussion of Twichell, or relegate him to an almost forgotten status, as in Ken Burns's acclaimed PBS series of 2001, entitled *Mark Twain,* where Twichell gets less than a minute of discussion in the course of a four-hour narrative.[3] The Burns documentary's almost complete silence on matters of religion is symptomatic of a scholarly disregard for the influence of organized religion in literary culture. But in reporting on a culture steeped in religion and belief, as nineteenth-century America most certainly was, such a disregard is bound to provide only part of the story.

This volume will consider how Twain's social and cultural environments were deeply indebted to Christianity of a specific time and place in American history. Much of this debt was positive for Twain, so much so that he could occasionally wax eloquent about Christianity as "the most precious and elevating and ennobling boon ever vouchsafed to the world." But these environments were also fairly shot through with evidence of the numerous religious controversies then confronting the American church. In trying to capture both the obvious and the far-flung aspects invoked by the topic of spirituality, this book attempts a sort of cultural biography of Mark Twain's religious ethos, one focusing on the positive contributions of American religion in the life and works of arguably our most famous author. Obviously we must also discuss religion's negative dimensions, just as Twain often did. But the positive dimensions are the ones that have been most ignored and that deserve most of our attention. The quasi-religious ethos of Twain's adult life—particularly in Hartford, Connecticut, and Elmira, New York—was marked by an intellectual, orthodox Christianity, much of it configured as responses to the spiritual crises at work against it. This muscular version of an intellectually geared faith was modeled in the lives of many of Twain's chief companions, but perhaps none more obviously than the man who became widely known in his lifetime as "Mark Twain's pastor," the Reverend Joseph H. Twichell. The manifestations of Twichell's faith had a central yet underestimated influence in the literary production of Mark Twain, but as with religion in general Twichell's influence has been overlooked.

To a much larger extent than most scholarship has recognized, a culturally engaged writer like Mark Twain was forced to confront religious topics during the period of his greatest work. Religious conflict, and even spiritual crisis, characterized American culture during Twain's lifetime. As the Gilded Age got fully under way after the Civil War, the fervid evangelical Christianity of the antebellum period began to explore new directions. These rapid changes were largely the result of what historian Paul Carter has called "the spiritual crisis of the Gilded Age."[4] More broadly, during the period of Twain's artistic maturity (1870–1900), Christianity and religion in general underwent several philosophical attacks that issued in some of the most sweeping changes in the history of the American church. Such attacks came on several fronts: the widespread impact of Darwinian theories of evolution; the popularization in America of the German higher criticism of the Bible; the growing interest in theories of the unconscious and human psychology; rapid advances in astronomy; the lingering grief and trauma from the Civil War, which spawned widespread epistemological doubt about God, providence, and the American mission; and the widely publicized heresy trials of several leading clergymen, such as David Swing and Charles Briggs. Between 1878 and 1906 almost every major Protestant denomination experienced at least one heresy trial, usually of a seminary professor, and almost always these trials were highly publicized and politicized.[5] In fact, the emerging spiritual crisis may be best exemplified by the most famous trial of all: that of Henry Ward Beecher in 1874–75, where America's greatest preacher stood accused of adultery as well as, in effect, heresy. But perhaps most sinister of all factors were simply the corrupting effects of growing wealth, ease, leisure, and prestige upon Christian America. By the turn of the century, the steady increase in the nation's wealth resulted in spiritual laziness, self-satisfaction, and moral complacency, and became a major topic for Sunday sermons to the faithful.[6] Similarly, screeds against wealth and greed were a common topic for Mark Twain.

Despite the manifold crises facing the church during Twain's adulthood, it is no exaggeration to say that the 1870s and 1880s must be identified as the period when American Christianity faced two primary intellectual challenges—specifically from, first, the German higher criticism of the Bible and secondly from Darwinian evolution. Much has been made of the spread of theories of evolutionism into mainstream American culture, and generally it is well known how the ideas of Charles Darwin, Herbert Spencer, and Thomas Huxley affected traditional beliefs about the creation as narrated in the book of Genesis.[7] Conversely, very much less is commonly known about the spread of higher criticism or its effects on virtually every area of modern biblical criticism. Protestant churchmen of the second part of the nineteenth century were much more alarmed about the implications of the higher criticism than they were about evolution; in fact, many of the leading lights of the church, including Beecher, Josiah Strong, Phillips Brooks, and others, embraced the basic tenets of evolution. One historian has claimed, "Of all intellectual currents within American Protestantism in the late nineteenth century, none was more controversial than the higher criticism of the Scriptures. The movement that submitted the Bible to historical analysis proved to be one of the most crucial challenges the American churches were to face."[8] The uncanny emergence of these two philosophically related phenomena at almost exactly the same time (and, more to the point, during the major period of Twain's career) constituted a devastating double-barreled attack on the traditional dogmas of the Christian church. The result was a spiritual crisis that rocked the world of American evangelicalism—a crisis from which American Christianity is still trying to recover.

In a striking manner, Twain's own spiritual development—and spiritual crises—mirrored many of the major trends and developments in American religion.[9] His movement from a rather primitive form of Protestant Christianity, through deism, and later into more scientific and psychological forms of belief roughly squares with the general movements detectable in the nation as a whole. Twain was a highly curious and widely read cultural observer, and he dabbled at various times in virtually all of these emerging areas of spiritual import: scientific theories that bore upon religious belief, such as those of Darwin and Spencer; biblical criticism and the historical nature of the Bible; religious eccentricities ranging from Mormonism to Christian Science to spiritualism and the occult; and scholarly breakthroughs in fields as diverse as astronomy, geology, comparative religion, and anthropology that related directly to issues of faith. Considering "the spiritual crisis of the Gilded Age," it is hard not to notice how much it coincides with Twain's struggles as well as the emergence of his darker, more utilitarian approach to religion. As a result, the major trends and developments in American religion throughout the post–Civil War era, during which Twain published his most important literary works, provide a fascinating lens through which his literary life and works can usefully be perceived. As it turns out, many of his literary works respond, implicitly or explicitly, to issues at the center of the spiritual crisis of his age.

Thus a religious sensibility is helpful in recovering the ideological structures that reigned in the eastern states where Twain resided for the most productive period of his career. Curiously, however, most critics have remained silent on the subject of Twain and American religion, or else they have told only part of the story. The neglect of religious or Christian approaches to literary or cultural histories may even suggest an institutional bias against such methods in graduate schools and publishing venues over the past several decades. The sociologist Christian Smith, drawing upon Pierre Bourdieu, describes what he calls the "habitus" of research universities today as involving "deeply internalized mental schemes that correspond to and reinforce particular social conditions, and that operate often prereflectively through human actors." This habitus of mind, Smith suggests, is one that has resulted more and more in what he describes as "academic anti-religion."[10] To whatever extent we are willing to consider such a view, it might help explain why the religious sensibilities and interests of a major literary figure like Mark Twain have been overlooked for so long. In addition, "religion" itself has unfortunately come to be considered by many a bad thing, lumped together as it often is with particular institutions that have been historically oppressive. For example, the church's complicity with the rise of American empire has by now been thoroughly recognized (a complicity Mark Twain wrote about frequently one hundred years ago). Thus today it has become a commonplace to reject the term *religious* in favor of the more postmodern term *spiritual,* which is less burdened with negative connotations.

One unfortunate result of these factors has been the marginalization of the positive and edifying effects of religion in American literary culture. This marginalization has helped foster a caricature of Mark Twain as an acidic, cynical, and finally even blasphemous observer of American religious life. One typically thinks of an old, despair- and grief-ridden white-haired man shaking his fist at a silent God, snarling in rage at the weak-minded and hypocritical American church, and writing devastating critical assaults against the contents of Holy Scripture. Arguments have even been advanced that Twain was for all practical purposes an atheist.[11] These reductive depictions feature Twain sarcastically dismissing the teachings of any number of preachers and authors as wild hogwash, including well-known American religious figures such as

Beecher, T. DeWitt Talmage, Elizabeth Stuart Phelps, Dwight Moody, Brigham Young, Mary Baker Eddy, and General Lew Wallace. All of these versions present important insights about Twain's religious views that are not inaccurate, but they provide only half of the story. Indeed this half of the story has been well represented over the years.[12]

Today, as the habitus of the academy begins to shift to a more inclusive view of religion, work is beginning to burgeon in this area. Critics are noticing more and more that Twain demonstrated a strong affinity with American manifestations of religion, particularly Protestant Christianity, throughout his career.[13] This affinity began as early as his close relationship with his mother, Jane Lampton Clemens, and her keen interest in the frontier Protestantism of his Missouri youth. Beyond Hannibal the most obvious signs of Twain's continuing religious quest would include such things as his friendships with preachers and pastors; his charitable giving and consistent church attendance in both Hartford and Elmira; his continual reading of books related to theology; his great fondness for church music such as hymns; his deep immersion in African American spirituals and jubilees; his strong attractions toward and often financial support for Social Gospel good works and the people who carried them out; his powerful sense of sympathy for the poor and oppressed of all nations; his consistent attempts to think theologically and to provide solid ethical training in a good deal of his published work; his strong personal interest in the welfare of the Chinese, the Jews, the American Indians, and many other marginalized groups; his passionate commitment to versions of the American civil religion; his almost religious fervor for the Union heroes of the Civil War; his resounding critique of the southern Lost Cause ideology; his lifelong philosophical examination of the nature of mankind; his frequent meanderings into questions of mind science, the occult, and the survival of the human soul after death; and his almost obsessive desire to foster an idealized version of the happy Victorian home, with wife Livy as the angel of the household.

But as has already been claimed, perhaps the most obvious illustration of Twain's spiritual inclinations, and one of the best places to start, is in his choice of friends. Throughout his career as world-famous author, his most intimate male relationship was with his parish pastor in

Hartford, Connecticut. The friendship with Joe Twichell is crucial in any attempt to come to terms with Twain's views of the Christian life and the spiritual conflicts that marked his most productive years. And yet numerous scholars have labored under the inaccurate impression that these two brilliant men carried on a friendship that was decidedly nonreligious, so much so that this odd notion has become almost a truism in Twain biographical criticism. But this claim must be rejected once and for all. Twain's initial biographer, Albert B. Paine, was responsible for suggesting that the Twichell-Twain friendship was nonreligious. But Paine's information came primarily from a despondent Twain near the end of his life. William Dean Howells appears to have believed the same thing, and many critics have followed their lead in dismissing either Twain's religious sentiment or the orthodox commitments of his closest friends, including Twichell.[14]

According to Paine, a decisive moment came in Switzerland in 1878. Significantly it occurred just "a day or two" after a conversation revealing the tender side of Mark Twain toward his pastor: "Twichell, finding him in a responsive mood—a remorseful mood—gave his sympathy, and spoke of the larger sympathy of divinity."[15] Apparently only days later Twain supposedly confessed his lack of belief to Twichell: "Joe . . . I'm going to make a confession. I don't believe in your religion at all. I've been living a lie right straight along whenever I pretended to. For a moment, sometimes, I have been almost a believer, but it immediately drifts away from me again."[16] This episode, claimed Paine, ended for all practical purposes any talk that these two friends would ever have on religion again: "So the personal side of religious discussion closed between them and was never afterwards reopened."[17]

But we should compare Twain's account several decades after the fact with Twichell's version written within days of the supposed argument. In a letter to his wife, Harmony, Twichell described an evening with Twain in Switzerland, probably only a day or two prior to the falling-out that Paine describes. It is difficult to date various sections of the letter, but it seems to have been composed over several days, with the following passage written on August 10 or 11, 1878. Indeed it also appears likely that here Twichell is describing the incident that ostensibly set the table for Twain's confession of disbelief days later:

> Mark and I had a good talk after dinner this evening on religion. A good talk, I say: he got to speaking of himself in a way that gave me a chance to declare gospel truth to him. "Romola" started it. Mark observed that he had been seeing himself as in a looking glass in the skillful uncovering of the workings of motive which characterize the book. And presently he said "There's nothing that makes me hate myself so, and feel so mean as to have Livy praise me and express a good opinion of me, when I know all the while that I am a humbug, and no such person as she takes me to be." He said this very heartily, and I sympathized with him, dear, and told him that I knew just how it was, having experienced the same humiliation from a like cause myself. And so we got into the subject of character and the state of the heart, and the application of Christ's gospel to the wants of a sinful man.
>
> People don't know Mark's best side. I am more persuaded of it than ever. It isn't at-all strange, of course, and I wish it was different. Would that the grace might touch him with power and lead him into larger views of things spiritual than he has ever yet seen!! He is exceedingly considerate toward me in regard of everything, or most things, where he apprehends that my religious feelings are concerned. Now to-day he wanted very much to go three or four hours by rail on our way to Lucerne, and so divide the ten hours tedious journey we must make tomorrow. There is no Sunday here, you understand, and all the trains run as usual, and travel is in full tide. But when he saw that I objected to it,—on the mere hint—he dropped the matter at once, and with perfect good nature, and hasn't referred to it since. And when we kneel down together at night to pray, it always seems to bring the spirit of gentleness upon him, and he is very likely to be affectionate after it. After all, coarse as he is in streaks, he is a genuinely loveable fellow.[18]

Twichell's comments suggest a kind and loving friendship between two men who utterly respect each other. We should note here, for example, the mention of Twain's compliant participation in prayer and Sabbath observance with his pastor and good friend. The passage commences with a brief reference to George Eliot's novel *Romola* (1863), which we know from notebook entries Twain had purchased and begun reading on August 10, either the day before the passage was written or perhaps even the day of the "good talk after dinner this evening on religion." *Romola* is a story of fifteenth-century Florence, at the crucial moment of the emergence of modern Europe. The title character, Romola, is an idealistic young woman who becomes deeply disillusioned, partly due to the political realities of this turbulent period of Florentine history. She marries a man named Tito Melema, a newcomer to Florence who rapidly gains power through a series of political maneuvers. He betrays Romola's father, selling him into slavery after his political use has run out. Tito stands for the extremes of self-promotion and self-interest that lay at the heart of the emergent Machiavellian approach to modern political intrigue.

Among other things, Twain's reading of *Romola* had clearly pricked his own conscience, as we know from his notebook jottings: "At last I came upon the only passage which has thus far *hit me with force*—Tito compromising with his conscience & resolving to do, not a bad thing, but not the *best* thing."[19] Twichell had commented in his letter to Harmony that Twain reacted to the novel's characterization of Tito as if he were "seeing himself as in a looking glass in the skillful uncovering of the workings of motives which characterizes the book." If Twain did see himself mirrored in the character of Tito, it testifies to his perception of his own corrupt motivations, including betrayals and self-interested manipulations. In effect, it is a confession of a profound sense of moral failure. In this context, it is intriguing that Twichell remarks on Twain's "spirit of gentleness" and his "best side," even as he makes clear his sense that Twain needs more of God's grace and a fuller revelation of God's power in his life.

The upshot is that Twichell's letter reveals a tender moment of pastoral counseling. One hardly gets the sense from this letter of impending religious animosity between these two men. It is significant that Paine's rendition of the manifestation of such animosity just days subsequent is completely reliant on Twain's memory of the events almost thirty years later. The lack of animosity is confirmed by the fact that Twain wrote an apology to Twichell at the end of the trip: "Ah, my boy, it has been such a rich holiday to me; + I feel under such deep + honest obligations to you for coming. I am putting out of my mind all memory of the times when I misbehaved toward you + hurt you; I am resolved to consider it forgiven, + to store up + remember only the charming hours of the journeys, + the times when I was not unworthy to be with you and share a companionship which to me stands first after Livy's."[20] Although Twain does admit here to some sort of "misbehavior" that apparently "hurt" Twichell, these remarks do not have the feel of a spiritual falling-out, as suggested by Paine's account.

Thus evidence suggests that the religious quarrel between these two friends is little more than a fabrication almost thirty years after the fact. And certainly the book that issued from the trip, *A Tramp Abroad* (1880), shows no animosity from Twain toward his traveling companion. If anything, it provides a touching and fond evocation of the mannerisms and character of Harris, Twain's fictitious traveling companion who is based upon Twichell. Twain does poke fun at his good friend on occasion—"he was a rabid Protestant"—particularly in his sarcastic jabs at Harris's apparent prejudice against Roman Catholics.[21] But significantly that section is followed immediately with commentary on Harris's moral sympathies, punctuated with Twain's clear admiration for Harris. In addition *A Tramp Abroad* is distinctive among Twain's books for its attention to the theme of the sublime, especially its sensitivity to the beauty of nature as representative of God's grandeur. This American version of the sublime was a major aspect of American landscape painting of the mid-nineteenth century, and it owes a literary debt to the transcendentalists of Concord, such as Emerson and Thoreau.[22] Certainly attention to the sublime is notable among Twain's other writings, particularly in some of the most beautiful passages of pastoralism to be found in *Adventures of Huckleberry Finn* and *Life on the Mississippi.* But in *A Tramp Abroad,* the experience of the sublime in nature is often linked specifically to God. Regarding the breathtaking views of the Jungfrau region in Switzerland, Twain writes: "One had the sense of being under the brooding contemplation of a spirit, not an inert mass of rocks and ice,—a spirit which had looked down, through the slow drifts of the ages, upon a million vanished races of men, and judged them. . . . the Great Spirit of the Mountain breathed his own peace upon their hurt minds and sore hearts, and healed them; they could not think base thoughts or do mean and sordid things here, before the visible throne of God." Regarding the glaciers near Zermatt, he writes: "It is all magnificent. That short valley is a picture gallery of a notable kind, for it contains no mediocrities; from end to end the Creator has hung it with His masterpieces." Perhaps the most famous moment of the sublime is Twain standing before Mont Blanc in France:

> [it] had a mellow something about it which was very different from the hard white glare of the kind of daylight I was used to. Its radiance was strong and clear, but at the same time it was singularly soft, and spiritual, and benignant. . . . It was a spectacle to take one's breath, for the wonder of it, and the sublimity. . . . There is no simile for it, for nothing is like it. If a child had asked me what it was, I should have said, "Humble yourself, in this presence, it is the glory flowing from the hidden hand of the Creator."[23]

While it is true that sometimes Twain lifted passages like these from travel books in order to lampoon them, these passages have an authentic ring and are presented without irony.

It is notable that these triumphant moments of sublime revelation all take place in the company of Joe Twichell. It is also worth observing that Twain's depictions here of a mysterious and perhaps unknowable God reflect the more poetical and less certain visions of God that intellectuals widely embraced after the Civil War. This poetical approach to God was championed most famously by Horace Bushnell, Joe Twichell's spiritual mentor and friend of Mark Twain, and to some extent it signals the effects of the higher criticism.[24] As such, Twain's versions of God's grandeur interrogate evangelical certainty and thus are symptomatic of the issues at stake between him and his pastor—as well as issues at the heart of the spiritual crisis of their age. Twain signals his nostalgia for an older style of pre-scientific faith (and pre-higher criticism) at the conclusion of the Mont Blanc passage: "We have not the reverent feeling for the rainbow that a savage has, because we know how it is made. We have lost as much as we have gained by prying into that matter."[25] Nevertheless, Twain's rendering of his experience at Mont Blanc, along with numerous other episodes in *A Tramp Abroad,* are some of the most beautiful expressions of a fundamentally theistic position in any of his writings—even though they memorialize the very days when he supposedly had forever given up "religious discussion" with Twichell. And they are representative of Twain's general view of God, revealed in his private notebook as late as 1898: "He is the perfect artisan, the perfect artist. Everything which He has made is fine, everything which He has made is beautiful; nothing coarse, nothing ugly has ever come from His hand. Even His materials are all delicate, none of them is coarse. . . . The contemplation of it moves one to something of the same awe and reverence which the march of the comets through their billion mile orbit compels. This is indeed a God!"[26]

Aside from these materials, much more evidence over the remaining decades of their lives indicates that we must dismiss Paine's characterization of the Twain-Twichell friendship as ceasing all connections with religion after 1878. In fact almost countless spiritual discussions and religious activities can be documented. Even Paine contradicts himself on this issue. For example, in his comments on some letters between Twain and Twichell in 1902, Paine notes that the exchange typifies their "regular arguments on theology . . . arguments that had been going on between them for more than thirty years."[27] Paine says this despite his having claimed that religious discussion ceased in 1878. A more accurate depiction of their friendship would note that it was often geared toward issues of religion, morality, and ethics. The fact is that the Twain-Twichell correspondence, despite the earlier misconceptions that the religious aspects of the friendship diminished or even disappeared after 1878, often features serious reflection on religious topics and concerns. The letters make it clear that these two men carried on a friendship that was profoundly shaped by the religious belief and the ethical and moral character of Twichell, a minister of unusual gifts and of wide-ranging intellectual interests.

Furthermore Twain's relationship with Twichell was an extremely intimate one. Almost from their first meeting, Twain and Twichell formed a deep personal attachment to one another. Indeed, it was probably the single most important friendship of Twain's life after that with his wife Olivia. Certainly this idea is confirmed in Twain's own words in the letter to Twichell after the tramp through Europe: "I am resolved to store up and remember only the charming hours of the journeys and the times when I was not unworthy to be with you, and share a companionship which to me stands first after Livy's."[28] Similarly, Twain compared Livy and Twichell in a 1902 speech: "She has been the best friend I have ever had, and that is saying a good deal; she has reared me—she and

Twichell together—and what I am I owe to them."[29] The Twain-Twichell personal letters so brim with filial piety and genuine devotion that one critic has labeled them "love letters."[30] And yet somehow Joe Twichell, and all that he stands for, has not been a major interest of Twain scholars.

It is also curious that Twichell, a firm believer, would allow himself to become so attached to a man considered by many to be a strident infidel. So we might begin by also asking, what was it about Twain that so many have misunderstood but that his attachment to Twichell seems to suggest intuitively? The letters of recommendation from his western acquaintances, written in 1869 to convince Jervis Langdon that Twain was worthy to wed his beloved daughter Olivia, all gave one-sided interpretations of Twain that emphasized a wild and dissolute, if not ungodly, lifestyle. Ironically, even to this day, the predominant view regarding Twain's moral and religious nature is similarly negative in most critical appraisals. But Twichell seemed to understand that there was another part to the story—he truly believed that "people don't know Mark's best side. I am more persuaded of it than ever."

My contention is that Twichell was correct about this more hidden side of Mark Twain. There is abundant evidence of Twain's strong religious proclivities throughout his life, and yet most people still don't recognize "Mark's best side." It even makes sense to summarize America's most famous author in the same way that he once summarized himself—as "a moralist in disguise."[31] Unfortunately, until fairly recently scholarship has not attempted to analyze Twain's engagement with religion, particularly as a social dynamic. Part of this aversion may have to do with the negative connotations of *religion* for many people these days. At the outset, I would like to introduce a fluid and open understanding of the term *religion,* one that invokes the overall ideologies and beliefs that inform a person's view of the cosmos, the individual, and society. In describing my use of *religion,* Paul Carter's phrase depicting a "spiritual" crisis may in some ways be very apt, but in others not so helpful. It helps us today because in the present moment *spiritual* has become such a favored term. Frequently one hears from intelligent adults the distinction that they are "spiritual, but not religious," a phrase that has become so conspicuous that Robert C. Fuller used it as the title of his influential volume discussing the phenomenon. According to Fuller, until very recently *religious* and *spiritual* were basically synonyms. But now as many as 20 percent of Americans describe themselves without irony as "spiritual, but not religious."[32] The abandonment of the term *religious* for purposes of self-identification apparently refers to the speaker's skepticism toward "organized religion," even though that speaker desires to be understood as a person of metaphysical curiosity and even perhaps commitment. On the other hand, *spiritual* can seem otherworldly, somehow disconnected with the activities of our daily lives—and thus it is a highly privatized phenomenon.

This sense of spirituality could hardly be further from the truth of most forms of nineteenth-century American Christianity, which was so focused on the real conditions of our world that it became known as Social Christianity. Somehow in our own day, religion and spirituality have become divorced from morality and ethics—a disconnection based to some extent on the influence of the so-called "secularization hypothesis" posited around the middle of the twentieth century by numerous influential social historians and critics. This hypothesis rests on the unproven premise that America—like other Western societies—would become increasingly secular to the point that virtually all religious activity would inevitably disappear. If this were true, morality and ethics, which were extremely important to the survival and viability of democracy, must be divorced from religion as quickly as possible. But we are now into the twenty-first century, and the complete secularization of America has not commenced. Indeed in some ways America seems even more religious than ever. More importantly the desire to separate the spiritual from the secular has been widely critiqued and rejected by numerous scholars. As Robert McAfee Brown has argued, this mistaken desire can be called the "Great Fallacy" of American thought: the fallacy, deriving from Greek gnosticism, that somehow we can separate the spiritual realm from the "unclean" social or material realms. Brown correctly points out that the Great Fallacy, which insists on an opposition between the secular and the spiritual, generally benefits the powerful, the wealthy, and the status quo. By keeping the world as it is and by emphasizing salvation and redemption as otherworldly activities, the Great Fallacy ends up frustrating and ultimately stagnating the work of the Kingdom of God in the here and now. Brown and many other contemporary theologians plainly reject such a notion and demonstrate how the Great Fallacy has fostered a philosophical disaster in the American

Christian church, affecting areas as diverse as the environment, biochemical research, education, labor and unions, and even diet and medicine.[33] Here I want to join a number of recent critics who question these distinctions and reject the employment of a dubious sacred versus secular opposition.

Certainly the boundary between spiritual and secular America would have been unthinkable for most Americans during Mark Twain's lifetime. The insistence today that a person can indeed be quite "ethical" even if that person is not "religious" might have baffled many Americans of the Gilded Age. This confusion would seem to be based on changing preconceptions about what ethics and religion actually are, but it also reflects the nineteenth century's unwillingness to separate the sacred from the secular. Religion, according to some of today's formulations, might mean doctrinal assertions, such as the existence of a transcendent being, or might involve participation in some sort of religious community. But one might just as easily argue, as I am doing, that ethical behavior itself demonstrates certain elements of religion. As one philosopher has put it, religion is most simply one's "orientation to ultimate reality"—a definition typical of many other recent attempts to boil down the idea of religion.[34] In this sense religion is an umbrella term, and under it spirituality, ethics, and morality become aspects of one's set of ultimate beliefs about the cosmos and human society.

I am not the first to suggest that religion originates in the attempt to represent and order beliefs, feelings, imaginings, and actions that arise in response to direct experience of the sacred and the spiritual. This insight was reflected in arguably the major work of the philosophy of religion produced in Mark Twain's lifetime, William James's *The Varieties of Religious Experience* (1902). There James defines religion as "the feelings, acts, and experiences of individual men in their solitude, so far as they apprehend themselves to stand in relation to whatever they may consider the divine."[35] Obviously, according to this definition, religion includes ethics and morality, since both involve one's "feelings, acts, and experiences." While in former days the sacred and spiritual might have mainly meant the institutions of the Christian tradition, it need not do so, according to James's formulation: the sacred might reside in any number of values or creeds, such as human freedom, the Declaration of Independence, and equality. And according to James's "principle of pragmatism," conviction and action are solidly joined in the real activities of our everyday lives: "Beliefs, in short, are really rules for action; and the whole function of thinking is but one step in the production of habits of action."[36] Religion is essentially one process of belief by which an individual creates meaning on a sustaining basis, in relation to whatever that individual considers divine or godlike, and from that meaning lives and acts a certain way. Pragmatically speaking, religion becomes one of many forms of belief that affect our habits. But as James argued, religion is also a highly personal affair that begins with "individual men in their solitude," a focus that presages our postmodern code word for religion par excellence, *spirituality.*

Socially, individual beliefs coalesce to form what Robert Bellah and his associates have called the "moral ecology" of a particular time and place. Bellah describes moral ecology as "[the] web of moral understandings and commitments that tie people together in community."[37] Bellah's desire was to locate "a moral language that [would] transcend [America's] radical individualism."[38] His ideas here echo the earlier formulations of Americanists such as Sacvan Bercovitch, who theorized ideology as "the ground and texture of consensus . . . the system of interlinked ideas, symbols, and beliefs by which a culture—any culture—seeks to justify and perpetuate itself; the web of rhetoric, ritual, and assumption through which society coerces, persuades, and coheres."[39] However, one crucial weakness of Bercovitch's formulation is its abstractness, its lack of embodiment. Bellah goes beyond Bercovitch by insisting that such a moral language is not good enough in and of itself: there must always be a "living reenactment that gives cultural ideals their power to organize life."[40] That is, moral ecologies are always crucially dependent on the social lives of their participants.

A major symptom of the move toward the privatization of religion in our culture is the extent to which considerations of a person's religious life have been limited to one's intellectual assent to or dissent from doctrine. Certainly such an emphasis has marred our understanding of Mark Twain's religious life by insisting on it being primarily the story of his rejection of doctrine. But an emphasis on mere dogma represents just one aspect of religion. Granted, for North American Protestants it has been perhaps the crucial aspect by which all others have been judged or measured. But when we place our focus on doctrine, we exclude other areas of Twain's life that clearly affirmed his religious sensibility—including his participation in the Social Christianity of Hartford and Elmira. As James stated, "beliefs are really rules for action." Indeed Twain's embrace of and consistent participation in aspects of Christian social life, along with its effects in his thinking and writing, have caused one commentator to make the claim that, for all practical purposes, throughout Twain's life he was "ethically" a Christian: "For in his life, truth, honor, and lofty ideals are the fabric of his character. No one ever held a greater admiration for the ideals of Christianity than Mark nor ever felt more remorse when those principles were degraded."[41] We might alter this phrase slightly to invoke James and suggest that Twain was in certain ways "pragmatically" a Christian. The germane point is the relative value of doctrinal purity as opposed to social activism and ethical behavior. It explains why Mark Twain, though he never believed all things that Christians are "supposed" to believe, did occasionally state unequivocally his intention to "be a Christian. I shall climb—climb—climb toward this bright sun that is shining in the heaven of my happiness. I shall be worthy—yet."[42] But it also may help us understand why he persisted in various Christian "habits of the heart" for as long as he did, even while doubting them internally or even castigating them in public. Indeed, late in life, he once admitted that he would have been better off if he had paid even closer attention to these habits of religion.

My approach in this book subordinates theory to praxis, meaning that I align myself with numerous influential thinkers today who envision Christian faith more as a social phenomenon than as chiefly a matter of intellectual assent.[43] As a result, this project is secondarily concerned with reconceptualizing religion as primarily a social activity and then showing how such a conception might help us reenvision a major writer like Mark Twain. As the theologian Stanley Hauerwas has recently argued, Christian ethics must always be considered a deeply social ethic. Hauerwas puts it this way:

> The notion that one can distinguish between personal and social ethics distorts the nature of Christian convictions. . . . The church does not have a social ethic; the church is a social ethic. . . . It is a call for the church to be a community which tries to develop the resources to stand

> within the world witnessing to the peaceable kingdom and thus rightly understanding the world. The gospel is a political gospel. . . . It is a politics of the kingdom that reveals the insufficiency of all politics based on coercion and falsehood and finds the true source of power in servanthood rather than dominion.[44]

Elsewhere Hauerwas restates his vision of the social element of the Christian faith: "Through the teaching, support, sacrifice, worship, and commitment of the church, utterly ordinary people are enabled to do some rather extraordinary, even heroic acts, not on the basis of their own gifts or abilities, but rather by having a community capable of sustaining Christian virtue. The church enables us to be better people than we could have been if left to our own devices."[45]

Hauerwas's vision of the communal nature of ethics shows how dependent we all are on those around us in forming our codes and even our vocabularies. Alasdair MacIntyre has claimed that the cultures to which we attach ourselves are always dramatic proclamations about what matters most to us. Cultural traditions are always attempts to incarnate and model arguments about the meaning and destiny of the members of those traditions. But at root they are also concerned primarily with disseminating to followers a moral language rooted in real experience.[46] And so this book will also attempt a recovery of the moral language and cultural traditions that Mark Twain drew upon in creating his literary legacy. A moral ecology is a manifestation of what a person thinks about himself and his world, what he values most—and postbellum Hartford was such a manifestation for Mark Twain.

In these contexts, religion is understood as profoundly social rather than merely intellectual; incarnational rather than merely propositional; this-worldly rather than otherworldly; and holistic rather than merely dualistic or Gnostic. Religion is resistant, in other words, to the Great Fallacy and thus opposed to the status quo. And yet the liberal Protestantism of the late nineteenth century is not today considered very subversive and in fact struggled to manifest itself as such. Still, it bore much fruit. Twain's literary achievement is often directly indebted to the Social Gospel's vision of cosmic hope, and Twain's use of hopefulness greatly complicates his view of the profound fallenness of humanity. The overall impact of Mark Twain's religious experience on his personal life and writings, and in particular the genteel Congregationalism that was at the center of post–Civil War Connecticut and New York, has been underestimated—an oversight that has hampered attempts at coming to grips with Twain's artistic achievement. But our critical oversight may owe as much to a recalcitrant unwillingness to stretch our concept of what really counts as "religious." For example, Twain's involvement in the propagation of the cultural memory of the Civil War, including his critiques of southern Lost Cause ideology, his support for Unionist civil religion, and his frequent sermonizing on the idea of America, can all be understood in a religious frame. In this context, Twain becomes a much more "religious" figure than he is traditionally thought to be. And the story of Mark Twain's engagement with the "spiritual crisis of his age" will invite us to see his literary and public career in an entirely new light—as a profoundly moral and religious one.

1

Mark Twain's Roots

Hannibal, the River, and the West

The Declaration of Independence of 1776 makes its primary appeal to "the laws of nature and nature's God"—a phrase that highlights a harmony between the spheres of science and theology, physics and metaphysics. The recognition of this harmony was a staple of the early republic's Enlightenment-style deism, shared by Jefferson and his cohort of founders. However, by the time of the Declaration's one-hundred-year celebration in 1876, a moment that coincided with Mark Twain reaching his peak powers as a writer, the laws of nature and the laws of God seemed to be not at all harmonized, but greatly at odds with each other. Scientists were making grand proclamations that called into question the so-called laws of religion, while theologians were rethinking traditional ideas in light of science's rapid changes. As Twain came to maturity as an author, "two apprehensions, of 'revealed' religion and of reason and science, were becoming aligned against each other. . . . Two ways of knowing, two avenues to Truth, were in conflict."[1]

If we recognize the pervasive manner in which this opposition typified nineteenth-century America, we will not be surprised to see how it typified the life and times of Mark Twain. To begin with, it provides a shorthand for understanding the religious influence passed on to him from those two most formative teachers, his parents. According to this gendered model, Sam's mother, Jane Lampton Clemens, would be most closely associated with the "feminized" revealed religion of an older order, while his father, John Marshal Clemens, would be associated with the emerging "masculine" sensibilities of science, reason, and ultimately business and industry. The influence of his parents came in the form of a tension between these two competing ways of knowing—one that was similar to the growing antagonisms within the general culture.

Young Sam's emerging faith in God is seen most prominently in his desire to manifest and to foster sympathy for others, and his primary model for this guiding moral sense was by his own admission his mother, Jane. Once he noted "it is at our mother's knee that we acquire our highest and noblest and purest ideals but there is seldom any money in them."[2] This humorous quote is itself gendered, setting the maternal instinct of religion against the masculine concerns of breadwinning. In a memoir Twain wrote on the occasion of his mother's death in 1890, her "large nature and liberal sympathies" are the dominant themes (figure 1):

> The greatest difference which I find between her and the rest of the people whom I have known, is this, and it is a remarkable one: those others felt a strong interest in a few things, whereas to the very day of her death she felt a strong interest in the whole world and everything and everybody in it. In all her life she never knew such a thing as a half-hearted interest in affairs and people, or an interest which drew a line and left out certain affairs and was indifferent to certain people. The invalid who takes a strenuous and indestructible interest in everything and everybody but himself, and to whom a dull moment is an unknown thing and an impossibility, is a formidable adversary for disease and a hard invalid to vanquish. I am certain it was this feature of my mother's make-up that carried her so far toward ninety.

Twain recalled that "[s]he had a slender small body, but a large heart; a heart so large that everybody's griefs and everybody's joys found welcome in it and hospitable accommodation."[3] This implicit biblical allusion refers to a Christian's ability to sympathize with whatever emotion another person is experiencing, as in Romans 12:15: "Rejoice with those who rejoice, and weep with those who weep." Strikingly, the first mental "photograph" of Jane that Twain gives in the essay is of a grief-stricken mother moaning intensely over the dead body of his older

1. Jane Lampton Clemens at 85. Courtesy of the Mark Twain Project, Bancroft Library, University of California, Berkeley.

brother Benjamin in May 1842. Twain recalled how she had asked him and the other children to place their hands, one by one, on Benjamin's still cheek. He never forgot her anguish and immediately recalled it at the outset of his moving sketch in tribute to her.

Much of Twain's description of his mother avoids strictly religious vocabulary in describing what is essentially a religious or moral characterization. However, by invoking her "liberal sympathies," claiming that she had a large heart that exercised grief and joy with any person, and in particular by depicting her as a figure of bereavement over lost children, Twain is calling upon major features of the religious sensibilities and moral ethos of his time. In nineteenth-century America, the rise of sympathy as a moral category is most often associated with the Scottish "Common Sense" philosophers, whose leading thinkers included the Earl of Shaftesbury, Adam Smith, Francis Hutcheson, Thomas Reid, and Hugh Blair. Hutcheson, for example, drew upon Shaftesbury's supposed discovery of a "moral sense" and then described additional "finer powers of perception." The outworking of these moral sensibilities required, according to Hutcheson, the exercise of the "benevolent affections," meaning charitable acts done solely for the good of other human beings, and "sympathy," which was "an ability to feel along with others both in 'compassion' for their troubles and in 'congratulation' for their happiness." According to Gregg Camfield, Hutcheson's theory of the moral sensibility became a central precept for the Common Sense school: "the sympathetic social impulse was the fundamental precondition of society and in turn of moral behavior."[4] Without the moral sense, society could not possibly cohere, nor could it ever progress.

This understanding of sympathy became important in sentimentalism. We can characterize sentimental ideology as "the cultural expression of the desire for union. Sentimentalism is a manifestation of the belief in or yearning for consonance—or even unity—of principal and purpose. Sympathy complements the work of sentiment: each can be defined as a set of registered impulses psychologically connecting an individual to things and people outside of him or her."[5] This desired psychological connection originates in the sentimentalist's assumption that a code of Christian morality and theology is shared by the sentimental writer herself (or himself), the individuals whom she or he addresses, and the object or objective of "the work of sentiment." The term *sentimental* applies to literature that "paradoxically both assumes and seeks to bring about an emotional and moral alliance between reader and text (an alliance at once so mystical and material that critics generally read it as excessive), an intimacy that is rooted in common cultural assumptions about virtue and piety."[6]

In Hartford, Mark Twain became next-door neighbors with Harriet Beecher Stowe, one of the movement's most exemplary figures. Her novel *Uncle Tom's Cabin* exemplifies the cultural work of popular, pietistic sentimentalism: "to assure us that we can and do feel culturally sanctioned and even socially prescribed emotions strongly."[7] The emphasis on feeling correctly is commonly seen as the major motivational focus of *Uncle Tom's Cabin,* as in the well-known passage in the "Concluding Remarks":

> There is one thing that every individual can do,—they can see to it they feel right. An atmosphere of sympathetic influence encircles every human being; and the man or woman who feels strongly, healthily, and justly, on the great interests of humanity, is the constant benefactor to the human race. See, then, to your sympathies in this matter! Are they in harmony with the sympathies of Christ? Or are they swayed and perverted by the sophistries of worldly policy?[8]

One can only be sympathetic insofar as one is in touch with the transcendent—as manifested through the "atmosphere of sympathetic influence" that surrounds each of us.

Typically sentiment was gendered as a feminine trait in Mark Twain's world. It is certainly true that much of Twain's early work emphasized his masculinity and to some extent his disdain for the sentimental. However, much of his greatest achievement derives from his dependence on the human desire to form union and solidarity with others—and as such, is sentimental in temperament. Twain's essay on his mother was an exemplary moment in his career as a sentimentalist, and it shows that despite his frequent satires of emotional excess, sometimes sentiment was not only appropriate but even necessary. It also reveals a man who believed that his own moral attributes originated at his mother's knee. One of his most important fictional depictions of his mother is the character of Mrs. Carpenter, the mother in the "Hellfire Hotchkiss" stories (1897). Written several years after the death of his mother, these stories involve the gendered expectations for a lively young lady but also narrate the parental wisdom being dispensed to a young man, Oscar Carpenter, who sets out to make good in the world. Carpenter's mother serves him well in providing encouragement and strength, and the character can be regarded as a loving tribute to Twain's own mother, Jane:

> I know now that she was the most eloquent person whom I have met in all my days, but I did not know it then, and I suppose that no one in all the village suspected that she was a marvel, or indeed that she was in any

> degree above the common. I had been abroad in the world for twenty years and known and listened to many of its best talkers before it at last dawned on me that in the matter of moving and pathetic eloquence none of them was the equal of that untrained and artless talker out there in the western village, that obscure little woman with the beautiful spirit and the great heart and the enchanted tongue.[9]

The keywords "spirit" and "heart" resonate with important aspects of the romantic and sentimental Christianity that peaked in nineteenth-century America.

Despite his powerfully masculine persona, Mark Twain (and young Sammy) yearned strongly for the guidance and love of the feminine others in his life. One critic recently put it this way: "In both the personal and literary realms, he was a man voluntarily controlled and influenced by women. Women shaped his life, edited his books, provided models for his fictional characters, and, through their correspondence, heavily influenced his fiction and literary works."[10] In general, these women tended to be women of faith; always, they were women of "liberal sympathies," and a chief model would always be his mother. Indeed if a woman did not meet such specifications, such as the wicked queen Morgan La Fey of *Connecticut Yankee,* she was hardly a woman at all.

Due to his mother's influence, young Sam became very familiar with the Sunday schools and church life of the antebellum frontier. He first went to Sunday school for about a year in a tiny brick Methodist church on the public square of Hannibal called the "Old Ship of Zion." On February 18, 1841, Sam's mother became a member of Hannibal's First Presbyterian Church, in whose basement young Sam attended the Sunday school that would stay with him throughout his life.[11] It was there that young Clemens was trained, as William Dean Howells once put it, "to fear God and dread the Sunday School."[12] The church Sam attended with his family (minus his father) based its doctrine on the Bible, with an emphasis on Old Testament texts about God's power, majesty, and wrath. Young Sammy was required to know the Bible: like others of his age, he had to memorize many passages and by his own admission had "read the Bible through" before he was fifteen.[13] As Sherwood Cummings puts it, "The Bible's imprint on his mind remained indelible under the palimpsest of later scientific knowledge."[14]

The positive imprint of the Bible and frontier religion, as rendered in sentimentalized and often humorous anecdotes about churchgoing, do appear in some of Twain's work. In a series of newspaper pieces published in 1866 while living in San Francisco, he remembers with some nostalgia his early church years. Some of the memories are not so flattering, to be sure. Twain took up the subject of the new "wildcat" religions then appearing in California. By "wildcat" he was lumping together a variety of spiritualist and other newly formed sects that preached either communion with the dead or, more generally, emotional and charismatic expressions of religious ecstasy. The articles make it clear that Clemens then found these kinds of behavior aberrant. But these were wildcat religions—offshoots, out of the mainstream. As such, this material makes Mark Twain appear conventional and conservative in his religious temperament, favoring the tried and true over the new and unconventional. In this context he still described himself as a Presbyterian, with a mildly satirical tone, yet in general he praised the regular activities of the First Presbyterian Church of Hannibal:

> We get up of a Sunday morning and put on the best harness we have got and trip cheerfully down town; we subside into solemnity and enter the church; we stand up and duck our heads and bear down on a hymn book propped on the pew in front when the minister prays; we stand up again while our hired choir are singing, and look in the hymn book and check off the verses to see that they don't shirk any of the stanzas; we sit silent and grave while the minister is preaching, and count the waterfalls and bonnets furtively, and catch flies; we grab our hats and bonnets when the benediction is begun; when it is finished, we shove, so to speak. No frenzy—no fanaticism—no skirmishing; everything perfectly serene.[15]

Throughout the rest of his career, he regularly self-identified as a Presbyterian. The sections of *The Adventures of Tom Sawyer* covering church life, despite a clearly satirical tone, contain as well sentimental details, such as the moment when the sermon reaches its climax: "[Tom] was really interested for a little while. The minister made a grand and moving picture of the assembling together of the world's hosts at the millennium when the lion and the lamb should lie down together and a little child should lead them."[16] While it is true that Twain does immediately deflate this transcendent vision by explaining Tom's inability to grasp it, the sheer wonder represented is a telling detail.

On the other hand, he certainly did recognize the negative legacy of his religious upbringing. Still some critics have been far too negative in their portrayals of Hannibal's harmful effects upon young Sam. The chief example of this is the very early depiction by Van Wyck Brooks, who perpetrated numerous distortions regarding Hannibal and his mother's religious influence: the town was a "desert of human sand! —the barrenest spot in all Christendom, surely, for the seed of genius to fall in. . . . [frontier Missouri] was not happy: it was a dark jumble of decayed faiths, of unconfessed class distinctions, of inarticulate misery. . . . It was a horde-life, a herd-life, an epoch without sun or stars, the twilight of a human spirit."[17] As Ron Powers has remarked, "Seldom has a recognized scholar been more drastically self-deluded, and with more destructive consequences, about the crucial resonance between an artist and the artist's formative habitat."[18]

Still we must concede that in Twain's mind, there were negative aspects to small-town life in Hannibal. Twain's Sunday school or church passages in *Tom Sawyer, The Gilded Age, Adventures of Huckleberry Finn,* and elsewhere are notable for their oppressive and enervating tone. Certainly Twain often poked fun at the silliness of the churches of his youth. In *Tom Sawyer* the key features of church life appear to be "showing off" and brainless conformity, such as in the story of the boy who "once recited three thousand verses [of Scripture] without stopping; but the strain upon his mental faculties was too great, and he was little better than an idiot from that day forth."[19] This comic episode suggests (and criticizes) the way religious language is consumed by the general populace: memorization without meaning or reflection that precludes any in-depth examination of the religious texts themselves. In many ways, the idiot child of Twain's anecdote is representative of all the evolving (or devolving) generations who consume the language without reflection and are won over by the art and in turn have forsaken the underlying reality (attitudes memorably captured in the posthumously published essay "Corn-Pone Opinions"). Later Tom is able to trade a variety of materials for the colored tokens in order to be presented with the prize Bible before the learned and honored guests by Judge Temple, who takes the opportunity to wax eloquent about this fine young Christian boy: "it's all owing to right bringing up."[20] Similarly, in *The Gilded Age,* the corrupt Senator Dilsworthy addresses a Sunday school with reverence and pious charm, ending by claiming that "All that he is, he owes to Sunday-school."[21] The irony of the speech consists of the allusion to the Sunday school as source of "all that he is"—meaning, hypocrisy, hidden corruption, and the ability to manipulate institutional religion to foster docility and conformity.

These examples and many more underscore a religious skepticism that attacks the prevailing myth of the small town and the Sunday schools—a myth of which Twain became profoundly aware at an early age. The small town, with the church and its Sunday school squarely at its center, became reified in the minds of many Americans as abstract symbol of all things good, pure, and right about their society. The mythic concept of the town was attacked by a number of savage critics of middle-class American civilization who reached an apogee of influence just after World War I in the movement known as the "revolt from the village," led by the likes of Sherwood Anderson and Sinclair Lewis. But this revolt began much earlier, in the antebellum period with the masters of Southwestern humor, and reignited just after the Civil War ended and the Gilded Age commenced. In Edward Eggleston's *The Hoosier Schoolmaster* (1871), for example, one long and memorable chapter entitled "The Hardshell Preacher" pokes good fun at the small-town church run by the "Hardshell" type of minister: "prodigiously illiterate, and often vicious. Some of their preachers are notorious drunkards."[22] Besides the sheer delight created by Eggleston's remarkable ear for dialect, this chapter is easily compared with similar sections in *Tom Sawyer* and *Huckleberry Finn:* the interminable, drowsy sermon; Tom playing with a pinch-bug (in Eggleston's book, a green lizard); and the satirical references to old-time revivalism when the King in *Huckleberry Finn* becomes a revivalist at a camp meeting associated in antebellum times with such groups as the "New York Perfectionists," the "Millerites," and the "Campbellites." Twain often poked fun at this sort of revivalism, as in the brief autobiographical note recorded in his youth: "Campbellite revival. All converted but me. All sinners again in a week."[23]

Twain's personal "revolt from the village" rises to perhaps its greatest height in his later story "The Man That Corrupted Hadleyburg," which reveals a vision of small-town religion that is both powerless to change the hearts of the people and highly negotiable when money is on the table. This story is commonly taught and analyzed, and yet readers often miss how much the tale invokes religious issues. The story of

Hadleyburg ends with the sinister implications of changing the town motto from "Lead us not into Temptation," a direct quotation from Jesus' version of the Lord's Prayer, to a newer one: "Lead us into Temptation." This switch emphasized Twain's rejection of an outward moral piety that does not match an inward holiness—such as he discovered his father to be guilty of. Temptation, or testing of faith and belief, becomes vital to intellectual and spiritual freedom and integrity. Holiness is phony if never tested. And small towns, church leaders, and sometimes justices of the peace were unable to sustain their integrity upon a cold, scientific dissection—such as the one Sam's father underwent upon his death.

Sam's father had never managed to find his proper place in the world. And the Clemenses, as a result, never had quite enough money. In March 1847 John Marshall Clemens was running for the position of circuit court clerk in Marion County, in another of his attempts to achieve financial equilibrium along with some social prestige. For a brief moment in time, he appeared to be a popular enough candidate to win the election and along with it to provide a lifestyle worthy of what he perceived to be his social stature. Unfortunately he was caught in a storm and contracted pneumonia, and within a brief time declined toward his death on March 24. Sam, his older brother Orion, his sister Pamela, and his mother were there at the end, when John Clemens motioned for Pamela, embraced her, whispered, "Let me die," and presently did so. He did not say good-bye to any of the others directly, including Sam—nor even his wife, Jane. Sam also recalled, late in life, that at his death, his father acknowledged a faith in Christianity: "The Presbyterian preacher had said, 'Do you believe on the Lord Jesus Christ, and that through his blood only you can be saved?' 'I do.' Then the preacher prayed over him and recommended him."[24]

The death of his father was shocking enough. Although theirs was not a warm and intimate relationship, Sam loved and respected his father, as most boys do. Beyond the normal grief that the eleven-year-old Sam must have endured, however, was an incident that was potentially one of the most traumatic of his entire life, one that revealed in certain ways the growing spiritual awareness of the young boy who would become Mark Twain. The episode involves the presumed hidden presence of Sam Clemens during the autopsy performed on his father, alluded to in later autobiographical remarks. Twain's presence at his father's autopsy has long been a matter of speculation among literary scholars. Little direct evidence can prove that he was there or for that matter whether the episode even took place. Mark Twain later recalled witnessing in 1847 an uncle's postmortem "through the keyhole," but no uncle of his died that year. His brother Orion wrote extensively about the autopsy, perhaps even in graphic detail, in his presumably lost autobiography, although it may turn up one day in an old trunk.[25] What we do know is that Mark Twain and his friend William Dean Howells both read Orion's manuscript, and Howells advised Twain, "Don't let any one else even see those passages about the autopsy. The light on your father's character is most pathetic."[26]

While the extent to which Sam did indeed witness all or part of this autopsy "through the keyhole" continues to be a controversy among Twain scholars, Phillip Fanning has recently presented a reasonable hypothesis that may ultimately explain the chain of events. In short, his version of the events considers the possibility that Jane Clemens ordered an autopsy because she believed that her husband had contracted syphilis, most likely from a prostitute. Perhaps he had committed adultery on his long trip south on the Mississippi to New Orleans, a well-known center of iniquity by this time. Without the suspicion that some other disease may have hastened his death, there would have been no need to perform an autopsy. Fanning's hypothesis places Orion at the scene of the autopsy, with Sam in the anteroom watching through a keyhole. It is also possible that the attending physician gave a running verbal commentary as he performed the process, a commentary that Sam might have been able to overhear as well.

The gist of Fanning's hypothesis is that the autopsy uncovered the fact that the father had indeed contracted syphilis, considered at the time a deadly plague that was in effect "just punishment for having sinned"—a religious interpretation not unlike some of the things that have been implied or openly stated in our own day about the AIDS virus.[27] It would certainly explain why Howells said that "the light on your father's character is most pathetic." John Clemens, by one account, was renowned for his "stern Puritan morality." Despite his confirmed status as a Whig, the *Democratic Gazette* spoke glowingly of his "public spirit [and his] high sense of justice and moral rectitude.'"[28] But this examination might have shown him to be just as fallen and fallible as any other man.

Further, the deathbed conversion of an aging skeptic, perhaps motivated not by genuine faith but simply the extreme terror regarding his imminent demise, compounds the perception that he turned out to be either a pathetic hypocrite, a man of no real conviction, or at best a man of great religious confusion. John Clemens's lifelong chastisement of religion was of no use to him when it really mattered and was apparently rejected in the final moments of despair. Sam knew his father to have been "sternly just and upright," but "he attended no church and never spoke of religious matters, and had no part nor lot in the pious joys of his Presbyterian family."[29]

Rather, Sam's father is probably best typified as a freethinker, a category of religious sensibility sharply on the rise in the nineteenth century with roots in Enlightenment deism and manifested most publicly in the Masonic movement of which John was a member. Mark Twain would follow his father into both of these avocations in later years, to varying degrees. Although freethinking or "freethought" is generally considered to be the equivalent of agnosticism or even atheism, in its antebellum forms it need not have been so understood. Rather, freethought was "a phenomenon running the gamut from the truly antireligious—those who regarded all religion as a form of superstition and wished to reduce its influence in every aspect of society—to those who adhered to a private, unconventional faith revering some form of God or Providence but at odds with orthodox religious authority."[30] Along this spectrum of freethinking, the former version emphasizing antireligious zeal would generally come after the onslaught of the Civil War, evolutionary science, biblical criticism, and the influence of the preeminent "freethinker" of the century, Col. Robert G. Ingersoll, whom Mark Twain greatly admired later in his life. John Clemens would have been closer to the earlier, deist version of freethinking—asserting the reality of God but questioning the authority of earthly institutions claiming to speak for that God. Such a milder form of freethought made its most obvious American appearance in the writings of Thomas Paine, especially *The Age of Reason*, a book that Twain swallowed whole and nearly memorized in about 1857. It is conceivable that Twain heard most of Tom Paine's ideas from his father and uncle in his youth, but Twain later claimed to have read Paine only when he was a cub pilot. He remembered reading *The Age of Reason* "with fear and hesitation, but marveling at its fearlessness and wonderful power."[31] Arguably it was of all books the one most definitive in forming the philosophy of the mature Mark Twain, although perhaps in an unconscious way that remains hard to document. Nevertheless, Sherwood Cummings has shown the very close connections between Mark Twain's written declarations of faith and Paine's volume, arguing that perhaps these close paraphrases resulted from "unconscious memory."[32] And yet Paine's work was probably more influential in terms of its approach to religious issues than any answers it may have provided. The deism of Paine and others was more a critical movement toward enlightened and open thinking than some set of doctrines or religious practice. Deism's originating force was in its desire to adapt Christianity to the many changes it would face in the emergence of the modern world.

Twain's later reaction to Paine's *The Age of Reason* was undoubtedly prepared by the many conversations he overheard involving his father and uncle. John Clemens shared many of Paine's ideas with his brother-in-law John Quarles, married to Jane Clemens's sister. Quarles was the first of the clan to move to Missouri, and he first encouraged the Clemenses to follow them to the tiny town of Florida, where Sam was born. Quarles owned a farm on which young Sam spent many summers, and they enjoyed a strong relationship that Twain remembered throughout his life. It was on Quarles's farm, for example, where Sam first grew close personally to slaves, learning to enjoy their stories and embrace them as human beings—at least to the extent that a boy in 1840s Missouri could do so. Thus did Quarles's freethought bear some little practical fruit in the young life of Sam Clemens, in opening up in some slight way the possibility of rethinking the nature of African Americans. Although Quarles is most often remembered by scholars for the free and open environment of his farm, perhaps he should be recalled even more for the iconoclastic views of religion that he shared with Sam's father. Quarles was "known to have unorthodox religious beliefs"—particularly on the question of human destination and damnation, which led him into Universalism.[33]

The effects of a father's premature and perhaps scandalous death on the growing religious sensibility of an eleven-year-old are not to be underestimated. For one thing, it made Sam feel even more guilt over past sins and his need for reform. It is not too much to say that Sam Clemens remained throughout his life a bit of a sexual prude. He was on occasion the giver and receiver of bawdy humor, to be sure. For example, he openly stated his considered opinion that "No Protestant child exists who does not masturbate. That art is the earliest accomplishment his religion confers upon him."[34] And of course he participated fully in the social masculinities of his bachelorhood: as a printer's apprentice, a steamboat pilot, and out west as prospector and newsman.[35] He once wrote a letter suggesting that while in California he occasionally slept with women for more than bodily warmth, and Louis J. Budd long ago described young Sam as a bachelor more than willing to indulge in the escapades of youthful sexuality.[36] But the overall evidence suggests a man, especially after attaining a national fame, of chaste, monogamous loyalty. Although of course we can never know much about his sexual adventures out west, it seems reasonable to believe that he remained faithful to his wife, Livy, after their marriage and that the claims made recently of his supposed homosexuality seem particularly out of character in this regard.[37] In other words, I am suggesting that the father's ostensible "stern Puritan morality," which may have been revealed to be fallible at least in the area of sexual purity and loyalty, contributed to a lifelong near obsession of Mark Twain's—almost as if he needed to prove his superiority to his father. In terms of the greater culture, we might understand young Sam's horror to rest on the shocking realization that the outward religious morality turned out to be a sham. The autopsy itself, a penetrating examination of a human body in search of disease or decay, becomes in this sense a metaphor of the emerging powers of science to investigate the truth claims of an entire way of life.

Fanning also suggests that the lingering effects of the events described here are to be seen explicitly in two important literary depictions, neither one of which was ever published in Twain's lifetime. The first is a long passage edited out of *Huckleberry Finn,* in which Jim tells Huck that his former master, a medical student, ordered him to warm up a corpse in preparation for dissection. As the body is heated, it falls off the table and onto Jim, causing him to flee in horror from the lab. The medical student goes to find the body on the floor and proceeds to "chop him up." Immediately following this excised scene, Huck and Jim discover a house floating down the river and upon investigation find a naked dead man, face down. Jim goes in alone to discover that the body is in fact Huck's father but keeps this fact a secret until the end of the novel. The room in which the body of Pap Finn is found is generally conceded to be a brothel.[38] These two scenes, one cut out of the final volume and one left to stand, bring together the death of the protagonist's father, a gruesome tale of human dissection, and an old-fashioned whorehouse—suggestive of the possibility that those three things were somehow tied together in Twain's mind when he wrote this.

The second possible literary expression of the lingering effects of the autopsy is in "Autobiography of a Damned Fool," a long unfinished tale that was not titled by Twain but by Paine much later. There Twain imagines a narrator (a thinly veiled copy of Orion) telling his own story. Among other things, the tale is notable because it begins prominently with the death of the father: "I was eighteen then, and a printer's apprentice. My father's funeral brought me suddenly and violently face to face with the great concerns of the hereafter. During many nights I could not sleep for thinking of my perilous situation. I resolved at last upon an immediate and thorough reform of all my ways."[39] Although the tale is ostensibly in the voice of his brother Orion, we know from a number of Twain's childhood reminiscences that he was much given to sleepless nights of guilt, fearfulness of thunderstorms, and even sleepwalking.

These two passages suggest the guilt and fear experienced by the young boy, as well as Twain's grief and anger over his father's pathetic life and demise, both of which became features of much of Twain's literary output. Its lasting clarity is demonstrated by the fact that Twain would comment a month before his own death, "My father died this day 63 years ago. I remember all about it quite clearly."[40] The excised passage from *Huckleberry Finn* foregrounds the sheer personal horror of the experience. While the "Autobiography of a Damned Fool" is meant to be a burlesque of a character much like Orion, the irony is that many of the emotional and spiritual crises are ones with which Sam Clemens was familiar. For example, young Sam made a solemn commitment of reform to his mother just after John Marshall Clemens died. "In a burst of 'heart-wringing' grief and remorse for past disobedience, [Sam] stood beside his father's coffin and promised his mother 'to be a better boy.' "[41] In addition, "Autobiography of a Damned Fool" foregrounds the narrator's comic ambivalence regarding religious truth: he flits from orthodox Christianity to agnosticism, atheism, and Mohammedanism. Though meant to deride brother Orion's recurrent metaphysical changes of heart, this constant shifting also catches more than a little of the spirit of the age in which Mark Twain achieved his fame. As such, the burlesque of Orion's religious waffling is discernible in Twain's own life: he was, as Fanning puts it, "a man caught in a spiritual maelstrom, casting about for something, anything, to believe in."[42]

Thus, in his two parents, Sam Clemens was faced with living and breathing embodiments of two competing religious sensibilities. For one thing, these two represented many of the gendered conventions of religion, as understood by many Americans of the period. His father was the more rational and unemotional, while the mother was the more merciful, sympathetic, and spiritually inclined. Jane held more strictly to revealed biblical faith, while John was more skeptical, worldly, and scientific. Both had character strengths and personal weaknesses. Twain suggested their relative strengths in a famous quip in 1881: "I am a border-ruffian from the state of Missouri. I am a Connecticut Yankee by adoption. I have the morals of Missouri and the culture of Connecticut culture, and that's the combination that makes the perfect man."[43] Although it is generally not understood as such, this statement can be read as a revealing confession of the religious and gendered conventions illustrated by his parents. It occurs in what is ostensibly a speech on the Pilgrims and is thus conceived in a religious context, specifically the first meeting of the New England Society and its celebration of its ancestors. However, instead of saluting the original settlers of New England, Twain emphasizes here his Missouri roots. Connecticut's contribution clearly is secondary, adopted, and "cultural." Among other things, this cultural contribution surely includes the Social Christianity of his neighborhood and friends. And, throughout the speech, Twain undermines the legacy of the Pilgrims by showing how they persecuted a variety of marginalized voices in America, including Indians, women, and Quakers. The speech overall reflects the ongoing struggle between the spiritual haves and have-nots, and the most famous quotation, stated above, signifies the two poles of a paradox that were his seemingly mismatched parents. Hank Morgan of *Connecticut Yankee* had only one side of the equation:

"I am an American. I was born and reared in Hartford, in the State of Connecticut—anyway, just over the river, in the country. So I am a Yankee of the Yankees—and practical; yes, and nearly barren of sentiment, I suppose—or poetry, in other words."[44] But Mark Twain knew that the "sentiment" and "poetry" were just as important as the pragmatism of the Yankee, spiritually speaking.

More generally, Sam Clemens's religious journey had at its foundations the teeming religious controversies that characterized American Christianity of the antebellum period. A common mistake made by many historians of American Christianity is to posit that it ever was a singular, hegemonic system of belief. It never was, nor is it today. Extensive polling data show the very wide levels of disagreement that contemporary Christians have on a variety of subjects, and this in-house debating has characterized the American church for a very long time. Arguably it is a major reason for the great vitality and expansiveness of the American church. In the case of Sam Clemens, his religious sensibility commences with two major, competing sets of roots: the conservative Protestant evangelicalism that characterized his mother's set of beliefs and, more generally, his childhood in Hannibal; and the freethinking yet deeply rational and nativist set of beliefs held by his father John. And yet even these generalizations are enlightening, since both parents said and did things that were in opposition to the descriptions set forth here. Jane Clemens, for instance, loved to dance (not proper for a conservative Christian), while John Clemens, as mentioned earlier, apparently confessed the blood of Jesus on his deathbed (not proper for a freethinker).

The competing versions of God, the gospel, and the nature of humanity were simply in the air of Sam's youth and had huge ramifications for how young Sam understood the world. To get serious about historical religion, one must begin by questioning and complicating what basic terms like these actually mean. An important clue to a reliance on limiting preconceptions is to be found in the tendency, for example, to generalize about the Calvinism of the early republic. In particular, the years of Sam Clemens's youth were marked by large controversies within the Calvinist Protestant churches of America, several of which were so crucial that they would literally end with schismatic separations. Furthermore these issues ultimately were reflected in the major themes of Twain's writing career. Understanding the nature of humanity, and the opposition of free will versus determinism, for example, is arguably the primary burden of Mark Twain's writings as a whole.

In fact the definitions of Calvinism as given by Twain critics oversimplify the interesting dynamics of Sam's religious world. One writes, "Presbyterians amplified the currents of brooding, theological mysticism that flowed on the American frontier. Deriving from the chilly Puritanism of the sixteenth-century ascetics John Calvin of France and John Knox of Scotland, this church in Twain's boyhood still sought to develop a model society based on strict discipline and a Moral Sense enforced by the terror of an eternal Hell."[45] Another writes, "Frontier Calvinism dominated [Jane's] family's mentality and was the hallmark of Hannibal's views about ultimate issues."[46] The dark, popular version of Calvinism has been well expressed by William Shurr to include the following precepts: "The monstrousness of a deity who allows the undeserved suffering of the innocent and who shows his love by wrath, the visceral conviction that the mass of men are irredeemably predestined to destruction, the gross popular abandonment to belief in miracles and special providences, and the final bind that man is responsible for his actions even though not free to determine them."[47] The "darker" elements of a deterministic view of salvation, such as guilt and fearfulness, are well-known elements of Sam's early years: the terror during thunderstorms, the sleepwalking, and the belief that sinfulness wrought real wages in the lives of young people. It is also true that, like all frontier towns of the period, Sam's Hannibal was teeming with shady characters, dying children, murder, mayhem, and occasional drownings in the river, all fodder for metaphysical brooding and fear. Later in the century, this particular set of assertions about popular Calvinism led many intellectuals to the conclusion that belief in this sort of God was not only unthinkable but also probably immoral—a position that Mark Twain would finally come to agree with.[48]

However, while it is wrong to say that old-style Calvinism was of no consequence in the Hannibal of Sam's youth, it was really just one part of the religious story of America. To begin with, Sam Clemens grew to manhood in the immediate aftermath of one of the most definitive religious eras in American history. The Second Great Awakening in America is usually depicted as running roughly from 1800–1830, but its impact went well beyond 1830. Some historians even argue that the Second Great Awakening extended almost until the brink of the Civil War, as manifested in the widespread revivals in the northeast in 1857–58. The Second Great Awakening culminated in the teachings of Charles Finney, whose "New Light" theological innovations influenced the thinking of the general culture. In particular Finney's emphasis on human agency and the freedom of will became hallmarks of religious and political rhetoric before the Civil War. As one historian has noted, the "transformation of American theology in the first quarter of the nineteenth century [had] released the very forces of romantic perfectionism that conservatives most feared. . . . As it spread, perfectionism swept across denominational barriers and penetrated even secular thought."[49] Another has articulated this phenomenon most cogently: "a religious and political ideology described most accurately as perfectionist became pervasive in Jacksonian America and remained normative to the end of the century; . . . widespread reading of the Bible and growing reverence for its authority was a principal factor in shaping that ideology; and . . . the combination of the millennial with the American dream was a prime catalyst, and not simply one of its fruits, of the quest for personal and social holiness."[50]

This vigorous movement also fostered what Nathan Hatch has called the "democratization of American Christianity." Hatch argues that "turbulence and bitter struggles for authority . . . characterize[d] American Christianity from 1790 to 1820": "To the consternation of respectable clergymen, the terms of that debate were set largely by people who had not known status, influence, or power. This stringent populist challenge to the religious establishment included violent anticlericalism, a flaunting of conventional religious deportment, a disdain for the wrangling of theologians, an assault on tradition, and an assertion that common people were more sensitive than elites to the divine."[51] A characteristic figure of this democratizing effect was David Nelson, founder of the First Presbyterian Church of Hannibal that Jane Clemens and her children attended. Nelson, originally a staid deist, was converted to the cause of zealous perfectionism and abolition after hearing Theodore Weld lecture in 1835. His presence and later expulsion from Hannibal must have become part of local lore on the subject of wildcat religion. Nelson's activism came at just the time when Hannibal churches were becoming divided over slavery—an "ideological earthquake . . . [with] Hannibal itself at the epicenter."[52]

Nelson symbolized the Wesleyan emphasis on immediate conversion, agency, and embodiment, showing deep sympathies for blacks long before it was considered proper to do so. He was a local version of other, nationally known firebrands, like Barton Stone and Alexander Campbell, all of whom "found traditional sources of authority anachronistic and groped toward similar definitions of egalitarian religion" years before Ralph Waldo Emerson made a more permanent literary expression of these same concerns. Stone was known to characterize his own resignation from the Presbyterian denomination as the "declaration of our independence." And Campbell, the colorful and extremely influential church leader who founded the group that later became known as the Disciples of Christ, asserted in 1830 that July 4, 1776, was "a day to be remembered as was the Jewish Passover. . . . This revolution, taken in all its influences, will make men free indeed."[53] Sam Clemens, growing up in Hannibal, not only knew about these movements, he had personal experience with these two key leaders of the democratization of American Christianity, Campbell and Stone. Both of them had left the Presbyterian Church in protest over doctrinal differences. Partly because Campbellites were religious rebels, their sect was of great interest to both Sam and his father, particularly in their rejection of narrow creedal statements, their questioning of the predestination doctrine regarding who was truly saved, and their desire to seek a cosmic unity of all humanity. When Sam was eleven years old, Campbell visited Hannibal, and Twain later recalled the great excitement that his visit engendered: "that was the first time in my life that I had realized what a mighty population this planet contains when you get them all together."[54] Later young Sam was involved in the printing of Campbell's sermon, which was produced in the print shop where Sam worked. His fellow printer Wales McCormick had been rebuked publicly by Campbell for taking the Lord's name in vain, so Sam and Wales conspired to make some alterations to the sermon. Where Campbell had said "Great God" they put "Great Scott," and where he had said "Jesus Christ" they put "J.C." When Campbell discovered their little joke, he stormed into the print shop and demanded corrections.

Sam had even more direct experience with Barton Stone, who was the grandfather of Will Bowen, Sam's best friend, and for a while lived in Hannibal with the Bowen family. Stone, like his mentor Campbell a former Presbyterian, found the doctrine of predestination particularly egregious. Once Stone walked in on Sam and Will playing cards, at which he admonished them for involvement in sinful practice and took the playing cards away from them. Twain later joked that he had hid them in his baptismal robe and that they came floating out one day when he was in the river baptizing believers.[55] Thus there is a certain irony involved in both of these famous preachers, known for questioning dogmatic religion, showing themselves at times to be quick to anger, judgmental, and self-righteous in the presence of the young Missourians. Both of these incidents were memorialized much later by Mark Twain as instances of staid religion, but in fact young Sam Clemens found aspects of the teachings of both Campbell and Stone rather attractive, especially their willingness to question ossified belief and tradition.

More generally, religious firebrands like Campbell, Stone, and Nelson embodied a newer, more subversive form of American Protestantism. It was oppositional in its emphasis on individual freedom, prophetic outrage at injustice, and democratic self-determination. Later, upon his departure from Hannibal, Sam would meet up with entire subcultures of America whose lifeblood consisted of similar oppositions—though not from a religious perspective. As a printer in such cities as Cincinnati, Philadelphia, and New York, a cub pilot on the Mississippi, and as a prospector and journalist in Nevada and California, Clemens would make fast friends with the citizens of an emergent bohemianism throughout America at midcentury. Twain's attraction to the bohemian life was awakened in his wide early travels. In late May 1857, after lengthy lessons from Horace Bixby on the art and science of steamboat piloting, Sam Clemens disembarked in New Orleans for some extended rest and relaxation. He had several weeks to test his journalistic eye in the city that had already become notorious for its seedy underside, its spicy foods, its musical entertainments, and its marginal lifestyles. As a trading center for the burgeoning Mississippi shipping industry, New Orleans had become one of the major crossroads for cultures and ethnicities from around the world, not unlike Twain's future residence, San Francisco. In New Orleans, Clemens was struck by the colors, smells, and sounds of the city, which were brought together by the great diversity of the people: "groups of Italians, French, Dutch, Irish, Spaniards, Indians, Chinese, Americans, English, and the Lord knows how many more different kinds of people."[56] As one biographer has put it, for Clemens, "the variety was an asset, the differences desirable, the community both tactilely sensual and raucously harmonious, his first experience with the American marketplace as a polyglot, multi-ethnic epitome of the national culture. His sheer pleasure in New Orleans was a step toward his gradual transcendence of Missouri slave culture provincialism and his increasing discomfort with xenophobia."[57]

To put it into today's parlance, it was the beginning of the multicultural awareness of Sam Clemens. His wide travels on the river as a pilot and later out west as a government bureaucrat, prospector, and finally journalist awoke in him a latent humane sympathy for others different from himself. At the same time, these travels underscored his sensibility that the world was itself a huge and complicated place peopled by ethnic groups with competing visions of the truth. He would write later that "I got personally and familiarly acquainted with about all the different types of human nature that are to be found in fiction, biography, or history. . . . When I find a well-drawn character in fiction or biography, I generally take a warm personal interest in him, for the reason that I have known him before—met him on the river."[58]

The "warm personal interest" expressed here for whatever characters he might come across translates into a generous and humane sympathy for the other. It also involves what the Russian theorist Mikhail Bakhtin called "insideness," which is "the ability to share otherness on the social level and on the psychic level." Joe B. Fulton describes the relation between Mark Twain's ethical stance and the emergence of his realism, which Fulton calls "ethical realism," and he shows that such an ethics emerged fruitfully from Twain's wide exposure to people who were different from himself. Bakhtin's concept of insideness focuses on seeing the world from the standpoint of the other: "I must empathize or project myself into this other human being, see his world axiologically from within him as he sees this world; I must put myself in his place." Fulton is correct to see a similarity between Bakhtin's desire for insideness and Twain's emerging aesthetic of realism, which so often involved the reader in getting inside those who are fundamentally different from himself.[59] The similarity is articulated in a letter from Twain to his literary mentor, William Dean Howells, dated January 21, 1879, praising Howells for his success in the art of realism: "And only you see people & their ways & their insides & outsides as they *are,* & make them talk as they *do* talk. I think you are the greatest artist in these tremendous mysteries that ever lived. There doesn't seem to be anything that can be concealed from your awful all-seeing eye. It must be a cheerful thing for one to live with you & be aware that you are going up & down in him like another conscience all the time."[60] Realism succeeds, according to Twain here, insofar as it gets inside its characters as they *are.*

New Orleans is also where Clemens first encountered the sheer carnivalesque qualities of the Mardi Gras, an experience that he described with great pleasure and yet also some moralizing restraint. Two years after his first visit, he arrived in March 1859, just as the celebration was beginning, "in blissful ignorance" of what he was about to encounter: "fine, fancy, splendid, ugly, coarse, ridiculous, grotesque, laughable costumes." Erotically costumed women were undoubtedly of particular interest to Sam, but he wrote home to his sister Pamela that "their costumes and actions were very trying to modest eyes." People were dressed up in every conceivable costume: "representing giants, Indians, nigger minstrels, monks, priests, clowns,—birds, beasts—everything."[61] His laughter in all of this is similar to the carnivalesque laughter described by Bakhtin: "Carnival laughter is the laughter of all the people. . . . It is directed at all and everyone. . . . The entire world is seen in its droll aspect. . . . It buries and revives. . . . It is also directed at those who laugh. The people do not exclude themselves from the wholeness of the world. They, too, are incomplete, they also die and are revived and renewed."[62] Bakhtin's analysis participates in a religious vocabulary here by noting how the carnival allows the celebrants to be revived; laughter somehow completes them. This sort of laughter acts as a revivifying agent, allowing all participants to enjoy momentary relief from all of the pressures and the responsibilities of their lives as workers, spouses, partners, parents, children, parishioners, and so forth. During carnival all such responsibilities are laid aside; all forms of conscience are laid waste. The carnival is thus a celebration of our common humanity, our alikeness. Such insight is apocalyptic in its spiritual and revelatory nature and as such is able to revive us and sustain us for the next leg of our journey.

Clemens seemed to understand intuitively the importance of this kind of event in the study of his native land: "I think that I may say that an American has not seen the United States until he has seen the Mardi-Gras in New Orleans."[63] The carnivalesque celebration of our common humanity would become a major trademark of Mark Twain for the rest of his career—a trademark, again, that can be understood from a religious perspective.

The carnivalesque mode of experience that Clemens found in New Orleans leads directly to the sort of bachelor's bohemianism that characterized his lifestyle from roughly the steamboat piloting years (1857–61) through his times out west (1861–67)—almost a full decade of his adulthood. The term *bohemian* was in fact an emerging term of the same period, and it is useful in understanding the moral and ethical sensibilities that would affect Clemens throughout his career. Generally bohemianism is associated with unconventional lifestyles, but it has been "stretched to cover so many different and sometimes opposed ways of life and such a remarkable assortment of groups, communities, and individuals" that it has become rather hard to define. Without a doubt, almost all bohemians of Clemens's era must be included in the growing numbers of artists and intellectual types who would call themselves freethinkers—meaning they resisted dogmatic assertions about the spiritual life. More specifically they participated in "the bohemian myth—the idea of the artist as a different sort of person from his fellow human beings—[which] is founded on the idea of the Artist as Genius."[64] In this sense, a bohemian has similarities with the Emersonian vision of the poet as prophet. Probably the most famous instance of bohemian America in the years just prior to the Civil War was the group of artists and writers who congregated in Pfaff's Tavern in Manhattan, including Walt Whitman. Before joining up with this group, Whitman "was disaffected and drifting, a perfect candidate for bohemia . . . [which consisted of] disaffected Democrats, footloose rebels with laughter at their lips and gloom in their hearts."[65] Bohemia "welcomed artistically inspired, politically disaffected renegades living in carefree disarray"; it "rejected hypocritical morality," "repudiated conventional working hours and domestic arrangements," and "educated itself to self-expression."[66] In Whitman's own words, his great pleasure in this environment at Pfaff's Tavern "was to look on—to see, talk little, absorb," and one of his biographers has noted that "Whitman's place of honor was not at the head table . . . but off to one side, where he could observe as much as participate."[67] Such observation had profound effects on Whitman's ability to sympathize with these marginalized characters and to recreate in his poems accounts of their peculiar "insideness"—abilities that became his hallmark, in many ways.

Similarly Sam Clemens immersed himself in the culture of bohemianism during his bachelor years, particularly out west in San Francisco. There he not only sought out marginalized people but often wrote about them in the newspapers. His writings of this period often described street people, prostitutes, criminals, actors, singers, other performers, and Chinese opium addicts. One of his subjects was the homeless street schizophrenic "Emperor Norton," who claimed to be the ruler of the city. Part of his regular beat for the *Morning Call* was drama, which meant he had to cover "the six theatres, one after the other; seven nights a week three hundred and sixty-five nights in the year." This beat, as well as other work for the "self-consciously literary and bohemian *California* and the *Golden Era* enabled him to maintain irregular work patterns, an addiction to night life and drinking, and a pose that combined ostentatious laziness, artistic pretense, and wild woolliness. . . . [The pose was] of an unkempt bohemian with populist impulses."[68] According to Randall Knoper, Twain's immersion into this bohemian lifestyle, and his interest in people on the fringe of society, is most relevant to his search for an acceptable form of masculine behavior. However I believe these days of what we might call "sowing his wild oats" were formative as well in terms of Mark Twain's spiritual quest. Ironically, after many years of bohemia, perhaps the one thing he learned was that bohemianism would not sustain him for the rest of his life. Additionally these years opened him up to the views and passions of a wide array of American characters. Just as the bohemian experience affected Whitman, it fostered in Mark Twain a deeper appreciation of all the various kinds of people who make up this place we call America. As such, bohemia had a powerfully leveling effect, a democratizing effect that is itself deeply spiritual.

And yet bohemianism had its limits. By the fall of 1864 Twain was broke and suffering from depression and loneliness. Partly this can be attributed to the bohemian culture to which he had become attached. It featured a mood much like what Walt Whitman had experienced in New York just a few years earlier: "Unable to cope with the national crisis, they were playing a desperate game of evasion. Their carefree, carpe diem attitude showed that fifties individualism had sunk toward anarchic decadence. Not surprisingly, Poe was their patron saint, and several of them cultivated melancholy. Ostensibly full of life, they in fact embodied death."[69] This description of Manhattan bohemia just prior to the Civil War captures much of the spirit of its West Coast counterpart. In particular the similarity exists in the way in which the bohemian mindset ultimately issues in a profound melancholia—just the attitude in which Mark Twain found himself languishing near the end of his California years. Bohemian culture was on the cutting edge of the emergence in the general culture of what Jackson Lears has called "weightlessness"—meaning, a sense of displacement, a loss of moral foundations, and a general fear that life was becoming more and more "unreal."[70] A lingering depression apparently became Twain's predominant mood from the fall of 1864 until his departure from California in December 1866, culminating at some point in thoughts of suicide. He alleviated much of this melancholia through his friendships with ministers that became a crucial aspect of these years. And even though today we know much more about the brain chemistry of depression and the emotional and psychological aspects of suicide, it is important to emphasize as well that contemplation of suicide entails a profound "spiritual crisis"—and that it was clearly considered so within the context of nineteenth-century American culture.

The story of Twain's supposed flight into suicidal despair is a recurring theme in much Twain biography. Biographers still debate the extent to which he actually came close to pulling the trigger or the precise time that he did so. The standard account is based on a letter Twain wrote to his brother Orion and his sister-in-law Mollie in October 1865, and on a marginal notation he wrote in a book near the end of his life in 1909. The letter of 1865 states, "You are in trouble, & in debt—so am I. I am utterly miserable—so are you. Perhaps your religion will sustain you, will feed you—I place no dependence in mine. Our religions are alike, though, in one respect—neither can make a man happy when he is out of luck. If I do not get out of debt in 3 months,—pistols or poison for one—exit me. [There's a text for a sermon on Self-Murder—Proceed.]"[71]

The marginal note was inscribed more than forty years later when Twain, while reading through the letters of James Russell Lowell, noticed a passage in which Lowell describes suicidal thoughts. Lowell writes, "I suppose scarce a young man of sensibility ever grew his shell who didn't, during the process, meditate suicide a great many times. I remember in '39 putting a cocked pistol to my forehead—and being afraid to pull the trigger, of which I was heartily ashamed, and am still whenever I think of it." In the margins, an aging Twain responds:

> Down to the "trigger" I am with him, but no further. It is odd that I should stumble upon this now, for it is only two days ago since something called to my mind my experience of 1866 & I told it at dinner. I put the pistol to my head but wasn't man enough to pull the trigger. Many times I have been sorry I did not succeed, but I was never ashamed of having tried. Suicide is the only really sane thing the young or old ever do in this life.[72]

Among other things, the scarcity of evidence has led commentators to wonder when the actual events Twain mentions here might have occurred. The answer is clouded by the fact that in these final years, Twain often confused dates, names, and other details from his past. According to Robert Hirst, general editor of the Mark Twain Papers, "Our collective best guess when we published *Letters 1* was that Clemens was off by a part of a year in saying he raised the pistol in 1866."[73] However, Fred Kaplan has placed the date a couple of years earlier.[74]

Recently Phillip Fanning has presented a plausible theory that examines the lingering feud between Twain and Orion, which is traced to the family's Tennessee land, a 288,000 acre tract of real estate purchased decades earlier by their father outside of Jamestown, Tennessee. The attempt to gain substantial wealth from this land had haunted the Clemens family for many years. Orion had even relocated his family to Jamestown in 1857–58, at which time brother Sam had admitted to him in a letter, "I am glad to see you in such high spirits about the land, and I hope will remain so, if you never get richer. I seldom venture to think about our landed wealth, for 'hope deferred maketh the heart sick.'"[75] The reference is to Proverbs 13:12, and the upshot of the verse is that Sam had by 1858 basically given up ever expecting any gain from the land.

The nearly obsessive hopefulness that many frontier Americans had in the possession of land as a means toward wealth can hardly be overestimated in the antebellum period. At the same time, land scams, false claims, and trumped-up speculations regularly took advantage of this obsession. The theme that can be called "hope deferred" is depicted perhaps most powerfully in the early books *Innocents Abroad* and *Roughing It,* but it was a theme that permeated the career of Mark Twain. Richard Lowry has discussed Twain's investigation of and interest in the various kinds of "claims" made by not only touring companies, tour guides, and guidebooks but also prospectors, famous authors, and newspaper writers themselves, who were often given shares in stocks and then asked to trump them up in their columns. In this thoroughly modern scheme of things, value is always already mere expectation, promotion, and finally recirculation—all of which is fraught with anxiety and fear.[76] The "sickness of heart" that is evoked in Twain's allusion to Proverbs here is an advanced form of Lowry's "anxiety and fear," a spiritual sickness unto death, as it were.

Fanning contends that a telegram from land speculator Herman Camp, sent sometime in January 1866, contained an offer to buy the property. Twain desperately wanted to sell the land, as he had for many years, but Orion apparently refused the offer because the land would be used for wine production. Thus did Orion's persistent legalistic morality, long a feature of his personality and a thorn in his brother's flesh, prevent the infusion of large sums of money into the Clemens family. According to Fanning, Twain's suicidal depression is linked directly to this series of events, culminating in Orion's lamely pietistic decision-making—another painful episode of hope deferred. Whether we grant that these events might actually induce suicidal thoughts, Fanning is probably correct in depicting the frustrations that Mark Twain experienced in dealing with his religious brother. At the very least the incident as related by Twain many years later can be understood as a metaphor for the depth of his disillusionment during this period.

But the San Francisco years, often seen as representative of Sam Clemens at his most irreligious, document a chain of events that finally issued in the steady spiritual maturation of Mark Twain. These events go from the rootless lifestyle of bohemia, through a near suicidal depression, and into a state of mind in which a sense of spiritual calling played a prominent, and perhaps crucial, role. One of the great ironies of this period is the fact that the letter that documents Twain at his lowest level spiritually, the notorious suicide letter of 1865, also contains what might be called the spiritual highlight of the same period: Mark Twain's announcement that he has finally located his true "calling" in life. Just at the lowest point of despair, Twain also experiences one of his great moments of clarity. To Orion and Mollie, he writes:

> And now let me preach you a sermon. I never had but two powerful ambitions in my life. One was to be a pilot, & the other a preacher of the gospel. I accomplished the one & failed in the other, because I could not supply myself with the necessary stock in trade—i.e. religion. I have given it up forever. I never had a "call" in that direction, anyhow, & my aspirations were the very ecstasy of presumption. But I have had a "call" to literature, of a low order—i.e. humorous. It is nothing to be proud of, but it is my strongest suit, & if I were to listen to that maxim of stern duty which says that to do right you must multiply the one of the two or the three talents which the Almighty entrusts to your keeping, I would long ago have ceased to meddle with things for which I was by nature unfitted & turned my attention to seriously scribbling to excite the laughter of God's creatures.[77]

This passage is remarkable in its apparent agreement with very conventional understandings of religious calling—that each person has been granted gifts by the Almighty, that sometimes it takes a long time to understand what those gifts are, and that once they are discovered, one must apply "stern duty" to get the most out of them. In emphasizing this final point, Twain here invokes Jesus' parable of the talents, from Matthew 25:14–30.

Readers might well question the extent to which Twain actually believed in the direct experience of God's voice in the calling, of course—as suggested by the quotation marks he employs around the term "call" on both occasions of its use. Traditionally a calling indicates a sense that there has been some sort of communicative action between God and the hearer, and it would be a bit of a stretcher to imagine Mark Twain suggesting that he has somehow been in communication with the Almighty. However, it is plausible that Twain at this time in his life might have believed in the possibility of a "still small voice" of God that operates largely through intuitive, implicit means, and such a belief is at least suggested by the vigor and the passion of this letter.

There is also a certain irony in the fact that the bohemian yearning for movement and the open road, culminating in Twain's engagement to write travel letters from Europe and the Holy Land, also led Twain to the people who would eventually become his anchor and home for the major period of his writing career. In effect his wide travels and his carnivalesque lifestyle began to take its toll, and his desire to settle down reached its peak. These effects would culminate in the period of time during which Sam Clemens truly "became" Mark Twain, at least spiritually speaking: the courtship of his future wife, Olivia Langdon, and ultimately the move to Hartford, Connecticut, the city that was becoming symbolic of the greatest shifts in liberal Christianity of the entire century. Mark Twain's wide-ranging bohemian experience, thus, never fully erased the moral and ethical impressions of his Missouri youth, and their effects are clearly seen in the early journalism, sketches, and travel letters from the Sandwich Islands (Hawaii) that together served as the springboard into his lecturing career, his return to New York, and the rapidly growing national fame to follow.

Related to his search for meaning and purpose was Twain's lifelong interest in members of the clergy and his propensity for church attendance, which also were features of his wide travels and his more settled experiences in Nevada and California. As early as his initial trip to St. Louis in February 1855, he wrote home to say how the Presbyterians there were neglecting the needs of a widow and her children: "The sight brought to mind the handsome sum our preacher collected in church last Sunday to obtain food and raiment for the poor, ignorant heathen in some far off part of the world; I thought, too, of the passage in the Bible instructing the disciples to carry their good works into all the world—beginning first at Jerusalem."[78] The allusion to Luke 24:47, the reference to the "heathen" of other lands, and the prophetic assertion of justice all bespeak a fairly standard Christian conscience at this early stage. Similarly he wrote home from Philadelphia, "I always thought the eastern people were patterns of uprightness; but I never before saw so many whiskey-swilling, God-despising heathens as I find in this part of the country. I believe I am the only person in the Inquirer office that does not drink."[79] In his journalistic work, "about a fourth of what he published before 1866" treated matters of social justice and public welfare; "he took himself seriously as an overseer of the public conscience and yearned to set it straight," according to Louis J. Budd.[80] Issues with which he became entangled included political corruption, poor court procedures, unfair police tactics, and the oppression of marginalized groups such as Chinese immigrants, among many others.

Meanwhile he tended to maintain relationships with ministers and often with churches as well. In Nevada Twain had some contact with both, even though, as one historian has put it, "it was probably the most secular place in America during the mid-nineteenth century."[81] His brother Orion, with whom he had traveled to Nevada to work for the territorial government there, became both an elder and a treasurer of the First Presbyterian Church of Carson City. Sometimes Orion enlisted his brother's help in fund-raising activities. One example is when Twain gave a humorous speech in January 1863 to raise money for the completion of the church building for First Presbyterian. In agreeing to do this service, Twain wrote to the trustees of the church: "Although I am not a very dusty Christian myself, I take an absorbing interest in religious affairs, and would willingly inflict my annual message upon the church itself if it might derive benefit thereby." His friend Clement Rice reported that the benefit raised $200 and also had more spiritual benefits: it "helped to keep up the effervescing spirit of the good work in behalf of that same, ever-present, gaping skeleton of a church."[82] One minister with whom Twain became especially good friends was Franklin Rising, a young easterner who lived in Virginia City at the same time Twain did, beginning in 1862. Twain notes in several places his attendance at church services at which Rising preached and in one newspaper article states somewhat comically, "Mr. Rising is our Episcopalian minister, and has done as much as any man among us to redeem this community from its pristine state of semi-barbarism."[83] Rising was destined to become the model for a key character in one of the most masterful comic sketches Twain would ever produce: the tale of Buck Fanshawe's funeral from *Roughing It.* The tale involves the humorous encounter between Scotty Briggs, an ardent gambler whose friend Buck Fanshawe has lately died, and the town minister. Buck was owner of the town's most "sumptuous saloon," and Scotty has been given the task of arranging a funeral for him. In carrying out the task, he meets the town minister, "a fragile, gentle, spiritual new fledgling from an Eastern theological seminary, and as yet unacquainted with the ways of the mines." Much of the humor in this episode centers on the competing vernaculars at work in the conversation: Scotty's miner's slang against the refined and more articulate eastern nuances of a seminary graduate:

> "Are you the duck that runs the gospel-mill next door?"
> "Am I the—pardon me, I believe I do not understand?"

It is obviously a burlesque of two men not quite able to speak each other's language. More generally the conversation homes in on crucial questions of faith and spirituality as well. The parson asks Scotty several questions about the character of Buck Fanshawe: "Did he feel a dependence upon, or acknowledge allegiance to a higher power? . . . Had he ever been connected with any organization sequestered from secular concerns and devoted to self-sacrifice in the interests of morality?" Scotty is "stumped": the fancy theological style of the questions is meaningless in the context of a mining town in Nevada. However, finally the minister asks, "Was he a good man," and here Scotty is well able to respond. He describes the manly deeds performed by the deceased, including feats of strength and taking good care of his mother. The tale ends with the discovery that Scotty Briggs became "the only convert to religion that was ever gathered from the Virginia roughs; and it transpired that the man who had it in him to espouse the quarrel of the weak out of inborn nobility of spirit was no mean timber whereof to construct a Christian. . . . He talked to his pioneer small-fry in a language they understood!"[84]

Twain's story shows that even the roughest of the miners has an "inborn nobility of spirit" to which the eastern theologians can appeal, and he highlights the need for some moral spokesperson to take up actively the "quarrel of the weak," by which Twain refers to the various injustices of the land. It became a matter of learning how to communicate gospel truth to them, in their own words: "It was my large privilege, a month before [Scotty] died, to hear him tell the beautiful story of Joseph and his brethren to his class 'without looking at the book.' I leave it to the reader to fancy what it was like, as it fell, riddled with slang, from the lips of that grave, earnest teacher."[85] The emphasis here is on the wondrous narrative power of a Bible story like that of Joseph and his brothers in Genesis, as related in the honest vernacular of a humble storyteller like Scotty. The passage is a major early example of Twain's keen interest in the real language of real Americans, an aspect of an emerging realism that is highly ethical, insofar as it attempts to reproduce the "insideness" of the character speaking. Regarding the value of religion out west, and specifically the importance of someone like Franklin Rising, Twain does not denigrate religion or Christianity per se so much as he celebrates the common man and the necessity of some sort of faith (even in the most secular place in America). Later in life Twain said of Rising, "He and I were fast friends. I used to try to teach him how he ought to preach in order to get at the better natures of the rough population about him."[86] It seems that this episode from *Roughing It* highlights a similar theme: that, after all, it is still possible to "get at the better natures" of the ruffians around them—many of whom, like Scotty Briggs, will be found to have already an "inborn nobility of spirit."

In San Francisco Twain's close affiliations with ministers and churches surpassed that of Nevada. He wrote home to his mother about ministers, "There are [no people] I like better to converse with—if they ain't narrow minded and bigoted they make good companions."[87] This remark is consistent with Twain's interest throughout life in what he considered the best kind of Christian thinking—one that is educated and broad minded. And yet, despite these ministers' great learning, he considered them "regular bricks . . . All those of high rank and real influence I visit, dine and swap lies with, just the same as ever."[88] That is, he greatly enjoyed their company as storytellers and jokesters, men who were learned but not stuffy and shy about enjoying life. This certainly describes the kind of intellectual powers he discovered in those who became his close allies in San Francisco: Dr. Henry Scudder, pastor of a large Presbyterian church, and the Reverend Horatio Stebbins (a "regular brick"[89]), a Harvard graduate who helped establish Stanford University and the University of California. Indeed it is correct to see his friendships with ministers, both in California and later in Connecticut and New York, as largely based on their status as some the best-educated and most liberally minded individuals he would ever come across. One of the most impressive ministers that Twain befriended in California was Dr. Henry Bellows, a Unitarian pastor who became an influential intellectual force as editor of the *Christian Examiner* from 1866–69. Bellows, according to Twain, was an "able, upright & eloquent man—a man of imperial intellect & matchless power—he is Christian in the truest sense of the term & is unquestionably a brick."[90] This remark reveals interesting things about Twain's concept of a "true" Christian: first, that he most certainly did have an idea about true Christianity, and second, that it was crucial that a real Christian man be both "imperially intellectual" and a "real brick"—meaning, a regular guy who was generally amusing to be around. It is useful to know of Bellows's future endeavors; as editor of the *Christian Examiner*, he led "one of the most important of American religious reviews . . . because of its distinctive work in literary criticism, and its comment on social, philosophical, and educational problems."[91] Bellows advocated a Christian intellectualism strongly engaged in the cultural works and social situations of contemporary America—a view that Twain was typically drawn to as well. In particular Twain must have been quite intrigued by Bellows's insistence on combining Christian belief with a thoroughgoing literary criticism. Thus do Bellows's aesthetic and cultural ideas help us to imagine the kinds of dinner conversations these friends might have enjoyed just prior to his taking over the reins of the *Christian Examiner*.

During his San Francisco years, Twain also visited occasionally the Calvary Presbyterian Church, whose pastor, Dr. Charles Wadsworth, became one of his favorites. Wadsworth is memorialized in a sketch published in 1866 entitled "Reflections on the Sabbath": "[he] never fails to preach an able sermon; but every now and then, with an admirable assumption of not being aware of it, he will get off a first rate joke and then frown severely at any one who is surprised into smiling at it. It is like throwing a bone to a dog and then arresting him with a look just as he is going to seize it."[92] In particular Twain liked Wadsworth's criticism of unrealistic Sunday schools, a theme that Twain used on many occasions later in his own work.

It is within the context of Wadsworth's church that Twain announced famously that he considered himself a "brevet Presbyterian," suggesting that even on the battlefields of these most uncivilized and bohemian settings, he maintained an allegiance to faith as a sort of rank or honor. Indeed it may be true to say that it was precisely because of these several, brilliant Christian ministers, whose social company Mark Twain came to value so much during these years, that Twain remained willing to self-identify as a Christian at all. It is even worth speculating how these refined and educated ministers of the gospel were able to come to the aid of the young and brilliant journalist, who so recently had been struggling perhaps even to the point of suicidal despair. We should remember that the final years of life in California featured a very close proximity between this suicidal despair and the announcement to the world that Mark Twain considered his authorial gift to be a kind of spiritual "calling." Often, as the saying goes, it is darkest just before the dawn. It is altogether plausible that the San Francisco clergymen had a hand in the beginnings of the transformation of the wild humorist of the West into the more mature and steady New Englander that Twain would become in just a few more years.

2

Mark Twain's Wife

The Moral Ethos of the Victorian Home

In June of 1867, a young and fiery Missouri journalist dined and drank with the editors of the *New York Tribune,* discussing among other things the nature of the travel letters he would submit to them in the coming months. Samuel Clemens was restless, curious, and just on the verge of becoming one of the most unusual and influential voices in American cultural history. His eyes stalked his listeners with a charged and mildly sarcastic attitude. He had been commissioned to travel via steamer as one of many pilgrims on an ocean journey to the cultural holy land of Europe, and then on to the spiritual Holy Land of the Middle East. The voyage aboard the *Quaker City* was conceived by members of Henry Ward Beecher's Plymouth Church in New York City—perhaps the most famous church in America at that time. Beecher's church was so well known that young Sam had visited there frequently, and with his letters of introduction had met and become friends with the famous preacher. Beecher was himself originally announced to be one of the pilgrims on the *Quaker City* journey—along with famed Civil War General William T. Sherman—but both had to withdraw at the last moment. The trip was advertised as a once-in-a-lifetime opportunity to experience the world's most important shrines, and Sam Clemens could hardly wait to begin: he wrote home to his family in Missouri that he was "wild with impatience to move—move—Move!"[1]

As it turned out, the pilgrimage aboard the *Quaker City* would initiate the social transformation that would define the greatest years of his life. That transformation would include religious elements—although, as with the voyage's religiosity, Sam had mixed emotions about some of those elements, especially when he sensed shallowness or cant. Most of the other passengers were pious, genteel, a bit stuffy, and wealthy enough to afford the $1,250 fee. For most of them, the journey was understood in largely spiritual and moral terms: a lifelong dream to visit the greatest cultural and religious capitals of the Western world, ending in Palestine to view the sites of the gospel, including those places where the Savior Himself was known to have walked. In keeping with these purposes, they held daily prayer meetings that included group singing out of the *Plymouth Collection of Hymns,* services that were superintended by one of the three accompanying Congregational ministers. The veteran newspaper man who would soon become known to the world as Mark Twain preferred the company of several of the more "splendid, immoral, tobacco-smoking, wine-drinking, godless" pilgrims, with whom he could swap stories, play cards, swear openly, and generally carry on in a fashion not in keeping with the more rigorous piety of the others.[2] Twain and his roommate, Daniel Slote, the owner of a successful stationery company in Brooklyn, surrounded themselves with a group of younger men who were drawn to their looser lifestyle and funnier tales. One of these was the eighteen-year-old heir of a wealthy lumber and coal dealer from a growing city called Elmira in upstate New York. Their friendship began rather brusquely when the teenager suggested to the much older Sam Clemens how he might play his hands in a card game, to which Sam responded, "Young man, there's a prayer meeting going on forward in the dining saloon and they need you there."[3] Despite this introduction, Charles Langdon became intrigued by the stories of mining in Nevada and California as well as the adventurous life of a steamboat pilot that Sam would tell. By and by they became good and lifelong friends.

From all outward appearances, this group consisted of men beyond the pale of religious pilgrimage and reverence for the holy. And yet later in the voyage, as the ship rested in the harbor of Smyrna, Charley Langdon pulled out an ivory miniature likeness of his beautiful twenty-two-year-old sister Olivia and showed it to Sam. Sam was deeply moved as he studied the face of the woman who would become his wife Livy (figure 2). He was fascinated in hearing about her recent illnesses and how she had somehow been miraculously healed of Pott's disease through the prayers of a faith-healing minister named Newton. Sam told Charley that he wished to meet Olivia at some point, but he certainly knew even then that a wide gulf separated him from the genteel social realm of the Langdons. Later that year, over the holidays of December 1867 while visiting in New York, Sam was invited by Charley to dine with his family, where he met for the first time Olivia and her father, Jervis Langdon. A few days later, on New Year's Eve 1867, he joined them in attending a reading by Charles Dickens. Appropriately enough, young Sam Clemens made his first visit of 1868 to the Langdon family at the house where they were staying in New York. Even then, it appears, Sam Clemens had fallen in love, the realization of which would commence a different sort of pilgrimage. In a roundabout manner, the voyage of the *Quaker City* had initiated a religious quest that would produce effects in the life and writings of Mark Twain for a very long time—if not for the rest of his life.

In his desire to court Olivia Langdon, Twain understood that he was crossing an unseen boundary, that he was entering new and perhaps "dangerous water"—which is in effect what the name Mark Twain actually means.[4] Above all, Twain would need to gain the approval of Olivia's protective and wise parents, especially her father Jervis. The elder Langdon was a self-made man of energy and high moral virtues whose strong abolitionist views were a hallmark of Elmira during its rapid growth before and during the recently ended Civil War. Jervis Langdon had given much of his great wealth to the building of Park Church, of which he was a founding member. In 1854 he almost single-handedly convinced the Reverend Thomas K. Beecher, a member of America's most elite ministerial clan and half brother of Henry Ward Beecher, to become pastor of Park Church, where he remained for many decades until his death in 1890. Langdon also donated profusely to the sustenance of the Underground Railroad and its stop in Elmira, and became friends and supporters of many abolitionist leaders, including Frederick Douglass and Wendell Phillips, both of whom stayed in the Langdon home. Langdon in many ways was a living incarnation of all that the town of Elmira represented: blessed with excellent natural resources, energized rapidly by the growth of transportation such as railroads and

2. Olivia Langdon, future bride of Samuel Clemens. Courtesy of the Mark Twain Boyhood Home and Museum, Hannibal, Missouri.

canals, and given to progressive religious activities. In short, Langdon had become, like Elmira, a beacon for the reform-minded Social Christianity that would remain the most influential religious movement in America for at least the rest of Mark Twain's life. And Twain desired earnestly to marry into his family.

But Langdon was nervous about accepting the court of this raw humorist from the West, and so he requested letters of recommendation. Both parents were put off by his ragged and curly head of hair, his wisecracking manner, his penetrating blue-green eyes, and his heavy southern drawl. The letters were not especially flattering, urging caution in allowing Mark Twain to court their daughter. One called him a "humbug"; another said he would doubtless "fill a drunkard's grave."[5] But Jervis Langdon sensed something in the young man who wanted desperately to marry his daughter. When they met to discuss the letters, Twain was obviously apprehensive. Neither seemed to know how to begin. Finally Jervis Langdon looked him straight in the eyes and asked, "What kind of people are these? Haven't you a friend in the world?"

Twain responded, "Apparently not."

Despite this confession, Mark Twain was met by what were perhaps the most sympathetic and kindhearted words that he would ever experience. Jervis Langdon said to him, "I'll be your friend myself. Take the girl. I know you better than they do!"[6] It is reasonable to believe that this anecdote, more or less, reflects a real episode. Historical or not, the spirit of Langdon's remarks can be compared with Joe Twichell's comments, quoted earlier: "People don't know Mark's best side. I am more persuaded of it than ever." Similarly, Livy wrote to a confidante early in her marriage of her desire that the public might get "to know something of his deeper, larger nature."[7] These three successful easterners discerned another side to Mark Twain that had gone unperceived by so many others. These three, guided by their shared perception of the finer side of Mark Twain, became his chief Christian mentors throughout the most crucial period of his personal spiritual journey (although Jervis Langdon only lived through the summer of 1870): the several years from roughly 1867 (when he traveled to Europe and the Holy Land, and met his future wife) through 1873 (when the move to Hartford appeared permanent with the purchase of a large lot in the Nook Farm neighborhood). According to Jeffrey Steinbrink, these years make up the period during which the former Sam Clemens worked at "getting to be Mark Twain." This mentoring process, in which the wild bohemian of the west reinvented himself as a Christian husband and parishioner (another sort of religious "claim") in one of liberal Protestantism's most prominent locations, engendered a virtual transformation in his outward behaviors and demeanor.

Twain's decisive need to be mentored had been sparked by comments he received while in Hawaii in 1866 from Anson Burlingame, a highly intellectual, moral, and talented U.S. diplomat whose attention and interest Twain prized at this early stage of his career. Burlingame's advice, which touched Twain deeply, was to seek out those men superior to himself: "What you need now is the refinement of association. Seek companionship among men of superior intellect and character. . . . Never affiliate with inferiors; always climb."[8] When Burlingame died, Twain's eulogy in the *Buffalo Express* on February 25, 1870, revealed his heady respect and admiration for the diplomat. In particular, the eulogy lists those moral attributes to which Twain would aspire: "he had outgrown the narrow citizenship of a state, and become a citizen of the world; and his charity was large enough and his great heart warm enough to feel for all its races and to labor for them. He was a true man, a brave man, an earnest man, a liberal man, a just man, a generous man, in all his ways and by all his instincts a noble man."[9] Burlingame's advice to "climb" is echoed in a letter Twain sent to Mary Fairbanks, a fellow passenger on the Plymouth journey whom he called affectionately "Mother," in November 1868: "I shall do no act which you or Livy might be pained to hear of—I shall seek the society of the good—I shall be a *Christian.* I shall climb—climb—climb—toward this bright sun that is shining in the heaven of my happiness until all that is gross & unworthy is hidden in the mists & the darkness of that lower earth whence you first lifted my aspiring feet."[10] In the same month, he wrote to his sister Pamela, "I do nothing that is not thoroughly *right*—I am *rising.*"[11] The triple verb "climb—climb—climb" from the first letter can be contrasted with his proclaimed "impatience to move—move—Move!" from a few months earlier.[12] We might say that the desire to climb—as opposed to movement for movement's sake—is more directed at a particular goal and in that sense more transcendental. The second letter to Pamela confirms Twain's conscious association of doing right with rising—meaning his connection of moral virtue with social influence and prestige. Twain's simple choice of words indicates a changing attitude toward his life and career from the wanderlust of his youth to a more goal-oriented, and metaphysical, concept of the future. This yearning to "rise" and to "climb," which includes both spiritual and social maturity (and undoubtedly financial growth), required mentoring and guidance, and Twain turned to those whose example he could depend upon. Thus a sort of cultural discipleship began to be enacted in Twain's relationships with several easterners, including Livy and her father Jervis Langdon. Later, more long-term companions shaped him: his spiritual mentor Twichell and his literary mentor William Dean Howells.

Much has been made of Twain's embrace of Christianity during this crucial period at the outset of his eastern literary career, all set in motion when he fell in love with Olivia Langdon. She was a complex figure with intellectual and moral concerns that represented much of the Victorian American culture. The sentimentalized religious piety that resonates throughout the courtship letters of 1868–69 has led some critics to make the dubious assertion that Twain's "conversion" to Christianity was nothing more than a series of rhetorical moves initiated to insure that the Langdons would endorse the courtship of their refined daughter to such an outlandish, somewhat boorish roughneck from the Far West. Clearly, Twain was a rhetorical genius as a writer, and without a doubt, it is a difficult business discerning the real from the fake in any writer's personal letters. Nevertheless, in Twain's letters of this period one confronts numerous bald statements of Christian faith: in February 1869, for instance, when Twain writes to Livy's mother, "But now I never swear; I never taste wine or spirits upon any occasion whatsoever; I am orderly, and my conduct is above reproach in a worldly sense; and finally, I now claim that I am a Christian."[13]

Most critics have questioned and summarily rejected Twain's confession, describing Twain as merely "[a]cting the part of returned Prodigal, of sinner turned Christian," thus emphasizing its trickery over its authenticity.[14] Moreover, whereas some have tended to belittle what they consider to be Twain's vaguely spiritual turn for greater gain, the ambiguity of this topic has resulted in many ambivalent reactions from some critics. Susan Harris, for example, while at first stating that Twain's religious proclivities constituted "a series of feints designed to convince the entire Langdon family that he was a viable suitor" later admits that Clemens may have been in fact "genuinely struggling to become a Christian." Harris further states candidly that "retrospection facilitates our skepticism. . . . [It is] difficult not to be struck by [the love letters'] apparent sincerity. . . . Clemens's struggles to achieve faith were perfectly sincere." And yet Harris's conclusion is largely in agreement with most critics, whom she says "have found it difficult to believe his professions, knowing first that he was a master manipulator of traditional forms, and second, that he gave up religion soon after the wedding."[15] Among other things, it seems wrong to say that Twain "gave up religion" after his marriage—unless one is drawing upon a very narrow definition of what "religion" actually is. Clearly, shortly after the marriage, some of the piety did disappear, and Twain did begin to slip away from whatever doctrinal orthodoxy he may have attained.

And yet the yearning for belief revealed in these letters is symptomatic of a religious nature that is not easily erased. James D. Wilson has asserted that the love letters reveal "graphically and, I think, convincingly the depth and sincerity of his quest for religious faith. . . . During the period from Christmas 1868 to the Epiphany, January 6, 1869, Clemens seems Augustinian in his concentrated and agonized examination of conscience," a reference to St. Augustine's earnest quest, centuries before, to discover true faith in God.[16] Presumably Wilson's comment underscores not just the lengthy and at times emotionally painful process of seeking and achieving conversion; it also suggests the similarly besmirched sexual purity of the seekers. The reference to Augustine also suggests what many consider the essential character of religion itself—its insistence that each person's life reveals something that he loves ultimately—what Paul Tillich called "ultimate concern." According to one philosopher, this "irresistible tendency to fix on an ultimate unifying concern for [one's] life" is equal to the "attempt to find the 'rest' of which Augustine spoke in the opening pages of his *Confessions.*"[17] Mark Twain's search for rest in some set of unifying meanings about life, in whatever degree, is thus easily construed as a religious quest, not unlike St. Augustine's.

Wilson's comparison (one of the more audacious in Twain scholarship) has the great benefit of announcing to the world that at least one judicious scholar considers Mark Twain's religious quest of this period to be both arduous and genuine. Furthermore, as Wilson has noted, this religious impulse had been fully awakened in Twain well before his encounter with Livy.[18] But Twain's religious quest of this period was not merely for the sake of attaining a properly evangelical conversion experience. Again, it is only within the contexts of a narrow and calcified understanding of "religion" that one would be compelled to see it that way. A more fluid and social understanding of religion would include matters of mood, motivation, and moral ecology. Twain's "Augustinian" quest targeted not just mere conversion but along with it (and arguably even more importantly) a sanctified and holy vision of married life and the home that was at the core of American belief of the time. In the apt phrase made famous by Barbara Welter, the "cult of true womanhood" was the standard vision of how woman were to behave as wives and mothers of genteel Victorian households.[19] Twain sought initiation into Victorian America largely through an earnest embrace of the codes of this cult. And yet Olivia "grew up in a community alive with ideas of new roles for women. . . . [she] entertained during her courtship some hope that she could play an active role on the public stage of life." But Twain argued against such a life, instead painting a future in which she would be "a powerful force for good within her limited world": the Victorian home. Twain extolled this role as sacred and compared Livy to one of his great idols, Joan of Arc.[20] If one biographer's claim that he "[made] Livy his religion" has limited value for some critics, it does have the ring of truth in suggesting the extent to which Mark Twain's idea of home and hearth motivated him in this crucial period.[21] In one of his love letters, he writes, "Goodbye, Livy. You are so pure, so great, so good, so beautiful. How can I help loving you? Say, rather, how can I keep from worshipping you, you dear little paragon."[22] Another waxes, "Oh. Livy darling, I could just worship that picture. . . . It is an angel-beauty—something not of earth."[23] And yet lest we make too much of the "spiritual" aspect of the courtship, we should admit that he venerated all that she represented, including cash: "her peaceful spirit derived as much from the Langdon wealth as from the progressive Christian faith that saw her through her treatment and cure."[24]

It is a curious fact that some of Mark Twain's most famous episodes depict male escape from female domesticity. Any list of examples would include the almost archetypal "lighting out for the territory" that ends his most famous novel. Both *Tom Sawyer* and *Huckleberry Finn*, however, revolve largely around these issues of young men seeking refuge from the "sivilizing" ways of their female supervisors. And yet both novels also often betray a yearning for domestic bliss. Thus it would be wrong to conclude that this view of boyish rebellion characterized the adult author in a full and satisfying manner. As Michael Kiskis has put it, "Mark Twain never wanted to escape the 'domestic.'"[25] Kiskis has shown us recently that critics of Mark Twain have tended to overlook Twain's devotion to the domestic culture of this time period. Kiskis begins his analysis by drawing upon distinctions critic Gillian Brown makes about the competing modes of nineteenth-century American literature, which she labels as "individualism" vs. "domesticity": "[these modes] have long been figured as . . . distinct and oppositional trajectories. . . . [I]n this androcentric, if not misogynistic, account of American culture, literature records the battle between the masculine desire for freedom and the feminine will toward civilization."[26] Kiskis agrees with Brown's contention that critics would be well served to view these themes not as competitive but as synergistic. Since Twain has often been seen primarily as a champion of freedom and individualism, for example, we tend to forget his unabashedly sentimentalized discourse regarding home, hearth, and Livy. That is, by focusing so much on the one side of the equation, we tend to forget the other.

Here I would like to follow Kiskis's desire to locate Mark Twain in the context of "the 'Other American tradition' of literary domesticity," especially by emphasizing the religious aspects of this tradition far more than Kiskis does in his own research.[27] It is clear from some of the language that Mark Twain employed when speaking of this home life that he viewed it as sacred, for example. Shortly after the children began arriving, Twain started keeping a journal specifically for the purpose of recording charming remarks the young girls made as they grew up. Titled "A Record of Small Foolishness," this diary contains a biblical quotation on its title page: "And Mary treasured these sayings in her heart." It is a reference to Luke 2:51, in which chapter Mary witnesses numerous amazing events and prophecies regarding the boy Jesus. The allusion indicates a sacralizing of not just the mother Livy but, importantly, of the children as well, especially Susy, the oldest: it "conveys his attitude of almost religious devotion to his wife and family," as Victor Doyno has put it (figure 3).[28] As we have already seen, the love letters to Livy literally drip with sentimentalized, religious discourse, but such language continued well into the many years of their lives together as well. To some extent, Twain was coached into this discourse by Mary Fairbanks, who perhaps as much as anyone urged him to court Livy. It was Fairbanks who argued that a "good wife would be a perpetual incentive to progress"[29]—a reference to an important category of Victorian religion, social improvement. It resonates with other letters of the period, such as another to Fairbanks quoted earlier: "I shall climb—climb—climb—toward this bright sun that is shining in the heaven of my happiness."[30]

3. Mark Twain and family. Courtesy of the Mark Twain Project, Bancroft Library, University of California, Berkeley.

These and many other statements document Mark Twain's need, and his evident desire, for moral improvement, not merely economic advancement. They also show that he recognized his need for feminine influences in order to succeed at such a lofty, sacred goal. In an 1885 description of Livy, Twain writes,

> Her spirit is serene, tranquil. She has not the support which is afforded by anger. . . . The mother of my children adores them—there is no milder term for it; and they worship her; they even worship anything which the touch of her hand has made sacred. They know her for the best and truest friend they have ever had, or ever shall have; they know her for one who never did them a wrong, and cannot do them a wrong; who never told them a lie, nor the shadow of one; who never deceived them by even an ambiguous gesture . . . they know her for one whose promise, whether of reward or punishment, is gold, and always worth its face, to the uttermost farthing. In a word, they know her, and I know her, for the best and dearest mother that lives—and by a long, long way the wisest.[31]

Besides the obvious gestures toward religious vocabulary here, it is interesting how the ending of the long passage seemingly figures Twain as himself just one of the children: "[the children] know her, and I know her, for the best and dearest mother." Of course, Livy usually referred to Twain as "youth," and like his affectionate naming of Mary Fairbanks as Mother, this passages slips into a similar sensibility. Mark Twain is conscious of having received precisely the same treatment that the children have received from their mother Livy. He has never been lied to by her or been given ambiguous gestures, and so on. Such a reading of this passage supports a view of Livy as moral standard-bearer within the sacred home and in particular of the extremely high view of her moral character as consistently sketched by Mark Twain. While we may doubt the ability of any human to attain such high standards, it seems clear that Twain did not doubt it—or at least that he desired to maintain a mythic conception of Livy and to present her publicly in this manner.

The effects of settling down and embracing a moral ecology superintended by the angel in the Clemens household were crucial in establishing the literary views of a world-class author. It is possible to identify a number of themes within Mark Twain's writings that were fostered by his emerging sense of Christian identity of this period. Certainly it would be going too far to suggest that Twain's literary achievement rested primarily on what might be called a Christian aesthetic. For one thing, it would be impossible to locate a single, monolithic version of what a Christian aesthetic of literature might actually be; there are a variety of Christian aesthetics, with some loose alliances among and between them. Secondly, accusing Mark Twain of premising his work fully on Christian aesthetics would repeat the mistake of telling only one part of the story. Nevertheless, it is striking how central many of these themes became in his most important works, especially of the so-called major period that coincided with his residence in Hartford. It is probably fair to say that these themes appeared most obvious in the early years of the marriage and dissipated thereafter. But aspects of this "theory" of literature and culture are present in almost all of the major works until the move away from Hartford—and in many even beyond that.

The liberalized Christianity with which Mark Twain willingly surrounded himself worked its way into his consciousness and eventually into his work as social critic and moral storyteller. Specifically, five aspects of Mark Twain's writings show affinities with Christian approaches to literature and culture of the same period. This list is not meant to be definitive, of course, but it does suggest major assumptions of a biblical and Christian approach to literature and culture. Obviously Twain often questioned, satirized, rebelled against, or even flatly denied aspects of these concepts at times throughout his career. Nevertheless, his works can be analyzed and understood as enactments of the cultural conversations about these ideas. Finally, this brief outline provides a basic vocabulary of ideas and terms for use throughout the rest of the story.

Emphasis on Human Responsibility as Opposed to Determinism

Mankind is responsible for moral actions. Much of humans' uniqueness inheres in their being held responsible by God for their actions. This liberal vision of mankind's moral agency reflects "the movement . . . towards the positing of some dynamic and practical version of what Schopenhauer calls 'the will'. . . . The general tendency observable in the history of philosophy between Kant and Hegel or Schopenhauer [is] roughly speaking a movement from an emphasis on knowledge to an emphasis on will."[32] In American religious history it is dramatized in the debates between strict Calvinists and more liberal Arminian views of mankind's moral agency. Much of Mark Twain's writing can be understood as participating in this debate, but the extent to which his work champions free will and moral change is often overlooked. Sometimes, by focusing on the later, more pessimistic writings, critics have emphasized only his deterministic worldview. Moreover, his output is concentrated in the period of the rise of realism and naturalism in American fiction—movements that also called into question the extent to which humans were free moral agents. In the case of naturalism in particular, human agency was typically rejected. However, and despite Twain's attractions to determinism, the emphasis throughout his work is on the moral improvement and enlightenment of mankind—major precepts of Social Christianity.

Sympathy and Solidarity

Among humanity's responsibilities is to love and respect each other as having been made in the image of God. One philosopher states that "each is to exhibit solidarity with the other, to stand in his stead, to love him as he loves himself, to seek his fulfillment as he seeks his own. Indeed, in seeking the other's, he will find his own."[33] Among many other examples, this statement is a fine description of the moral action in novels like *Huckleberry Finn* or *The Prince and the Pauper.* Today we often speak of human solidarity or identification, but in the nineteenth century this emotion or "sentiment" was frequently described as sympathy, and it became increasingly the work of the human heart.

It is not an exaggeration to say that Mark Twain's Christian sensibility is seen most prominently, in both his own life and in the moral effects of his many writings, in his desire to manifest and to foster sympathy, a term brimming with Christian connotations. We can hardly overstate the importance of human sympathy for those influenced by this way of thinking. Without the moral sense, society cannot possibly cohere, and it certainly can never progress. In addition to its impact in the general field of philosophy, the Scottish Common Sense philosophy had an important impact on American literary culture, in which sympathy became the highest ideal of human sentiment. While attempts to define sentimentalism have proliferated greatly over the past two decades, a simple way of understanding sentimental literature is to see its authors as attempting to create and sustain human sympathy and solidarity among their readers. Historically, discussions of sentimentalism as a literary mode have excluded male writers like Mark Twain, although the analysis of male sentimentalism is a growing trend. It is now becoming clear that in many cases Twain shared certain aesthetic aims with these sentimental writers (who were mostly women) and that often his finest passages abounded with sentimentalism. This is apparent in his warm depictions of domestic life, especially as presided over by kind and moral women. Perhaps the best examples are his fond descriptions of both his own mother, Jane, and his wife Livy, and his heart-wrenching elegies for his two daughters much later in life. As Michael Kiskis has said about Twain's elegy "The Death of Jean" in 1909, "Frankly, I have found no piece so likely to destroy conventional notions of Mark Twain.

. . . It challenges the established paradigm and is, therefore, relegated to the ash heap of sentimentalism."[34] By now there should be little doubt that much of Twain's literary magic fits with one recent description of sentimentalism: "the cultural expression of the desire for union. . . . a manifestation of the belief in . . . unity—of principal and purpose."[35] Twain hoped to build and sustain a social union that would encourage a "more perfect union"—even an intimacy rooted in common cultural and moral assumptions. To whatever extent a work of literature fosters such human solidarity, it can be called sentimental, according to this understanding. Thus was Mark Twain a powerfully sentimental author.

Humanity's Fallenness and the Apocalyptic Power of Humor

An excellent observation about humor's apocalyptic power is made by Stanley Brodwin, who notes that humor is made possible through sympathy, by which he means close identification. Our alikeness, what we might call our "Adamness," allows humor its eschatological effect. According to Brodwin, "Mark Twain's Adamic Diaries reveal his understanding that his profound comic sense had theological roots; that it was a manifestation of man's fallen state and a dread cure for it that few men knew how to use; and that his 'kinship' with Adam gave him a universal relationship through which his deepest theological insights into the humor of the absurd could be illuminated."[36] Here Brodwin asserts a theological framework for understanding Twain's comic work, one premised on a certain view of humanity in general as being ultimately fallen and imperfect. Humor functions as a constant reminder that humanity is not perfectible, as the Pelagian view might have it; humanity is finally both hideous in its errors and amusing in its sameness.

Brodwin's explanation is easily compared to some interesting observations by the British commentator Malcolm Muggeridge, who described the purpose of gargoyles on church steeples. According to Muggeridge, gargoyles are placed on steeples so that those who ascend the steps are always confronted with their own human frailties even as they are being entranced by the beautiful spires of the cathedral. The gargoyles are present as a constant reminder of the laughable nature of all human achievement, this side of paradise. Muggeridge states that the gargoyle is "laughing at the inadequacy of man, the pretensions of man, the absolute preposterous gap—disparity—between his aspirations and his performance, which is the eternal comedy of human life."[37] Oddly enough, these gargoyles are not only humorous, they are brimming with hope, because it is within the context of our common humanity that our greatest hope is to be discovered. Furthermore, a cosmic and transcendent hope is not primarily located within humankind alone, but must somehow be aided by a benevolent God for its successful prosecution. The gargoyle, thus, is a constant reminder of our shared fallenness and neediness.

Additionally, Muggeridge notes that a gargoyle is attached to the physical exterior of the sacred building, the church steeple, which points forever toward heaven. Its location suggests that humor is itself a proper, and perhaps vital, feature of the heavenly journey. Humor is in keeping with the best of the Christian tradition—and was even exemplified, like all positive human traits, in the life of the Master Himself. Indeed it seems shocking to many today to be told that Jesus Christ was quite a humorist, but that is precisely what Elton Trueblood and others have shown.[38] If Jesus used humor, there is to be a strong endorsement for its use as a tool of teaching and wisdom. For example, Jesus often displayed an acute awareness of and criticism of hypocrisy and cant among religious leaders precisely by satirizing them. Mark Twain shared with Jesus a propensity to burlesque those members of the clergy who in His view did not live up to their roles as Christian models. For both Jesus and Mark Twain, as for most people, ministers and priests must meet an even higher standard than the members of their flocks. And for both of them, the tool of choice was often humor.

Culture as Teleological, with Shalom ("Oughtness") as the Goal

Cornelius Plantinga invokes the Hebrew concept of "shalom," which he defines as "the webbing together of God, humans, and all creation in justice, fulfillment, and delight. . . . shalom means universal flourishing, wholeness, and delight—a rich state of affairs in which natural needs are satisfied and natural gifts fruitfully employed, a state of affairs that inspires joyful wonder as its Creator and Savior opens doors and welcomes the creatures in whom he delights."[39] Nicholas Wolterstorff also provides a similar reading of the concept of shalom: it is the idea of "man dwelling at peace in all his relationships: with God, with himself, with his fellows, with nature. Shalom is a peace which is not merely the absence of hostility, though certainly it is that, but a peace which is at its highest level enjoyment. To dwell in shalom is to enjoy living in nature, to enjoy living with one's fellows, to enjoy life with oneself."[40] The forming of right relations ultimately brings with it an enjoyment or relishing of existence that cannot be exceeded. This vision of social arrangements constitutes the heart of the Old Testament prophetic tradition, illustrated most powerfully in Isaiah.

These utopian passages might seem otherworldly, even impossible. But according to Plantinga and Wolterstorff, this rarified concept of shalom constitutes the biblical goal of our hopes as human beings on planet Earth. At its most basic level, says Plantinga, the term shalom is best translated as "the way things ought to be." This sense of the "oughtness" in the world is the basis of all social and cultural criticism, and it has its own roots in the prophetic tradition. Obviously it is not limited to a theistic view, as even so skeptical a theorist as Terry Eagleton has grudgingly drawn upon the concept of oughtness: "You cannot describe someone as oppressed unless you have some dim notion of what not being oppressed might look like, and why being oppressed is a bad idea in the first place. And this involves normative judgments, which then makes politics look uncomfortably like ethics."[41] Eagleton's gesture toward "oughtness" here is symptomatic of a growing awareness among theorists that in applying postmodern versions of relativism, our culture has lost something important. In Mark Twain's time, however, "normative judgments" were a commonplace, and an alliance between politics and ethics was certainly nowhere felt to be uncomfortable.

Mark Twain's own clear sense of the "oughtness" of our lives is rampant throughout many of his works but is perhaps most clearly illustrated in his response to an article in the *Christian Union* in 1885—a relatively unknown piece in the Twain canon. This essay is the source of the illuminating description of Livy as sacred mother quoted earlier: "The mother of my children adores them—there is no milder term for it; and they worship her; they even worship anything which the touch of her hand has made sacred. They know her for the best and truest friend they have ever had, or ever shall have."[42] Perhaps it goes without saying that Twain's emphatic response provides his conception of the ways and manners of domestic life as it "ought" to be, in every "Christian" home. This point is supported by the fact that the piece in the *Christian Union* came as a response to an incident regarding the disciplining of a young boy by his father and mother. The magazine solicited from its readers responses under the title, "What Ought He to Have Done?" This question invokes the biblical concept of shalom—the way things ought to be. Whether the *Christian Union* or Mark Twain was conscious of this specific invocation or not, the philosophy of "oughtness" is so crucial to a culture steeped in the biblical tradition that it goes without saying that it redounds with the spiritual ramifications of its origins. As we shall see, "oughtness" or shalom is a central preoccupation of Twain's career.

Lament as Protest Theism

Much of Mark Twain's output centers on what theologians like to call the "problem of evil"—meaning the existence of great pain and suffering in a world that is supposedly made by a good and benevolent Creator. The concept of protest theism has been suggested by Stan Goldman to describe Herman Melville's difficult relationship with God. Goldman argues that Melville was

> neither an agnostic nor an atheist . . . [he searched for] the limits within which a nonsectarian faith is possible and life endures meaningfully. Protest theism is a response to God that allows the human to protest against the physical and spiritual limits imposed upon the human by the divine: undeserved suffering, death, divine self-concealment, and the presence of doubt. Melville's protest theism daringly reminds God of His promises, judicially tries God for his breach of promise. . . . [It] continuously questions the nature of God's absolute love, justice, and goodness, prompted by the agonizing disparity between God's biblical promise of presence, protection, and peace and God's fulfillment in absence, suffering, and war. Protest theism is a protest against human fate.[43]

Goldman's description of Melville's state of mind can be easily applied to Mark Twain. To put it in a biblical frame, protest theism involves calling into question God's commitment to bringing about a world of shalom. One can only protest if one believes he knows how the world ought to be. The obvious presence of unexplainable pain and suffering seems on its surface to be perhaps the strongest argument against the world ever becoming what it ought to be.

As Mark Twain aged and increasingly was faced with the pain and suffering of his own personal world, this protest grew to the point of outrage and led him to question the moral acceptability of belief in a God who would allow so much pain. However, we must also attend to Twain's preoccupation throughout the major period with the problem of pain—one that can rightfully be understood as one of the major preoccupations of his career. And once again, the logic of this preoccupation necessitates a view of how the world ought to be. This logic has deep affinities with the Christian approach to society and culture, and indeed with faith itself. As the theologian Jürgen Moltmann explains, "faith, whenever it develops into hope, causes not rest but unrest, not patience but impatience. It does not calm the unquiet heart, but is itself the unquiet heart in man. . . . Peace with God means conflict with the world, for the goad of the promised future stabs inexorably into the flesh of every unfulfilled present."[44] In Moltmann's formulation, protest is always the natural outgrowth of hopefulness that the future will be different from, and morally superior to, the present. For Moltmann, the unquiet hearts of men like Melville and Twain do not speak of a lack of faith, but rather the opposite.

These five major themes, each of which can be loosely identified with nineteenth-century versions of a Christian approach to culture and the arts, were also preoccupations of Mark Twain, particularly during his residence in Hartford and Elmira. Two excellent, relatively brief pieces of writing that illustrate these themes are "About Smells" and "The Indignity Put Upon the Remains of George Holland by the Rev. Mr. Sabine." Both were written during the short time Twain lived in Buffalo, at the very beginning of his married life, as he was trying to establish his writing career in the East. "About Smells" is a response to Brooklyn minister DeWitt Talmage, a popular fire-and-brimstone preacher whom Twain had actually misread in 1870. Twain believed that Talmage wished to separate the higher class members of his congregation from the lower, fearing the wealthy might be offended by the body odors of the working class. But in fact the entire context of the sermon, which Twain later read, showed that Talmage meant it to be a sarcastic attack on such an idea. Twain's response in "About Smells" reveals a man indignant at the suggestion that pews be rented for a fee or that one group of believers be treated differently from another. In general, it shows his indignant rejection of what he regarded as the pompous proclamations of the bourgeois clergy:

> We have reason to believe that there will be laboring men in heaven; and also a number of negroes, and Esquimaux, and Terra del Fuegans, and Arabs, and a few Indians. . . . Talmage is of the same material as that used in the construction of his early predecessors in the ministry; and yet one feels that there must be a difference somewhere between him and the Savior's first disciples. . . . Is there a choir in Mr. T's church? And does it ever occur that they have no better manners than to sing that hymn which is so suggestive of laborers and mechanics:
>
> "Son of the Carpenter! Receive
> This humble work of mine?"
>
> Now, can it be possible that in a handful of centuries the Christian character has fallen away from an imposing heroism that scorned even the stake, the cross, and the axe, to a poor little effeminacy that withers and wilts under an unsavory smell? We are not prepared to believe so, the reverend Doctor and his friend to the contrary.[45]

It is worth pointing out that Twain later apologized to Talmage and admitted his misunderstanding of Talmage's basic point: Twain wrote that Talmage "is a very excellent man and . . . his heart is in the freeing of the churches."[46] But the episode and the brief essay speak volumes about the emergence of a Christian sensibility in the works of Mark Twain. Besides his outrage at the condescending approach to any members of a congregation, Twain here invokes a hymn by Charles Wesley, "Son of the Carpenter," that celebrates the work of the hands of everyday laborers as things giving glory to God. In particular the hymn operates by noting that Jesus was himself a laborer. Likewise, Twain describes the Twelve as mainly fishermen who undoubtedly had a "fishy" smell about them. The essay lists a number of disenfranchised groups who deserve better treatment by the churches. Finally, however, most prominent in all of this is a strong gesture toward shalom: Twain's argument against his perception of Talmage indicates that he truly believes things ought not to be a certain way. His ending claims that Christianity has fallen away from its former glories, becoming little more than "a poor little effeminacy." Far from dismissing the church as obsolete, the burden of this piece is to suggest a direction that is truer to the church's meaning and purpose. Twain is concerned here with the church fulfilling its proper and holy calling, as welcomer of all peoples. Furthermore, Twain is under the impression that this essay may have some effect among his readers. He is modeling here a belief that writing about these things matters and that humor can change people for the better.

Even more persuasive on these points is a related piece written a year later, "The Indignity Put Upon the Remains of George Holland by the Rev. Mr. Sabine." This essay arose in response to Twain learning that the Reverend William Sabine, an Episcopal rector in New York City, had refused to allow a memorial service for a deceased actor named George Holland to be held in his church on Madison Avenue. Sabine echoed Christians' widespread disregard of all forms of popular culture, including the theater. In particular, Sabine charged that the work of the popular stage did not teach any moral lessons to audiences, and as a result was a waste of time. Mark Twain's powerful rejection of Sabine's view expresses many of the themes I have outlined. On the one hand, Twain violently opposed the fact that Sabine regarded Holland as somehow different or inferior to the other members he was supposedly called to serve. In this sense the article mirrors the argument of "About Smells." But in showing his support for allowing the funeral of Holland, Twain creates here one of the most important documents of his emerging aesthetic sensibility that he ever penned. The argument is a sustained attack on Sabine's notion that the arts do not bring about moral good and that only the Christian clergy do so. Instead, says Twain, Sabine should recognize that

> We are all instruments for the carrying out of God's purposes; it is not for me to pass judgment upon your appointed share of the work, or to

> praise or to revile it; I have divine authority for it that we are all sinners, and therefore it is not for me to discriminate and say we will supplicate for this sinner, for he was a merchant prince of a banker, but we will beseech no forgiveness for this other one, for he was a play actor.

Twain takes his greatest offense in Sabine's claim that not only do actors not provide moral lessons, but in fact they are "obstacles to moral progress." He counters with shining examples: "Where was ever a sermon preached that could make filial ingratitude so hateful to men as the sinful play King Lear?" For Twain,

> nine-tenths of all the kindness and forbearance and Christian charity and generosity in the hearts of the American people today, got there by being filtered down from their fountainhead, the gospel of Christ, through dramas and tragedies and comedies on the stage, and through the despised novel and the Christmas story, and through the thousand and one lessons, suggestions, and narratives of generous deeds that stir the pulses, and exalt and augment the nobility of the nation day by day from the teeming columns of ten thousand newspapers, and NOT from the drowsy pulpit![47]

Twain's response to Sabine goes even further in connecting the work of culture with the work of the gospel of Jesus Christ:

> All that is great and good in our particular civilization came straight from the hand of Jesus Christ, and many creatures, and of divers sorts, were doubtless appointed to disseminate it; and let us believe that this seed and the result are the main thing . . . whosoever, in his way and according to his opportunity, sows the one and produces the other, has done high service and worthy. . . . [the theaters] till nine-tenths of the vineyard, and the pulpit tills the other tenth.

The metaphor of the vineyard and the sowing of the seed is a familiar one in Christian accounts of human culture, of course, and Twain's use of it here suggests his agreement with a holistic and all-encompassing influence of the gospel in all areas of human commerce and culture. This version is closely aligned with the traditional Calvinistic view of culture as depicted first in the works of John Calvin himself, and then as hashed out in the reformational version of what H. Richard Niebuhr called a "transformational" approach in his classic work *Christ and Culture*. To some extent this vision had been rejected by many church leaders of Twain's time, and his argument makes a plea for its recovery. We might compare Twain's concerns here with those of David Hegeman, who has identified the difference between what he calls "redemptive history" and "culturative history" of the created order. According to Hegeman, the church has long been preoccupied with redemptive history to the exclusion of a balanced focus on its culturative mission. In other words, the church has obsessively focused on its "redemptive" mission to save souls—and perhaps to a large extent, as the author suggests, this is justifiably so. However, an insidious aspect of this narrow focus is that Christians have forsaken their culturative mission to the earth and its civilizations. Indeed mankind's culturative calling actually was its original calling. Thus does Hegeman attempt "to help the Church recover a biblical vision for culture-making; culture has a central place in God's overall purpose for the human race."[48]

Mark Twain made a similar plea in "The Indignity Put Upon the Remains of George Holland by the Rev. Mr. Sabine." In his own manner, and without the theological sophistication, Twain calls upon the church to recognize the culturative contributions of artists and actors that are in fact more in keeping with the heart of reformed theology:

> No, I am not trying to rob the pulpit of any atom of its full share and credit in the work of disseminating the meat and marrow of the gospel of Christ; but I am trying to get a moment's hearing for worthy agencies in the same work, that with overwrought modesty seldom or never claim a recognition of their great services. . . . it is fair and just that somebody who believes that actors were made for a high and good purpose, and that they accomplish the object of their creation and accomplish it well, protest.

In all of this, of course, there is a great deal of personal interest. To a large extent we can read this essay as a sort of self-apology for the work that Mark Twain believed he had done in the past and would continue to do. Here he protests those who might consider actors, including himself, as serving no real "high and good purpose." Indeed the essay ends by invoking the "theatrical ministry" of George Holland, a ministry that "had for fifty years softened hard hearts, bred generosity in cold ones, kindled emotions in dead ones, uplifted base ones, broadened bigoted ones."[49] What Twain asserts for Holland is, of course, precisely what he asserts for much of his own work—both are ministries, ones involved primarily in changing the human heart. And that is precisely as it should be—it is within the right and proper working of the artistic endeavor as a culturative process. Thus are George Holland and Mark Twain recognizable as coworkers in the same vineyard of the Lord.

Undoubtedly some readers may still wish to reject the view of Mark Twain as an apocalyptic writer focused on "Christian" concerns by arguing that it was not his intention or that later he would question and reject these particular views. However, although I do believe that often Twain's intentions and motivations were rooted in such Christian categories as hope, shalom, charity, or sympathy, they need not be so rooted dogmatically in order to issue in an apocalyptic message, or the changing of the human heart. We have it from the best authority that this is so, Mark Twain himself, who stated at one point, "Even here in this humble capacity I am doing what you are always doing—preaching. The art of preaching is to influence you. From the pulpit and from the mouths of all of you the preaching goes on all the time. Our words and our acts are not for ourselves, but for others. . . . We are preaching all the time, even if we do not know it."[50] Twain concedes here that we cannot control how our lives are interpreted by others, and of course that is doubly true for our literary productions.

One useful description of this phenomenon comes from the work of J. R. R. Tolkien, who disliked being called an author of allegory and responded by coining the term "applicability" to refer to a story's appeal to the "freedom of the reader." For Tolkien, allegory is overshadowed by the "purposed domination of the author." In contrast, a story filled with applicability invites multiple readings and morals, thus transcending a story with a thinly concealed agenda, which is little more than propaganda.[51] Tolkien's concept of applicability should help us get around the potential problem of whatever Mark Twain's actual intentions might have been. We need not be overly concerned about whether Twain was self-consciously trying to be apocalyptic or whether he always aimed at achieving social and moral shalom. Rather, we can appeal to the inherent Christian applicability of Twain's artistic work, much of which derives from his apocalyptic tendencies. This insight should inform our analysis of Mark Twain, insofar as he seemingly was never able to shake the hope deep down inside—or at least, not until he was an old, tired, grief-ridden man. Indeed Mark Twain was often and deeply moved by expressions of human hope. To the extent that Twain utilized the apocalyptic mode whose goal is the "the achievement of shalom," his work is part of one of the great strains of the American project, itself deeply tied to the Christian traditions. As such, we can take him at his word—that he actually believed, as he said in 1902, that we are "preaching all the time, even if we do not know it."[52] Twain confirms this approach in another essay written late in life, where he provided what turned out to be one of the most profound and explicit explanations of his main profession in life, that of a humorist: "Humor must not professedly teach, and it must not professedly preach, but it must do both if it would live forever. By forever, I mean 30 years [after which the topics become passe or commonplace]. . . . I have always preached. That is the reason I have lasted thirty years."[53] By now we can admit he has lasted far longer than a century and largely because of his culturative work; not "preachy" by any means, he was nevertheless a preacher of shalom, the way things ought to be.

An awareness of these features of Twain's cosmic vision helps clarify how seemingly irreverent or antireligious screeds fit into a pattern of cosmic shalom. During this pivotal period in which Twain's dream of achieving a sacred domestic bliss seemed on the verge of fulfillment, he was publishing works that appeared to struggle with the implications of the full achievement of that dream. During these crucial years when he was forging his own "Christian" identity, Twain completed and published two early masterworks that attack and disparage institutional religion and romantic idealism, and yet which both also yearn for the time of settling down. His first best-seller, *The Innocents Abroad* (1869), spends much of its energy lambasting the hollow spirituality of Twain's fellow passengers on the voyage to Europe and the Holy Land. A major theme is the crass commodification of the cultural and religious sites being visited. Twain directs much of his critique toward the fictitious William Grimes, the supposed author of a highly romantic and pietistic travel book called *Nomadic Life of Palestine.* Grimes was a thinly disguised pseudonym for William Cowper Prime, whose own *Tent Life in the Holy Land* (1857) was the common guide for many of Twain's companions. *Innocents* criticizes the deceptive ways of the social negotiation of value throughout Gilded Age culture, as exemplified in such travel guides, which program their readers to respond in predetermined ways.

In addition, however, *Innocents* reveals a strong anti-Catholic prejudice —which cuts against the first principle of resisting such knee-jerk responses. His prejudice mirrored the sentiments of the Masonic Lodge of which he became a member, as well as the growing nativism in America.[54] According to this view, Twain equated Catholicism with ignorance, with the desire for knowledge and progress frequently shown to be blasphemous in the eyes of the church. The church, in fact, is actively engaged in deception (for example, "Jesuit humbuggery"),[55] while the churchgoers are gullible and often base. These views culminate in Twain's visit to Italy: "We were in the heart and home of priestcraft—of a happy, cheerful, contented ignorance, superstition, degradation, poverty, indolence, and everlasting unaspiring worthlessness. And we said fervently, It suits these people precisely; let them enjoy it, along with the other animals. . . . *We* feel no malice toward these fumigators."[56] Twain's anti-Catholic strain would persist throughout his career: a much more vitriolic criticism of Romanism, influenced by his reading of Lecky's *History of European Morals* in 1874, is apparent throughout *Connecticut Yankee,* where the church is depicted as the main reason for the stupidity and backwardness of the entire civilization; it also provides the opening context of *No. 44, The Mysterious Stranger.* These attitudes also reflect the thorough revulsion toward Rome dictated by Twain's Protestant youth, a revulsion influenced by popular anti-Catholic diatribes like Samuel F. B. Morse's *Foreign Conspiracy* or Lyman Beecher's *Plea for the West* (both 1834). Twain undoubtedly also encountered anti-Catholicism in sermons by Horace Bushnell and other Congregational preachers that he heard during the Hartford years.

In *Roughing It* (1872), similar attacks are brought to bear on social structures of the Wild West. Forrest Robinson writes, "Nothing in [Twain's] response to [the] world is at all stable or predictable. . . . Humans are everywhere in thrall to fictions of their own devising."[57] Thus, Twain's pioneer is infected by a "vision of a whole mountain of gold and silver [which] overwhelmed the senses of thousands of investors and brought them to financial ruin."[58] At one point, describing the mounting anticipation of crossing "an absolute desert," Twain ends his commentary on the romance and drama of the situation by writing, "The poetry was all in the anticipation—there is none in the reality."[59] One religious reality Twain considers is Mormonism, another marginalized group eschewed by nativists and Masons alike. He discusses Mormonism in some detail, particularly in a long section ranging through much of chapters 12–17 and then in an extended appendix at the end of *Roughing It.* When he encounters a Mormon "Destroying Angel," he responds with, "but alas for all our romances, he was nothing but a loud, profane, offensive, old blackguard!"[60] The section also contains a lengthy dismissal of the Book of Mormon: "so 'slow,' so sleepy; such an insipid mess of inspiration. It is chloroform in print."[61]

These two books epitomize irreverence, an antireligious flippancy so prevalent that Louis J. Budd has labeled it the "dominant quality" of Twain's achievement.[62] Despite Twain's irreverent lampoons, however, both books also contain moments of strong sentimentality. These moments are exemplified in *Innocents,* for instance, after a long tirade against standard tourist accounts of the Holy Land, which are ridiculed for their predictability and their sectarian nature: "Presbyterians . . . found a Presbyterian Palestine."[63] And yet the chapter ends with a demonstration of the author's own experience of the sublime power of place. On one dark evening in Palestine, Twain waxes eloquently about the Saviour: "In the starlight, Galilee has no boundaries but the broad compass of the heavens, and is a theater meet for great events; meet for the birth of a religion able to save the world; and meet for the stately Figure appointed to stand upon its stage and proclaim its high decrees. . . . One can comprehend it only when the night has hidden all incongruities and created a theatre proper for so grand a drama."[64] The regularity of such observations has caused Leland Krauth to go so far as to assert that "while it is seldom acknowledged, the moments of seriousness in the text far outnumber those of comedy. . . . Twain's moral outlook [in *Innocents*] is almost stodgily traditional. . . . [T]he heart of civilization . . . is predictably religion and the morality that derives from it."[65] Krauth is surely correct in pointing out what many have obviously missed—yet the critical consensus continues to highlight the nearly complete undermining of any such traditional belief, exemplified by Forrest Robinson's emphasis on the romantic traveler's eventual "discovery of hollowness, pointlessness, collapsed illusions, willful deception, hapless self-deception, and defeat."[66]

Despite his antireligious satire, Twain desired to move into the higher realms of the staid eastern establishment, and thus we should consider how these critiques encode a conservative impulse. This impulse accounts for Twain's numerous social, moral, and ultimately religious criticisms, all worthy of inclusion in the tradition of the American jeremiad. According to Perry Miller, the historic jeremiad consisted of "lamentations over the 'declension' of New England and tirades against its lengthening list of sins." Like John the Baptist's similar wailings, these rhetorical creations were meant to be delivered publicly: "on the great occasions of communal life, when the body politic met in solemn conclave to consider the state of society, the one kind of sermon it attended . . . was a jeremiad in which the sins of New England were tabulated over and over again."[67] Though clearly much more secular in tone, a vast amount of Twain's work can be understood as contributing to the long line of American prophets who utilized their favored mode, the jeremiad. This rhetorical mode illustrates the close intertwining in American social and cultural history of religion with political and other forms of thought. As a raving Jeremiah speaking out against the social and ethical injustices of an age, Twain becomes much more than merely "a moralist in disguise."[68] He becomes, rather, a profoundly religious and spiritual presence. Although we may be tempted to view Twain's jeremiads as radical acts of rebellion, they can also be understood as the most conservative and even primordial religious acts of the American civil religion: they embody a strong desire for union and solidarity, and ultimately serve to support and glorify his vision of American shalom—a peculiarly American religion.

3

Mark Twain's Pastor

Joe Twichell and Social Christianity

On November 12, 1874, Mark Twain sat with Joe Twichell next to a stove in a rickety country tavern, leaning into the warmth of the fire on a chilly New England evening. He and Twichell had hiked twenty-eight miles that day from their homes in Hartford to the village of Westford, the first stage of a lengthier journey. Twichell, a former champion athlete at Yale and Civil War veteran, was not very worn down by the walk so far. Mark Twain, however, had inflicted himself with some fairly cruel and unusual punishment that day, and so he sat massaging his aching legs as well. As they warmed themselves and waited for dinner to be served, the two friends exchanged smiles as they listened to a crusty member of the working class express himself in phrases that were not for the faint of heart. Twichell described the man they encountered that night at the tavern as "a sublimely profane hostler whom you couldn't jostle with any sort of mild remark without bringing down upon yourself a perfect avalanche of oaths." His reference to the man's colorful language as "sublime" indicates that the minister shared Mark Twain's more obvious amusement. Also present that evening was a "mellow inebriate who recommended kerosene for Clemens's lameness, and offered as testimony the fact that he himself had frequently used it for stiffness in his joints after lying out all night in cold weather, drunk."[1] Altogether, it was a memorable evening that illustrated the easy fellow-

4. Joseph Twichell, 1875. Courtesy of the Mark Twain House and Museum, Hartford, Connecticut.

ship these two seemingly different personalities were able to share (figure 4).

They had left Hartford about twelve hours earlier. Around 8:30 on a pleasant Thursday morning, Mark Twain set out with Joe Twichell intending to walk all the way from his Hartford home to the literary fortress of North America known as Boston—a distance surpassing one hundred miles. A few days before this, Twain had notified his agent, James Redpath, and his good friend William Dean Howells, both of

Boston, about the preposterous attempt, insuring that the newspapers would cover it. Twain and Twichell took to the road that Thursday morning, with Twichell "carrying a little bag" and Mark Twain sporting "a basket of lunch."[2] They had hoped to make it all the way to Boston on foot, and in time for dinner on Saturday evening, thus covering more than thirty miles per day in their Barnum-like stunt. The record is inconclusive regarding Twain's possible use of kerosene on his sore legs. Nevertheless, we do know that the next morning Mark Twain was physically unable to continue the pilgrimage on foot after about six miles, whereupon he wired Howells and Redpath that he must give up the attempt and would arrive instead that evening by train. Even though they did not complete the trip on foot, Twain noted in the telegram, "this demonstrates the thing can be done."[3] They dined at Howells's that evening and the next, meeting with many of the leading literary and cultural lights of the city. Howells later recalled, "I never saw a more used-up, hungrier man than Clemens. It was something fearful to see him eat escalloped oysters."[4]

Although Howells joined Twain and the newspapers in making out the entire venture to be a grand joke, the symbolism of the episode is revealing. In 1874 Boston stood as the hub of the cultural universe for emerging literary talents like Mark Twain. Boston was the preeminent manifestation of what American unity and civility might actually look like for educated Americans. In the post–Civil War ethos of the North, a desire for national unity intensified. Most citizens desired to recreate and reinvigorate prewar consensus and get back to the business of everyday life. The culture was embodied in the activities of the literary establishment based in Boston, home of the so-called "Brahmins," symbolized by the "schoolroom" or "Fireside" poets Henry Wadsworth Longfellow, Oliver Wendell Holmes, James Russell Lowell, and John Greenleaf Whittier. Boston was also the home of Ralph Waldo Emerson, author of America's "intellectual declaration of independence," as Holmes famously dubbed "The American Scholar."[5] Among other things, these poets and the literary culture that they represented were undergirded by a religious ethos indebted to many of Protestant evangelicalism's central principles.

It is not too much to say that Boston evinced a religious aura for those pilgrims from the outback who ventured into it, a cultural mecca that drew acolytes from all about the young nation. Testimony to this claim comes from the memoirs of various writers regarding their first visits to Boston. When Howells first arrived from the Midwest in 1860, he described himself as "the passionate pilgrim from the West [who] approached his holy land at Boston."[6] One biographer's description of Twain's walk to Boston signals his awareness of this same mystique: "the celebrated humorist was setting out on foot for the Holy Sepulcher accompanied, as a princely pilgrim should be, by his confessor and almoner."[7] As such, the fact that Twain's destination was Boston should not be understood as mere coincidence. Rather, Boston as destination of the lengthy pilgrimage of Mark Twain, in the solemn company of his minister, takes on a moral and religious sense.

Twain's sojourn to Boston also represents his awareness that he was finally "arriving" on the national literary landscape. Just weeks before the trip, at the end of September 1874, he had moved his family into the ostentatious mansion at 351 Farmington Avenue in Hartford. At a cost of more than $120,000 and featuring a billiard room and a mantelpiece from a Scottish castle, this edifice became the permanent symbol of Mark Twain's success in the East. It is also significant to remember that it was during the month of the walk to Boston that Twain saw his first publication in the *Atlantic Monthly*: "A True Story," a tale told in the voice of an ex-slave woman. This achievement served notice to his "arrival" on the scene of that most highly esteemed national periodical, edited by the man fast becoming the dean of American letters, his close friend Howells. Curiously, a few weeks before the walk to Boston, Howells had requested another piece for an upcoming issue, but initially Mark Twain seemed unable to come up with anything. On the morning of October 24, he wrote Howells that his "state of weary and endless confusion" would not allow him to produce anything worthy of the *Atlantic*. However, that same afternoon, Twain took one of his regular hikes with Joe Twichell through the woods, after which he wrote again to Howells. He had been telling Twichell about the "old Mississippi days of steamboating glory and grandeur as I saw them (during 5 years) from the pilot house." Twichell responded, "What a virgin subject to hurl into a magazine!"[8] This suggestion marked the beginning of Twain's series "Old Times on the Mississippi," the first installment of which was completed by Twain in a month and printed in the January 1875 *Atlantic*. The tales of the steamboat men appeared in that issue alongside poems by Longfellow and Holmes, and an installment from *Roderick Hudson* by Henry James. Twain was thrilled to be able to write for the more educated *Atlantic* audience: "it is the only audience that I sit down before in perfect serenity (for the simple reason that it don't require a 'humorist' to paint himself striped & stand on his head every fifteen minutes)."[9] The new house in Hartford, coupled with his new authorial presence in the quintessential journal of the Gilded Age, meant that Mark Twain, nearing the height of his powers, had finally arrived as a permanent presence in New England literary culture. Or so he hoped in 1874.

The fantastic attempt to walk to Boston, and more generally the regular walks Mark Twain took with Joe Twichell, represent the journey by which the wild humorist of the West was finally able to enter the staid culture of the Fireside poets and the conservative pages of the *Atlantic.* Twain's sketches about steamboating, considered by many some of the brightest and liveliest writing that he ever produced, were inspired by that autumn hike with Twichell. This was not a unique occurrence, as Twichell often served a similar role on other walks. On almost every Saturday afternoon when he was in Hartford, Mark Twain would take a long walk with Joe Twichell. Most commonly they would hike out to Bartlett's Tower, a local landmark about five miles out of town on a large hill from which the entire city could be viewed.[10] The synergetic effect of the long discussions and storytelling that were at the heart of these jaunts was described by a newspaper writer who interviewed Twain in 1874: "Mr. Twichell sometimes gains ideas from his companion which he embodies in his sermons and Mark Twain obtains information from his pastor which he works up into comical and humorous stories, and makes note of every joke which unconsciously falls from the clerical lips."[11]

Of course, the audacious qualities of the walk to Boston, and the self-serving nature of the stunt as advertisement, simultaneously mock the more religious reverence of earlier pilgrims. In this sense, the walk to Boston is also a conscious critique of the silliness of such reverent attitudes as those expressed above by the likes of Howells. Nevertheless, and despite his genuine irreverence, there was a side of Mark Twain that desperately desired to be recognized and embraced by those whom he considered to be the civil religious gatekeepers of Brahmin Boston, so much so that he was even willing to undertake a pilgrimage there, with pastor in tow. One writer has described a pilgrimage as

> a journey undertaken in the light of a story. A great event has happened; the pilgrim hears the reports and goes in search of the evidence, aspiring to be an eyewitness. The pilgrim seeks not only to confirm the experience of others firsthand but to be changed by the experience. Pilgrims often make the journey in company, but each must be changed individually; they must see for themselves, each with his or her own eyes.[12]

In this formulation, the story heard is of the greatness of Boston as literary mecca. It is no surprise that for Twain's entrance into Boston, symbolically and realistically, Joe Twichell was at his side. And yet each must see for himself. Of course, Twain had already used the theme of pilgrimage in his first best-seller, *Innocents Abroad,* whose subtitle was *A New Pilgrims' Progress.* There, as here, he both utilized and burlesqued the traditional idea of the pilgrimage. He was changed by these experiences, becoming both enlightened and disappointed by the objects of his search, so that his pilgrimage became a profoundly divided and ambivalent modern version. He had to "see for himself," and what he saw was a glass half full, and half empty. But even more spectacularly, Twain turned the idea of pilgrimage completely on its head, particularly with the walk to Boston. He did this by himself becoming the story, the object of the gaze. The story of his "heroic" walk ran in papers throughout the nation, and thus did the pilgrim become the focus of a pilgrimage.

Mark Twain's arrival into the cultural ethos of New England is signaled by much more than just the failed attempt to walk to Boston. Other features of his life during these formative years of the mid-1870s reveal similar ambivalences. On the one hand we can see them as distinct from the kinds of activities he might have done in California, for example. But on the other hand, even while doing them, he indicates a discomfort or a sense of inauthenticity. For instance, in Victorian New England it was not unusual for genteel Americans to collect albums or notebooks in which friends and family would be asked to inscribe poems, memories, or other light prose or verse. In a book of so-called *Mental Photographs,* Mark Twain was asked by one Charles J. Rosenbloom to provide responses to forty questions, which he did on May 14, 1876.[13]

One's answers to the questions were meant to provide insight into the person's character, and Twain's comments certainly are suggestive:

3. Favorite tree?
   Any that bear forbidden fruit.
14. Favorite poet?
   Robert Browning, when he has a lucid interval.
18. Favorite character in history?
   King Herod.
25. What trait of character do you most admire in man?
   The noblest form of cannibalism—love for his fellow man.
33. What do you most dread?
   Exposure.
37. What are the sweetest words in the world?
   "Not Guilty."
38. What are the saddest words in the world?
   "Dust unto dust."
39. What is your aim in life?
   To endeavor to be absent when my time comes.
40. What is your motto?
   Be virtuous and you will be eccentric.

These remarks suggest several things about Mark Twain. First, they reveal a preoccupation with such Christian concerns as the fall of mankind, the threat of exposure, the burdens of sin, the finality of death, and the importance of virtue and sacrificial love. Second, one is able to read some of these responses as if the writer wants simply to dismiss or ridicule genteel American Christianity. To call King Herod his favorite character in history is to invoke the name of one of the most cruel and violent kings who oppressed the Jews at the time of Jesus. Third, some of the responses were certainly written in earnest. For example, Twain was known to have what one critic has called an "infatuation with" Robert Browning's poems, many of which took the form of dramatic monologues by religious figures or meditations on faith and metaphysical concerns, and he often read them aloud to his family and friends.[14] Finally, some of the responses here certainly were not written in earnest, such as the several merely amusing remarks for his friend (favorite gem—"The jack of diamonds—when it is trump"; favorite book—"Vanderbilt's pocket book"). Overall, one senses the scribblings of a man with metaphysical preoccupations, one who is simultaneously irreverent toward and yet also intrigued by the "matters of life and death," as religion is sometimes described. Twain's motives for these inscriptions, like his motives for undertaking the walk to Boston, seem at once reverent and irreverent.

And yet the culture of the *Mental Photographs* volumes, and Twain's participation in it, foreground the religious connotations of the New England culture in which Twain composed his passing remarks in 1876. Twain's engagement with this culture ran very deep: he lived for almost two decades as a member of the genteel community of Nook Farm outside of Hartford, Connecticut. For Twain, Nook Farm was a sort of compromise to the Bostonian power center ruled by the Fireside poets and the Harvard divines, insofar as it provided a bit of distance both geographically and ideologically. Nevertheless, his neighbors included some of the most influential thinkers and writers of the period, such as Horace Bushnell, Harriet Beecher Stowe and her sister Isabella Beecher Hooker (with numerous visits by their siblings, including Thomas K. Beecher of Elmira, New York, and Henry Ward Beecher, perhaps the most famous preacher of the nineteenth century), the publisher Elisha Bliss, and Charles Dudley Warner, author and editor of the *Hartford Courant.* Moreover, the neighborhood also featured a vibrant and socially active church where Twain not only attended but often pitched in to help: The Asylum Hill Congregational Church, pastored by the Reverend Joseph H. Twichell.

Jeffrey Steinbrink has eloquently told the story of the formative years of the emerging "Mark Twain," which he believes culminated with the move to Hartford in the summer of 1871 and the completion of the manuscript of *Roughing It,* published in 1872. This was the period, according to Steinbrink, when Clemens began and completed the process of "getting to be Mark Twain."[15] However, according to Steinbrink's reading, the arrival in Hartford should be recognized as the completion of a process rather than the inception of another crucial stage of Twain's emerging sense of self and ideology. The importance of Hartford's moral ethos in the process of "getting to be Mark Twain" is clear, however, when Twain writes Twichell in February 1869: "my future wife wants me to be surrounded by a good moral & religious atmosphere (for I shall unite with the church as soon as I am located,) & so she likes the idea of living in Hartford."[16] Initially the somewhat stiff easterners showed little regard for the "wild humorist," until the widespread success of Twain's first two best-sellers, *The Innocents Abroad* (1869) and *Roughing It* (1872) solidified his writerly status as more than just a vulgar journalist from the Wild West. Despite the cold reception he received from some in the literary power centers of Gilded Age America, Twain persisted in his desires for the lifestyle promised by the denizens of Hartford. Steinbrink correctly underlines the key aspect of his interest in this particular location: "Clemens's persistent regard for Hartford, despite the snub, was no doubt reinforced by his affection for Joe Twichell, his ties to Bliss [the publisher], and his appreciation of Olivia's friendships there, but from the outset what had chiefly drawn him to the city was his sense of its upright and elevating character."[17]

Steinbrink's account of Clemens's "getting to be Mark Twain" is invaluable but I think truncated. Indeed I would like to consider more fully the society and culture that were at the heart of the process of "getting to be Mark Twain." It was not just before Twain's move to Hartford that he "became" Mark Twain. The move to Hartford was the crucial moment when he made clear his desire to plunge into a particular social and religious way of life. Relocating to Hartford represented, so to speak, his full and final public "conversion" to and embrace of the genteel moral ecology in which the author we know today as Mark Twain was matured and fully formed. Specifically we should consider the brand of puissant, intellectually vigorous, yet consistently orthodox Christianity that was incarnated in the life of Joseph Twichell and to some extent manifested in the social life of Twichell's Asylum Hill Congregational Church of Hartford. More generally, we might begin to describe the city of Hartford as a symbolic manifestation of certain religious and moral ideologies that were predominant during the second half of the nineteenth century. Hartford's role as a leader in the emerging Social Christianity movement meant that the city was a hotbed of the major themes of that movement, such as American destiny, Christian progressivism, and a romantic view of humanity coupled with a growing emphasis on charitable good works.

Hartford's moral ecology not only drew Mark Twain and his family to settle in Nook Farm, it maintained a central influence in Twain's literary and cultural production from 1871 onward. Among many other key life decisions, Mark Twain decided early in his married life that he wanted to relocate, perhaps permanently, to the city of Hartford—and specifically to that section of the city called Nook Farm and populated by the likes of the Twichells, the Stowes, the Beechers, the Blisses, and the Warners. That neighborhood boasted several other ministers besides Twichell; two others in particular also became close friends of Mark Twain: Nathaniel Burton and Edwin Parker, both of whom, like Twichell, were intelligent and eloquent spokespersons of many of the better aspects of Christianity to which Mark Twain was consistently sympathetic. Just like his bohemian years out west, Twain not only respected the office of the ministry, but also immensely enjoyed the company of certain clergymen (the highly educated yet also warmly humorous variety) and made them a permanent and vital part of his social identity. He had great respect for the ministry itself, which he once called "the highest dignity to which a man may aspire."[18] He once told his brother Orion that he had had in his early life only "two powerful ambitions," to be a riverboat pilot and to be a "preacher of the gospel: I would rather be a shining light in that department than the greatest lawyer that ever trod the earth."[19] Given Twain's reverence regarding the ministry, and given the fact that he spent countless hours in the company of ministers like Twichell, more needs to be understood about the influence of Congregational Hartford on America's favorite son. As such the story presented here is in the spirit of augmenting Steinbrink's account by presenting the Hartford years as crucial to the process of a "young" Sam Clemens (who was almost thirty-six) "getting to be Mark Twain."

The Reverend Joseph Twichell, along with his close friends and fellow Congregational ministers Burton and Parker, were dedicated to forms of "Social Christianity" that rose to prominence in many northern churches in the years following the Civil War. Social Christianity, the movement toward a social manifestation of the gospel within specific communities, drew upon the instincts of Twichell's mentor, Horace Bushnell, a stalwart who was one of the three or four most influential American theologians of the century. Protestant and Catholic leaders began to take seriously the severe problems arising especially within urban communities of the 1870s and '80s, including urban decay in slum areas, the rising tensions between labor and capital, rising crime rates, alcoholism, prostitution, and homelessness. Leaders of the Social Christianity movement, or what became known later as the "Social Gospel," responded to these problems by asserting the possibility that through diligent moral effort, Christians might help reform American political and economic institutions for the betterment of all, especially the oppressed. Adherents of the Social Gospel envisioned the Kingdom of God to be at work within human communities through believers and thus at work for social progress through a compassionate and just service to the needy. As such, the Social Gospel was an eschatological movement of Christian ethics—meaning that it proposed to move toward a specific telos and preached a progressive view of human society that is not only possible but ordained by God. Social Gospellers, that is, were eschatological insofar as they were (and are) aiming at a particular vision of social and cultural justice, or shalom. They aimed at a particular goal, and they believed that such a vision was inevitable according to the sanctions of God. Theirs was a vision of a socially incarnated Kingdom of God, "on Earth as it is in Heaven," as Jesus prays in the Lord's Prayer (Matthew 6:10). For Mark Twain, Joseph Twichell not only incarnated the very best aspects of the Social Christianity of the Gilded Age, but also represented the most viable Christian example of virtuous and wise manhood that Twain had ever encountered. During this period, a gendered version of the faith arose that also had profound effects upon the institutional church and its activities. What became known as Christian manhood, or "muscular Christianity," developed as a general response to what was widely perceived as a growing feminization of Christianity, and it influenced movements as diverse as the rise of college athletics to the initiation of the Young Men's Christian Association (YMCA).[20] Symptomatic of this movement was the fact that for many of the years Twain resided in Hartford, Christian manhood was a primary topic of Twichell's preaching. It was a version of Christianity for which Mark Twain had deep affinities.

Given the depth and seriousness of this relationship, closer attention should be paid to the actual moral and ethical dimensions of Twichell's worldview. The Social Christianity that formed the core of Twichell's religious ethos and of Twain's most productive years as an author grew directly out of the more general religious tendencies of what Sydney

Ahlstrom has called "the golden age of liberal theology."[21] The "liberalism" that flowered to unprecedented degrees after the Civil War can be associated broadly with a liberation of mind and an embrace of new and different ideas. Theologically speaking, liberalism tended heavily toward the Arminian view of humanity, with an emphasis on man's freedom and the natural tendency toward altruistic and ethical action. Instead of focusing on man's sinful nature due to the Fall, as traditional Calvinists might, liberal theologians described faulty child-rearing, poor ethical and moral training, or lack of social reform as the fundamental causes of human error. Thus liberal theologians placed heavy emphasis on moral teaching and ethical preaching, and in so doing they argued for the creative, autonomous, and nearly godlike nature of the human spirit—a rarified view bordering at times on the ancient heresy of the church known as Pelagianism. As such, the church's view of humanity was turning away from a realistic determinism of Calvin and to a more sentimentalized romanticism associated in an earlier period with the likes of Emerson and the Transcendentalists.[22]

Horace Bushnell was the leading light for this movement and, theologically speaking, its most important influence. His famous volume, *Christian Nurture* (1847, 1860), for example, can be considered a cornerstone of the shift toward undermining the dogma of original sin and initiating a new system of religious and moral education. Among other things, Bushnell also propounded a complex theory of the American civil religion, forcefully asserting that America was founded on the twin ideals of Protestantism and Republicanism: "It was Protestantism in religion producing republicanism in government."[23] Bushnell's essay "City Planning" (1864), along with his active profile in the city of Hartford, showed his strong desire to develop a holistic view of an urban area and to create within that area an embodiment of ethical and moral society. The social ethos of Bushnell, the Social Gospel, and liberal theology in general, with its pragmatic call to active participation in life's cosmic struggle toward some vaguely utopian future, were the hallmarks of cultural Hartford during the Gilded Age and were prominent themes in the life and ministry of Mark Twain's pastor, Joseph Twichell. Twain recognized Bushnell's great impact on Twichell, and on America, when in 1902 he called him "that greatest clergyman that the last century produced."[24] Strikingly, one of the most famous preachers of the Social

Gospel, Washington Gladden, said almost the exact same thing a few years after Twain did: Bushnell was "the greatest theological genius of the American church in the nineteenth century."[25]

If Bushnell was the century's most influential theologian, then Hartford must be considered its exemplary city of faith. Certainly Hartford best represented the spirit of moral uplift that ultimately propelled the Social Gospel of American Christianity, being as it was the longtime home of Bushnell, whose mentorship largely sealed the beliefs and ministry style of his many protégés, including Twichell. Nonetheless, Hartford maintained just enough distance from the stultified Brahminism that Twain associated with the "hub of the universe," Boston—an ethos that commanded from many Americans of the period an almost religious devotion. This ethos was one that both Twain and Howells would satirize and sacralize, depending on their moods. The "distance" between Twain's Missouri roots and his aspirations in Brahmin New England is helpful in explaining the motives behind the walk to Boston with Joe Twichell. It also helps explain perhaps the most famous social gaffe of Twain's career: his speech at John Greenleaf Whittier's birthday celebration in 1877. There Twain presented a humorous sketch of western hoboes pretending to be Whittier, Longfellow, and Emerson. Unfortunately some observers—and perhaps Twain himself—were offended by what they perceived to be a tasteless lampooning of the famous poets. Twain's speech was not an uncommon or even unexpected feature of such a celebration, although he quickly regretted what he considered a massive error of judgment. More than anything, the controversy illustrates the tensions at the center of Twain's identity of this period: easterner vs. westerner, northerner vs. southerner, genteel vs. corn pone.[26] And yet Twain longed for the cultural acknowledgement of the Boston Brahmins. Despite their considerable physical distance from Boston, ultimately Hartford's ideological leaders had much in common with their somewhat more prestigious elder brothers in Massachusetts. Within this quasi-religious context, much of Mark Twain's social thinking grew to maturity. Initially Twain's quest for a serious use for Christian faith, as evidenced in his commitment to the Social Christianity of Hartford's moral ecology, was largely genuine.

Mark Twain knew the religious implications of living in Hartford, and yet he could hardly wait to leave Buffalo to move there. Beyond the general ethos of the city of Hartford, Mark Twain had identified a number of embodiments of Social Christianity, one of whom became the most convincing and ultimately the most influential one of his adult life: his pastor Joe. Twichell incarnated the physically powerful yet intellectually sophisticated Christianity that Mark Twain considered to be the truest and most worthy form. On many occasions they worked together for the betterment of the world, as in the following anecdote recorded by Twichell on July 17, 1877:

> In the evening MT read us the remaining two acts of the Comedy—a fitting way to quiet our minds after the day's excitement, occasioned as follows.
>
> He had come up from New York partly to inquire into the matter of a burglar having been detected hid in his house one evening since he left. From the cross-examination of his domestics who have the house in charge, he was led to suspect very strongly that the supposed burglar was the lover of one of them—an English girl Lizzie Wills. It turned out that probably his suspicion in this respect was not warranted, but in the course of his inquiry into affairs, he learned, what resulted in the poor girl's confession that she ought to be married and on her part desired to be. The lover had promised and postponed. Mark undertook to help her out. Dispatching her to find the recreant and get him to come to the house that afternoon, and sending for a policeman to be there also, he came over to see me and engage my service. I told him to go and get a license, which he did, and got back to our house at about 4 o'clock where we waited till 6. When his servant George appeared announcing that the above named were all on the way (the policeman in citizen's dress "shadowing" the unsuspecting couple) to the house. We went over: I was placed in a chamber adjoining the study where Mark took his position, and whither he summoned the girl and man to see him. A very long talk followed (which I could hear little of) in which Mark, by reasoning and exhortation, keeping his temper perfectly, finally demanded the fellow to say "yes." I was called in straightway and the business finished. . . . I never had performed the marriage service with such mingled feelings. I felt great sympathy for the bride and groom and gave them the best counsel I could. Mark ordered up cake and wine. The witnesses (the servants) expressed their congratulations—things really took a cheerful tone. Then Mark stepped

> out of the room and soon returning gave each a check for $100 to begin life with. It was a thing well done and we were very thankful that it was concluded.[27]

This episode highlights a number of attributes that Twichell shared with Twain. Both appeared to have "great sympathy for the bride and groom." Twain's generosity and concern here are mirrored on countless occasions by Twichell. And both men had the highest esteem for the sacrament of marriage and the honor of young women. Most importantly, these actions all were motivated by the sympathetic imagination of Mark Twain, who "ordered up cake and wine" for the celebration.

One important reason that Twain was so attracted to Twichell was the man's great humility. Twichell was often in demand as a public orator and guest preacher, and he occasionally was actively recruited for other pastoral positions. Yet Twichell's humility was obvious in the friendly manner he had with all those who knew him, especially in the fact that he would allow them to call him, affectionately and simply, "Joe." Although this might appear fairly standard today, in postbellum New England it was almost unheard of to address an esteemed minister of the gospel in such a manner. This tendency is noted, for example, in an article titled "The Hartford Minister's Meeting," by Rev. William L. Gage, that appeared in the *Hartford Courant:* "my mind runs to [Parker's] 'glorious' brother Twichell, still profanely called Joe by those who know him best. That adjective and that pet name are at once the epitome and the eulogy of his character, and all that I might write would simply expand what those two words hint."[28] The author is correct to point out that the use of the informal "Joe" is highly indicative of Twichell's humble character—even while being thought simultaneously as quite "glorious." Sometimes Twichell makes clear his own humility in his letters to Twain, such as several instances where he laments the fact that he had at times not been a very good minister. For example, on July 13, 1881, he writes, "We have had many and many a good time together, my dear old fellow; it has been a bright streak experience to me all through; but, oh dear me, how I do wish I had been a better pastor to you. God bless you, spite of me." On October 2, 1881, he says, "I'll try to be a better minister than ever *to you,* Mark, i.e. I'll try to *be* one, which I often fear I haven't been at all. I've got the affection any how, whatever else is wanting."[29]

An illustration of Twichell's humility came in May of 1888, when he was offered a new job as pastor of Church of the Covenant, a Presbyterian congregation in New York. This offer would have provided income nearly double Twichell's current salary, along with free use of a beautiful parsonage. Twichell, although greatly flattered, turned it down. But the offer caused much introspection, as did his fiftieth birthday two weeks later on May 27, 1888. The episode reveals how highly Twichell was valued by prestigious churches. But his insistence to remain in Hartford indicates his own sense of calling and vocation in continuing in the "field" in which he was already long at work, which meant more than the money and prestige that moving to a bigger pond might bring him. These qualities were among those featured when his own congregation gave him quite a surprise of their own for that birthday. Twichell learned the evening of his fiftieth birthday, by the calling of a committee of his parishioners, that they would give him the fully paid-off deed to his house on Woodland Street, along with a fund of some $10,000 for adding on to it or furnishing it, as he and his wife, Harmony, would choose. Twain gave a brief speech at the formal celebration at the church on May 28, 1888: after many solemn and eloquent praises, Twain's remarks consisted mainly of funny reminiscences and satirical attacks on the strongly romanticized tributes given earlier. Twain was among the more generous supporters of this gift to the Twichells, despite Twain's own mounting financial difficulties, and the moment typifies the very strong bonds of love and friendship that the parish held for their beloved pastor. The following morning, Twichell wrote to thank his good friend—a letter, again, brimming with genuine humility:

> [29 May 1888]
> Tuesday Morning
> Dear Old Mark:
>
> I find myself this morning wanting to tell you how thankful to you I am and *we* are for the part you bore in our reception last night.
>
> I appreciate that it must have seemed, on some accounts, rather rough on you to be asked to *appear* on such occasion. And had I been consulted about it—which I was not—I would have spared you.
>
> All the more am I affected with gratitude toward you, that you did not spare yourself, but took up the cross and accommodated yourself with

> such kindly grace to the situation, with your difficulty in which, proud as I was to have you there, I was in acute sympathy.
>
> I hope you understand that by submitting to be called out, as well as by what you said, you gave great pleasure to many worthy people.
>
> And may I say that in the tone and air of a long familiar friendly sentiment toward me, bred and nurtured in a personal relation, that pervaded your charming talk, you perfectly met that particular propriety of the occasion which I judge you aimed to meet.
>
> I never heard you read anything better than you read the verses with which you closed—which is saying a great deal.
>
> Dear old fellow, heaven only knows how I love you, and what unspeakable desires for your happiness live in my heart.
>
> I have learned to what extent Harmony and I are beholden to Livy and you for our sudden elevation in point of material fortune. There again I would have had you spared. What an expense to you we are! It is too bad. But the people didn't know.
>
> As I said last night, we can't yet quite get hold of so strange a fact as that we are worth ten thousand dollars! You had the sensation of it once, I suppose, but you have forgotten all about it now. We are trying, struggling, to climb into it. We shall get there, I guess, but it is a dizzy job.[30]

Another incident arose a year later in 1889, when Twichell declined an honorary doctoral degree that was offered by Williams College. In keeping with his character, Twichell did not openly comment on his reasons, but in his journal he makes it clear that his refusal was a function of his own humility and even embarrassment about being called "doctor": "it was my distaste for the title that was my most conscious motive for asking to be excused." In his journal, Twichell appended to these comments a brief clipping from the *Springfield Republican:* "'That is very like Joe Twichell' will be the mental comment of those who know the man."[31] The newspaper's observation indicates that Twichell was clearly well known for his modest and genuine integrity. Nevertheless, after this date he was often referred to in the popular press as "Dr. Twichell."

The extensive documentation of Twichell's admirable and tireless work as a community pastor is impressive, even in the context of a time period in which it was common to wax eloquent regarding even mediocre church leadership. Twichell was a man who clearly cared for his flock, and they knew it. Twichell kept extensive records of virtually all of the ministry work that he did among his parishioners. Calling these records his "Parish Calls," Twichell maintained an alphabetical listing of each church member, underneath which he listed the dates of meetings or counseling sessions, basic topics of conversation, as well as the key verses of Scripture that, apparently, he called upon by way of advice or sympathy. These remarkable records demonstrate a true pastor's heart for his people. Twichell's diligence indicates a desire to maintain long-term relationships above and beyond a mere level of friendship. In their level of detail and personal insight, Twichell's extensive "Parish Calls" read almost like the records of a physician.

Since these were for the church members only, the Clemenses are not recorded throughout their years in residence. Indeed critics have often made the point that Mark Twain never did join the Asylum Hill Congregational Church, a point that supposedly supports the view that he disparaged organized religion or that his refusal to join somehow manifested a fundamental distrust of the church as an organization. But James D. Wilson has made a cogent observation regarding nineteenth-century families' tendencies to belong only to a single congregation:

> An examination of the membership records of the Park Congregational Church in Elmira, New York, however, reveals that Olivia maintained family membership there without interruption until at least 1891. Clemens' failure to register his family as members of Asylum Hill church [sic] in Hartford—where they did, after all, maintain a pew—need not imply repudiation of church doctrine or reluctance to embrace the religious community there; more plausible is the assumption that the family would officially belong to only one congregation, and that was the one in Elmira—where Olivia's father Jervis had been a founder and charter member, Olivia a communicant since childhood, and Sam and Olivia were married in February 1870.[32]

Interestingly, despite the fact that they were not officially members of his church, Twichell treats the Clemens family as church members in his pastoral records, at least in the first years of their habitation in Hartford. Twichell lists the Clemenses and has the following dates, apparently for what he considered to be his more "official" parish visits: December 5 and 21, 1871; January 2, 15, and 27, June 13, October 7, and November 20,

1872; November 27, 1873; and February 23, 1874. Of course these were by no means the only times they met. The formal nature of these records indicates a different sort of visit was at hand on each of these occasions. Generally, however, it is certain that Twichell always was at the ready to be Twain's pastor throughout the rest of their career as close friends. Even as late as March 18–21, 1895, Twichell comments: "Had a visit from our dear friend M. T., temporarily on this side of the Atlantic on business. He seemed tired and down-hearted by reason of recent pecuniary losses, yet we enjoyed seeing him, and especially because he *was* under a cloud were glad he came."[33] Such comments indicate that Twichell seemed not only willing to interact on the level of pastor but indeed to enjoy his work as minister and encourager of the downtrodden. They betray the fundamentally pastoral heart of Joe Twichell. It is notable again in comments in the journal dated June 13, 1875: "Mark Twain and WDH walked home from church with me, and subsequently I went to Mark's and dined with them. . . . When leaving[,] Howells followed me to the door and we had on the threshold quite a talk on religious subjects and I was sorry that we couldn't have more. He seemed very humble and earnest, and vastly loveable."[34] These and other comments support a view of Twichell as a man truly concerned with the spiritual well-being of other men.

Thus it is important that in the later years, including even the times after Livy's death in 1904 when Mark Twain was most bitter and impassioned against virtually everything, he never said anything negative or disparaging about Joe Twichell. Indeed the opposite seems to be true. For example, in the autobiographical dictation dated January 12, 1906, Twain remarked on Twichell's conversation and manner among other men:

> if he talked, it was easily perceptible that it was because he had something to say, and he was always able to say it well. . . . Joe Twichell could get together the most impossible Christians that ever assembled in anybody's congregation; and as a usual thing he couldn't run his church systematically on account of new deacons who didn't understand the business—the recent deacons having joined their predecessors in the Penitentiary down there in Wethersfield.[35]

At Twain's sixty-seventh birthday celebration, he said: "Another of my oldest friends is here—the Reverend Joe Twichell—and whenever Twichell goes to start a church I see them flocking, rushing to buy the land all around there. Many and many a time I have attended the annual sale in his church, and bought up all the pews on a margin and it would have been better for me spiritually and financially if I had staid under his wing."[36] Although the speech is clearly in a humorous vein, the touching confession that Twain considered that his life "would have been better for me spiritually and financially" is quite telling. We might compare these comments with those from Deacon John Keep, who described Twichell in a *Courant* article in 1915: "You have in a most remarkable manner taken the hearts of all. . . . [T]he original inspiration for the development west [in Hartford] was due to . . . Mr. Twichell's church. The Hill has become what it is because of the good providence that brought Mr. Twichell to live and work among us. If he had been a different type of man, his coming would have been an incident instead of making an epoch in the city's history."[37] Keep agrees with Twain to the extent that both men attribute much of the greatness of Nook Farm and West Hartford to the presence of Twichell and his church. And although, in the speech cited above, Twain indicates that his life might have been much better had he "staid under [Joe's] wing," other comments indicate that Twain often did see himself as protected under the pastoral wing of his good friend—or else badly affected by his stubborn refusal to remain under Joe's close scrutiny. In one revealing letter to Twichell dated June 24, 1905, Twain writes: "I have used you as an equilibrium-restorer more than once in my time, + shall continue, I guess." In another dated January 19, 1897, from London, Twain explains his grief over the death of his favored daughter Susy and says he wants no letters from anyone except Joe, who has "something divine" within him.[38]

Twichell's unusual humility, his easy familiarity with people from diverse backgrounds, and his great skill as a pastor who truly cared for and understood the members of his flock, all combine as aspects of sympathy, a term used commonly by friends to describe Twichell's humane spirit. As the passage from Twichell's journal admits regarding the secretly planned wedding of Lizzie Wills, the main sentiment both he and Twain experienced was "great sympathy for the bride and groom."[39] It is interesting, for instance, that when it came time for Twichell to compose a eulogy for Mark Twain in 1910, he focused on his dear friend's sympathy as a mark of the noblest aspects of his character:

> Along with his penetrating insight of the weaknesses of humanity went an equally keen appreciation of its nobler aspects and capabilities. What was honorable he most heartily honored. He was not wanting in generous tolerations, high admirations, deep reverences, yes, and deep humilities. No one could be much in his company without perceiving that he was of a singularly affectionate nature. He was quickly responsive to any appeal to his sympathy, especially to his pity. I have seldom known a person so easily moved to tears.[40]

Given the central importance of sympathy in this culture, it is not surprising that this virtue is frequently attributed to Twichell, as in a letter to him from the Reverend Thomas K. Beecher of Elmira, dated June 14, 1875: "I am equally persuaded that there is a sweetness, a cheerfulness, a love of mankind and an interest in their airs illustrated by you, the want of which is in me a fearful defect."[41] Twain himself associated the quality with his pastor: "Twichell, with his big heart, his wide sympathies, and his limitless benignities and charities and generosities, is the kind of person that people of all ages and both sexes fly to for consolation and help in time of trouble."[42] Of all of these generous comments by and about Twichell, perhaps the Christian associations of the virtue of sympathy are most easily missed by today's readers. Sympathy in late nineteenth-century Hartford, however, was fundamentally a religious virtue marking God's common grace in the lives of believers and unbelievers alike. And it was an attribute not only associated with women but was in keeping with the masculine belief that came to be known in this era as "muscular Christianity."

Twenty-first century readers might bristle at the concept of Christian manhood because of its gendered nature, but the Christianity of the Gilded Age and its aftermath distinguished sharply between male and female social roles. Sympathy was a trait shared by both sexes, however, and it was understood to be a defining trait of Christian manhood. Not surprisingly, the formation of a "muscular Christianity" was a major topic of consideration throughout the preaching career of Joe Twichell. Mark Twain would have heard his friend preach on it many times, since Twichell made it a regular part of his lectures and sermons. It was particularly common in his speeches to younger men, such as his many sermons at the Yale College Chapel, and, as the *Yale Record* noted about

Twichell in 1875, he could "appeal strongly and personally to that better nature which exists somewhere in every man."[43] On November 20, 1887, he spoke again to students at Yale: "There are words and actions which are the insignia of a Christian man, and while it is sometimes convenient not to confess oneself it is always desirable for a man, especially in college, to fly his flag. Nowhere does the church suffer more from silent Christians than in college."[44] On February 24, 1888, at the Sixth Annual Conference of the College YMCA of New England at Boston, Twichell's address titled "Manhood" included these words: "in this race of the Christian life, the prize of which is manhood . . . your experience is a trying one—and a sorely trying one at times. . . . The Christian gospel was the gospel of true manhood. The call of Jesus to us, summed up, was, be men. . . . their calling was to a fulfillment of the most essential conditions of the largest, truest, and freest manhood."[45] In his sermon to the Clinton Avenue Congregational Church of Brooklyn, New York, on January 14, 1895, he made a similar plea: "Youth has its highest calling in manhood. The Christian gospel is the gospel of true manhood, indeed rightly interpreted, of manhood throughout, body, intellect, spirit. . . . Christ is the basis of all true manhood."[46] One of the finest summaries of Twichell's thought on sympathy as an expression of true manhood comes in his address on May 29, 1892, to the Scroll and Key Society at Yale's Battell Chapel, given at the invitation of President Dwight:

> Largeness of manhood all 'round is conditioned on a thing, that is of the essence unselfishness—an inwrought, deep-grained, rooted sense of it that brings the common interest home to our feelings of a personal concern. For it is unquestionably out of that public spirit that all our finer loyalties arise, in the experience of which we may come to our proper stature as men, and so dwell in a spacious world and prove life worth living. . . . that public spirit is but another term for broad and fervent human sympathy. . . . The principal studies of the collegian lead into regions warm with human interest—eminently literature, history, philosophy. They naturally tend to make the student feel the pulse-beat of the world's great life, to feel the oneness of it.[47]

Note that the originating premise of Twichell's comments is his interest in identifying the "largeness of manhood." While it might seem today, especially after a century of modern attacks on the religious sensibility, that sympathy is a sentimentalized and largely feminine characteristic, the nineteenth-century church viewed sympathy as a central goal for the truly Christian man.

Twichell's concept of Christian manhood can also be illustrated with a few exemplars. One of these would be Charles Dudley Warner, Twichell's parishioner and good friend (and Twain's coauthor of *The Gilded Age*). In a March 14, 1885, article on Warner published in the *Critic*, Twichell wrote, "He is a communicant in the Congregational Church, and a constant attendant on public worship."[48] In his published remarks on the occasion of Warner's sudden death on Oct. 20, 1900, after dining in very joyful humor with Twichell and several others, Twichell noted especially Warner's faith: "He was a man of positive Christian character. Never was he ashamed of Christian confession. . . . he always asked a blessing over the food. He always knelt in prayer before retiring at night. . . . [he showed a] Christian faith in the immortality of the soul."[49] Twichell obviously placed much esteem on the mundane habits of regular churchgoing and prayer. These were the signs of true Christian manhood.

Much more revealing are Twichell's comments on Henry Ward Beecher. On March 13, 1887, after Beecher's death, Twichell wrote in his journal: "So passes the greatest man I ever knew. . . . No mind has had such influence on mine, unless it be Dr. Bushnell; and no character, unless it be my father."[50] Twichell had long considered Beecher a public embodiment of some of his own most cherished values, both as an orator and as a Christian witness to the gospel. Twichell preached a memorial sermon about Beecher on the Sunday following the news of his death, later published in the *Hartford Courant* on March 14, 1887; Twichell's text was Jeremiah 20:9: "But if I say, 'I will not remember Him, Or speak anymore in His name,' Then in my heart it becomes like a burning fire shut up in my bones; And I am weary of holding it in, And I cannot endure it." Among other things, Twichell's choice of text here implies that the importance of remembering Beecher is similar to the need to remember God, the object of Jeremiah's statement. Moreover, the need to speak of Beecher literally fills the orator with a charismatic unction not unlike that of a burning fire—in biblical symbolism, the very presence of God's spirit.

Excerpts from the sermon reveal Twichell's sense of the greatness of his deceased colleague:

> The great outstanding fact of his life is that he was a preacher. . . . in the strictest sense of the term, the main product of his incomparable genius was preaching. . . . In 1874 he said to his own people "I have worked hard from three considerations—the love that I have for God, the love that I have for my fellow men, and because I could not help myself. I was made to be a preacher, and I have preached just as fountains run. The apostle said, 'woe to me if I preach not the gospel,' and I suppose my experience may come somewhat within the scope of his meaning. . . ."
>
> One who was present wrote that while he was saying this, [Beecher] seemed to lose consciousness of his audience: his voice, although clear and distinct, became low and gentle; he was carried away by one of those very inspirations which he was describing; and when he spoke of the revelation of Christ to himself, as one who loved men because they needed love, his face underwent a marvelous change; it seemed transparent with a radiant light, like a sunset glow on the Alps. . . . He spoke what he had to speak as by the dictation of an overpowering inward command. . . . He on another occasion, speaking of his interior experience in the act of preaching, when under the sway of profound emotion, said "I feel as though all the ocean were not strong enough to be the power behind my words, nor all the thunders that were in the Heavens . . . There are times when it is not I that is talking, when I am caught up and carried away, so that I know not whether I am in the body or out of the body. . . . I see things, and I hear sounds, and seem, if not in the seventh heaven, yet in a condition that leads me to understand what Paul said—that he heard things which it was not possible for a man to utter."[51]

Among other things, this view of Beecher is brimming with the famously charismatic aspect of his preaching style, including a mystical sense of being "caught up" into the very presence of God. Mark Twain was known to share a deep admiration for Beecher's oratorical style.[52] Twichell's tone and allusions depict Beecher as a prophet of God and suggest his own strong endorsement of Beecher as model preacher and man of God. Twichell, in other words, longed to be a preacher of such power and transcendent splendor as Beecher occasionally manifested—

and this aspiration speaks plainly of Twichell's fairly conservative yet somewhat mystical brand of Christianity that marked his own preaching style and career. It is revealing that shortly after this sermon, on May 22, 1887, Twichell filled the pulpit of his fallen hero at Beecher's Plymouth Church in New York, where he preached on the "Coming Man"—the perfect manhood, marked by his wide sympathy, that is coming in the world—certainly a major theme, if not the major theme, shared by the preaching ministries of both Twichell and Beecher.

Sadly Twichell understood that the spiritual crisis of the age made personal integrity and convictions about truth much harder than they had ever been previously—as illustrated by the scandalous adultery trial of Henry Ward Beecher in 1874–75. But Twichell's concept of Christian manhood, along with his embodiment of those principles, still managed to influence much of Mark Twain's own achievement. For example, Twain's railing against mankind, when considered as a manifestation of the classic American (and Christian) jeremiad, also assumes the desirability of a concept of shalom: a pristine and virtuous form of manhood from which present-day manhood has fallen or been corrupted. In other words, Twain's blasts against man can only make sense, and indeed can only be constructed, in relation to another version of mankind that is not damned, not fallen, and not hypocritical. This kind of Christian manhood is best represented not only in the sermons and speeches of Joe Twichell, but perhaps most importantly in the kind of life Twichell actually lived, as emblem and example of his own preaching. The synergy between Twichell's preaching and his life was what Mark Twain admired most about his good friend. It would be impossible to admire fully the one without the other.

Today we typically refer to this synergy as a man's "integrity." This notion thus stands in opposition to one of the key foes in much of Twain's writing: hypocrisy. Twichell must be understood foremost as a man of integrity whose personal life and character were nearly identical incarnations of his Christian belief and preaching, something that Twain had not always found to be the case with the clergy. Such integrity was in fact quite a liberating force of mind, for which Twichell should be applauded at this stage of American history. One of the best illustrations was Twichell's strong and vocal opposition to the Republican James G. Blaine in the 1884 presidential election, for reasons of corruption and Blaine's anti-Chinese stand. In the context of postbellum Connecticut, voting against the Republican Party was quite the radical leap for almost all good Christian parishioners of Joe Twichell. This even included Twain, who actually presided at a meeting of the mugwumps, a dissident political party with which he was associated. At that meeting in Hartford in October 1884, he pledged his continuing belief in the "greatness and righteousness of the principles of the Republican Party," despite the fact that he would not be voting for Blaine.[53] A few weeks earlier, Twain had written to his friend Howells about the coming election: "I only urge you not to soil yourself by voting for Blaine. It is not necessary to vote for Cleveland. The only necessary thing to do, as I understand it, is that a man shall keep himself clean (by withholding his vote for an improper man) even though the party and the country go to destruction in consequence."[54] Oddly, some biographers have thought that Twain exaggerated the public outcry against Twichell's stand against Blaine—so much so that Louis J. Budd remarked that "it has been a commonplace that Twain badly overstated the resentment of his Republican friends and the related pressure on Twichell."[55] However, it appears that Twichell actually did experience heaping condemnation for his stand against the immorality of Blaine's political views. According to one historian, Twichell received an abundance of criticism at that time, and some even charged that he should lose his pulpit, simply because he failed to support a Republican.[56] One letter to the *Hartford Times,* printed on October 20, 1884, complained openly about the "insulting attempt to browbeat and annoy Mr. Twichell because he will not vote for Mr. Blaine and has the manliness and courage to say so."[57] Twain himself authored a "Mock Oration on the Dead Partisan" shortly after the election, satirizing those who voted for Blaine simply because he was a Republican:

> he was a slave; not a turbulent and troublesome, but a meek and docile, cringing and fawning, dirt-eating and dirt-preferring slave; and Party was his lord and master. He had no mind of his own, no will of his own, no opinion of his own; body and soul he was the property and chattel of that master. . . . And the desire of his heart was to make of a nation of freemen a nation of slaves like to himself.[58]

Significantly, Twichell's outspoken stand left a strong impression on Mark Twain. Twain admitted later that he prepared the article entitled "The Character of Man" just after these political events—probably early 1885—and that it was based primarily on Twichell.[59] Regarding the recent election, Twain writes: "Surely if anything is proven, by whole oceans and continents of evidence, it is that the quality of independence was almost wholly left out of the human race. The scattering exceptions to the rule only emphasize it, light it up, make it glare." The crucial example is Twain's discussion of Twichell's vote for conscience' sake against Blaine: "The preacher who casts a vote for conscience' sake, runs the risk of starving. And is rightly served; for he has been teaching a falsity—that men respect and honor independence of thought and action."[60]

Twain's remarks on this occasion typify much about his own thinking on the issues of Christianity and the church. Indeed it would be untrue to the spirit of Mark Twain to suggest that these remarks were in some sense mere public rhetoric, since he spent much of his writing and public life speaking out against hypocrisy. Interestingly a case can be made that hypocrisy as a philosophical and religious category has its origins in Christianity. Dallas Willard has noted that in classical Greek, the term *hypocrite* originally meant actor and eventually became linked to those who practiced deceit. But Willard argues that "it was Jesus alone who brought this term and the corresponding character into the moral vocabulary of the Western world."[61] Jesus's emphasis on this concept is in keeping with Christianity's keen interest in the issues of the inner heart, as opposed to merely the outer appearances. An abhorrence of hypocrisy is among the central features of the teaching ministry of Jesus Christ. In accord with this insight, Twain's vision comports with the Christian idea of a moral and ethical community that somehow modeled for the world a set of relationships by which we might live our lives humanely and sympathetically with one another. Much of Twain's irritation with the Christian church in America can be understood as participating in the jeremiad tradition, insofar as Twain felt betrayed by the callous and shallow nature of Christianity as incarnated in the American church. In other words, perhaps Twain is not castigating Christianity itself so much as contrasting the sad state of Christianity as he typically saw it with the pure and undefiled vision of Christian morality and ethics provided by the very best of Hartford's Christian culture, as manifested by the likes of Joe Twichell.

Appeals to one's conscience are in fact deeply religious in connotation. Twain's meditations on conscience are some of his most enduring works, such as "The Facts Concerning the Recent Carnival of Crime in Connecticut," where Twain questions the necessity and purpose of conscience; or *Adventures of Huckleberry Finn,* where he laments the way culture, including the church itself, can deform a conscience. But Twain apparently regarded Twichell as a man of pure Christian conscience in the fullest and most admirable sense of the phrase. "The Character of Man" indicates that Twain admired any man who votes his conscience, but sadly the folks in Twichell's church were much less accepting of their pastor's failure to pass the Republican litmus test, a point that Twain recalled to the end of his life. In his dictation of February 1, 1906, Twain remembers the church's vote on Twichell's impeachment—Twichell's salvation coming largely, as Twain remembered it, when one man stood up for him on the basis that he helped maintain and raise the real estate prices in town! Twain ends this section with discussion of the sacred need for political independence among ministers.[62] Christian manhood was for Twichell nothing less than the way men ought to be, and as such it illustrates biblical shalom—the ideal toward which Christian men must aspire, by God's good graces.

Crucially, Twichell did not just talk the talk—his life was exemplary of one who walked the walk. And the pilgrimage toward God involved not just the heart but also the mind. Like many liberal congregations of the North, Twichell's church functioned throughout this period as a sort of educational institution, presenting to the members information and analysis of a variety of topics of local, national, and international interest as well as multifaceted cultural events, such as readings by literary figures or speeches by political leaders. Twichell's church mirrored a common trait of the era's genteel congregations in undertaking a sort of lyceum function for the parishioners. This educational function was in keeping with general principles of Social Christianity that appealed to the maintenance and growth of the "mind of Christ" among believers, to the directive to "study to show thyself approved," and to the church's status as the "pillar and ground of the truth" (1 Cor. 2:16; 2 Tim. 2:15;

1 Tim. 3:15). That is, although Twain satirized the coarse ignorance of Christians during the nineteenth century, in fact the genteel leaders of the golden age of liberal Christianity were deeply involved in the intellectual debates that were fomenting throughout North America and beyond. It was within the bounds of the church's ministry, especially given the spiritual crisis of the age, to provide thoughtful and intellectually rigorous presentations on the issues of the day, so that the believing community, as it were, could speak fluently and persuasively as learned and spiritually motivated social observers.

There should be no doubt that this aspect of the Asylum Hill Church was of immediate interest to such a curious and widely read parishioner as Mark Twain. In fact one of his greatest challenges to both the church itself and to the society in which he lived was precisely to eradicate the opposite spirit, that which remains uneducated and close-minded. As Mark Noll has memorably put it about later forms of American Christianity, "The scandal of the evangelical mind is that there is not much of an evangelical mind."[63] Noll's comment reflects his view of a historical decline in the intellectual lives of evangelicals since the nineteenth century, during which the evangelical mind predominated. But by the final decades of the nineteenth century in America, Christians had begun a startling retreat from the life of the mind, a phenomenon associated with the rise of modernism and Darwinism and detailed convincingly in the works of several notable historians.[64] The upshot is that by the time of Twain's residence in Hartford, large segments of the church had already begun moving away from learning and intellectual pursuits. This movement would accelerate greatly as the nation approached the new century.

Anti-intellectualism and cultural retreat were attitudes that Twain often castigated in his writings and speeches, associating them broadly with medievalism, slavery, and the institutional church. On this point, Twain drew once again upon W. E. H. Lecky. In his *History of European Morals,* Lecky constantly critiques the church's attempts to maintain the common people in the throes of ignorance, superstition, and above all "passive, unreasoning obedience."[65] In Lecky's view, the church is basically the great enemy of free thought and expression, insisting on reverence for rank and subservient respect and giving "the servile virtues the foremost place in the moral type."[66] Twain commented on this fallen and mistaken version of the faith when he scribbled in the Lecky volume at one point, "Christianity, then, did not raise up the Slave, but degraded all conditions of men to the Slave's level."[67] The church's enslavement of the human mind was a major theme as early as the European sections of *Innocents Abroad.* Regarding Italy, Twain says, "We were in the heart and home of priestcraft—of a happy, cheerful, contented ignorance, superstition, degradation, poverty, indolence, and everlasting unaspiring worthlessness."[68] Twain expanded his idea of mental slavery among religious devotees to include the enslavement of wage workers, as seen in a revealing illustration from *Connecticut Yankee.* This three-part drawing by Dan Beard, included in the first edition, shows a king over a bound peasant, a southern planter over a bound slave, and a postwar industrialist over a worker. Each has the same words underneath—"Brother!—to dirt like that?"[69]—meaning, "Are you suggesting that I am a brother to this pathetic creature?" This line emphasizes the hierarchies of society and the unwillingness of aristocrats or the wealthy to embrace their subordinates as equals. Such hierarchies embody enslavement while simultaneously rejecting the sympathies with which one might identify with the poor and downtrodden.

In short, Twain abominated the enslavement of the human mind and spirit, and he associated it, as did Lecky, with the offices of the church. But most reformed theologians also abominate intellectual withdrawal and would counter that the spirit of the Scriptures aims at precisely the opposite of Christianity's cultural abandonment and anti-intellectualism. First, the spirit of the gospel is largely a vision of liberation. Secondly, the life of the mind, the investigation of the created order, and the embrace and understanding of the languages, literatures, and cultures of the various ethnic groups around the globe seem most fitting for the true followers of the Creator. This view has long been a staple of Christian theories of education, including theories of the humanities and the liberal arts.[70] In fact, for centuries Christians had referred to the created order as the "second book," God's alternative inscription of truth, after the Bible. On at least one occasion Twain made reference to his awareness and endorsement of this position when he wrote, "[God's] real character is written in plain words in His real Bible, which is nature and her history."[71] Twain's mention here of nature and science as the "real

Bible" should not be taken as unorthodox, given the long history of seeing nature as the "second book."

In fact, Twain was aware of the limitations of his and Lecky's critiques, largely because of the kind of Christian community of which he found himself a part. Twichell and the Asylum Hill Church modeled a progressive form of intellectual pursuit from a Christian perspective that was typical of the liberal gospel of its time in its multicultural and far-flung interests. This form appealed to Mark Twain. Again, he drew much upon Lecky's view that there was a direct connection between imagination and sympathy. As Howard Baetzhold explains, Lecky believed that "if benevolent feelings thus depend upon prior 'realisation,' then any influence that can increase the range and power of the imagination (the 'realising faculty') will help to develop sympathy and compassion. And of all such influences, education is the foremost."[72] In other words, we are granted increased sympathy in direct relation to our power to imagine, which is directly related to our education. We can sympathize with Chinese Americans, ex-slaves, Roman Catholics, or Jews, to the extent that we know and understand them as people.

Joe Twichell made sure, as headmaster of the church and its educational function, that his congregants were exposed to some of the finest thinking of his day. He would agree that compassion and sympathy could be fostered by learning about the world and its inhabitants in more detail. Twichell's insatiable curiosity is clear from the range of topics covered in the frequent lectures given at the church: lectures on literature, poetry, and on such authors as Oliver Wendell Holmes, Thomas Carlyle, and Ralph Waldo Emerson; Richard Burton's occasional lectures on American literature; presentations on the disabled, the blind, and the deaf; and an extensive travel series covering the Eskimos, the Arctic Sea, Greenland, the Far East, Africa, and of course Europe. Twichell frequently preached sermons, or else hosted guest speakers, covering such topics as race relations, foreign cultures, science, archaeology, and ecumenical relations among the different churches, including improving relations with Roman Catholics and Jews. Indeed we also know that literary stars themselves sometimes appeared at the church: for instance an evening with Eugene Field and James Whitcomb Riley was held at the church on April 12, 1898. Even the master, Mark Twain, was a somewhat regular speaker at the church, as we know from the reminiscences of William Lyon Phelps:

> At church-meetings, held on some weekday night, Mark frequently entertained the audience, which crowded the room every time it was announced that he would speak. I remember on one occasion, as Mr. Twichell preceded him up the stairs leading to the platform, the audience burst into tumultuous applause. Mark, pointing at Twichell's back, called out to the audience, "He thinks it's for him."
>
> Three of these occasions I remember very well indeed. . . . First, I heard him read in 1876 from the novel just published, *Tom Sawyer;* he chose the episode of Tom's fight with the citified boy. Second, I heard him read from *Huckleberry Finn* from manuscript, some time before the year 1885, when it was published. Third, I heard him recite his own ghost-story "The Golden Arm," and I remember the shriek of surprised horror that rose from the audience when he reached the climax.[73]

Twain's numerous appearances typified the voracious curiosity and well-rounded intellectual climate of the Asylum Hill Church. By associating with Twichell over such a long period of time, Twain heard lectures and sermons on a myriad of topics beyond simply the gospel, and discussed these topics with Twichell and other Christian believers. Twichell's approach to culture as a passionate Christian was broad and thorough, one that recognized the dominion of God's Kingdom in every area of life, including the arts, and that took genuine glee in uncovering new areas of knowledge that were unfamiliar and mysterious. Such a vision of education and learning appealed to Twain's inherent sense of seriousness with which he approached his literary work.

As part of his schooling to fulfill that role, Twain regularly participated in another aspect of the church community—the Monday Evening Club of Hartford, founded by Horace Bushnell, Calvin Stowe (husband of Harriet Beecher Stowe), and James Hammond Trumbull (who supplied Twain and Warner with the chapter headings for *The Gilded Age*). The club regularly featured topics of religious concern, serving up moral and ethical uplift alongside sandwiches, beer, and cigars. Besides its well-known founders, the club included many of the leading intellectuals of the state: Joseph Hawley and Henry Robinson (both of whom served as Connecticut state governor), Charles Dudley Warner, and the city's three popular Congregational ministers, Joseph Twichell, Edwin Parker, and Nathaniel Burton (and later his son Richard). As a group, these men might be considered an elite collection of Victorian "sages," meaning intellectuals who try to "see life and the world over again, see it with a more searching, or perhaps a more subtle and sensitive gaze." The model for a sage was the biblical prophet, whose primary calling was to diagnose "the spiritual condition of an age." Thus the Monday Evening Club was also largely in the business of spiritual diagnosis, one carried out in the face of the growing ontological despair that Jackson Lears has called "weightlessness."[74] It became a large and growing aspect of Twain's public persona and would remain so for the rest of his life.

Fortunately we have the rare monograph of Howell Cheney that details the topics for every meeting of the club starting in 1869. Cheney's volume illustrates the range of topics covered by the various members, each of whom was required to present an essay to the entire group approximately once every year or two. Richard Burton, for example, spoke on "Divorce" in 1871; "Individualism" in 1873; "Reverence" in 1875; "Originality" in 1877; "Love and Truth" in 1879; "Funeral Rites" in 1880; "Agnosticism" in 1881; "The Vague Element in Language" in 1884; and "The Use of the Beautiful in Sacred Things" in 1886. Edwin Parker's topics included "Capital Punishment" in 1871; "Ritualism" in 1871; "Influence of Climate on Man" in 1874; "Immortality" in 1876; "Calvinism" in 1877; "Agitation against the Jews in Germany" in 1881; "Individual Indebtedness to Society" in 1887; and "Books that Have Helped Me" in 1888.

Joe Twichell spoke on the following topics:

> "Women's Suffrage," Nov. 22, 1869; "Tennyson," April 15, 1872; "Mobs," March 16, 1874; "Is This a Degenerate Age in the United States?," Dec. 13, 1875; "Is Restriction of Suffrage in This Country Desirable?," Jan. 29, 1877; "Charles Lamb," Nov. 18, 1878; "The Pitcairn Islanders," Jan. 19, 1880; "Physical Training in College," Jan. 8, 1883; "Industrial Education," March 17, 1884; "The Classical Education," Jan. 11, 1886; "Education Old and New," April 2, 1888; "The Scheme for a National University," March 11, 1889; "David Livingstone and African Explorations," March 3, 1891; "Some Causes of Some Changes in Recent Religious Thought," Feb. 13, 1893; "Review of Lord Salisbury's Paper on the Limitations of Science,"

> Feb. 11, 1895; "The Military Element in the Nation," March 27, 1899; "The Confederate Apologia," Feb. 26, 1906; "Military Elements in a Nation," Feb. 24, 1908; and his final talk, "Hartford in Literature," Jan. 31, 1910.

Twain was a regular and committed part of the group whenever he was in town, presenting all told thirteen papers over fifteen years to the other members:

> "The License of the Press," March 31, 1873; "Universal Suffrage," Feb. 15, 1875; "The Facts Concerning the Recent Carnival of Crime in Connecticut," Jan. 24, 1876; "Advantages of Travel," March 26, 1877; "Decay of the Art of Lying," April 5, 1880; "Phrenography," Nov. 21, 1881; "What is Happiness?" Feb. 19, 1883; "Southern Literature," March 3, 1884; "A Paper Left Unfinished for the Club to Complete, Each Member as He Thought Best," April 28, 1884; "Knights of Labor—The New Dynasty," March 22, 1886; "A Protest against Taking the Pledge," Oct. 11, 1886; "Machine Culture," Feb. 26, 1887; and "Consistency," Dec. 5, 1887—the last Twain talk given at the Monday Evening Club.[75]

Twain need not have attended those lectures to be influenced by them, since their contents were discussed in his conversations with other club members, and Twichell and others (including Livy) frequently reported the club's activities in their letters to Twain when he was on the road. Women, though they were not officially allowed entrance into the club's meeting rooms, also listened in on the debates and discussions: "the wife of the host was always invited and it was customary for her to ask several friends to sit with her, usually in the hall or on the stairs."[76] Thus Twain certainly would have had further discussions with his wife Livy about the meetings—or, when he was absent and she was invited to sit on the stairs, she would probably give him summaries of the evening's events.

The listing of topics here suggests numerous of Twain's writings undertaken either at about the same time as a talk or sometimes much later. For example, Twichell's talks on "Mobs" and then the "Degenerate Age" of America in 1874–75 might have influenced Twain's thinking as he began the process of composing his tales of Tom and Huck; Burton's discussion of the "Agitation against the Jews in Germany" might have been a seed begetting Twain's later sympathies with the Jews while living in Austria; his talk on "Calvinism" in 1877 might have encouraged Twain's obsession with determinism and religion; and Twichell's lecture on "The Pitcairn Islanders" in 1880 was surely a response of sorts to Twain's own piece, "The Great Revolution in Pitcairn," published two years earlier in 1878. Sometimes Twain's topics are obvious extensions of earlier talks, as in 1875 when Twichell's talk "Is Restriction of Suffrage in This Country Desirable?" is followed the next month by Twain's essay on "Universal Suffrage." At times Twain's topics indicate his playful attitude, as when he presented "A Paper Left Unfinished for the Club to Complete, Each Member as He Thought Best," as well as a willingness to test potentially controversial new angles, as in the most famous piece he read to the group, "The Facts Concerning the Recent Carnival of Crime in Connecticut." Some of his theoretical musings almost certainly were seeds for works written soon after them, as in the case of "Knights of Labor—The New Dynasty" in 1886 and "Machine Culture" in 1887, which relate to *Connecticut Yankee.*[77] He lectured on "Southern Literature" in 1884 just as *Huckleberry Finn* was being completed and as he was beginning "A Private History of a Campaign that Failed." One of the most important talks Twain gave was "What is Happiness?" in 1883, which became the seed for much of his later thinking about mankind and ultimately turned into his philosophical musings in *What is Man?* and elsewhere during his final years.

Thus the Monday Evening Club should be understood as a vital source of information, intellectual stimulation, and critical feedback for Mark Twain. It was "central to [his] intellectual development"[78]—and, I would add, to his spiritual development as well. The club's great influence should be clear, despite some predictable burlesques of this genteel fellowship in his latter years. In a dictation of 1906, Twain reminisced about this learned and somewhat eccentric group. There Twain spent much energy satirizing the Monday Evening Club, several of whose members, he recalled, droned on and on, making no sense or blathering endless pietistic platitudes, and so on. Twain called Trumbull, for example, "the most learned man in the United States . . . and yet if there was a prize offered for the man that could put up the most uninteresting ten minutes' talk, you wouldn't know whether to bet on him or on Perkins." In this dictation, Twain even dismisses the majority of what his friend and collaborator Warner said. The only one who does not get utterly satirized is Twichell: "Joe Twichell . . . if he talked, it was easily perceptible that it was because he had something to say, and he was always able to say it well." (Indeed Twain admired much of Twichell's writing, as when he encouraged his friend to publish the essay on Charles Lamb, which Twichell did.) Not surprisingly, Twain's memory of the group emphasizes the centrality of his pastor: "Twichell could get together the most impossible Christians that ever assembled in anybody's congregation."[79] Despite this dictation's fairly heavy ridicule (written many years later), the emphasis should be on his faithfulness to the club: Twain's consistent participation, the potential influence of the various papers of the other members, and the obvious manner in which the club acted as a sort of writing group where he could test some of his material on his learned and generally sympathetic listeners.

Most importantly, this writing and discussion group also signifies Twichell's attempts to embody Social Christianity and to model it within the confines of the Asylum Hill Congregational Church. The club was a moral undertaking from first to last and reflected the liberal Christian values of lifelong learning and education that later generations of church folk would largely neglect and even chastise. At its best, the club was a social embodiment of the very best instincts of its members. In 1910, on the occasion of Parker's fiftieth year in ministry, Twichell published a tribute to him:

> Dr. Parker's service in the Christian ministry has fallen in a period masked by extraordinary movement and change in the intellectual world, involving widespread fresh agitation and debate touching the great questions of religious truth. No one among us has been more alive to this circumstance, more profoundly appreciative of its significance, or more sympathetic toward the perplexities of faith incident to it, than he, as has been manifest in his teaching. In the pulpit he has been eminently a man for his time. Of one thing his people, and all who have known him, have always been sure—of his entire intellectual veracity.[80]

The Monday Evening Club's desire to achieve such "veracity" was a noble one. But there were daunting new cultural challenges to its achievement. Twichell, Parker, Twain, and the rest lived in a period that was most difficult for attaining such intellectual veracity. By invoking the "widespread fresh agitation and debate touching the great questions of religious truth," Twichell is referring to the controversial arguments of the European theologians whose "higher criticism" brought scientific scrutiny to bear upon the Scriptures. The roots of modern biblical criticism emerged from several theorists, most of whom worked in Germany in the late eighteenth and early nineteenth centuries. At that time, "scholars began to use literary analysis, archaeological discoveries, and comparative linguistics to gain a better understanding of the Old Testament."[81] Among the more prominent names was Julius Wellhausen, whose work on the authorship of the Pentateuch suggested multiple authorship (the so-called JEDP theory, or the documentary hypothesis) rather than it being the single work of Moses. Later critics took on the far more ticklish subject of the New Testament. Ferdinand Baur propounded a theory of the origin of the New Testament that emphasized differences and contradiction among the major writers of the gospels and epistles. David Strauss (1835; reviewed by Theodore Parker in the *Christian Examiner* in 1840; available in George Eliot's English translation in 1846) and Ernest Renan (1863) wrote identically titled studies of the *Life of Jesus*, in which they reconsidered the historicity of the gospel accounts. As these ideas were disseminated throughout the churches of Europe and America, profound changes in the popular approach to the Bible became commonplace as conservative believers began to express their mounting opposition.

A symptom of these changes, and arguably one of the most controversial moments in nineteenth-century American church history, occurred during the period leading up to May 21, 1881—the date on which the first Revised Version of the King James New Testament was offered to the public. As the *New York Times* put it, modern studies in various fields like science, geography, archaeology, and philology made a new translation "almost a necessity." Published by Oxford, with advance orders for a million copies, the book was sold on sidewalks in major cities, and demand was so great that it resulted in major traffic jams and over thirty editions in the first year alone, making it perhaps the single fastest-selling volume in American history until that time.[82] Thus the new version of the Bible that emerged in 1881 was symbolic of an entirely new way of reading and thinking about the Bible that was emerging at just about the same time. This new approach to Scripture was becoming so popular that church leaders Washington Gladden and Lyman Abbott both later remarked that for all practical purposes, the "New Bible" became at that time an entirely new book.

The New Bible occasioned new ways of reading it, including the demythologization of its tales and heroes at the hands of the German higher critics, an approach that quickly gained in popularity. Evidence of the dissemination of modern biblical criticism in the general culture appeared in a number of novels, all best-sellers at the time, which reflected the new vogue of the scientific criticism of the Bible, as well as the attendant anxiety over it. In fact, according to one historian, 1888 "marks a peak in the growth of the nation's awareness of higher criticism because in that year two significant novels on religious issues appeared: *John Ward, Preacher* by Margaret Deland and *Robert Elsmere* by the British author Mrs. Humphrey Ward."[83] These novels both dramatize the falling away of once idealistic and zealous young evangelical preachers, mainly as a result of their encounters with attacks on the nature and fallibility of Scripture. Not surprisingly, both novels were largely reviled in popular reviews, especially in the religious press. Moreover, Twain owned both volumes and on different occasions commented that he had read them (he greatly satirized Deland's book but strongly praised Ward's).

Most prominently, the higher criticism's dismissal of the historic biblical characters is central to the dramatic action in *The Damnation of Theron Ware* (1896), a novel by Harold Frederic, in which a young and idealistic minister encounters a variety of secular and spiritual forces that tend, over the long run, to drive out the love of God and his fellow man and turn Ware into an aging and jaded agnostic. Ware, a small-town Methodist minister, comes under the influence of certain "degenerated" town sophisticates, including a Roman Catholic priest and a dilettantish, sexually provocative young woman given to pagan goddess worship. Looming just beneath these figures, however, is the sinister presence of the German higher criticism. Thus one of the most dramatic moments of the novel occurs when Ware discovers incredulously that some of the religious leaders, including the priest Father Forbes and the strange Hawthornesque intellectual Dr. Ledsmar, no longer consider the biblical heroes to be historical at all. Specifically Ware hopes to become learned in order to produce the definitive historical treatment of the patriarch Abraham. Upon revealing these plans, he is met with a lukewarm reception, as well as the stunning observation that Abraham, in all probability, never existed anyway. It is a classic example of the glib pronouncements that the higher critics were delighted to make to unenlightened preachers such as Ware: "I fear you are taking our friend Abraham too literally, Mr. Ware . . . Modern research, you know, quite wipes him out of existence as an individual. The word "Abram" is merely an eponym—it means 'exalted father . . . Abram is not a person at all: he is a tribe, a sept, a clan."[84] By the end of Frederic's novel, the sinister theological "masters" have virtually destroyed the naïve understandings of popular Christianity.

While the culture was dealing with these remarkable changes with regard to the Good Book, Mark Twain was thinking about them as well. The changes are suggested by Twain's famous metaphorical distinction between the "Pilot and the Passenger," which appears in "Old Times on the Mississippi" (a work that later was greatly expanded into the book *Life on the Mississippi*, 1883). This especially lucid and elastic passage can be related to a multitude of social and cultural conversations, but its religious connotations have been overlooked. "Old Times" depicts the young cub pilot looking in wonder upon the work of the steamboat man as the "one permanent ambition" of his boyhood. The full pilot of these boats was "the grandest position of all. . . . [he] had a princely salary. . . . Two months of his wages would pay a preacher's salary for a year."[85] In fact, the magic of the riverboats bordered on the religious: the appearance of the boat on a drowsy summer's day, for instance, immediately changed the scene: "all in a twinkling the dead town is alive and moving," an image reminiscent of Paul's metaphor of the Lord's return in a "twinkling of an eye" (1 Cor. 15:52).

The naïve passenger's magical vision changes very quickly once the young Clemens is employed full-time under a strong and challenging tutor, the pilot Horace Bixby: "I began to fear that piloting was not quite so romantic as I had imagined it was." For the boy, harsh reality begins to set in when Bixby calmly assures him that "there's only one way to be a pilot, and that is to get this entire river by heart. You have to know it just like A B C."[86] This monumental change, which unfolds in one of the most beloved passages in all of Twain's writing, laments the transition of the boy from mere passenger to savvy and mature pilot:

> The face of the water, in time, became a wonderful book—a book that was a dead language to the uneducated passenger, but which told its mind to me without reserve, delivering its most cherished secrets as clearly as if it uttered them with a voice. And it was not a book to be read once and thrown aside, for it had a new story to tell every day. . . . Now when I had mastered the language of this water and had come to know every trifling feature that bordered the great river as familiarly as I knew the letters of the alphabet, I had made a valuable acquisition. But I had lost something, too. I had lost something which could never be restored to me while I lived. All the grace, the beauty, the poetry had gone out of the majestic river! . . . No, the romance and the beauty were all gone from the river.[87]

It is possible to read this passage as a suggestive religious metaphor in which, for example, the river represents the Bible and/or simple Christian faith. Several features of this passage support such a view. The "face of the water" echoes the opening lines of Genesis: "the spirit of God was moving on the face of the waters" (Gen. 1:2). The river is directly called a "book"—one written, like the Bible, in a "dead language." This book "utters" its "secrets" with a "voice"; it also is one that needs to be read "every day." For "uneducated" readers, this book remains filled with "grace, beauty, and poetry"; however, once the reader is educated, it no longer is. When read in the context of the sustained critical deconstruction of the Bible as text that was almost simultaneously becoming the most important challenge facing traditional faith, this passage takes on a new life and points not only to a turning point in the life of the pilot but also the turning point in the spiritual crisis of the entire age. The upshot of such a reading is to realize that, above all, the spiritual crisis of Twain's era largely derived from a crisis in the understanding of the Bible, especially as authoritative source of truth. Older, more romantic, and less scientifically scrutinized versions of the Good Book were giving way to more technical and skeptical ways of reading and knowing. Suddenly, it seemed, the old ways of knowing truth were not just being challenged by the intellectuals; they were crumbling before the eyes of regular folks as well. It was indeed becoming a "New Bible."

Thus the epistemological revolution characterized by Twain as a conversion of the passenger into the pilot includes not only the jejune transition of the romantic into the realistic. It also invokes the revolution underway in the fields of theology and biblical exegesis throughout North America as well. This revolution constituted a shift away from a sentimentalized version of humanity to a more cynically realistic version. Twain's fortunate fall from the innocent romance of his boyhood youth to the studied maturity of his piloting years can serve as a tautology of the revolutionary innovations of thought in a multitude of scholarly worlds. The pilot is the mid- to late-nineteenth-century scientific version of Emerson's transparent eyeball in *Nature*: one who knows each and every detail, yet now without romance, without sentimentality, and without remorse. The loss of innocence depicted in the "Old Times" passage, when combined with the revolutionary impact of approaches to the "New Bible" around the time of the tale's composition, comports with Twain's famous statement of faith in a letter to his brother Orion in 1878: "Neither Howells nor I believe in hell or the divinity of the Savior but no matter, the Savior is none the less a Sacred Personage, and a man should have no desire or disposition to refer to him lightly, profanely or otherwise than with the profoundest reverence."[88]

Twain's confession resonates with the conclusions of the German higher criticism—the historicized, and thus demythologized, new versions of figures like Jesus, still "sacred," but no longer God. Related are numerous sustained attacks on religious romanticism Twain undertook, such as the long story, "Extracts from Captain Stormfield's Visit to Heaven." "Captain Stormfield's Visit," apparently written mostly around 1867–71 but not published until 1907–8 in *Harper's*, describes one person's long journey to and in the heavenly realm.[89] Twain's fantastic vision of the hereafter is evident throughout "Captain Stormfield's Visit"; this extremism is part and parcel of the deistic view of the universe that by the time of the story's composition had become Twain's primary religious ideology. Specifically, "Stormfield" began as a response to Elizabeth Stuart Phelps's 1868 best-seller *The Gates Ajar;* more generally, it is a response to the romanticized view of the afterlife that predominated throughout much of women's fiction of that period—much of it in reaction to the horrific deaths of loved ones in the Civil War.[90] Twain took umbrage with these glorified views of death and of the afterlife, which reflected the widespread acceptance of a "domestic heaven." Perhaps the best example of this was Phelps's *The Gates Ajar,* which offered "homes restored, families regathered, and friends reunited."[91] According to Ann Douglas, *The Gates Ajar* constitutes the culmination of an entire genre of fiction that she labels "consolation literature": "All the logic of *The Gates Ajar* . . . suggests to the reader: you are going to end up, if you are well-behaved and lucky, in a domestic realm of children, women, and ministers (i.e. angels), so why not begin to believe in them now?"[92]

Evidently, Livy Clemens shared such a romantic view of the afterlife.[93] For Twain, however, such a view was much too small, greatly exaggerating the close relationship between Heaven and Earth. Thus "Captain Stormfield's Visit" can be read as Twain's satirical rebuke of the smallness of the American concept of God and His Heaven. Much of the opening section is devoted to the lengthy adventure involved in approaching Heaven, part of which involves racing a comet. Upon arrival, readers learn that there are billions of planets and that the earth is itself of so small consequence that it is called the Wart. The mistaken and sentimental ideas about Heaven are condescendingly allowed to dictate the actions of the angels and the redeemed, such as when believers from America arrive expecting a huge welcome, which is exactly what they get. But after time, it becomes apparent that Heaven is no democracy, and that the prophets or great personages of the Bible are hardly accessible to common folk. In short, new arrivals learn quickly how deceived they were on earth about the nature of the afterlife. Like much of Twain's attack on romanticism, he ascribes the guilt to the romantic ideas as presented in various written works on the subject. Further, he names several historical figures, such as T. DeWitt Talmage and Dwight Moody, who bear responsibility for misrepresenting Heaven to their flocks.

But it would be a mistake to read the tale as the author's rejection of God or Heaven. Indeed the story betrays the heart of one interested in capturing the true grandeur of God and His Heaven. He rails against the eviscerated and mundane versions that have been perpetrated onto the reading public. What seems to bother Twain most here is that the vision of the Almighty is just not transcendent enough. Once more, we can read this story from the vantage point of the pilot's demythologizing power to reveal the truth to the unlearned passengers. But here the mythos being deconstructed is the product of an emasculated church rapidly in decline toward the anti-intellectualism and sentimentality that would become its hallmarks early in the next century. Under these circumstances, it is plausible to ask whether such a critic of Christianity speaks as one who is clearly outside of and opposed to the tradition, or as one from within.

4

Mark Twain's Liberal Faith

The Social Gospel on Asylum Hill

At a dinner in St. Louis in 1902, during a period when he is generally considered to be at his most antireligious, Mark Twain made some memorably spiritual remarks. According to a reporter of the event, at the end of the many speeches, Twain stood and said he

> wanted to preach a sermon, since he was as reverend as anybody. He took for his text a story of St. Francis, how he asked one of the Brothers to go with him into the village to preach. Arm in arm they walked down the hill, rejoicing in the soft spring sunlight, talking of the love of God, happy in their fellowship. On through the village they went, up the hill on the other side, then back again to the monastery gate, without stopping. "But are we not going to preach today?" asked the Brother. "We have preached," said Francis. "We have been happy in the love of God and the glory of His sunlight—that is our sermon for the day."[1]

Twain claims here that we are always "preaching" whether we know it or not. It is a vision of an incarnated Kingdom of God that bespeaks the Social Christianity of his day. It also betrays the steady influence of his good friend and pastor, the Rev. Joe Twichell: the long walks of fellowship remind us of the countless hikes Twain took with Twichell up and down the wooded hills surrounding Hartford.

But Joe Twichell was hardly the only model of Christian character available to Mark Twain. The city of Hartford was fortunate enough to have the services of Father David Hawley, a dedicated social worker whose calling in life was a full-time ministry to the indigent, the estranged, and the forgotten of nineteenth-century urban America. Hartford, like virtually all northern cities, experienced explosive growth after the Civil War, burgeoning from a population of 13,555 in 1850 to 37,743 in 1870, an increase of 178 percent in twenty years.[2] Hawley supervised Hartford's City Missionary Society—formerly the Young Men's City Missionary Society—from 1852–61 and then from 1863 until his death in 1876. Hawley's basic outreach was to the poor, providing clothing, food, and pastoral care. He particularly reached out to the foreign-born of the city, many of whom were Roman Catholic, and his friendship to them earned him the title of Father, his moniker for all who knew of his work. Mark Twain was among those Hartford residents who became friends and supporters of Father Hawley's ministry.

Hawley's outreach exemplified in spirit and pragmatic effect the emerging Social Gospel movement in urban America of that period. The Social Gospel grew out of the near-utopian optimism that sprang to life after the Civil War came to an end. As life in America tried to return to normalcy, urban centers sprang to life as well—many of these cities doubled or even tripled in population between 1850 and 1870. Among the most influential of the Congregationalist Social Gospellers, and another direct disciple of Horace Bushnell, was Washington Gladden, whom Sydney Ahlstrom called "a major awakener of the American Protestant social conscience" who "saturated his liberalism with social concern."[3] This concern derived largely from the realities of urban poverty. In his memoir *Recollections* (1909), Gladden recalls the power of the urban nightmare he first entered in 1860:

> The city, from the first day, was a thing stupendous and overpowering, a mighty monster, with portentous energies; the sense of its power to absorb human personalities and to shape human destinies was often vivid and painful. . . . the contact with the strenuous life of the great city was a revelation. . . . Everything was alive, yet there was a vivid sense of the impersonality and brutality of the whole movement, of the lack of coordinating intelligence.[4]

These themes of impersonality and brutality were major tropes of realism, the emerging literary mode in the decades after the Civil War.

The literature of realism illustrated the implications of Darwinian science: it depicted city dwellers as bestial rather than angelic and their lives as premised on economic competition where only the fittest survived. Realism also emphasized the dangers and mysteries that were becoming increasingly associated with the cities. Louis J. Budd notes that "editors saw an urgent need as well as profitable opportunity to document the new social contexts. . . . The competing, burgeoning metropolitan newspapers featured the twists of daily survival or success; periodicals featured breathless essays on changing facts and attitudes."[5] Not coincidentally, most of the great writers of American realism and naturalism cut their teeth as journalists covering the dark urban scenes of the period. Besides Twain, William Dean Howells, Twain's literary mentor, was the most obvious example. One of the best literary expressions of the threatening tone of the new urban landscape appears in Howells's novel *A Hazard of New Fortunes* (1890): New York "seemed to him lawless, Godless; the absence of intelligent, comprehensive purpose in the huge disorder and the violent struggle."[6] But the list of journalists turned novelists would also include almost all of the other leaders of the movement: Ambrose Bierce, Stephen Crane, Theodore Dreiser, Harold Frederic, Frank Norris, and Willa Cather, among others. Dreiser recalled in his memoir the darkness of his own initiation at the age of twenty into the hell of urban reporting in Chicago: "from that time dates my real contact with life—murders, arson, rape, sodomy, bribery, corruption, trickery and false witness in every conceivable form."[7]

Thus, to a rather large extent, the rise of realism and then naturalism in American literature owes a lot to the rapid changes in the urban settings of the North, which became a central focus for the journalism of the day. At the same time, the religious communities of the North earnestly began the search for a direct response to these alarming trends in the cities. We can even go so far as to say that the religious emergence of Social Christianity has much in common with the literary emergence of realism and naturalism: both, it seems, were powerful attempts to deal with the frightening changes in America's urban landscape. Both were shaped significantly by the sheer scale and horror of the Civil War. Both drew heavily from the emerging scientific studies in fields like psychology and sociology in shaping their views of humanity. Furthermore, both were interested in forging the bonds of sympathy between the social classes and among all members of the American democratic experiment. Perhaps most significantly, true responses to the growing problems of the urban nightmare, for both Social Gospellers and writers of realism, could only issue from people who had, as Dreiser put it, "real contact with life." Some writers went so far as to disguise themselves as members of the lower classes in an attempt to achieve authentic, "vital contact" with the poor.[8] In its goal of focusing on the commonplace and the everyday individuals of the working class and the poor, realism can be understood as largely a moral and ethical project.

Although today it is rarely discussed from this perspective, some early commentators made the connection between realism and Christianity. In 1874, for example, George Parsons Lathrop published one of the first accounts of realism, in which he describes

> the dawn of a new epoch. Christ's thought, however slow to manifest itself firmly in the details of our social, political, and religious organization, has assuredly taken root in the novel. Pity and charity, love, or admiration for the poor, the common, the unfortunate, and the unrecognized nobility of the world, are what it is continually endeavoring to arouse and propagate. . . . Our heroes and heroines are taken from the rank and file of the race, and represent people whom we daily encounter.[9]

Lathrop's direct comparison between the spirit of Christ and the recognition of the value and worth of each individual has somehow fallen out of theoretical considerations of literary realism. But in one of his great discussions of his theory of the practice of realism, William Dean Howells in 1886 affirmed its ability to extend social awareness and "widen the bounds of sympathy."[10] Similarly, in its efforts to gain a fuller and truer understanding of each individual within the domain of their influence, and to study the unseen forces and systemic realities that determined much of their existence, Social Christianity can be understood as largely a cultural and social project sharing provocative connections with literary realism. As a result, perhaps we should not be so surprised that realist artists like Twain and Howells were so drawn to many of the themes of the Social Gospel.

Father Hawley's work in Hartford typified the rise of the Social Gospel, as Social Christianity came to be called, after the Civil War, providing a flesh and blood embodiment of Social Gospel principles for the parishioners of the Asylum Hill Church. While Hawley was technically not a member of the Asylum Hill Church, he was certainly an affiliate and colleague, and was often supported both financially and in prayer and service by that congregation. Joe Twichell had spent at least two full days working with Father Hawley in 1873. His aim was to determine if there were worthy poor among the flock, or if they were merely poor due to their own improvidence, laziness, or vice. His personal experience led him to believe that it was indeed a worthy mission—and that many of the poor had a genuine need. As a result, he urged his flock to serve and support Hawley's work. It was an exhortation that Twain would have heard on several occasions. Indeed the Nook Farm community as a whole, and Mark Twain in particular, were great supporters and friends of the City Missionary Society and Father Hawley. Twichell and Twain often spoke at the Morgan Street Mission, Hawley's headquarters. When Twain moved to Hartford, Father Hawley was the single full-time social worker of the town, and Twain was immediately attracted to him because of his "generous selflessness," describing him as "a man whose tireless zeal was unique among his fellows."[11] In 1875 a number of prominent citizens asked Twain to give a benefit lecture in support of Hawley's work. Twain at first said that he had permanently quit the lecture field and would not return to it "unless driven there by lack of bread," but he later agreed to do the performance because, he lamented, "I am confronted by a lack of bread—among Father Hawley's flock!" He insisted that all must pay for the lecture, himself included—which he did! The performance at the Opera House lecture raised $1,200 for Hawley's mission.[12] Even after Hawley's death in 1876, Mark Twain and a quartet of women singers performed at the Morgan Street Mission on January 18, 1877: "Twain told the class and teachers several stories and of his duel. There were 115 present."[13]

Twichell often spoke about Hawley's works and occasionally included information about him in his sermons. In December 1873, Father Hawley was the central topic of Twichell's sermon at Asylum Hill: "He *knows* the poor. . . . the work of Father Hawley in this city is a grand work of Christian charity, in which he ought to be supported by all needful sympathy and cooperation. . . . His heart is with the poor; he makes their cause his own; he cares for them; he is identified with them; so much so, that what is done for them he feels as if it has been done for him."[14]

Twichell also gave one of the main orations at the memorial service after Hawley died in 1876, reasserting many of the same themes:

> At the end of twenty-five years of labor, Father Hawley had a fresher and quicker sympathy with suffering and with sorrow than he had at the beginning. . . . Father Hawley was a Christian man. . . . [he] has done in all these years a great service for the cause of Christ in this city, and the Christian Church in this city, in that he has set forth in living form the likeness of the Lord Jesus Christ; and our Christian religion is weak, weak, for lack of more representation of that sort.[15]

Mark Twain's version of a Christian ethic can be extrapolated from his high esteem and actual support for Father Hawley's urban mission. Twain admired those who incarnated the Christian ethic to "do unto others as you would have them do unto you"—as opposed to those who merely parroted such Christian pieties but lived in some other manner. This was the church's great failing, in Twain's eyes. We might usefully compare Twain's position with other critiques of the church presented before him by some of America's great writers, such as Frederick Douglass and Harriet Beecher Stowe. Douglass ends his *Narrative* by reminding his readers of his position within the church:

> What I have said respecting and against religion, I mean strictly to apply to the slaveholding religion of this land, and with no possible reference to Christianity proper; for, between the Christianity of this land, and the Christianity of Christ, I recognize the widest possible difference—so wide, that to receive the one as good, pure, and holy, is of necessity to reject the other as bad, corrupt, and wicked. . . . I love the pure, peaceable, and impartial Christianity of Christ: I therefore hate the corrupt, slaveholding, women-whipping, cradle-plundering, partial and hypocritical Christianity of this land.[16]

Douglass qualifies as a sentimentalist insofar as he works to create sympathy in his readers, to foster certain sentiments. This passage also conveys his commitment to shalom: he describes a vision of the way Christianity ought to be, as opposed to how it is at present.

Harriet Beecher Stowe similarly aimed at both altering the sentiments of her readers and preaching a version of shalom, the pure vision of the Kingdom of God. *Uncle Tom's Cabin* urges its readers to embrace an emotional union with or sympathy for the novel's characters and crises—the quintessential rhetorical goal of sentimentalists. *Uncle Tom's Cabin* may be the century's most important and powerful example of sentimentalism, not simply because it models certain features that are often associated with sentimental literature. Additionally *Uncle Tom's Cabin* serves as the great example of sentimentalism precisely because of its moral effect on the reader. As Joycelyn Moody puts it, "In this case, the purpose of sentimentality is to induce the process by which the reader's desire for psychic union with characters and tropes is aroused. . . . the ideological work of the sentimentalist is to assure us that we *can* and do feel culturally sanctioned and even socially prescribed emotions strongly."[17] In other words, sentimentalists are in the business of fostering among readers a precise way of feeling. As Stowe exhorts her readers in the novel's famous "Concluding Remarks": "There is one thing that every individual can do,—they can see to it they feel right. . . . See, then, to your sympathies in this matter! Are they in harmony with the sympathies of Christ? Or are they swayed and perverted by the sophistries of worldly policy?"[18] Analysis of the historical discussion of the Twichell-Twain friendship reveals their sentimental connection, particularly the importance of the term *sympathy.* Regarding Twain, Albert B. Paine wrote, "something in his heart always warmed toward any laborer in the vineyard, and if we could put the explanation into a single sentence, perhaps we might say it was because he could meet them on that wide, common ground—sympathy with mankind."[19] To the extent that we understand sympathy as a mystical connection between individuals, the concept is religious. In the nineteenth century, sympathy was a decidedly Christian concept with deep roots in the New Testament concept of community and oneness in the body of Christ, and in the theological history of the Western church.

Despite what many think, Twain regularly participated in the social and religious activities of the Asylum Hill Congregational Church, throughout his major period from 1872–89. Innumerable newspaper reports attest to his and Livy's regular attendance: as late as 1887, for example, one paper reported that Twain "attends church regularly, being fond of the eloquent sermons of his friend, Dr. Twichell."[20] Twain sympathized with the ministry of the Asylum Hill Church over a long period of time, meaning he identified closely with it. The family's interest in the church extended beyond mere attendance to financial and voluntary support in a variety of ways. For instance, Twain often helped with collections for missionary work, even as he often chastised American missionary efforts. Scrutiny of the existing parish records shows not only that Twain often donated money for many causes, including foreign missions, but also that he frequently gave more than anyone else. Furthermore he sometimes offered his personal appearance at fund-raisers, which greatly enhanced the success of such meetings, as in the case above with Father Hawley. Perhaps most strikingly, Twain frequently contributed to Twichell's local mission project, the American Chinese Educational Mission, which sponsored Chinese students for study in the United States, culminating at Yale University. For instance, in a listing of subscriptions to help pay for the college expenses of Yung Kwai at Yale in March 1882, the name "S. L. Clemens" is prominent in his generous donation of twenty-five dollars each year for three years—one of the highest amounts among the participants.

Some may be surprised that Mark Twain gave willingly on many occasions to the missions activities of the Asylum Hill Church, given his vehement opposition to Christian missions in many of its forms during his lifetime. This opposition grew as he aged and found its most articulate form in some of the most sweeping and sustained critiques he would ever publish, including sections of *Following the Equator* (1897) and such essays as "To the Person Sitting in Darkness" (1901). He also would challenge some of the premises of missions work metaphorically in such fictions as *A Connecticut Yankee in King Arthur's Court.* In Twain's mind, much of the work of missions was strongly associated with the more sinister workings of imperialism—a view he shared with an earlier American novelist, Herman Melville. As several critics have forcefully shown, Twain was nearly obsessed with imperialism and colonialism in the last years of his life, and he penned some well-known critiques of cross-cultural missions movements.[21] And as Richard Gamble has recently shown, the late nineteenth-century church was deeply implicated in America's march toward world dominance (although the church's intentions were mostly good ones), a fact never lost on Mark Twain.[22]

An emphasis on this version of Twain's view of missionary activities and the rise of American empire has perpetrated what has clearly become the consensus opinion: he was fervently opposed to such activities. And so it is perhaps surprising to many readers that there are various other moments when Twain strongly endorsed the rise of Christian civilization in the future. Some of these statements appear in *Following the Equator,* a late book often written off as largely a pessimistic screed. There, for instance, Twain waxes eloquent with regard to some benefits of imperialism: "All the savage lands in the world are going to be brought under subjection to the Christian governments of Europe. I am not sorry, but glad. . . . The sooner the seizure is consummated, the better for the savages. The dreary and dragging ages of bloodshed and disorder and oppression will give place to peace and order and the reign of law."[23] Richard Bridgman correctly concludes that Twain "was not being ironic." Bridgman qualifies his view by going on to say that, "[if] these hopeful sentiments . . . represented Mark Twain's best judgment as he came to the end of his last extensive journey, in fact he would shortly be obliged to repudiate them."[24] In a related matter, Howard Baetzhold claims that, when Twain wrote in the margins of his copy of Lecky's *History of European Morals* that "Christianity is the most precious and elevating and ennobling boon ever vouchsafed to the world," this notation "seems to imply Clemens's wry exasperation with the historian's efforts to present both sides concerning the Church's influence."[25] But it is unclear why Baetzhold thinks Twain is being ironic in this case. Perhaps, as I have already suggested, Twain took this inscription very seriously. It is also important to recall that Twain worked feverishly on *Following the Equator* in those torrid and emotional months after the death of his daughter Susy in August 1896, just at the very end of the journey. As I will suggest later, severe grief and pain enhanced Twain's desire that the world's "disorder and oppression" would ultimately be replaced with more "peace and order"—a hope, not uncommon among bereaved parents, that ironically appears to expand during the grief process, acting somehow as a tribute and memorial to the departed child. Finally, and most significantly, are Twain's concrete activities over many years in support of Christian ministries and the increase of Christian influence.

Mark Twain's engagement with cross-cultural missions outreach is thus more complex than some accounts have suggested, particularly those carried out in his home country among the immigrants, as in Father Hawley's mission, or in the work of the Chinese Educational Mission of Yung Wing and his close friend, Joseph Twichell. The Chinese Educational Mission was a long-term attempt to bring promising young Chinese students overseas to study in New England, and Twain's ongoing support of it might surprise those who tend to label him as opposed to missions outreach by the Christian church. The Chinese Educational Mission should be considered a major success of Twichell's career, despite the continual political problems that arose. Not the least of these problems was the fact that the Chinese governmental leaders were divided over the goals and philosophy of the program. Obviously the program hoped to introduce the Chinese students not just to the American way of life but also to the Christian gospel.

Much of the success of this program can be attributed to Twichell's insistent vision along with the very fine leadership team he employed to carry it out. Chief among these leaders was Yung Wing, the first Chinese student at Yale College and the man responsible in 1871 for bringing over a number of promising boys from some of China's most important families to study in Connecticut. While living in the homes of members of the Asylum Hill Church, these boys attended Hartford Public High School. Five officials of the Chinese government accompanied these boys and lived in a house at the corner of Collins and Woodland streets in Hartford, not far from the Twichells. The education was to include instruction in both English and Chinese; college education would take place at Yale or any number of other participating schools. Due to growing stress between the Chinese and American governments, the mission was forced to discontinue its activities in 1881.

Yung Wing described Twichell as his "life-long friend." In 1874, when Wing was sent by the Chinese government to investigate the treatment of Chinese laborers in Peru, Twichell accompanied him. Twichell frequently spoke out against the growing hostility against Chinese laborers, or "coolies," and against the Chinese Exclusion Acts, a set of statutes that institutionalized this sort of bias. Wing became a member of the Asylum Hill Church in 1887 and married an American woman, Mary Kellogg, with whom he had two sons. Twichell presided at the wedding ceremony. When Wing was recalled to China in 1895, his son, Bartlett, lived with the Twichells, a generous arrangement that inspired Wing:

> This is only a single instance illustrative of the large-hearted and broad spirit which has endeared [the Twichells] to their people both in the Asylum Hill church and outside of it. I was deeply affected by this act of self-denial and magnanimity in my behalf as well as in the behalf of my son Bartlett, whom I felt perfectly assured was in first-class hands, adopted as a member of one of the best families in New England.[26]

While back in China, Wing joined the reform movement, at which time the Empress Dowager marked him as a danger to the regime by setting a price on his head. Wing was forced to flee China and returned to live out his days in Hartford in 1902.

Yung Wing, the key spokesman for Chinese-American activists, was also an acquaintance of Mark Twain. Twain fully embraced Wing's work, hosting, for instance, a reception for him in his Nook Farm home in 1877. More important is the astonishing story of Twain's great assistance to the Chinese Educational Mission at critical moments. This story must be considered in the context of the program's inception as a tangible expression of the American Social Gospel. A few years into the program's existence, the Chinese government attempted to close it down. Twichell made extensive journal entries about the fate of the mission, as in the following excerpts from December 1880:

> [20th] During the month of October (I think) Yung Wing, in consequence of new perils having arisen, threatening the existence of the Mission, chiefly through the alarming representations made to the Chinese Government by Woo the Commissioner, asked me to draw up a circular, to be signed by the heads of all the higher class of institution at which students had been placed, expressing the opinion that the scheme of the Mission was excellent, its success so far manifest and that its abandonment was greatly to be deplored. . . .
>
> Wing wrote to me asking me to go to New York and see Gen. Grant,

and try to enlist his services on behalf of the Mission, the prospect of which was by this time darker still. As the subjoined letter will show, I went to my friend Mark Twain and solicited his good offices in aiding me to gain access to Gen. G. with whom he had acquaintance. He readily undertook to do this and wrote to Gen. Grant asking for both of us an interview with him the following Tuesday at New York. He also described to him the nature of the errand we were coming on, and enclosed to him a copy of my Lecture on the Mission. . . .

Dec. 21st [1880]. We were at the Fifth Ave. Hotel betimes in the morning, were received most kindly by Gen. Grant, who launched out in as free and flowing a talk as I ever heard, marked by . . . intelligent and benevolent views, on the subject of China, her wants, disadvantages & c. Now and then he asked a question, but kept the lead in the conversation. At last he proposed of his own accord to write a letter to Li Hung Chang, advising the continuance of the Mission, asking only that I would prepare him some note giving him points to go by. . . . Thus we succeeded easily beyond expectation, thanks, very largely, to Clemens' assistance.

The following Monday the letter came to M.T. at Hartford and was forthwith mailed to the Am. Consul Genl. at Tientsin, to be forwarded to the Viceroy. And may God prosper it. It was five pages, well written, going right to the marrow of the subject, and was calculated, coming from him, to have effect, I should judge.[27]

We can measure the results, temporary as they turned out to be, by the tone of a letter dated March 10, 1881, from Yung Wing to Twichell:

My Dear Friend,

General Grant's letter has done its work. . . . I think the mission has passed its most critical crisis. Could you go [to] see our friend Mr. Clemens and tell him confidentially what good he is capable of doing.[28]

Two weeks later, Twichell writes:

Yung Wing arrives from Washington full of business. The Chinese Gov. (so he is advised) is soon to embark on a great Rail Road enterprise, and he wants the United States to get in ahead of England and all the world in furnishing the men and the capital involved in carrying out the proj-

> ect. It is for the welfare of China that this should be. Gen. Grant's services are again required. Accordingly M.T. is called on for counsel and aid. He writes to Gen. Grant at once. Answer comes promptly that he is on the point of setting out for Mexico, but will be sure to seize an opportunity en route to write to Li Hung Chang making recommendations in the line of Yung Wing's ideas. Also, comes a telegram from John Russell Young, Gen. Grant's intimate friend and companion around the world, saying that he is desired by the General to learn more about the matter. M.T. and Y.W. therefore go to New York, meet and hold long talk with Mr. Young, and find that it was better to see him than General G.—matters could be more thoroughly discussed, and some important things said to the Gen. *through* him than could have been said immediately. . . . The Lord seems to be opening his way to greater usefulness. We shall see.[29]

This passage again shows the central agency of Twain in the workings of Twichell's ministry to the Chinese.

However, and despite the powerful influence of the likes of Grant and Twain, the mission was facing eminent closure. On July 7, Twichell writes: "Yung Wing called to say that the new alarming dispatches from China of which I had heard, and which I had written him a note about, were in his opinion, not what they seemed. . . . They *seemed* to seal the fate of the mission, and when he told me what they were I doubted if his hope of a lighter meaning was justifiable." And finally, on July 9, 1881: "Another dispatch from China received yesterday removes all doubt. *The Mission is doomed*!"[30]

Despite the ultimate demise of the program, it signifies the growing sympathies that Twain had for the Chinese and by extension for other immigrant groups—sympathies shared and fostered by his pastor. As late as 1900, Twichell and Twain carried on an extensive discussion of China in their correspondence, especially as the imperialist powers competed for power in the emerging nation. Twain writes, "It is all China, now, + my sympathies are with the Chinese. They have been villainously dealt with by the sceptred thieves of Europe, + I hope they will drive all the foreigners out + keep them out for good. I only wish it; of course I don't really expect it."[31] Twain's attitude toward Christian work in China had greatly changed by 1901. In 1868, thirty-three years earlier, he had strenuously endorsed the Burlingame Treaty with China: "[the

Treaty] confers science, mechanics, social and political advancement, Christianity."[32] By 1901, however, Twain often wrote strong attacks on missions work in China, especially criticizing Robert Ament and Judson Smith of the American Board of Foreign Mission. One of the most devastating rhetorical pieces he ever wrote was on this topic, "To the Person Sitting in Darkness," published in 1901 to widespread public controversy. Today it must surely be listed among his great tours de force. And yet it is easy to forget how committed this essay remains to the rightness of the pure gospel, which Twain refers to as "the grace and gentleness and charity and loving kindness of our religion."[33] Like Frederick Douglass and Harriet Beecher Stowe, he contrasts this pure gospel with the corrupt version being perpetrated in its stead. As such, "To the Person Sitting in Darkness" operates in the mode of the jeremiad and thus speaks as one from within the church ("our religion") rather than as one outside. While certainly favoring extending "grace and gentleness" to the Chinese, he feared that the imperialistic American church was no longer capable of it.

In a note to Twain during the winter of 1877–78, Twichell urged him to read excerpts from Omar Khayyam's "Rubaiyat" printed in the morning papers. "Read it, and we'll talk it over. There is something in it very like the passage of Emerson you read me last night, in fact identical with it in thought. Surely this Omar was a great poet. Anyhow, he has given me an immense revelation this morning." Twain responded that he had already read the poem and "was still steeped in the ecstasy of delight which they had occasioned; no poem had ever given me so much pleasure before."[34] This exchange shows another facet of the curious synergy that these two men shared: a passion for the exotic and the mystical that clearly went beyond the bounds of a staid, traditional version of Christianity. Twichell's interest in the Near East caused him to host a presentation by theology professor Duncan McDonald on "The Creed of Islam" at the church in 1894. Twichell's far-flung interest in other cultures and ethnicities was a regular feature of his ministry activities, as evidenced by his work with the Chinese mission. As a result, he became well-known as a leader in what we might call today the multicultural movement. Testimony to this was the fact that Twichell was appointed to the Advisory Council on Religious Congresses of the World's Congress Auxiliary in connection with the World's Columbian Exposition of 1893. This appointment gave Twichell the idea to host a "Columbian bazaar" on March 10, 1893, at the Asylum Hill Church. It comprised what today we might call a multicultural festival, with booths representing various nations, their cultures, foods, and so on, including prominent ones for the Chinese and Japanese.

As he did with the Chinese, Twichell had a long interest in and sympathy for the Japanese. Indeed Twichell's commitment to ethnic groups throughout the world, but perhaps in particular to China and Japan, might arguably be one of his preoccupations as a minister of the gospel—and a particularly progressive one for this period in American religious history. For instance, Twichell attached into his journal one stunning photo of a Japanese young man: the subject is identified in Twichell's handwriting as "Inajiro T. Tajori—Yale college class of 1878 treasury official of the Japanese government and instructor in Tokio [sic] University. . . . The main expense of his education—including a year of post-graduate study—was borne by members of the Asylum Hill Cong. Church."[35] Additionally, the progress of Christianity in Japan was the topic of an address by the "Rev. K. Tsumachima of Tokio," at the Asylum Hill Church on May 7, 1896. Tsumachima was a graduate of Doshisha University, founded as a Congregational university in the ancient capitol of Kyoto, and he did seminary training at Yale. Tsumachima was very optimistic about the future of Japan as a Christian nation, primarily focusing on its unity as a single race of people with unmixed blood and 2,700 years under a single dynasty. And on October 5, 1899, the "Rev. Minosuke Yamaguchi of Tokio lectured on home life in Japan" at the Asylum Hill Church. His presentation included one hundred illustrations by the stereopticon, and he described the Japanese as the "Yankees of the Orient." While none of these latter events would have been attended by Twain, they nevertheless indicate the degree to which Twichell's passion for the Japanese, and more generally his interest in multicultural understanding, was a significant part of his character and ministry.

Related to Twichell's multicultural burden was his strong advocacy for building ecumenical relations among the different faith communities in Hartford, including improving relations with Roman Catholics and Jews. Twichell tried to build an ecumenical bridge between his Congregational base and other denominations of the Christian church. In particular, Twichell was a forerunner in his attempts to build a coalition with the marginalized Roman Catholics of Hartford. Considering that most Protestants still harbored prejudice against Catholics in the latter part of the century, Twichell's activities along these lines were progressive and indeed somewhat heroic. This progressivism is all the more admirable because of his strong prejudice against Catholic religion in his early career. His own "conversion" from an entrenched Protestant fear and paranoia about Romanism can be dated fairly precisely: it began with his war service with a jovial and loving Catholic priest, Joseph B. O'Hagan. His devotion to O'Hagan deepened at Fredericksburg, where they slept together under shared bedding on the open battlefield, a story that Twichell often drew upon as a sermon illustration. One historian notes,

> Mr. Twichell used to speak frequently and affectionately of Father O'Hagan . . . nor did he fail to relate how, in the late watches of a cold and sleepless December night, they had shared their blankets on the field of Fredericksburg. Both agreed that Heaven was pleased at the spectacle and many beheld in the incident an ostensible proof that fair-minded men can readily establish a working union among the churches without either annulling dogmatic differences or violating conscientious preferences.[36]

O'Hagan, a Jesuit, went on to become president of the College of the Holy Cross in Worcester, Massachusetts. Twichell recalled O'Hagan in an obituary in December 1878: "For whole months we were daily companions, and we often slept under the same blanket. As Christian ministers we were continually thrown together in scenes with the effect to make us forgetful of our differences and mindful only of our sympathies."[37] Note the crucial ethical deployment here of the need for sympathies: Twichell, especially in the war-torn surroundings of their fellowship, realizes that difference is what has brought the bloodshed and that in this context he and O'Hagan had much more in common than they had earlier supposed. On at least one occasion Twichell brought Mark Twain along on a visit to see O'Hagan in Boston. Twain was pleased that he could joke with the priest about the childish prejudices Protestants harbored about Catholics, a fact he reported with glee to his friend Charley Stoddard in a letter. Twain's derisive treatment of priestcraft, influenced by Lecky and others, was on full view in books throughout his career. Ranging from *Innocents Abroad* to *Connecticut Yankee* to *No. 44, The Mysterious Stranger,* these texts illustrate that Twain was somewhat bound by the prejudices toward Catholicism that reigned in his Missouri youth and that were largely representative of Protestant attitudes throughout his lifetime. Here again, Twichell's progressive attitude was undoubtedly influential in Twain's intellectual growth toward at least a mild embrace of other religions.

Much of Twichell's ecumenical activity was undertaken in conjunction with his great friend Edwin Parker, pastor of Second Church in Hartford and himself another protégé of Horace Bushnell. Twichell and Parker served together on the committee to form the YMCA in Hartford, directly as a result of the encouragement they both experienced at Dwight Moody's 1878 revival meetings. The big controversy at the time was whether the YMCA should be restricted to "orthodox" believers or should be open to anyone, and thus be evangelical in its attempt to reach out to those from other faiths and beliefs. Many conservative Christians, including Moody, worried about allowing access to Universalists or Unitarians—let alone Catholics! The committee settled on the Apostles' Creed as a decisive confession, although in its meetings with the famous evangelist, Moody confessed he did not know the creed, or what it was. In his published account of these matters, Parker emphasizes his and Twichell's great dislike of the simplistic evangelical litmus tests of the likes of Dwight Moody and their wish not to separate Christians from Christians.[38]

The YMCA controversy demonstrates why evangelicalism began to be associated with close-mindedness after the Civil War. Opposed to this, Parker and Twichell were known for their open-minded embrace of Catholics and Jews. Twichell clipped and saved an 1894 article from the *Hartford Courant,* presumably because he agreed with Parker's friendly stance toward the Catholics: "I stand up to be counted with the Roman Catholics; they are my friends."[39] This was a rather brave remark for 1894 preachers, given the history of Protestant-Catholic prejudice in nineteenth-century America. It was also brave of Parker and Twichell to express sympathy for the Jews of Hartford. In 1889 Twichell's Asylum Hill Church gave three dozen settees to the Congregation of Russian

Jews on Front Street. "Christian and Jew" was the topic of a meeting on March 23, 1898, at the Charter Oak Street Temple, a Jewish synagogue. That night, both Twichell and Parker spoke. Parker stated that "the God of your fathers is the God whom we also acknowledge and adore. . . . Let us honor the common Father by regarding each other, in all brotherly kindness, as His children."[40] At this time, Twain was in Vienna, where he was appalled by the treatment of the Jews and corresponded with Twichell regarding it. Twain addressed the deep anti-Semitism of the era in such works as "Stirring Times in Austria" and "Concerning the Jews," both composed during his stay in Austria and published in America. Twichell applauded his efforts in a letter: "What you say of the Jews recalls talk I used to hear about them from dear old Prof. [Calvin] Stowe. He was wont to affirm that their survival and masterfulness—due to an inextinguishable and incomparable Vitality—was a phenomenon without parallel and a *miracle.*"[41]

Twichell was fondly remembered by his flock and his community for his sympathetic gestures toward all of these largely marginalized groups. One writer noted how "Twichell's mellow maturity, derived partly from his Civil War Chaplaincy, led to an ecumenicity to which the *Catholic Transcript,* at the time of his death in 1918, credits the good relations among the sects of Hartford."[42] Another cited the editorial that appeared in the *Catholic Transcript:*

> we can and do testify to his tolerance, his broadmindedness, his Christian spirit and his worth as a moral and intellectual force in the city. When Bishop Tierney died, Dr. Twichell spoke of him as a friend he admired and valued. . . . It is our conviction that the presence and example of Dr. Twichell had much to do with the killing off of whatever anti-Catholic sentiment existed in Hartford in former days. Eminently sane and gifted with a sense of humor, a man of heart and of natural benevolences, he frowned on rancor, and sect bigotry had no place in his life or in his dealings with his fellowman. . . . His departure leaves a void in the life of the community.[43]

Twichell thus modeled an ecumenical embrace of other denominations that went against the grain of much close-minded evangelicalism of his day. His version of the Social Gospel was broadly inclusive of peoples from all nations and ethnicities, one that could be said to imitate the glorious host surrounding the throne of God in the book of Revelation.

Of course the primary issue of inclusion at this time had to do with the treatment of African Americans. The transformation of Mark Twain's views on race occurred within the context of his friendship with Twichell, his participation in the Asylum Hill Church, and his residence primarily in Hartford. The changes also were fostered by steady personal contact with black Americans as well. For example, Twain was well known to hold a lifelong admiration for African American forms of music, including the spirituals and jubilees, forms that drew upon the images of that glorious host around the throne. Twain was extremely fond of African American styles and frequently mimicked them in his own performance of standard hymns and spirituals. Twichell often records in his journal episodes of Twain having sung spirituals and other religious hymns at public meetings and private parties. On October 26, 1877, Twichell wrote: "to MT's to attend a neighborhood reception given by him to Yung Wing and wife. . . . MT and Gen. Hawley sang negro religious songs."[44] Twichell's entry for March 8, 1884: "Friday, after a charming morning in Brooklyn (M.T. sang negro "spirituals" at the piano, deliciously) we went over to New York"[45] (figure 5). Another time, as Twain's housekeeper Katy Leary later reported, "Suddenly Mr. Clemens got right up without any warning and began singing one of them Negro spirituals. . . . When he got to the end, to the glory Hallelujah, he gave a great shout—just like the Negroes do—he shouted out the 'Glory, Glory, Hallelujah.' "[46] Perhaps most poignantly, in Florence, Italy, in 1904, as Livy was dying in a nearby room, Twain sat at the piano and sang the old jubilees "Swing Low, Sweet Chariot" and "My Lord He Calls Me." Upon hearing the songs, Livy said her last words: "He is singing a goodnight carol to me." Presently the songs ended, and Livy slipped away.[47] Tellingly, at the moment of his greatest heartbreak, Mark Twain turned to the old "Negro spirituals."

Twain so thoroughly loved various African American musical forms and traditions that he considered hearing the Fisk Jubilee Singers, which he did on several occasions, to be the greatest musical experience of his lifetime. The Jubilee Singers were a group of eleven young African

5. Mark Twain playing piano. Courtesy of the Mark Twain Project, Bancroft Library, University of California, Berkeley.

Americans, eight of whom were themselves former slaves, whose initial purpose was to raise funding for Fisk, a new college for freed slaves in Nashville, Tennessee. They rose to international fame during their tour of America in 1872 and then of Great Britain in 1873. Mark Twain's lifelong romance with the Jubilee Singers began very early in his marriage to Livy. While the dating of his first encounter is somewhat uncertain, he does write in a March 1875 letter from London that "I am expecting to hear the Jubilee Singers to-night, for the fifth time."[48] Since it is known that he heard them twice in England in 1873, it is highly likely that he was present both times they performed in Hartford in 1872. The first of these performances was on January 28, 1872, at the Asylum Hill Congregational Church. The next day the *Hartford Courant* claimed that the Jubilee Singers created "a sensation rarely equaled. . . . It is the first time that we at the north have heard the genuine songs of their race, executed with their faith and their feeling. It was like a revelation. . . . One heard in those strange and plaintive melodies the sadness and the hope of a trusting and a really joyous race."[49] This odd mixing of sadness and hope, in particular, was a common feature of many descriptions of the Jubilee Singers, as was the assertion that they were genuine. In addition, commentators often mentioned the strangeness, wildness, or weirdness of their songs. Mark Twain noted these features in 1873:

> I was reared in the South, & my father owned slaves, & I do not know when anything has so moved me as did the plaintive melodies of the Jubilee Singers. It was the first time for twenty-five or thirty years that I had heard such songs, or heard them sung in the genuine old way—& it is a way, I think, that white people cannot imitate—& never can, for that matter, for one must have been a slave himself in order to feel what that life was & so convey the pathos of it in the music.[50]

Twain's response rests largely on nostalgia, on his poignant memories of actual slaves in his youth. This tradition of soulful expression was given some attention throughout the literature of the period, perhaps most popularly in Stowe's *Uncle Tom's Cabin* but even earlier in several slave narratives such as Douglass's *Narrative.* After the Civil War, the tradition was given national exposure anew by Thomas Wentworth Higginson, longtime abolitionist, Harvard graduate, and commander of the first regiment of freed slaves fighting against the Confederates. During the war, Higginson became fascinated with the songs his soldiers sang and began collecting them. He published his findings and his meditations on the music after the war ended, first in the *Atlantic Monthly* in

1867 and then in book form as *Army Life in a Black Regiment* (1870). These songs, Higginson believed, were

> a stimulus to courage and a tie to heaven. . . . By these they could sing themselves, as had their fathers before them, out of the contemplation of their own low estate, into the sublime scenery of the Apocalypse. . . . There is no parallel instance of an oppressed race thus sustained by the religious sentiment alone. These songs are but the vocal expression of the simplicity of their faith and the sublimity of their long resignation.[51]

Later in life, Mark Twain would recall and write about the songs of a young Missouri slave by the name of Sandy, who was "singing, whistling, yelling, whooping, laughing" all day long. He had been separated from his family in Maryland and had been hired out to the Clemens family. When young Sam complained to his mother about Sandy's noisy personality, she became sad and whispered to him with tears in her eyes, "Poor thing, when he sings it shows that he is not remembering, and that comforts me; but when he is still I am afraid he is thinking, and I cannot bear it. He will never see his mother again; if he can sing, I must not hinder it, but be thankful for it. If you were older, you would understand me; then that friendless child's noise would make you glad."[52] This anecdote indicates that Twain associated Sandy's songs with relief from the sheer pain of his separation from his family. They represented the "sublimity of [the slaves'] long resignation" described by Higginson and engendered both in Jane Clemens and her son the deepest sympathies. "The genuine article," as Twain called the music of the Jubilee Singers, had the same effects: it redounded with a sentimental power that could foster the solidarity of white and black Americans.

Thus while some might argue that these episodes of Twain's enchantment with the Jubilee Singers speak more to aesthetic appreciation than spirituality, the religious content cannot be entirely ignored. Indeed Twain's romance with them was symptomatic of his moral solidarity with the suffering and pain that gave rise to these musical forms. Twain's attraction to this music rested largely on its power to engender sympathy for the oppressed victims of slavery and the power of the narratives the singers utilized most often. It is not an exaggeration to say that music by African Americans, particularly as embodied in the Jubilee Singers, was an extremely effective means of bridging the color line in the nineteenth century, and its effectiveness in building sympathy and respect among its listeners is evidenced in the life of Mark Twain. Lord Shaftesbury, one of their greatest supporters in Britain, specifically mentioned this function in one of his comments about them: "these Jubilee Singers have come here to see whether they can excite a like sympathy, and stir the hearts of the English people to join them in elevating the negro race to the position to which they are entitled by the laws of God and the great capacities with which he has endowed them." And the man who became their agent, Gustavus Pike, promoted them primarily on the grounds of the "spiritual and religious power" of their music, which "touched the hearts of Christian people everywhere and secured their sympathy and liberal aid."[53] Thus, besides his pure enjoyment of the artistic performance, Twain was like many other observers in understanding the Jubilee Singers as doing important spiritual work among their listeners. As such, this work foreshadowed African American music's even greater role during the civil rights movement in the 1950s and '60s as a redemptive element fostering sympathy among its white listeners.

By far the most pressing multicultural issue of post–Civil War America (and later, in DuBois's famous formulation, "*the* problem of the twentieth century"[54]) was the treatment of African Americans, and there was more than just music in the air. Joe Twichell was at the forefront of the movement to bring equity and justice to American blacks. Twichell worked hard to advance the cause of African Americans, and his progressive awareness, going all the way back to his antebellum days as an abolitionist, surely had at least some influence on Twain's emerging sensibility about African Americans. Twichell's sister Jane was married to Edmund Asa Ware, the first president of Atlanta University, one of the leading African American colleges. Their son, Edward Twichell Ware, who lived with Twichell and his family after Jane's death in 1890, would later become the third president, in 1907. Between these two Twichell relatives was Dr. Horace Bumstead, who served as president of Atlanta University for over twenty years, from 1886 to 1907. Bumstead, like Twichell, was a Congregational minister with an impressive Civil War record: he was commissioned as a major for the Forty-third Regiment of the U.S. Colored Troops. Twichell served as a member of the board of trustees of Atlanta University for many years, and he and Bumstead became friends and accomplices in the business of funding and overseeing one of the major black colleges of the century. At least once, Twichell spoke at the university's graduation ceremony, on May 29–30, 1894 in Atlanta. Later that year, on July 8, 1894, Twichell hosted Bumstead in Hartford. Bumstead's talk at the Asylum Hill Church addressed the noble work of black uplift in the South. Similarly Twichell's connections with Atlanta University put him in contact with several other important African American leaders, including W. E. B. DuBois and Booker T. Washington, who spoke on at least two occasions at the Asylum Hill Church. Twichell's connections put Twain in touch with the National Association for the Advancement of Colored People (NAACP) and its leaders, with whom Twain enjoyed a good relationship, largely due to their perception of Twain's respect for and sympathy with black America.[55]

Twichell's interest in and support of freedmen and the rights of African Americans typifies that of many church leaders with ties to Social Christianity. And yet no records show that Twichell gave even a single speech or sermon concerned specifically with race relations. While Twichell was proud of having been an abolitionist from his early days, his attitude toward African Americans was that of many other white gentlemen of his time period: altruistically interested in their advancement, yet somewhat patronizing in person. This tendency speaks volumes about Twichell's social milieu in the North and helps explain why some historians have generally not considered race relations a major concern for ministers of the Social Gospel. Much more damning are the countless racist statements about the African race that came from the pulpits of America's most influential clergymen. For example, Twichell's mentor Horace Bushnell spoke on many occasions against the Africans' ability to compete with Caucasians. Bushnell firmly believed, and openly preached, that African Americans would die out after emancipation. George Frederickson has gone so far as to say that Bushnell's influential views were a crucial source for many of the Christian racist and imperialist factions of the late nineteenth century. It is to Twichell's credit that he never endorsed these shameful quasi-Darwinian opinions. But there are compelling reasons why historians have criticized, sometimes savagely, the evangelical church's response to the race issues of the nineteenth century.[56] Sadly, the American church after the Civil War was generally no more progressive, and perhaps in many cases much less progressive, than the rest of the culture on the problems of the color line.

However, in a major revisionist account of this subject, Ralph Luker has questioned the conclusions of an entire generation of historians, many of whom took their cue from a highly influential 1932 essay by Arthur Schlesinger. According to Luker, historians have been influenced by earlier studies that emphasized what Rayford Logan called the "astigmatism of the social gospel" with regard to race. Luker argues that undue influence of earlier sources has fostered an "astigmatism of the historians," meaning that a large part of the story simply has been ignored because of the influence of the earlier information, and he provides extensive research into the church's advocacy of better relations between whites and blacks.[57] His volume goes on to document dozens of highly influential Christian leaders and workers whose achievements constituted the cutting edge of race relations progress during the Social Gospel era. Luker admits that the Social Gospel movement was highly fluid, which may be part of the problem. Its coherence can only be approximated "by taking a part of it as equivalent to the whole, and the part [earlier historians] make primary has never been one that includes race relations."[58] The fact is that many of the leaders he discusses were well known to Joe Twichell and Mark Twain, some personally, such as George Washington Cable and Booker T. Washington, and others by reputation and influence, including Washington Gladden, Walter Rauschenbusch, and the anti-lynching crusader Ida B. Wells, all of whom had strong ties with progressive, reform-minded churches.

Thus it appears that Social Christianity has been unfairly characterized over the years with regard to its record on matters of race relations. As Luker has shown in substantial detail, and as I have illustrated here in the case of Twichell, there were many ministers of the Social Gospel, broadly construed, whose lives indicate a strong burden for the plight of ethnic citizens, including African Americans. However, before we get too congratulatory, the church's accomplishments at this time with regard to race—even those as progressive as Twichell's—should be qualified. Luker rejects an uncritical embrace of Social Christianity's heroic stand: "neither point of view quite comprehends both the high lights and deep shadows of American social Christianity's record in race relations."[59] What he calls the "astigmatism of the historians" on this point suggests my own conclusions regarding Mark Twain's use of Social Christianity: we should couple a strong awareness of Twain's critique of religion with his fond embrace of many of the social activities and charitable works of the church, even well into the years after 1900. To understand fully Mark Twain's use of the Social Gospel, one must comprehend "both the high lights and deep shadows" of Twain's lifelong relation to matters of Christianity. We need to strike a balance that will illustrate the "high lights" so long overlooked. Such a balancing act will help to counteract any "astigmatism of Twain scholars" on matters of belief and religious ethos.

This approach is useful in broaching what has surely become the most lively (and for some the most dreaded) topic in all of Twain scholarship for the past couple of decades: the issue of race, especially with regard to African Americans. Over the past decade numerous collections of essays and individual studies have shaped the debate, and although there is no universal consensus on virtually any of this, it seems possible to make some general observations.[60] And yet no critic has suggested that Twain's conversion to a view that supported race relations and African American rights was even slightly encouraged by the ethos of Social Christianity described here. However, Twain's embrace of African Americans as a people was grounded on a metaphysical view of all peoples having been created equally by one God. That said, Twain clearly should not be applauded too loudly as a staunch advocate of equality and civil rights; he harbored aspects of the frontier racism of his youth until the end of his life. For example, he never seems to have lost his enthusiasm for blackface minstrelsy, which one critic has called a "national symbolic ritual of debasement," that is seemingly endorsed most clearly in *Tom Sawyer Abroad,* where "the minstrel element mars the trip."[61] Eric Lott recounts Twain's glee in taking his religious mother and an aunt to see a minstrel show in St. Louis, without their knowledge of what the evening entailed. Lott writes, "One almost senses Twain rubbing his hands together as he prepares to sink his mother into some real dissipation—a desacralizing impulse on the part of the son inspired by the unease minstrelsy has provoked in the writer."[62] Lott's conclusions are debatable, but even as we enter that debate we should rest assured that we are treading on uneven and difficult ground. Why did Twain continue to remember minstrelsy fondly? Did he enjoy the ridiculing of "helpless darkies," or did he respond on a more sophisticated level of irony to the stupidity of exaggerated stereotypes? Critics have posed the same question about several of his literary creations, including most obviously Jim in *Huckleberry Finn* and Roxy in *Pudd'nhead Wilson,* among others.

Several more specific observations should be put forward. First, Mark Twain did undergo a fairly radical "conversion" regarding relations with black Americans—largely as a result of close contact with them.[63] While specific dates are hard to pin down, there seems to be some consensus regarding certain events or moments of central importance. There were the numerous occasions when, as a youth, Twain witnessed the abuse of slaves, which finally led him to make one of his clearest anti-lynching statements in his early essay "Only a Nigger" (1869), a title that foreshadows one of the more controversial passages in all of Twain's work. In that passage, Huck lies to Aunt Sally about a steamboat explosion and is asked if there were "anybody hurt?" to which he infamously responds, "No'm. Killed a nigger."[64] This brief passage is indicative of the debate over Twain's racial views. It has been read both ways: factually, in the sense that it reveals the narrator's (and the writer's) inbred racist view that blacks were not human, and ironically, as demonstrating without approbation or endorsement that hateful view. Bernard Bell represents the first view in describing Twain and Huck as "kindred spirits."[65] But the growing consensus seems more in favor of a reading such as Jocelyn Chadwick-Joshua's, who sees the passage as highly ironic and chastises those critics like Bell who read it otherwise: "No reasonable reader misses this [irony]."[66] Most critics today seem willing to echo Chadwick-Joshua's notion that "no reasonable reader misses" Twain's heavy dependence on the ironic mode in understanding not only this passage but the entire final section of *Huckleberry Finn,* as well as other troubled, racialized texts like *Pudd'nhead Wilson.* Even today, however, there are admittedly still numerous, less-forgiving critics who continue to reject the "irony defense," agreeing with such harsh voices as John Wallace, who has become well known for his attacks on *Huckleberry*

Finn, which he calls "the most grotesque example of racist trash ever written."[67]

In plotting the narrative of Twain's conversion from calcified Missouri racist to enlightened New England liberal, one must understand the crucial influence of a number of Twain's close relationships with deeply religious African Americans. One of the most powerful experiences Twain had was listening to Mary Ann Cord tell her sad story of being a slave and losing her son to slave traders. Many historians see that moment in the summer of 1874 as a turning point—in at least two ways. Twain parlayed the tale into his first publication in the *Atlantic* as "A True Story," so that the conversion (and commodification) of it affected both his national career as author and his moral insight into the status of the slaves. The key trope is initiated in the narrator's opening question to Aunt Rachel: "how is it you've lived sixty years and never had any trouble?"[68] Aunt Rachel's tale, despite the naïveté of the questioner, is filled with pathos and trouble—a shocking revelation to the narrator who has cut his teeth on the stereotyped "happy darky" of much southern fiction about the slaves. And Cord's real life experience of maintaining faith in God through these trials was a powerful testimony of Christian endurance for Twain and his family.

Twain's relationships with other African Americans were among the more cherished in his memories. John Lewis, an Elmira farmer who, as Chadwick-Joshua points out, became a "folk hero of substantial dimensions" in Twain's eyes, also served as a model for Jim, a fact that argues for the moral integrity and heroism of Huck's companion.[69] Lewis, a Baptist (or "Dunkard," as Albert Paine wrote about him), often haggled over religious doctrine in the kitchen with Cord, a stern Methodist—discussions that often pleased Twain. Paine noted that Lewis was the more intelligent of the two amateur theologians and that Twain would sneak up to the kitchen window to eavesdrop on their debates, which often deteriorated into shouting matches: "theology invariably led to personality, and eventually to epithets, crockery, geology, and victuals." Despite this gentle sarcasm, Lewis is most famous for his heroic actions in saving the lives of the wife and child of Twain's brother-in-law Charley Langdon in the summer of 1877. As their buggy flew down the East Hill toward Elmira, Lewis intervened to slow the out-of-control ve-

6. Twain with John Lewis. Courtesy of the Mark Twain House and Museum, Hartford, Connecticut.

hicle. Twain never forgot this selfless act. He wrote in a letter to a friend that it was "the most marvelous [feat] I can call to mind." Afterward, Twain recalled the scene: "when he arrived hunched up on his manure-wagon and as grotesquely picturesque as usual, everybody wanted to go and see how he looked. They came back and said he was beautiful. It was so, too, and yet he would have photographed exactly as he would have done any day these past seven years that he has occupied this farm" (figure 6). Despite Lewis appearing grotesque and hunched over, Twain asserts here his inner beauty, one that is beyond the limits of mechanical photography to detect. The Clemens family rewarded Lewis with cash, a fancy gold watch, and ultimately a part of a pension after his working days came to an end. Lewis remained humble through it all: "divine Providence saw fit to use me as an instrument for the saving of those preshious [sic] lives."[70]

Lewis was not the only black man of genuine faith with whom Twain became intimate. Another African American, George Griffin, Twain's butler in Hartford for nearly fifteen years, had the great honor of residing in the third-floor bedroom adjacent to Twain's study. Twain and Griffin's intimacy testifies to a deep friendship that provided "a framework within which to continue a psychological and sociological transformation begun much earlier."[71] Twain remembered Griffin, as he did Lewis, particularly for his spirituality: "he was strenuously religious, he was a deacon of the African Methodist Church; no dirt, no profanity, ever soiled his speech, and he neither drank nor smoked. . . . Consider the influence of a glory like that upon our little kids in the nursery. To them he was something more than mortal."[72] Griffin is memorialized in a piece Twain wrote in 1906, "A Family Sketch," where he is recognized particularly for his intelligence and keen financial insight. According to Twain, "in some ways he was my equal, in some others my superior."[73]

Besides African Americans, Twain was in steady contact with a number of intellectuals of the period who were leaders in the promotion of equity between blacks and whites. Some of these influences were clearly of a decidedly Christian flavor, most obviously Joseph Twichell. Others would include Twain's adopted kin in New York, the entire Langdon clan led by the father Jervis, who was proud of his abolitionist history and his support for the Underground Railroad, which hosted a stop in Elmira. The Elmira contingent would also include the Reverend Thomas Beecher and members of his flock, with whom Livy and Sam fellowshipped when residing during the summers at Quarry Farm. Through the Elmira connection, Twain met and became friends with Frederick Douglass. In one instance he wrote a letter to president-elect Garfield in 1881 advocating Douglass for a federal position in the District of Columbia. In Hartford, Twain lived next door to Harriet Beecher Stowe—the little lady who mythically started the war. Although he sometimes chided her and her masterwork *Uncle Tom's Cabin,* he shared Twichell's respect for her achievements, the greatest of which he considered to be the social effects of her storytelling. Perhaps most significantly, Twain was greatly influenced by the writer and reformer George Washington Cable, whose stand against racial hatred and abuse marked him as one of the era's most progressive social prophets.[74] Cable's views of race were rooted in a biblical view of equality among humans coupled with a deep admiration for the ideals expressed in the Declaration of Independence.

Twain and Cable spent long hours together on a speaking tour in 1884–85, during which they surely discussed Cable's provocative ideas that would later coalesce into such volumes as *The Silent South* (1885) and *The Negro Question* (1888), two of the most subversive texts published by a southerner during Twain's lifetime. Twain was very impressed with Cable when he first spent time with him in New Orleans at the end of his trip down the Mississippi in 1882. In his book that issued from that trip, *Life on the Mississippi,* Twain remembers Cable as "the South's finest literary genius. . . . In him the South has found a masterly delineator of the interior life and its history. In truth, I find by experience that the untrained eye and vacant mind can inspect it and learn of it and judge of it more clearly and profitably in his books than by personal contact with it."[75] It is interesting that Cable is often remembered more for Twain's stinging ridicule of his legalistic religious idiosyncrasies, which Twain piled onto Cable as the long speaking tour in winter 1885 dragged on. He complained to Howells, "You will never, never know, never divine, guess, imagine, how loathsome a thing the Christian religion can be made until you come to know and study Cable daily and hourly." And yet he also fondly remembered the trip later in a missive to Cable: "Yes, sir! I liked you in spite of your religion. . . . And I have always said, & still maintain, that as a railroad-comrade you were perfect—the only railroad-comrade in the world that a man of moods & frets & uncertainties of disposition could travel with, a third of a year, and never weary of his company." Guy Cardwell identifies some of their affinities: "Both Twain and Cable had broken with a culture and had the hard problem of discovering or creating a new culture for themselves. They were close together on many important points of social doctrine. Both hated social injustice with the ardor of crusaders."[76] Cardwell's choice of language here denotes the religious fervor and "social" principles that these two men shared. Despite Twain's satirical comments to Howells, he was drawn to Cable, especially his ideas on social justice that were deeply rooted in a biblical theology. Cable deserves recognition as one of the era's most influential evangelical voices on behalf of the plight of African Americans.

Another important critic of Reconstruction, the treatment of African Americans, and the newly emergent Lost Cause mythos was former Union soldier and later carpetbagger judge Albion Tourgée, who wrote numerous novels and essays. Tourgée is important for a number of reasons, and Twain was familiar with his work, although they apparently never met. His novels, especially *A Fool's Errand* (1879) and *Bricks without Straw* (1880) (which Mark Twain is known to have owned), and his essays, including "The Renaissance of Nationalism" (1887), "The South as a Field for Fiction" (1888), and the volume of essays *An Appeal to Caesar* (1884), constitute perhaps the most sustained and well-known critique of southern ideology of the period. *A Fool's Errand,* one of the nation's biggest best-sellers of the 1880s, was often said to have done to Reconstruction what *Uncle Tom's Cabin* did to slavery. Tourgée was particularly interested in refuting the plantation school of southern writers, led by Thomas Nelson Page, whose depiction of romantic southern life and happy, carefree slaves mitigated the racial issues that Tourgée believed were at the center of the conflict. He denounced the fact that most southerners "believed that the slave loved his chains and was all the better physically and morally for wearing them"; and he was almost alone among national figures when he wrote that southern slaveholding society was "horrible beyond the power of imagination to conceive in its injustice, cruelty, and barbarous debasement of a subject race."[77] The nation risked forgetting these things by its overblown focus on romantic reunion. Both sides were depicted as fighting for "holy causes," which eliminated the need to investigate claims and to make moral decisions about causes and results.

Tourgée claimed that Civil War memory had become largely "Confederate in sympathy"[78] and that one result was that the nation simply ignored racial issues. He wrote, "About the Negro as a man, with hopes, fears, and aspirations like other men, our literature is nearly silent."[79] Going against the grain of what had already become an ossified ideology, Tourgée "dared to say, in season and out, that the war and its aftermath were all about race."[80] In his desire to redirect the American imagination to the issue of slavery and the plight of the ex-slave, Tourgée took on the religious fervor of a moral crusader, both against institutionalized racism as well as against the Lost Cause mythology of the Confederacy. Tourgée, who spoke and wrote from the perspective of Christian socialism, hoped "to arouse humanity to the exertion of its finest impulses, to work toward a day when justice and peace should really reign on the earth."[81]

Perhaps the high point of Tourgée's career was his argument before the U.S. Supreme Court in the Plessy v. Ferguson case (1896), when he powerfully spoke out against the notion of "separate but equal" facilities as constitutional. Although the court denied the case, it would later overturn this decision based on legal arguments almost identical to Tourgée's. Mark Twain kept a close watch on the entire legal process, which had begun many years before when Homer Plessy, legally black but by appearance white, entered a railroad car marked for whites only. The case was centered on the idea of the "one-drop rule," which stated that a person was Negro if they had even a single drop of Negro blood in their ancestry. The ridiculous judgments of the case at lower levels of the court system influenced Twain's conception of the plot in *Pudd'nhead Wilson,* which revolves around issues of racial identity.[82] As Susan Gillman has shown, *Pudd'nhead Wilson* "implicitly reminds readers that racial codes regulating miscegenation and classifying mixed-race offspring did not disappear after Emancipation, but instead were reenacted or reaffirmed, with even more rigorous definitions of whiteness, during the nineties when antiblack repression took multiple forms, legal and extralegal."[83] Twain's novel, in many respects, can be understood as a fictional reenactment of the silliness of rejecting Albion Tourgée's legal arguments.

The most pressing point in all of these examples is the extent to which Twain's changing attitudes on race were fostered by a social context in which both African Americans and progressive Christians were present, respected, and even admired. Social experience can often transcend theoretical objections—as it did with Huck in the case of Jim, or Twain in the case of Mary Ann Cord, John Lewis, George Griffin, or the Jubilee Singers. As such, very often the social trumps the theoretical. This insight underlies Twain's comments on one of the era's most respected black leaders, one who was both African American and progressive Christian: Booker T. Washington. From our perspective today, Washington remains a controversial figure for his apparent stance regarding such issues as segregation. But at the time he was widely regarded as the foremost spokesperson for his race in America. Twain gave a speech at Carnegie Hall on January 22, 1906, in support of Washington's Tuskegee Institute:

> At Tuskegee they thoroughly ground the student in the Christian code of morals; they instill into him the indisputable truth that this is the highest and best of all systems of morals that the Nation's greatness, its strength, and its repute among the other nations is the product of that system; that it is the foundation upon which rests the American character; that whatever is commendable, whatever is valuable in the individual American's character is the flower and fruit of that seed.
>
> They teach him that this is true in every case, whether the man be a professing Christian or an unbeliever; for we have none but the Christian code of morals, and every individual is under its character-building powerful influence and dominion from the cradle to the grave; he breathes it in with his breath, it is in his blood and bone, it is the web and woof and fibre of his mental and spiritual heredities and ineradicable. And so every born American among the eighty millions, let his creed or destitution of creed be what it may, is indisputably a Christian to this degree—that his moral constitution is Christian.
>
> All this is true, and no student will leave Tuskegee ignorant of it.[84]

Among other things, this speech is remarkable for Twain's forthright confession of respect for a "Christian code of morals" at such a late date. Twain celebrates here what is in effect a structured system of Social Christianity that was being practiced at Tuskegee. Furthermore this code is at the heart of the American character, says Twain. Of course it was a highly charged public moment before a staid and largely conservative audience, and so Twain can be accused of merely giving the audience what they wanted to hear. We might easily write this off as mere pomp and circumstance from the genteel Samuel Clemens and certainly not take it seriously. Another obvious problem with Twain's endorsement of Washington here is Washington's status among historians today as something less than the exemplary African American leader, especially in his disagreements with other black leaders like W. E. B. DuBois. This conflict is important since for many today an endorsement of and support for Washington may not be such a progressive stance. And yet Twain's speech does seem to ring true, without even a whisp of irony. After Twain's death in 1910, Washington remembered Twain in a tribute published in the *North American Review:* "I do not believe any one can read [*Huck Finn*] closely, however, without becoming aware of the deep sympathy of the author in 'Jim.' . . . I cannot help feeling that in this character Mark Twain has, perhaps unconsciously, exhibited his sympathy and interest in the masses of the negro people."[85] And perhaps, as Twain's 1906 speech suggests, it was this sympathy, a mystical social bond rooted in biblical theology, that should be understood as the center of Twain's version of the Social Gospel. If we are willing to grant that much, maybe we will even go a little further. Mark Twain might even agree with his own words; he might even say that, after all, he considered himself "indisputably a Christian to this degree—that [my] moral constitution is Christian."

5

Mark Twain's Civil War

Civil Religion and the Lost Cause

On the Fourth of July, 1876, the town of Hartford, like almost all municipalities around the nation, held a centennial celebration on America's hundredth birthday, featuring a public reading of the Declaration of Independence. The Reverend Joseph Twichell was Hartford's main orator that day. Twichell's solemn speech is filled with references to the myth of America as redeemer nation and the nature of the American covenant with God—just as we might suspect in 1876. His church on Asylum Hill held an evening service; there was no sermon (most parishioners had probably heard Twichell's lengthy speech earlier that day), but there were readings from Scripture, including Psalm 89 (remembering God's faithfulness); Exodus 20:1–17 (the Ten Commandments); Deuteronomy 28:1–20 (God's blessings for obedience and curses for disobedience); and Deuteronomy 29:10–13 (entering the covenant and becoming the people of God)—passages frequently applied to versions of the American mission at that time.[1] These readings were followed by prayer and songs: "Ye Nations Round the Earth Rejoice," "O God Beneath Thy Guiding Hand," and "My Country 'Tis of Thee"—a comfortable mixture of sacred and patriotic tunes.

All told, it was a daylong celebration of America's providential history as the nation officially turned the age of one hundred. Joe Twichell's invitation to be Hartford's keynote speaker testifies to his status as a major figure in Gilded Age civil religion. He frequently spoke or led prayers at other major and minor events commemorating America throughout New England and New York state. One reason for his growing influence was that Twichell was an outspoken disciple of what has often been called America's civil religion. In a story focused on spiritual concerns, we must continually recall the close intertwining in American social and cultural history of religion with political thought. Indeed the close connection of these two realms is illustrated by the term *civil religion* itself, pointing as it does simultaneously to the kingdoms of this world and to the Kingdom of God. This civil religion "borrowed selectively from the religious tradition in such a way that the average American saw no conflict between the two. In this way, the civil religion was able to build up without any bitter struggle with the church powerful symbols of national solidarity and to mobilize deep levels of personal motivation for the attainment of national goals."[2]

Mark Twain also attended many events featuring these "symbols of national solidarity," sometimes appearing on the same program with Twichell. For instance, Twain and Twichell often traveled together to West Point or veterans reunions, usually to speak on the same program to the officers and cadets. On February 28, 1881, Twichell writes, "To West Point with M.T. to attend and assist the entertainment below indicated [program attached] given by the literary society in the U.S. Military Academy." This program was called the "One Hundredth Night Entertainment" and included an address by Twichell and a reading by Twain. On June 8, 1881, they attended together the Twelfth Annual Reunion of the Army of the Potomac in Hartford, at which Twichell gave the blessing and Twain gave an address entitled "The Benefit of Judicious Training."[3] The next day, June 9, 1881, they went together by train to West Point, where along with Gen. William T. Sherman they were guests of Lieutenant Wood. They repeated the trip on April 2–5, 1886, and again on May 5–7, 1886. Twain's and Twichell's long and largely patriotic relationship with the principal war college of the nation has been well documented.[4]

Twichell's interest in American military history was not limited to book learning. He was a Civil War veteran with many tales to tell about his intense eyewitness experience of some of the most famous moments of the war. As chaplain of a regiment in New York's Excelsior Brigade, Twichell witnessed some of the Civil War's most dramatic battles, including Williamsburg, Malvern Hill, Second Bull Run (Manassas), Fredericksburg, Chancellorsville, and Gettysburg. Besides the hair-raising accounts of major battles, his letters from the front describe prayer meetings and sermons, hospital visits, matters of money and food, disease and filth, the internal politics of armies, the vagaries of weather, and the sheer pain of watching the life seep out of boys who have been mortally wounded. His stories of the war years, about which he sometimes spoke in public, were frequent topics of discussion during those many long walks in the woods with Mark Twain. Twichell's courageous service for the Union contrasts sharply with Twain's nonparticipation in the war. Although later Twain would mythologize his own war experience, he basically sat out the conflict in the hinterlands of the far West.

If Mark Twain represents the ambivalent fence-sitter who lit out for the western territory at the very beginning of hostilities during the Civil War, and only later became a convert to the Union cause, then Twichell represents those who from the very beginning pledged their lives to the Union and against the "infamous cause" of the Confederacy. Twichell's genuine burden for the Union—along with his conservative Christian orthodoxy—are well represented in his letters home during the war. Many of these letters depict a profoundly spiritual vision of not only the work of a Union chaplain, but indeed of the Union project itself. "It almost seemed as if loyalty to the Union were a recommendation to heaven," says Twichell. He recognizes the events of the war as under the guidance of "the Eternal Plan. . . . If I had no faith in God, and did not feel that the plan, the *plan,* is unfolding in ways of His appointment, I should go crazy." After Gettysburg, Twichell writes, "The Army of the Union has fought as if appreciating its Cause."[5] Thus, like most Federal supporters, Twichell weds the Union agenda with the Kingdom of God. According to one Civil War historian, "Most [chaplains] believed that love of country and concern for the souls of those whose lives were threatened impelled them to become chaplains. Equating the cause of their nation with the cause of God, they entered the army with clear consciences. . . . At a moment when all citizens were united in a common struggle, the duties of a minister and a patriot seemed to be thoroughly compatible, perhaps almost identical. Chaplains thought that they were in a unique position to inspire men to fight, protect them from the vices of camp, and bring their souls spotless to Christ in the world to come."[6] This description of Union chaplains, who were popularly called at the time "Holy Joes," is perfectly in tune with the Joe Twichell revealed in his stirring war letters.

Twain once remarked that Twichell's outstanding skills as an oral storyteller never seemed to carry over into his prose writing. But flashes of Twichell's ability are evident in many of his notes and letters written during the war.[7] One excellent example was composed at ground zero of the Union victory—on the battleground of America's most mythic struggle in the small town of Gettysburg in southeastern Pennsylvania. On July 5, 1863, Twichell wrote one of his many remarkable Civil War letters to his sister from the "3rd Corps Hospital—Near the battlefield":

> Another libation of blood has been poured out to liberty. Thousands of souls have been called to sudden judgment—thousands of homes are desolated. . . . the bugles sounded, and with a firm step with colors flying, the bravest men in the Army, marched into the open field. It was a splendid sight. . . . My eyes and heart followed the flag which I love best and I stood unsuspicious of danger, but full of anxiety. Of a sudden, from the left, a point not apprehended as concealing the enemy, a battery opened upon us, the most terrific fire I ever witnessed. . . . It was awful. For half an hour it raged incessantly. Grape, cannister, solid shot and shell, whizzed and shrieked and tore past us. The trees near by were torn and dismembered. . . . One of our boys was brought to us with both legs gone. Poor fellow, he lived but a few moments . . .
>
> It was the most terrible battle field I ever beheld. The stench was unendurable and the dead lay everywhere. In one place more than 30 were gathered together and the look of their bloated, blackened corpses was a thing to murder sleep. I saw where two Confederate officers had tried to screen themselves behind a stump, but a shell passing through had taken off both their heads. I grieve for our poor boys.[8]

This riveting account is one of the best extant examples of what Twain remembered as Twichell's "booming yarns" and illustrates his status as a "powerful storyteller."[9] It places Twichell at the epicenter of the American Civil War. The letter goes on to describe how Twichell was directly at the side of Major General Dan Sickles, destined to become one of the most celebrated and quirky heroes of the Union, when Sickles's leg was amputated. Twichell's choice of words and phrases typifies Unionist sentiment of the period during and after the conflict. Twichell underscores the religious nature of the conflict and the redemptive agency of the casualties: "Another libation of blood has been poured out to liberty. . . . the fruits of such a war as this amply pay the cost."

Elsewhere among Twichell's letters from the war period are ample illustrations that he understood his role to be consolatory, and specifically Christian, in nature. In a fragment of a letter to his Uncle Harry Hopkins, he writes, "Last Sunday afternoon we celebrated the Lord's Supper away in the heart of the woods, under a grove of oaks we sat down—some twenty fine men. Old Mr. Watson of the 11th Mass. administered the bread and wine, Eastman prayed and I talked. It was sweet and solemn, and as our hymns swelled through the still glades and died away in remote thickets, an unwonted, sacred calm was shed upon our souls. We may remember that spot after this life."[10] In another letter he tells his father, "I wish to witness the 'great day' which will blow the trumpet of freedom for the oppressed, and proclaim to the world that the Republic is not a failure," a passage that compares the wartime effort with the biblical apocalypse.[11] In one letter, he enclosed a brief poem called "After Battle" that he had composed, as he put it, "on the march up the Peninsula, soon after the battle of Williamsburg [which occurred May 5, 1862]"[12]:

They're left behind!
Our steps are turned away:
We forward march, but these forever stay
Halted, till trumpets wake the final day:—
Good bye! Good bye!

. . . .

They're left behind!
Comfort!—our heavy souls!
Their battle shout forever onward rolls
Till God's own freedom gather in the Jobs!
Good-bye! Farewell!

The sacramental quality of these passages would often be echoed in Twichell's public speeches regarding the events of the war for the next five decades. And they are not merely the religious platitudes of an evangelical Army chaplain, but are representative of the biblical perspectives and religious motivations shared by many of the soldiers from both sides (figure 7).[13]

Twichell's relationship over the years to the stricken General Sickles, both during the Battle of Gettysburg, where he lost his leg, and throughout the decades thereafter, placed Twichell in contact with what came to be considered the crucial command decision of Gettysburg, and perhaps even the war itself. Twichell became widely known for his association with the eccentric and singular hero of Gettysburg. In a newspaper account of 1905 entitled "Hartford's Joseph Twichell," the reporter said that

> Twichell frequently spoke at gatherings of Civil War veterans. On these occasions, he sometimes told the story of Major Gen. Dan Sickles's forward advance during the Battle of Gettysburg, an advance that Sickles apparently undertook against the explicit orders of Gen. Meade. However, claimed Twichell, it was that advance that led to the defeat of the Confederates at Gettysburg, and in fact may have been the decisive event of the War. In support of this assertion, Twichell would read a letter that he apparently had in his possession, written by Gen. Longstreet. There, Longstreet said that "he considered it the one thing that won the great battle for the Northern side."[14]

The highly eccentric aspects of Sickles's personality were perhaps the most notable features of Mark Twain's rather amusing reminiscences about meeting the aging hero. But we also know from this dictation that Twichell recounted the horrific experience on one of their hikes together: "Sickles lost a leg at Gettysburg, and I remember Twichell's account of that circumstance. He talked about it on one of our long walks. . . . I still carry the picture in my mind as presented by Twichell."[15]

Twichell's status as a veteran of the Union Army, and in particular as eyewitness chaplain at Gettysburg and as General Sickles's close aide and confidant, opened doors for him throughout the rest of his life. Twichell was often asked to speak or to lead prayers at various veterans' functions and memorials all over the northeast, up to and including the fiftieth anniversary of the battle at Gettysburg in 1913. For that event,

7. Joe Twichell in Civil War officer's uniform. Courtesy of Asylum Hill Congregational Church, Hartford, Connecticut.

attended by President Woodrow Wilson, Twichell traveled with Sickles to the Third Army Corps reunion and spent much time with him there as his right-hand man (Twichell himself was in his seventies and yet still fit). Many other times over the years, Twichell had reunited with his comrades or returned to the scene of the great battle to act in some official function to memorialize the site and the memory. He attended a gathering of veterans from Chancellorsville and Gettysburg in New York in May 1878 that included Sickles and General Joe Hooker, after which all three went to West Point. On July 1–2, 1886, Twichell delivered the prayer at a reunion of the Third Army Corps at Gettysburg, calling it in his journal "a very great occasion."[16] On July 2, 1888, at the laying of the cornerstone of the Excelsior Brigade Monument on the Gettysburg battlefield, Twichell delivered the main address, which included the following:

> Abraham Lincoln, you will recall, in that transcendent utterance of his which has passed into the liturgy of freedom forever, spoken above the ashes of these same dead, summoned the living to take from them increased devotion to the cause, their devotion to which, given here in its last full measure, had itself hallowed this ground far above the power of any to add or to detract. . . . No graves were ever so eloquent as these. What do they say? "Hear us, ye living, who once pressed out hands! We died while our blood was leaping in the pulses of our prime. Let your hearts beat ever true response to the high calling of a patriot's duty! We gave our lives; give yours freely, wholly, purely to the service of God and right and liberty."[17]

Twichell's address memorializes Lincoln in powerful yet predictable ways, alluding to famous motifs in Lincoln's "transcendent utterance," such as the "high calling" of the combatants and the "hallowed ground" of the battlefield.

In comparison with Twain's "war experience," the highlight of which is the dubious anecdote of the single fallen soldier in "The Private History of a Campaign that Failed"—an account both historically challenged and, in James Cox's words, a "patchwork of cliches"[18]—Twichell's accounts testify to a man who was an eyewitness to some of the most historically significant episodes in American history. Thus when Twichell spoke of Lincoln and Gettysburg, or the war in general, he did so with an authority not available to Mark Twain. Twain's close relationships with veterans of Twichell's caliber help explain his general reluctance to say much about the war throughout most of his career. Certain remarks Twain made over the years indicate his sense of shame at not having been a real combatant. Authentic war experience was a marker of manhood for many in the culture of the Gilded Age, which may explain why Twain felt it necessary to tell his brief tale of the war at all. In addition, Twain became more intensely pacifist in tone and message as he got older. However, Twichell's conscientious position was one that Mark Twain admired, and listened to with respect, during those long walks through the woods or at the dinner table with family and friends. Twichell's Union rhetoric, including his near worship of Lincoln, who had become the martyr-symbol of the American civil religion par excellence, was a major influence in Mark Twain's developing view of the Civil War.

Besides his pastor, Twain greatly admired many other Union figures, especially Civil War hero and former President Ulysses S. Grant, who became one of the passions of his major period. Twain's love for Grant was nearly a form of hero worship: "Grant embodied a laissez faire serenity and power that made him the prime exemplar for America after the Civil War."[19] Twain's high regard, combined with his deep sympathy for Grant and his family, who faced huge financial difficulties after being swindled out of most of their assets by a business partner, resulted in his contracting to have Grant's *Personal Memoirs* published with Twain's firm, Charles L. Webster and Company. The result was the largest single royalty payment in America up to that time, which Twain proudly presented to Grant's widow Julia after Grant's death from throat cancer.

In some ways Twain identified very closely with Grant—"Both of them were poor boys, unlikely successes, with hard-drinking pasts, who had succeeded through a combination of genius and hard work."[20] Grant was, like Mark Twain himself, a living embodiment of the American Dream. Justin Kaplan puts it a bit more fancifully: Grant was "touched by history and the Holy Ghost and achieved greatness."[21] More concretely, Grant represented the victory of the Union, along with its northern civil religion, over the fallen and corrupt Lost Cause ideology of the Confederacy. Thus Grant embodied a bit of religious symbolism for Mark Twain. And not just Twain: Kaplan writes that "even [General William T.] Sherman, a nonbeliever, said that he fought under Grant 'with the faith a Christian has in his Saviour.' To the North, during the war years, Grant seemed God's tool." General Sherman said in a speech of 1885: "Grant more nearly impersonated the American character of 1861–5 than any other living man. Therefore he will stand as the typical hero of the great Civil War in America."[22] If one writer exaggerates a bit when he claims that Twain "regarded publishing Grant's memoirs as the most significant achievement of his life," we can forgive him since, at the time, it was probably close to the truth.[23]

In 1879, not long after both Grant and Twain had returned to America from extended stays overseas, Twain participated in a weeklong reunion of the Army of the Tennessee in Chicago at which General Grant acted as guest of honor. At the final banquet at the Palmer House, Twain was "transfigured by oratory" as he listened to the patriotic rhetoric throughout the course of the evening. In particular, he was moved by the eloquence of Colonel Robert G. Ingersoll, a former Union cavalry officer who later became perhaps the nation's most famous orator and what one recent biographer has nostalgically called "the great agnostic during the golden age of freethought." It may seem ironic, given Ingersoll's status as America's leading freethinker and agnostic (which ostensibly means one who holds that ultimate reality is unknowable), that in his speech that night he made broad, metaphysical assertions about the meaning and purpose of the Civil War. However, "Freethinkers did not hesitate to describe atheism and agnosticism as faiths like any other, often using the term religion in a secular sense to define an ethical and metaphysical system grounded in the search for truth rather than in the conviction of having found the truth."[24] It is significant that nineteenth-century intellectuals understood what many seem to forget today: that any ideological system embraced with passion can be perceived as religious in nature. Ingersoll's speech that evening in Chicago did in fact present a religious view of America and the war, insofar as it advocated an "ethical and metaphysical system." Indeed, in terms of America's civil religion, Ingersoll's speech must be considered nothing less than a sermon on the gospel of America:

> [the soldiers of the republic] fought to preserve the homestead of liberty, that their children might have peace. They were the defenders of humanity, the destroyers of prejudice, the breakers of chains, and in the name of the future they saluted the monsters of their time. They finished what the soldiers of the revolution commenced. They relighted the torch that fell from those august hands and filled the world again with light. . . . They broke the shackles from the limbs of slaves, from the souls of masters, and from the Northern brain. They kept our country on the map of the world and our flag in heaven. They rolled the stone from the sepulcher of progress, and found therein two angels clad in shining garments—nationality and liberty.[25]

Much of this rhetoric sounds vaguely similar to themes that have emanated regularly from the Bush administration post-9/11 (generating great public concern about the threat and arrogance of an "American empire"), but in the aftermath of the Civil War these tropes and biblical allusions were widely applauded by almost all Americans (at least in the North). The Civil War, says Ingersoll, completes the work of the Revolution. The Union is the defender of all humanity, not just America. And the wartime victory succeeded in rolling away the stone that had sealed the tomb of the sacred and Christlike Union. The two angels within the tomb indicate the secularizing trends of postwar civil religion: they are clad in "nationality and liberty," with no reference to God or the Bible.

Ingersoll's speech ended with a toast to the great victors of the war. Significantly it also included a chastisement of the South's errors, particularly slavery, and emphasized the cultural work of the war as including a grand liberation of mind:

> The soldiers were the saviors of the nation. They were the liberators of man. In writing the proclamation of emancipation, Lincoln, greatest of our mighty dead, whose memory is as gentle as the summer air when reapers sing 'mid gathered sheaves, copied with the pen what Grant and his brave comrades wrote with swords. . . . The Southern people must submit, not to the dictation of the North but to the nation's will and to the verdict of mankind. They were wrong, and the time will come when they say that they are victors who have been vanquished by the right. Freedom conquered them, and freedom will cultivate their feelings, educate their children, weave for them the robes of wealth, execute their laws, and fill their land with happy homes.
>
> The soldiers of the Union saved the South as well as the North. They made us a nation. Their victories made us free and rendered tyranny in every other land as insecure as snow upon volcanoes' lips.[26]

Again, Ingersoll's claim that the South has been "vanquished by the right" assumes at least some version of a metaphysical shalom. Although he was the nation's leading agnostic, Ingersoll's lines reverberate with a sense of the cosmic meaning and destiny of the American republic. Its implications are worldwide: "tyranny in every other land" has now been made permanently "insecure." Finally, the notion of the salvation of the

South along with the North, as a result of the sacrifices of the soldiers, places the cultural effect of the war within another traditional metaphor of Christianity. And yet the redemptive force, again, is no longer Jesus, God, or the Bible; it is now the abstraction "freedom," which is the agent of many verbs for Ingersoll. According to Ingersoll, freedom conquers, cultivates, educates, weaves, executes laws, and fills the land with happiness. Ingersoll's vision here is a symptom of the period of American thought in which the object of faith is passing subtly away from God and the Bible and becoming more focused on an impersonal, nationalistic faith in America itself.[27]

Twain's reaction to Ingersoll's impassioned speech that evening was rapturous: "[Ingersoll is] the most beautiful human creature that ever lived," he wrote later to Howells. "I doubt if America has ever seen anything quite equal to it."[28] Twain was already familiar with many of Ingersoll's views on religion. Among the most important was Ingersoll's long-standing critique of any idea, belief, or superstition that effectively enslaved human beings. In his speech, Ingersoll rails against the "shackles" that bind "the Northern brain." Opposed to such slavery of the mind was "freethought," or freethinking, terms identifying the movement that questioned religious authority and the certainties of church dogma. While this movement is typically remembered as having been peopled with atheists or agnostics, many freethinkers were deists who believed in a watchmaker God but did not believe that He had any dealings with earth after the initial acts of creation. The patron saint of the movement was Thomas Paine, whose writings had enchanted Twain during his cub piloting days. Twain utilized the theme of freethinking most explicitly in *Pudd'nhead Wilson,* in which the title character and Judge Driscoll are the only two members of the "Free-Thinker's Society" of Dawson's Landing. Thus was Twain immediately drawn to the major themes of Ingersoll's oration—themes that appear implicitly in his own comic contribution to the night's events.

Basking in the leftover radiation of Ingersoll's speech, Mark Twain gave his famous speech in the presence of General Grant. It was well past 2:00 a.m. when Twain, the fifteenth and final speaker of the evening, rose to the platform to present what some consider his greatest public performance: the "Babies" oration in which he asked the 500 Union veterans to imagine Grant as an infant trying to put his big toe into his mouth. The speech, coming at the end of a long evening of mainly patriotic rhetoric similar to that presented by Ingersoll, was now filling a need for some comic relief, and Twain was happy to comply. Still, what people remember most about that speech—the snapper at the end, which reminds everyone that the mighty general was once just a slobbering infant—is preceded with a nod toward the audacious metaphysical statements that came earlier. The speech, in other words, does assert an American civil religion, even though it is dressed up in some mild satire. It begins with the calm assertion that we were once all formerly babies and thus "we stand on common ground." Every great man or woman, Twain reminds us, was once a baby, and "it was high time for a toastmaster to recognize the importance of the babies." Initially he praises the sacrificial work of the soldiers, who comprise the vast majority of his listeners. Ingeniously Twain describes the greatest commanders of men to be their own babies. Upon the baby's arrival in the household, "he took entire command. You became his lackey. . . . You could face the death storm at Donelson and Vicksburg, and give back blow for blow; but when he clawed your whiskers, and pulled your hair, and twisted your nose, you had to take it."[29] The babies, he says, are the truest commanders of the nation. And so the body of the speech is a mild burlesque of the beauty and peaceful happiness of the homestead, one that Twain was now associating with his own experience of fatherhood.

He then asks his listeners to imagine the nation in fifty years, at which time "our present schooner of state will have grown into a political leviathan." The leaders of the future, he says, are now rocking in their cradles. One is a future great scientist, now teething. Another is a future great historian, lying in his cradle—"and doubtless he will continue to lie until his earthly mission is ended." Finally we see a future commander in chief, "so little burdened with his approaching grandeurs and responsibilities," who is now "giving his whole strategic mind, at this moment, to trying to find out some way to get his own big toe into his mouth." This occupation of the future great president, says Twain, is precisely what the great General Grant was undertaking some fifty-six years earlier. There was a brief moment of silence before Twain presented the snapper: "And if the child is but a prophecy of the man, there are mighty few who will doubt that he succeeded."[30] Twain wrote proudly home to Livy that he stole the show, but his most triumphant note was with regard to Grant himself, famous for his stern and stoic demeanor: "I fetched him! I broke him up, utterly! . . . The audience saw that for once in his life he had been knocked out of his iron serenity."[31] Partly the success he valued so much was his ability to bring even Grant to tears of laughter—to slay him. And yet this is a sort of humor that is absolutely in love with its object. By focusing on our shared humanity, Twain is in this sense laughing at us all. Thus does Twain's Adamic sense of humor have a profoundly democratic effect. But also the speech serves as a paean to home life and the joys of parenting, and thus of sowing into the future of the nation itself. As such, it redounds with a quintessential American hopefulness. There truly was, for Twain, a great pleasure in being caught up in the majesty of Union memory mixed with hearth and home, and simultaneously being able to pull the rug out from under that majesty.

Yet General Grant signified for Twain America at its greatest, especially during Twain's heyday, the early- to mid-1880s when he completed *Adventures of Huckleberry Finn,* published Grant's memoirs, and then finished writing his personal memoir of the Civil War "The Private History of a Campaign that Failed." If anything, his adulation was heightened when the great general finally passed away in July 1885. Joe Twichell's reaction and sermon after Grant's death contains an eloquent expression of Grant's meaning to almost all northern Americans of 1885. His journal entry about the news of Grant's death states that "its occurrence moves the public heart in a manner wonderful to see—and glorious. In me it revives in full force all the loyalties, burning, unreserved, which as a youth, twenty years ago, I felt for my commander; and memories of great days, and scenes never-to-be-forgotten, with which he is associated."[32] On July 26, 1885, Twichell preached on the life of General Grant at Asylum Hill. His text came from Psalms 78:70–71: "He chose David also his servant, and took him from the sheepfolds. . . . he brought him to feed Jacob his people, and Israel his inheritance." Twichell's text compares Grant directly with the boy David as God's chosen vessel, and the message focuses on his understanding of Grant "as a Providential man."[33] Two weeks later, on August 8, 1885, Hartford held "Grant Memorial Services," and Twichell was asked to give the main address:

> Yea, the heart of a whole people is in that coffin. . . . We are a sorrowing nation, yet in our sorrow how blessed. The most precious wealth of any people is in its hero spirits. . . . They are the perennial spring of the inspirations of patriotism. Happy the nation whose heroes are good men. . . . To God we give the praise, for he is God's gift. His hand fashioned him. It was in the school of His peculiar providence that he came to his glorious stature. . . . at last came an hour when God touched him and called him by name, and he answered: Here am I. . . . A sacred cause, the most sacred of all causes, that of most vital moment, we believe, not only to the nation but to the world, to mankind—the holy cause of freedom, in distress, in extremity—beckoned him, saying 'follow me'; and he arose, left all, and followed it. . . . his sublime faith [in Freedom] . . . could be 'likened to nothing else but a Christian's faith in his Saviour,' for with him success was not his success, but something far, far greater. For this reason, that the spirit in him was the inspiration of such a cause, he could impart it—impart the qualities of his own serene courage, indomitable resolution, undoubting confidence, to the hosts he led, and to the Nation itself, as he did.[34]

This powerful oration, filled with King James language and style, declares that the fallen hero incarnates the "heart of the nation." As in the Sunday sermon, Grant is figured here as a sort of everyman David, who obediently rises to follow the Lord's commands. Typical of postbellum rhetoric, the cause is less that of biblical Christianity and more that of an idealized "freedom." Note the connection with General Sherman's comments above: Grant's faith was not specifically "Christian" but it is "likened" to a "Christian's faith." Grant's passion, says Twichell, is in a "sacred cause, the most sacred of all causes."

Grant typified what Twain called the "simple soldier," as opposed to the romantic Lost Cause versions in Confederate storytelling. In Twain's description, Grant was "the simple soldier, who, all untaught of the silken phrase-makers, linked words together with an art surpassing the art of the schools and put into them a something which will still bring to American ears, as long as America shall last, the roll of his vanished drums and the tread of the marching hosts."[35] In part, calling Grant a "simple soldier" foregrounds his role as democratic everyman. But additionally, Twain is impressed by Grant's highly concise and direct form of expression. Grant was able to put into his words "a something" that transcends the flowery language of a Walter Scott or a James Fenimore Cooper—or, of a Matthew Arnold, the writer who angered Twain when he openly criticized Grant for writing "an English without charm and high breeding."[36] In both of these cases Grant represents the antithesis of the aristocratic, romance-laden style of the Lost Cause. His language is direct, strong, and driven by assertive verbs. It was the emerging style of the realists, comprising a more down-to-earth language representative of ordinary Americans, a sort of meat-and-potatoes "democratic eloquence" that eschewed aristocratic pomp and Arnoldian "high breeding."[37] Grant's style of language thus represents a prime directive of Twain's civil religion: the democratization of voice, a manifestation of the heart of the people.

In these ways, Twain's allegiance to a rarified vision of the meaning of General Grant indicates much more than just his membership in a cult of personality. In addition, it indicates Twain's status as a strong disciple of the tenets of America's civil religion. Twain often copied Union discourse by following its two major objectives: the endorsement of the northern civil religion and the rejection of the southern civil religion, especially its myth of the Lost Cause. Twain shared with Twichell a desire to contribute to both of these ideological projects, and to some extent Twichell was his mentor in these areas. Indeed Joe Twichell's passionate embrace of the northern civil religion, including its emphasis on Christian manhood, equal rights for all, the abomination of slavery and racial hatred and prejudice, and the affirmation of Union saints such as Lincoln and Grant, aided and abetted the "conversion" of Mark Twain from southern sympathizer to northern acolyte.

Conversion, again, may seem too strong a term, but it is important to recall the religious sensibilities of both North and South during and long after the war years—sensibilities that support a view of the Civil War as America's religious war. For example, the Reverend Richard Wilmer was a Virginian by birth but became the Episcopalian bishop of Alabama. Wilmer maintained for many years after the war a blunt support of the Confederacy, stating in his memoir of 1887 that he and other southern leaders did so "to maintain the supremacy of the Word of God, and the teachings of the universal tradition. . . . [confederates were] a noble army of martyrs, . . . a small remnant," the agents of salvation for the nation.[38] Brigadier General William Nelson Pendleton, Lee's former chief of artillery and later rector at Grace Memorial Church in Lexington, Virginia, remarked that southerners were "related towards the government and Northern people somewhat as our Blessed Lord and the Apostles towards the Roman authorities and population."[39] Pendleton's and Wilmer's alienation from the United States federal government helps explain an even more extreme version of alienation: more than 10,000 southerners became permanent exiles, establishing Confederate colonies in Mexico, Venezuela, Brazil, and other nations.[40]

Long-lasting devotion to the southern cause may have reached its limits, however, in the life of Father Abram Ryan, parish priest of St. Paul's Church in Augusta, Georgia, who became known as the "Poet Priest of the Lost Cause." He served in Confederate infantry units as a full-time chaplain and later founded the fanatical pro-southern newspaper, *Banner of the South.* One historian describes him as a "melancholy, morose figure. A sad-eyed man with stooped shoulders and curly, unruly hair . . . He cultivated his unusual appearance by wearing a faded black coat that reached to his feet. . . . He was a poet of the dead, the Confederate dead. 'There's grandeur in graves— / There's glory in gloom.' "[41] Ryan, a nationally known incarnation of the Lost Cause sentimentality at its most lugubrious, might easily have served Mark Twain as self-parodying model for Emmeline Grangerford, the melancholy graveyard poet of *Adventures of Huckleberry Finn* (although credit for this is generally given to Julia A. Moore, the "Sweet Singer of Michigan"). Ryan conveyed his religious allegiance to the Confederacy in what was his most famous poem, "The Conquered Banner": "Furl that Banner, softly, slowly, / Treat it gently—it is holy."[42] As these citations suggest, Ryan became almost obsessed with the trope of the banner, an Old Testament symbol of the holy cause of a God-ordained army, which he featured in his most famous poem and in the title of his influential newspaper.

The postwar careers of the likes of the reverends Wilmer, Pendleton, and Ryan represented literally hundreds of others very much like them, both North and South. And yet Americans of the early twenty-first century do not generally consider the American Civil War to have been largely, if not primarily, a religious war. Many reasons exist for this cultural amnesia, including perhaps most notably the perception of the secularization of culture and society, and the privatization of belief.

Many contemporary Americans are embarrassed to believe that Americans of the past would have been motivated by sacred belief in prosecuting a bloody war. Perhaps in our own day of global terrorism, we are prone to consider religious fanaticism in the context of violence as decidedly antimodern, even anti-American. But the Civil War was very much a clash of religious worldviews; it was, as one judicious historian has argued, effectively a religious war deriving from a theological crisis.[43] One group of historians has noted that "surprisingly little attention has been devoted to the war as a religious experience and event. . . . [but] the findings [are] substantial. God was truly alive and very much at the center of this nation's defining moment. . . . it is now clear how, in fundamental respects, religion stood at the center of the American Civil War experience."[44] Our understanding of the war and its long aftermath is clarified when we realize that the Confederacy created its own distinct "civil religion" that not only motivated southerners during the war but also played a crucial role in the South's cultural development for decades afterward:

> The Southern public faith involved a nation—a dead one, which was perhaps the unique quality of this phenomenon. One of the central issues of American faith has been the relationship between church and state, but since the Confederate quest for political nationhood failed, the Southern faith has been less concerned with such political issues than with the cultural question of identity. . . . Because of its origins in Confederate defeat, the southern civil religion offered confused and suffering Southerners a sense of meaning, an identity in a precarious but distinct culture.[45]

Staggering documentary evidence from the years immediately after Appomattox in 1865 shows that Americans both North and South made sense out of the war experience through religious means. Civil War memory, in other words, was heavily invested in religious terms and images. The greatest rhetorical expressions of the meaning of the war, Abraham Lincoln's Gettysburg Address and Second Inaugural Address, are brimming with biblical images and theological belief. The death and apotheosis of Lincoln, to take one of the weightiest incidents, was steeped in Christian symbolism, and it was the topic of virtually all northern sermons in the weeks following the assassination (figure 8).[46]

Famous northern clergymen, such as Henry Ward Beecher and Horace Bushnell, gladly participated in the construction of the Union as holy political entity and the war as sacred national cleansing. Beecher was the featured speaker at the symbolic raising of the Union flag in Charleston harbor on April 14, 1865, at war's end. Bushnell's theological treatises were among the most influential statements regarding the metaphysical meanings of the war. His 1866 volume *The Vicarious Sacrifice* explored in great depth the spiritual work carried out by soldiers of both sides as somehow being crucial to the redemption of the nation as a whole. This volume developed a new approach to the atoning work of suffering as it shifted emphasis from the work of Jesus Christ on the cross to the sacrificial work of each individual American in the redemption of others. Bushnell's idea became prominent at the same time that many "children abandoned by their fathers . . . turned to the ways of their mothers and took Christianity out of the home to save the world." The preeminent Social Gospel figure Walter Rauschenbush is one of many raised by his mother in such a religious milieu. As Phillip Shaw Paludan has suggested, there is a strong connection between the emerging theologies of the North, as typified by Bushnell, and the postwar rise of the Social Gospel, often described as an ongoing war or crusade. As Paludan points out, "Social Gospel thinkers emphasized not a distant God but a more nurturing, more human divinity. And they adopted values of nurture and self-sacrifice to modify or in some cases reject the extreme individualism of their fathers."[47]

The connection between theological understandings of the war and the emerging religious ethos of the North, as typified by Union Republicanism, Social Christianity, the Social Gospel, and Christian manhood, has not been commonly explored in literary studies. And yet these religious themes permeated thinking about the nation in the aftermath of the Civil War. In fact, the manifestation of a unified religious and moral nation was considered by some to have become the primary effect of the war experience, as in Bushnell's statement: "These United States, having dissolved the intractable matter of so many infallible theories and bones of contention in the dreadful menstruum of their blood are to settle into a fixed unity and finally into a nearly homogeneous life."[48] Twichell, one of Bushnell's protégés, made these themes central to his ministry. And by extension, they had a lasting effect on Mark Twain.

8. Abraham Lincoln being raptured into Heaven by angels. Courtesy of the Lincoln Museum, Fort Wayne, Indiana [#3282].

Southern apologists also created and deployed their own religious analysis of the war experience, a version that became known as the myth of the Lost Cause. While many excellent historical accounts have examined the Lost Cause mentality, almost no literary analysis has drawn upon these histories; and further, few studies of Mark Twain have made use of these materials or even shown any interest or knowledge of the Lost Cause as a social and cultural phenomenon.[49] This is particularly surprising given the fact that Twain's writings can so easily be understood in the context of Civil War memory. He was a southerner merging into northern culture and thus highly conscious of his outsider status among the Yankee gentry. Generally critics have given short shrift to Twain's complicated response to the rapid embrace of the myth of the Lost Cause among Americans both North and South. This is unfortunate, since he provided extensive insider knowledge of that myth, a knowledge that he chose on many occasions to share with his reading and listening audiences. In fact Twain did respond to the Lost Cause ideology—and in doing so, provided his own religious interpretation of the Civil War. Attempts to outline Twain's heavy involvement in the cultural memory of the war are complicated and require a contextualized discussion of many aspects of postbellum northern ideology. But a description of the religious and moral lenses through which Americans viewed and tried to make sense of the war shows that many of Twain's views were characteristic of his time and social position.

The precise origin of the term Lost Cause is hard to pin down, but the concept and arguments that we now associate with it first made a big bang with the volume entitled *The Lost Cause,* published in 1866 by the wartime editor of the *Richmond Examiner,* Edward A. Pollard. There Pollard called for a "war of ideas" to continue indefinitely after the military defeat. Tellingly Pollard's manifesto stated unequivocally that the Civil War might have decided the "restoration of the union and the excision of slavery, but the war did not decide Negro equality."[50] The character of Pollard's insights may be judged from a quotation from another of his books, *Southern History of the War,* also published in 1866, in which he wrote, "The occasion of that conflict was what the Yankees called—by one of their convenient libels in political nomenclature—slavery; but what was in fact nothing more than a system of Negro servitude in the South . . . one of the mildest and most beneficent systems of servitude in the world."[51]

Thus, from its infancy, the myth of the Lost Cause clearly foregrounded a pro-slavery, racist agenda, and it never admitted to the evil of slavery or of racial prejudice. More generally, the myth of the Lost Cause constituted the means by which southerners and their sympathizers (including, as the decades ensued, many in the North) would choose to remember the war. Gary W. Gallagher has outlined the two primary motives that caused Confederates to create such a memory: 1) to justify their own actions and allow themselves and other former Confederates to find something positive in all-encompassing failure, and 2) to provide their children and future generations of white southerners with a "correct" narrative of the war.[52]

Gallagher's coeditor Alan T. Nolan has provided "The Claims of the Legend," a succinct version of what almost all Confederates and many northerners believed for decades after Appomattox (and which many Americans believe to this day)[53]:

> *Slavery Was Not the Primary Sectional Issue:* "Slavery was trivialized as the cause of the war in favor of such things as tariff disputes, control of investment banking and the means of wealth, cultural differences, and conflict between industrial and agricultural societies."[54]
>
> *The Abolitionists as Provocateurs:* "[Abolitionists] are seen as troublemakers . . . virtually manufacturing a disagreement between the sections that was of little or no interest to the people and had little substance."[55]
>
> *The South Would Have Given Up Slavery:* "The South would have abandoned slavery of its own accord. It was simply a question of time."[56] If this were true, the war was wasteful and vain.
>
> *The Nature of the Slaves:* "In the legend there exists two prominent images of the black slaves. One is of the 'faithful slave'; the other is what William Garrett Piston calls 'the happy darky stereotype'. . . . [In] 1863 . . . President Davis called the slaves "peaceful and contented laborers."[57] However, with Reconstruction and the advent of hate groups such as the KKK, African Americans were increasingly depicted as subhumans. A result was the creation of a third category that featured the shiftless, foolish, corrupt, sexually profligate, and ultimately demonic aspects of blacks.
>
> *The Nationalistic/Cultural Difference:* "[The] South created a nationalistic/cultural basis for the disagreement. . . . Northerners were said to be descended from the Anglo-Saxon tribes that had been conquered by the Norman cavaliers. The cavaliers were, of course, the ancestors of the Southerners according to this theory. It was written that the cavaliers were 'descended from the Norman Barons of

William the Conquerer, a race distinguished in earliest history for its warlike and fearless character, a race in all times since renowned for its gallantry, chivalry, honor, gentleness, and intellect.' "[58]

The Military Loss: "[The] Confederates had not really been defeated, they had instead been overwhelmed by massive Northern manpower and material. . . . [The] loss was somehow mitigated in the myth because it was said that winning had been impossible. . . . [And yet] the myth asserted that had the South won at Gettysburg, it would have won the war. The loss at Gettysburg was attributed to Lt. Gen. James Longstreet."[59] This is probably the most resonant aspect of the term "Lost Cause": In contemporary vernacular, a "lost cause" means precisely an unwinnable contest, such as in a sporting event.

The Idealized Home Front: "Southern culture is portrayed as superior, peopled by cavalier aristocrats and martyrs along with the fortunate happy darkies. . . . The 'moonlight and magnolias' culture as described by [Gaines] Foster is fully displayed in *Gone With the Wind,* America's favorite Civil War story. That story idealized the men and women of the plantation class, suggested the superior valor of Southern manhood, and is strongly peopled with happy slaves and gentle and indulgent masters."[60]

The Idealized Confederate Soldier: "He was invariably heroic, indefatigable, gallant, and law-abiding." Nolan is correct to note that he is not interested in disparaging southern soldiers, but that in fact to a large extent, the Confederate soldiers were the "principle victim[s]" of the Lost Cause myth.[61]

The Lawfulness of Secession: "The Lost Cause doctrine endlessly asserted that secession was a constitutional right. . . . those supporting it were not rebels or traitors; there had not been a rebellion or a revolution."[62]

The Saints Go Marching In: "Southern military leaders . . . are not evaluated simply in terms of their military and leadership skills and combat effectiveness. . . . they are also presented as remarkable and saintly creatures, supermen. . . . Generals Lee and Stonewall Jackson are the primary examples of this phenomenon."[63]

The upshot of Nolan's outline of the Lost Cause is its doctrinal quality—a quality betraying the quasi-religious nature of the myth itself. If one accepts a description of religion such as Clifford Geertz's—religion as a "system of symbols which acts to . . . establish powerful, pervasive, and long-lasting moods"[64]—then one can reasonably consider the myth of the Lost Cause as more than a set of historical suppositions. Instead these detailed assertions comprise the heart of the southern civil religion as it had developed by the beginning of the war and which continued to motivate people for many decades afterwards. Indeed many Americans still appear to believe these ideologies, as illustrated powerfully in Civil War reenactments or at screenings of films like *Gods and Generals* filled with viewers proudly wearing Confederate uniforms.[65]

David Blight has written that "nations build memories in the same way that religions build followings. In the wake of the war and Reconstruction, the defeated South, as well as the victorious North, needed a new religion of nationhood. . . . But the movement for a New South, and inherently therefore for sectional reconciliation, needed a mythos in which to flourish; the 'new' demanded an 'old' counterpoise for emotional fuel and sustenance."[66] By granting such a view regarding the religious qualities of nationalistic ideology, the critics and supporters of either project can be said to take on a religious mission and identity. As Nolan points out, the heart of the southern civil religion is a "caricature" based on falsehoods. Secession was decidedly not heroic; it was "mean and narrow and a profound mistake. Its leaders were wrong and authored a major tragedy for the American people."[67] But the promulgation of the Lost Cause myth did have two major, long-lasting effects in American cultural history, one positive and the other negative. The myth did facilitate reunion of the two warring factions, but it also fostered the nearly complete abandonment of the African Americans for the better part of a century. Blight has argued in great detail that the nation after the Civil War was required to choose one over the other, and the choice was reunion over racial reconciliation. Favoring white reconciliation came at the cost of elevated racial division between whites and blacks.[68] Ignoring the plight of the ex-slaves, and African Americans in general, and conveniently leaving out of the Civil War histories the critical importance of the slavery issue, became the historical consensus by the time of the 1876 election, which installed Rutherford Hayes as president in return for the removal of Federal troops from the south in the so-called Compromise of 1877. This political deal, in effect, cemented Lost Cause mythology in the minds of most Americans for a very long time.

In 1882 Mark Twain set out on an extensive tour of the Mississippi River Valley as a means of gathering information and impressions for the revision of his "Old Times" sketches into the volume that would become *Life on the Mississippi.* It was his first return since the Civil War to most of the river scenes of his triumphant steamboat piloting years and included stops in Hannibal, St. Louis, Vicksburg, and New Orleans, where he had friendly visits with George Washington Cable and Joel Chandler Harris, author of the Uncle Remus tales. The journey featured long days aboard a riverboat called the *Gold Dust,* headed for New Orleans. As the ship moved downstream, Twain experienced the "psychological and cultural regression of the slow, easy, lazy drift into a backward and defeated civilization."[69] But he was also required to do some hard work. The purpose of the trip was to gather interviews, anecdotes, and news accounts of the region: its history, geography, and the social and cultural conditions after the war. But what he ultimately learned about the present state of the beloved river country was the climax of a lengthy period of sustained reflection on the meaning, purpose, and effects of the Civil War—a period that would result in what one critic has called the "classic texts in Mark Twain's Civil War writings": *Life on the Mississippi, Adventures of Huckleberry Finn,* and "The Private History of a Campaign that Failed."[70]

Although these works treat many other topics, especially the first two, they go together well because of their common examination of America's religious war, particularly the myths and ideologies of the southern cause. They also provide inspired analysis of the changes that had taken hold in the South, which contrasted so significantly with growth and progress in the North, especially New England and New York. These regional changes were even more striking than Twain had imagined, so that he was both delighted and dismayed by what he found. He wrote to Livy, "That world which I knew in its blossoming youth is old and bowed and melancholy, now; its soft cheeks are leathery and wrinkled, the fire is gone out in its eyes, and the spring from its step."[71] The bottom of the river south of St. Louis was littered with the buried hulks of sunken steamboats—a ghostly legacy of both the river's untamable natural powers and the war years, and a poignant reminder of Twain's heroic days as a pilot. This image of the wrecked steamboats would become important in *Huckleberry Finn:* the *Walter Scott,* on which the corpse of Huck's despicable father was found. The memories of actual survivors of battles such as Vicksburg brought Twain face to face with of some of the most brutal tales of the war. Those tales are recalled in chapter 35 of *Life on the Mississippi,* entitled "Vicksburg during the Trouble." The frequent bombardment of the city would result in "frantic women and children scurrying from home and bed toward the cave dungeons—encouraged by the humorous grim soldiery, who shout 'Rats, to your holes!' and laugh."[72]

It is not surprising that this nostalgic trip would jar Twain's imagination back to the days when he, if ever so briefly, had his own personal contact with the Civil War. Young Sam had been working the river and was in New Orleans in January of 1861 when the state of Louisiana officially seceded from the Union; he was also there in April when Fort Sumter was fired upon, officially beginning the war. Almost immediately, his work on the river came to an end, at which time he headed back to Missouri. There, while in Marion County during June of 1861, Sam Clemens joined briefly with fourteen other young men to form a militia unit of the Missouri State Guard. They called themselves the Marion Rangers. During two weeks in the stifling summer heat, they marched, trained, slept out under the stars, and generally tried to act like actual infantry volunteers. For reasons that are not entirely clear, Sam left the Marion Rangers after those two weeks to join his brother Orion on a journey out west, where he would act as assistant to his older sibling, recently appointed secretary of the territorial government of Nevada. For many years, Twain never said much about this brief experience in the Missouri State Guard, whose ostensible goal was to protect the state from the threat of invasion. Perhaps he was hesitant to speak openly about it because of the possibility of being charged as a deserter or as simply a coward. But the trip out to the Mississippi in 1882, more than twenty years later, was a catalyst in bringing back the stories from that period.

Although various versions of his tale of service were published as narratives or presented as speeches over the course of his career, the most famous was "The Private History of a Campaign that Failed," where Twain claims that "I was in the Confederate army."[73] Twain often announced his initial allegiance with the southern cause: "I was born and reared in a slave state; my father was a slave owner; and in the Civil War I was a second lieutenant in the Confederate service."[74] Here we see a familiar pattern of Twain's enlarged version of his actual military involvement. However, the term "Confederate" does not accurately describe the outfit in which Twain briefly served (although numerous critics have called Twain a "Confederate"). It is more accurate to call him a member of the Missouri State Guard at a time of high tensions, as the state tried to determine its loyalties; his oath of allegiance upon entering the guard was to the state of Missouri, not the Confederacy. More generally, Twain's ambivalence at the outbreak of war reflected the general confusion, yet largely Unionist sentiments, of Hannibal and the state of Missouri from St. Louis northward. Terrell Dempsey notes: "The people of Marion County simply did not want to leave the Union. Secession had little support in the community. When a secession rally was held at the county seat in Palmyra on November 14, 1861, only a dozen people attended. . . . Seventy-two percent of the voters of Marion County voted for pro-Union candidates." According to Dempsey, by February of 1861, even after the newly elected pro-South governor of Missouri, Claiborne Fox Jackson, had tried to turn the public sentiment toward the Confederacy, "the issue of secession was dead in Missouri. It would not be revitalized when the shooting started."[75] Annie Moffett, Twain's niece, remembered the mixed emotions that everyone in St. Louis felt at the time; she also recalled that on one occasion, Twain "helped some boys make Confederate cockades and only shortly afterward became furiously angry with the same boys when they burned the Union flag."[76] Moffett believed that "[Twain] would gladly have given his life for his country, but he was a Southerner, his friends were all Southern, his sympathies were with the South."[77] Dempsey states, "There were Missouri Confederates, but the fact is that nearly three-quarters of the Missourians who took up arms during the Civil War served with the Union side."[78] Twain reported that when news of the first secession broke in December 1860 while he was piloting on the Mississippi, "My pilot mate was a New Yorker. He was strong for the Union; so was I."[79]

And yet time and again Mark Twain would claim to have once been a Confederate soldier and even a soldier of the Lost Cause. One overt example of his occasional embrace of the Lost Cause is in a speech in 1901, when he described himself as one of the "soldiers of the Lost Cause and foes of your great and good leader."[80] Analysis of Twain's repugnance for and critical appraisal of the Lost Cause mentality must remember that on some occasions he was willing to embrace it and even treat it as a sacred part of his youth—an attitude common in much post-Civil War discourse of reunion. His insistence that he was once a Confederate regular may be rooted in a desire to assure his audience that his ultimate rejection and critique of southern ideology came from one who was previously a full participant. His critique becomes most powerful from the vantage point of someone who was once an insider, a convert who was formerly steeped in the intricacies and grandeur of the Lost Cause myth. And yet Twain made more conscious efforts to reject and even satirize the remnants of Lost Cause ideology. He did this by responding, in effect, to many of the claims of the Lost Cause legend.

Mark Twain even invented his own nomenclature for the myth of the Lost Cause, a set of terms he deployed more generally to signify the entrenched and ossified ideology of the South. The most well-known term was the "Walter Scott disease," most famously described in *Life on the Mississippi.* Significantly, Twain named the sinking steamboat in *Adventures of Huckleberry Finn* after Walter Scott. The term "Lost Cause" historically derives from Scotland's attempts at independence from Britain, tales of which were memorialized in many of the works of Walter Scott, especially his Waverly novels. Twain read many of these novels, some of them almost obsessively at times.[81] As Connelly and Bellows put it, southerners "thrived upon Sir Walter Scott's accounts of the lost cause of Scotland in its quest for independence. An antebellum South embroiled in a power struggle with the 'churlish Saxons' of Yankeedom could identify with a heroic Ivanhoe."[82] The Confederate battle flag used the design of the Scottish cross of St. Andrew in a symbolic tribute to this lingering connection, and the Confederate historians also tried to link Robert E. Lee with the ancestry of Robert the Bruce. Southerners developed a craze for coats of arms and heraldry, a trend that Twain satirized on occasion. Given the overt connection between Scott and the term Lost Cause, it is surprising that no attention has been given to the obvious fact that Mark Twain's naming of the "Walter Scott disease" links it with his critique of specific southern mythologies of the postwar period. These mythologies would include the Lost Cause itself along with, more generally, the southern attempt to create a civil religion of its own, distinct from that of the North.

In other words, most critics have failed to recognize fully how Walter Scott served Twain as a generalized metaphor for fallen southern ideology. Twain is attributing the corruption of southern life to loyalties and beliefs that he merely associates broadly with Scott. Sir Walter Scott as cultural shorthand for corrupt southern ideology is depicted in Twain's own analysis of the Walter Scott disease: "[it] sets the world in love with dreams and phantoms; with decayed and swinish forms of religion; with decayed and degraded systems of government; with the sillinesses and emptinesses, sham grandeurs, sham gauds, and sham chivalries of a brainless and worthless long-vanished society. He did measureless harm; more real and lasting harm, perhaps, than any other individual that ever wrote."[83] Elsewhere Twain added to his list of objects and ideas associated with Scott by including duels, inflated speech, frilly architecture, "windy humbuggeries," and in general what he calls the "jejune romanticism" of the South. One of his most audacious claims is his statement that "Sir Walter has so large a hand in making southern character, as it existed before the war, that he is in great measure responsible for the war."[84] Such obvious exaggerations are not to be taken seriously, and yet at least two critics have written articles seriously debating Twain's charges against Scott.[85] But it is far more useful to realize that Twain is using Scott as a concise symbol for something much more complicated than a set of novels about the English and the Scots. Twain enlisted Scott as a metonymy for all things southern. He says as much when he most succinctly emphasizes the detrimental effect of Scott on "the character of the Southerner."[86] As such, as one critic puts it, "Mark Twain's indictment of Scott is more than an eccentric, hyperbolic flight of fancy, though it is that too. For all its absurdity it stands as a bold, imaginative, and sweeping criticism of Southerners and of Southern institutions." Another critic states that "Sir Walter Scott is the name of that discourse"—meaning, the "ongoing dominant discourse" of the South.[87]

Mark Twain took on this "dominant discourse" throughout his postbellum career, particularly in the major writings. We have already considered to some extent Twain's eventual rejection of southern versions of the true nature of the slaves and of African Americans in general. In more general terms, we should consider how Mark Twain vigorously championed views in many of his writings that contradicted major precepts of Lost Cause ideology.

The Idealized Home Front Combined with the Nationalistic/Cultural Difference

Twain portrays southern culture as fallen, corrupt, and swinish. The people of the South, typified by many of the characters in *Adventures of Huckleberry Finn* and *Pudd'nhead Wilson,* are lazy, unmotivated, unlearned, and credulous. Perhaps the most typical attitude of Mark Twain in his 1882 visit to the region, as documented in *Life on the Mississippi,* is grave and solemn disappointment. After his return from that trip, and when taking up the manuscript of *Huck Finn* once more in 1883, Twain began with a revealing and crucial critique of southern mob mentality: the shooting of Boggs and Colonel Sherburn's stinging invectives against the southern mob that is powerless against him.[88] In his discussion of *Connecticut Yankee,* James Cox has claimed that this book, "seen in a certain light, amounts to fighting the Civil War again."[89] Cox draws upon the work of earlier critics such as Henry Nash Smith, who considered the Arthurian kingdom, filled with chivalry, aristocracy, slavery, and superstition, merely "a projection of the benighted South." Similarly Smith considered Eseldorf (German for "Assville") from *No. 44, The Mysterious Stranger* to be much the same.[90] Twain constantly indicts southerners' honor and virtue in numerous other stories—so much so that the deconstruction of this idealized southern home front is one of the most prevalent of Twainian themes. For Twain, the South was becoming "one vast pigsty—a region of dirt, grime, and mud."[91] Far from embellishing the Lost Cause version of southern society, Twain became a convert to the northern civil religion as represented by his new homes in Connecticut and New York and his new friends like Twichell and Howells.

The Idealized Confederate Soldier

Perhaps here is where Twain's semiautobiographical tale "The Private History of a Campaign that Failed" fits most usefully. Although some critics have humorously concluded, like James Cox, that the story itself constitutes "a campaign that failed,"[92] there is much to commend in this essay. Stanley Mattson has raised some interesting questions about why the *Century* magazine even asked Twain to contribute the story, given the fact that their famous "Battles and Leaders of the Civil War" series was one of the hallmarks of solemn and serious war reminiscence: "It is precisely this staid and earnest quality of the entire series which lends particular interest in the patently maverick contribution . . . by an even more maverick contributor."[93]

Curiously, in the *Century*'s initial issue of the "Battles and Leaders" series in November 1884, Twain had published "An Adventure of Huckleberry Finn: With an Account of the Famous Grangerford-Shepherdson Feud." As Neil Schmitz says, readers of that issue "turned past Huck's account of Buck Grangerford's death . . . to find Warren Lee Goss's mud gritty 'Recollection of a Private'. . . . It put Mark Twain figuratively right in the thick of things, though up a tree, onlooking, *hors de combat*."[94] Twain's fictional feud, we learn from chapter 26 of *Life on the Mississippi*, had a real life basis in the tragic tale of the Darnells and Watsons, two families who faced off for many years, with much bloody violence for both families. As the narrator says, "Nobody don't know now what the first quarrel was about, it's so long ago." Nevertheless, the families "went on shooting each other, year in and year out—making a kind of religion out of it, you see."[95] In *Huckleberry Finn*, the feuding Grangerfords and Shepherdsons attend the same church, guns in tow, and listen to a sermon "about brotherly love, and such-like tiresomeness." Huck notes that "[the] men took their guns along, so did Buck, and kept them between their knees or stood them handy against the wall."[96] Arthur Pettit has documented many other connections between the feud in Twain's masterpiece and the actual feuds along the Mississippi that Twain encountered. In particular, he notes that the Darnell and Watson families, as in the novel, "[attended] the same church services. . . . 'Part of the church,' Clemens wrote in his river notebook, was 'in Tenn., part in Ky.,' with the aisle serving as neutral territory between the two armed camps."[97] The deadly feud of the novel causes the most shocking moment of Huck's journey—the horrific death of his pseudo-twin, Buck, discovered facedown in the river, shot to death. It is revealing that during the discussion of the feud in *Life on the Mississippi*, both at the chapter's beginning and just as the narrator begins describing the real-life feud, Twain invokes memories of the Civil War. This close association in Twain's mind suggests that the heavy ironies of the feuding "Christian" families can appropriately be extended to a consideration of the Civil War itself. In effect, both sides, as Lincoln noted in his Second Inaugural Address, "read the same Bible," and yet ironically the bloodshed and horror were the direct result. Twain's depictions of the feuding families thus relate directly to his critique of heroic renderings of the Civil War—especially those that "make a kind of religion out of it."

Mattson notes that of all the essays commissioned and published by the *Century* in its "Battles and Leaders" series, Twain's sketch "alone was cut from the subsequently published four-volume edition of the series."[98] One of the chief reasons, according to Mattson, is the fact that Twain's piece has a distinctly pacifistic tone. Twain describes the killing of the apparently Union soldier as "an epitome of war . . . all war must be just that—the killing of strangers against whom you feel no personal animosity; strangers whom, in other circumstances, you would help if you found them in trouble, and who would help you if you needed it."[99] In addition, Mattson suggests that the "conversion in 'The Private History' was immediate and complete."[100] Seeing the story as a sort of religious conversion tends to work against the postwar emphasis on reunion and toward an understanding of the war that celebrates the righteousness of one side against the wrongheadedness of the other. However, the conversion that Mattson has in mind is more fully blown: it is an utter rejection and denunciation of war in every respect. Of course, this rejection includes a view of war as a children's game, little more than an opportunity for showing off and an escape from the drudgery of everyday southern life. The fullness of Twain's ire against war is most forcefully represented in such later pieces as "The War Prayer," where the faithful beseech God to "help us to tear their soldiers to bloody shreds with our shells; Help us to cover their smiling fields with the pale forms of their patriot dead."[101] Moreover, in the context of the Lost Cause emphasis on the idealized Confederate soldier, Twain's war memoir counteracts a heroic view by depicting the soldiers, including himself, as "boys" who are on a lark. Curiously, in this way the tale takes on a bit of autobiographical confession: Twain is baring his own soul as well as uncovering the true nature of the vast majority of the boys who were forced into actually fighting the war. As Mattson concludes, the "Private History" "directs an arsenal of grape-shot at the entire concept of the glory of war."[102] But it goes beyond this general view. The "Private History" illustrates Twain's growing critique of the precepts of southern Lost Cause ideology and suggests that his consideration of the Civil War was much more pervasive than has previously been realized.

Sir Walter Scott was not the only metonymic representation of all things South. There was another: Tom Sawyer, especially as he is depicted in *Adventures of Huckleberry Finn.* For many years, critics have suggested that the novel breaks down upon Tom's appearance at the Phelps farm, a view that has spawned one of the longest running "feuds" in American critical history, featuring major names like T. S. Eliot and Lionel Trilling. Recently some critics have suggested a solution to this longstanding debate by understanding the Phelps farm episodes as metaphorical illustrations of the failure, and indeed even the comical nonsense, of Reconstruction.[103] If, as Arthur Pettit claims, Mark Twain generalized that "Northerners worked and Southerners dreamed,"[104] then Tom's dreaminess and playfulness, meaning his southernness, are what spoil Jim's liberation. Or perhaps a better verb for the effects of Tom's actions might be that they "complicated" Jim's release: "I should hope we can find a way that's a little more complicated than that, Huck Finn."[105] Tom wants to lengthen the process of emancipation indefinitely, as reflected in the coat of arms he designs with a motto that translates as "the more haste, the less speed."[106] In today's vernacular, Tom's motto might be restated this way: "What's the big hurry?" We have already noted that coats of arms are one of many things Twain associated explicitly with Walter Scott disease in *Life on the Mississippi.* More indicting is the sickeningly condescending motto, along with Tom's earlier statement that "I bet we can find a way that's twice as long. There ain't no hurry; let's keep on looking around." We can relate Tom's flippancy with some of Huck's observations of Tom:

> He said it was the best fun he ever had in his life, and the most intellectural; and said if he only could see his way to it we would keep it up all the rest of our lives and leave Jim to our children to get out; for he believed Jim would come to like it better and better the more he got used to

> it. He said that in that way it could be strung out to as much as eighty years, and would be the best time on record. And he said it would make us all celebrated that had a hand in it.[107]

The concept of "stringing it out" for eighty years foreshadows the critiques of "gradualism" by black leaders from W. E. B. DuBois to Martin Luther King Jr. And it seems both unpleasantly accurate and surprisingly prophetic in retrospect, given that the novel was composed approximately eighty years prior to the civil rights movement of the 1950s and '60s and published almost exactly eighty years prior to the two legislative victories that most historians believe signaled the turning of the tide: the Civil Rights Act of 1964 and the Voting Rights Act of 1965. Thus Jim's subservient relation to Tom "reflects that of the Negro in the Reconstruction, free at last and thoroughly impotent, the object of devious schemes and a hapless victim of constant brutality."[108]

We might compare this archly sardonic reading of Tom Sawyer with another, later Tom: Tom Driscoll from *Pudd'nhead Wilson.* In a passage that Twain wrote for *Pudd'nhead Wilson* but later deleted, he has Tom consider the true source of his own despair: "That which was high came from either blood, & was the monopoly of neither color; but that which was base was the white blood in him debased by the brutalizing effects of a . . . long-drawn heredity of slave-owning, with the habit of abuse which the possession of irresponsible power always creates & perpetuates, by a law of human nature."[109] As Shelley Fisher Fishkin notes, here Twain was willing to go further than any other white writers of the time "in his rejection of a hierarchy of color."[110] Twain's reference to the "brutalizing effects" of the slave system hearken back to antebellum writers who made similar arguments, including Harriet Beecher Stowe and Frederick Douglass. His claim that it was "the habit of abuse which the possession of irresponsible power always creates & perpetuates," is a fine description of Tom Sawyer's egotistical behavior in the final stages of *Adventures of Huckleberry Finn.* Moreover, this observation anticipates the far more detailed expressions of the idea in W. E. B. DuBois's masterwork *The Souls of Black Folks,* which would appear less than a decade after *Pudd'nhead Wilson.* There DuBois's descriptions of how southern blacks had been overtaken and re-enslaved by the ostensibly good intentions of Reconstruction sound very much like Jim's treatment at the hands of Tom Sawyer:

> [The] regular civil courts tended to become solely institutions for perpetuating the slavery of blacks. Almost every law and method ingenuity could devise was employed by legislatures to reduce the Negroes to serfdom,—to make them slaves to the State. . . . The crop-lien system which is depopulating the South is not simply the result of shiftlessness on the part of Negroes, but is also the result of cunningly devised laws as to mortgage, liens, and misdemeanors, which can be made by conscienceless men to entrap and snare the unwary until escape is impossible. . . . [Reconciliation] between the North and South . . . ought to be a source of deep congratulation to all . . . but if that reconciliation is to be marked by the industrial slavery and civic death of those same black men, with permanent legislation into a position of inferiority, then those black men, if they are really men, are called upon by every consideration of patriotism and loyalty to oppose such a course.[111]

Such debasement of black Americans is frequently chastised in Mark Twain's writings, but nowhere is it so powerfully illustrated as in Tom Sawyer's "humorous" treatment of poor old Jim. In effect, as James Cox puts it, the "joke" of *Adventures of Huckleberry Finn* entails the judgment against the morality Tom Sawyer represents and by extension the morality of what became the Jim Crow South: "For when Tom proclaims to the assembled throng who have witnessed his performance that Jim 'is as free as any cretur that walks this earth,' he is an exposed embodiment of the complacent moral sentiment on which the reader has relied throughout the book. And to the extent the reader has indulged the complacency he will be disturbed by the ending." Cox gets it right when he says that in writing his masterpiece, "Mark Twain reached the limits of his humor, which is to say he reached the threshold of his disillusion."[112] Thus does this brand of humor mask Twain's (and presumably his reader's) utter despair and disillusion.

Mark Twain forever felt the need to expose complacent moral belief and unholiness dressed up as authority. Accordingly such a reading helps rescue the ending of what many have considered "two-thirds" of the Great American Novel. More to the point, Tom's reappearance after all that Huck and Jim have been through would seem to indicate the bondage that remains in the American South even twenty years after the war ended. In that regard, Tom's reappearance is historically required. The dreams of the South, mythologized as the Lost Cause and associated in Twain's writings with Walter Scott and Tom Sawyer, have proven unworkable and ultimately deeply violent against African Americans. The violence may in the future even victimize the likes of Tom, as Twain suggests in the brief exchange between Huck and the doctor after Tom is shot:

> "How'd you say he got shot?"
> "He had a dream," I says, "and it shot him."
> "Singular dream," he says.[113]

If it is true, as historian Jeffry Wert has argued, that by "the first decade of the twentieth century, the basic elements of the Lost Cause argument had become entrenched in interpretations of the war,"[114] then it is now possible to see much of Twain's most serious writing and speaking to be opposed to that entrenched, "singular dream." Fittingly one of the major pieces that Twain worked on just as the new century was beginning was the unfinished novel *Which Was It?*, in which the slave Jasper purchases his freedom, only to be re-enslaved by his master after his bill of sale is destroyed. Twain explains that the mistreatments that Jasper faced "embitter him against the whole white race. That hate has grown in vindictiveness since, year by year."[115] This theme of re-enslavement and bitterness was on Twain's mind at the very moment that DuBois was completing work on his revolutionary collection of essays, *The Souls of Black Folk*. For both Twain and DuBois, exposing the "singular dream" of the South was a shared preoccupation of their greatest writing.

At Carnegie Hall on February 11, 1901, Mark Twain gave a speech entitled "On Lincoln's Birthday." The purpose of this event was the raising of funds for Lincoln Memorial University, a new college for African Americans. Such an event in honor of the college's namesake denotes the fact that it was an occasion of high civil religion. Twain appeared onstage with Colonel Henry Watterson, a former officer in the Confederate Army, whom he called a "reconstructed rebel." In this speech, Twain insists on foregrounding his own southernness along with Watterson's, as he had done in the various versions of his tale of service that were published as narratives or presented as speeches prior to 1901. It is one of Twain's lengthiest renditions of the religious elements of the Civil War itself, echoing passages from Lincoln's key speeches and invoking directly Lincoln's Gettysburg Address—a speech that Twain had once called "probably the finest prose passage that exists in the English language."[116]:

> For the hearts of the whole nation, North and South, were in the war. We of the South were not ashamed; for, like the men of the North, we were fighting for flags we loved; and when men fight for these things, and under these convictions, with nothing sordid to tarnish their cause, that cause is holy, the blood spilled for it is sacred, the life that is laid down for it is consecrated. . . .
>
> North and South we put our hearts into that colossal struggle, and out of it came the blessed fulfillment of the prophecy of the immortal Gettysburg speech which said: "We here highly resolve that these dead shall not have died in vain; that this nation, under God, shall have a new birth of freedom; and that a government of the people, by the people, and for the people shall not perish from the earth."[117]

Twain agrees here with crucial aspects of reunion discourse, as he equates all soldiers in terms of commitment and sacrifice, of putting their "hearts" fully into it. Both sides, he says, loved their "flags"—a patriotic comment that suggests perhaps a blind allegiance, such as powerfully symbolized in the carrying of the flag in Stephen Crane's *The Red Badge of Courage.* Religious language is invoked especially at the end of the first section and is even presented in the three-fold manner that Lincoln was so fond of ("that cause is holy, the blood spilled for it is sacred, the life that is laid down for it is consecrated"). And Twain directly quotes Lincoln's call to the entire nation to remember the mission of America and not allow the blood of the war to have been spilled in vain; rather, the war must issue in a "new birth," and the government of the Union must go forth into perpetuity.

In the final passage of the speech, Twain makes clear a desire to showcase his supposed former allegiance with the southern cause and his reliance on reunion discourse even more directly:

> The old wounds are healed; you and we are brothers again; you testify by honoring two of us, once soldiers of the Lost Cause and foes of your great and good leader—with the privilege of assisting here; and we testify it by laying our honest homage at the feet of Abraham Lincoln and in forgetting that you of the North and we of the South were ever enemies, and remembering only that we are now indistinguishably fused together and namable by one common great name—Americans.

Here Twain names directly the Lost Cause as his former allegiance and draws most obviously on the desire for reunion that marked postwar rhetoric. His self-identification as a Confederate plays fast and loose with the historical reality, but, again, confessing former ties with the Lost Cause mythos serves the rhetorical purpose of positioning himself as a convert. Indeed, in the terms given here, the entire speech becomes in the closing sentences an elaborate form of testimony. For Twain, the fact that two former southern rebels, both of whom were ostensibly Confederate officers, are honored on this solemn occasion commemorating the greatest of Union saints testifies to reconciliation and reunion. Furthermore Twain states that "we [Southerners] testify it" by genuflecting to the memory of Lincoln. The "it" in this case must surely be reunion and reconciliation. "It," says Twain, has been fully achieved—and this occasion is emblematic of that achievement. As Twain put it in an 1887 speech to Union veterans, "There is no North, no South any more."[118]

Although Twain did not often speak or write about Lincoln, this speech and other extant remarks make clear that he held high praise for this patron saint of Unionist nationalism. In fact, Twain's remarks supporting attempts to preserve Lincoln's Kentucky birthplace in 1907 contain a certain autobiographical ring:

> If the Union was to be saved, it had to be a man of such an origin that should save it. No wintry New England Brahmin could have done it, or any torrid cotton planter, regarding the distant Yankee as a species of obnoxious foreigner. It needed a man of the border, where civil war

> meant the grapple of brother and brother and disunion a raw and gaping wound. It needed one who knew slavery not from books only, but as a living thing, knew the good that was mixed with its evil, and knew the evil not merely as it affected the negroes, but in its hardly less baneful influence upon the poor whites. It needed one who knew how human all the parties to the quarrel were, how much alike they were at bottom, who saw them all reflected in himself, and felt their dissensions like the tearing apart of his own soul. When the war came Georgia sent an army in gray and Massachusetts an army in blue, but Kentucky raised armies for both sides. And this man, sprung from Southern poor whites, born on a Kentucky farm and transplanted to an Illinois village, this man, in whose heart knowledge and charity had left no room for malice, was marked by Providence as the one to "bind up the Nation's wounds."[119]

Twain shows here a familiarity with Lincolnian phrasing and style, including lines like "when the war came," the single word "malice," and the ending quotation, all of which echo the Second Inaugural Address. The statement clearly supports a Unionist view and brilliantly considers the position of a man like Lincoln as a "man of the border"—very much as Twain himself was. Like Kentucky, Missouri also raised armies for both sides; for people of these states, the war literally often meant "brother grappling with brother." Lincoln is also like Twain himself insofar as both "knew slavery not from books only, but as a living thing." Unfortunately here Twain slips briefly into Lost Cause mode in stating that Lincoln also knew "the good that was mixed with [slavery's] evil." Overall, this brief paean displays Twain's sincere regard for the mainstream view of Lincoln as the leader who through providence was able to save the Union. As such, it was a very predictable theological reflection on the war—especially in the period immediately after the war ended and Lincoln was murdered.

But Twain's speech also reveals an ambivalence that he shared with Lincoln as a "man of the border." Indeed it was precisely their status as liminal figures that allowed both Lincoln and Twain to see so deeply into the values and beliefs of both sides—and thus to assure the binding of the "Nation's wounds." The phrase "man of the border" also suggests the massive changes taking place in approaches to epistemology in American religion, changes that were exacerbated by the events of the

Civil War. Ideas of a providential American civil religion were tested to the limits by the sheer horror and irrationality of events like the battle of Fredericksburg, for example, where thousands of Union troops were ordered to cross a temporary bridge on the Rappahannock River into the town of Fredericksburg while Confederate troops fired at will into their ranks. Thirteen thousand Union troops died in that slaughter, to no apparent purpose. Such atrocities called into question convictions that had previously seemed unassailable. Certainty seemed to breed violence—and so certainty must be abandoned. Christian prayers in support of either side, in the context of horrific eyewitness accounts of the butchery at Fredericksburg, Antietam, or Gettysburg, seemed to become pagan acts of moral degeneracy in retrospect. The war's ramifications for religious belief have been staggeringly overlooked, but they contributed to the spiritual crisis of the period by contributing to an epistemological shift characterized more by doubt than certainty.[120] A growing atmosphere of doubt and confusion ultimately insured that the religious meaning of Abraham Lincoln, and of the Civil War, would need to go much deeper than most preachers had taken it in their simple analyses in the weeks and months after Lincoln's assassination in 1865. Mark Twain, along with many other northern intellectuals, somehow knew this intuitively. And Abraham Lincoln, as it turned out, was the great articulator of a newer, more nuanced version of the religious implications of the war. His meditations contained theological reflections far more subtle and profound than those of practically any other commentator, and they reflected prophetically the massive changes in social belief that would emerge in the war's great wake.

In this emerging epistemological context, a "man of the border" becomes one who, like William James a few years later, is convinced that "certainty was moral death."[121] The confusion, indecisiveness, and finally agnosticism of the post–Civil War era is discernible in seed form in Lincoln's almost sublime expressions in his Second Inaugural Address, although it is not often viewed in this manner. Lincoln makes three main observations there that signal this rapid shift. First, Lincoln repeats a view that was first stated in the Gettysburg Address: the victors must have Christian charity for the defeated foe. Such self-emptying love must resist sinister forms of self-righteousness, which derive from moral certainty. This is even more profound given the fact that at the time of the Second Inaugural's delivery, the war had not actually come to its conclusion. Second, Lincoln refrained from claiming the moral high ground for the Union victors alone. He did not take the opportunity to denounce the South and its soldiers or leaders, and he did not openly celebrate the righteousness of the Union. Finally, and perhaps most significantly, Lincoln articulated a progressively modern view of the providence of God as mysterious and obscure. Lincoln emphasized to his listeners his firm belief that the will of God is not easily discerned and is often affected by contingencies and human stupidity. While most commentators in the North spoke confidently about the ways of God in the aftermath of the war, Lincoln injected a strong note of modern uncertainty and, in the end, humility before a great and awesome God who is very difficult for mankind to size up.[122] As such, Lincoln's analysis anticipated major shifts in postbellum thinking. One might say that his brand of agnosticism was of a decidedly theistic brand—a notion that in the twenty-first century must sound like a contradiction. Lincoln believed in God, but like many deists of the nineteenth century, he had serious reservations about trying to read God's mind with any confidence.

Meanwhile, the more popular expositors of the war, like Henry Ward Beecher, Horace Bushnell, and Joseph Twichell, drew upon Lincoln when he fit their particular viewpoints of confidence and American exceptionalism. But they somehow missed the more progressive and mystical nuggets of wisdom that Lincoln offered—while the more agnostically inclined picked right up on those themes. Freethinking intellectuals like Mark Twain were drawn powerfully to Lincoln's thought for its nuanced questioning of American exceptionalism and its disavowal of self-righteousness or a clear understanding of God's will in the affairs of man. These ideas explain why Lincoln was also such a hero to both Robert Ingersoll and Walt Whitman, "the two defining voices of the golden age of freethought."[123] All seemed to understand intuitively what the historian Mark Noll has recently stated: "the Civil War proved to be the climax, but also the exhaustion, of the synthesis of common sense, republicanism, and evangelical Christianity" in America, and Lincoln was the prophetic voice signaling its demise. Lincoln was one of the very few clarion voices who recognized how the Civil War had called into question America's brazen confidence in a "clear-eyed moral certainty about God and His will."[124] Mark Twain's strong affinity with Lincoln was based on more than their shared status as natives of the border states of Kentucky and Missouri. He perceived correctly Lincoln's "borderline" status as both a believer of God and a doubter of man's ability to conceptualize or describe God.

Twain's observations of Lincoln emphasized conflict and uncertainty—a vague in-betweenness—an emphasis that would come to predominate the spiritual conflict in America after the Civil War. Twain's focus is remarkably similar to Nathaniel Hawthorne's famous analysis of his friend Herman Melville's conflicted soul, written in 1858:

> Melville, as he always does, began to reason of Providence and futurity, and of everything that lies beyond human ken, and informed me that he had 'pretty much made up his mind to be annihilated'; but still he does not seem to rest in that anticipation; and, I think, will never rest until he gets hold of a definite belief. . . . He can neither believe, nor be comfortable in his unbelief; and he is too honest and courageous not to try to do one or the other.[125]

Tellingly, in his magisterial biography, Allen C. Guelzo compared Melville's anxieties with Lincoln's spiritual confusion: "Lincoln was haunted by the sense of his own foreordained inability to believe or to be content in his unbelief. . . . He thought of himself as an 'accidental instrument' of providence and not a beloved son. . . . Like Herman Melville, Lincoln could 'neither believe nor be comfortable in his unbelief.' "[126] According to Guelzo, few commentators have "ever penetrated to the real heart of Lincoln's personal religious anguish, the deep sense of helplessness before a distant and implacable Judge who revealed himself only through crisis and death."[127]

In his brief comments on Lincoln, Twain memorably and subtly captured a bit of this anguish. The irony, of course, is that much the same could be said about Twain: what he wrote about Lincoln as "man of the border" is largely true for himself. Twain's analysis of Lincoln's spiritual struggles, like Hawthorne's comments on Melville, can thus be read as a revealing autobiographical reflection. But it is also a striking comment about the culture in general and about the Civil War as the transitional metaphysical event. As Andrew Delbanco puts it, "The Civil War was the great divide between a culture of faith and a culture of doubt. It began on both sides as a resurgence of mass belief, and ended as the last rally of a dying patient. . . . The Civil War may have been America's greatest religious revival, but it was also our spiritual suicide."[128] Perhaps the metaphor of a national religious suicide is too strong. But at the very least, perhaps we can agree that in the years after the Civil War, America as a religious nation was fast becoming, like Melville, a nation that could neither believe nor be comfortable in its unbelief. One might say that America became a "nation of the border." Twain signals his awareness that Lincoln was the key transitional figure in the emergence of this more modern and more nearly agnostic temperament toward God and providence by calling him a "man of the border." As such, Twain was among the first to recognize the important role that Lincoln played in America's ongoing spiritual crisis.

But besides these elements of doubt and uncertainty, both Lincoln and Twain should be remembered as prophets of an American hopefulness that initially might appear contradictory to agnostic doubt. Although William Dean Howells's famous comments are rarely understood in this sense, his reference to his good friend as the "Lincoln of our literature" suggests this metaphysical contradiction. Howells stated that Mark Twain possessed "the depths of a nature whose tragical seriousness broke in the laughter which the unwise took for the whole of him. . . . Clemens was sole, incomparable, the Lincoln of our literature."[129] The key is the recognition of a "tragical seriousness" that Howells calls the true source of Twain's comedy. Much the same might be said of Lincoln, a man known to have a rare humor. Howells's concept here of a "tragical seriousness" is similar to what Cornel West has recently described as a "tragicomic commitment to hope." According to West, this is "the ability to laugh and retain a sense of life's joy—to preserve hope even while staring in the face of hate and hypocrisy—as against falling into the nihilism of paralyzing despair."[130] Tragicomic hope must join a sense of joyful optimism with a sense of oppressive despair. Its crucial center is humor, but Howells reminds us that it is "unwise" to stop there. West's formulation of a "tragicomic commitment to hope" captures well this further aspect of the metaphysical view of the world that Twain shared with Lincoln. Poised between unquestioning faith and unquestioning doubt, both were cosmic thinkers somewhat ahead of their times. And both insisted on preserving hope for a better future—despite the constant threats of hate, hypocrisy, and suffering.

6

Mark Twain's American Adam

Humor as Hope and Apocalypse

In the fall of 1879, Mark Twain enlisted many of the most prominent members of Elmira society into a preposterous scheme to erect a memorial to Adam, "the Father of the Human Race," in their town. A committee, called the "Adam Monument Association of Elmira," was appointed to select a sculptor. Thomas K. Beecher, the prominent local minister, was chosen as president. This association went so far as to have letterhead produced; in their zeal they proclaimed, "The monument will rise. It only awaits approval of the model."[1] In his essay entitled "A Monument to Adam," which he published many years afterward, Twain recalled some of the reasons for his idea:

> Darwin's *Descent of Man* had been in print five or six years, and the storm of indignation raised by it was still raging in pulpits and periodicals. In tracing the genesis of the human race back to its sources, Mr. Darwin had left Adam out altogether. . . . Jesting with Mr. Beecher and other friends of Elmira, I said there seemed to be a likelihood that the world would discard Adam and accept the monkey, and that in the course of time Adam's very name would be forgotten in the earth; therefore this calamity ought to be averted; a monument would accomplish this. . . . People would come from every corner of the globe and stop off to look at it, no tour of the world would be complete that left out Adam's monu-

> ment. Elmira would be a Mecca; there would be pilgrim ships at pilgrim rates, pilgrim specials on the continent's railways; libraries would be written about the monument, every tourist would kodak it.[2]

Why this puzzling and rather irreverent focus on Adam? As the Gilded Age got fully under way after the Civil War's end, the fervid evangelical beliefs about human nature were forced to take new directions. Christianity had to evolve for several reasons, none more urgent than the emergence of scientific and intellectual movements that scrutinized the notions of humankind made in the image of God and the Bible as the holy, infallible, and authenticating expression of God. Simultaneously, educated Americans were being told by the "experts" that there was nothing particularly sacred or supernatural about either their Bible or their own species.

The sustained attacks upon biblical belief accelerated the spiritual crisis that coincided with Mark Twain's near obsession with the biblical Adam. The German higher criticism had the most radical effect on the way the Bible was "read" and understood in the latter half of the nineteenth century. But Twain's passage on Adam quoted above becomes notable for its overt connection of German criticism with Charles Darwin's evolutionary theories, which were then becoming popularly espoused in North America. Twain's mention of a specific volume, *The Descent of Man* (1871), is particularly relevant, for it is there that Darwin took up the problem of human origins. Darwin's explicit claim that humans are directly related to the animal kingdom was a far cry from traditional explanations of the special creation of human beings through Adam and Eve. Twain's memory of a "storm of indignation" being raised is accurate testimony to the loud public cries surrounding Darwinian pronouncements of the day. The famous Presbyterian leader Charles Hodge, for example, published his response *What is Darwinism?* in 1874 and answered the titular question quite clearly: "it is atheism." Perhaps the most popular critic of Darwin for evangelicals of this period was T. DeWitt Talmage, who opined in his diatribe of 1886, *Live Coals:* "I tell you plainly, if your father was a muskrat and your mother an opossum, and your great aunt a kangaroo, and the toads and the snapping turtle were your illustrious predecessors, my father was God."[3]

Darwinism posed a threat that would have serious repercussions—a threat of which Twain was well aware.

The simultaneous rise of modern biblical criticism—with its roots in Germany of the late eighteenth and early to mid-nineteenth centuries—began to influence the work of many American theologians. During Twain's adulthood, "scholars began to use literary analysis, archaeological discoveries, and comparative linguistics to gain a better understanding of the Old Testament."[4] The threat posed by this style of criticism was largely historical. It challenged and finally dismissed the "quaint" notion that a biblical figure such as Adam ever existed in the first place. Adam, for the biblical critics, was reduced to the level of metaphor or eponym. Again Talmage became the most well-known conservative spokesperson for the evangelicals on a number of issues related to biblical criticism's threat to orthodox Christianity. His most famous sermon, "The Splendors of Orthodoxy," delivered hundreds of times all over the country, was essentially a lengthy jeremiad aimed at the "advanced thinkers" who sought to destroy simple faith in God's word.[5] Once again this movement opposed to an historical understanding of the Bible was familiar to Mark Twain. In fact his veritable obsession with biblical figures, including primarily Adam, can be understood as an outgrowth of his engagement with the very issues being raised by biblical critics.

Moreover, given the extreme affinity that biblical Christianity had with the founding and the nurturing of a peculiarly American ideology, the simultaneous attacks of Darwinism and of the German higher criticism implicitly advanced criticisms against America's civil religion. Due to Christianity's close allegiance with political rhetoric throughout American history, any attack on the faith implicitly questions American political ideology. Key aspects of this ideology were famously captured by R. W. B. Lewis, who romantically described the "American Adam" as "an individual emancipated from history, happily bereft of ancestry, untouched and undefiled by the usual inheritances of family and race; an individual standing alone, self-reliant and self-propelling, ready to confront whatever awaited him with the aid of his own unique and inherent resources." In this version of the American myth, Adam is the romantic individual venturing out into the great unknown armed with grand resources and virtues: "His moral position was prior to experience, and in his very newness he was fundamentally innocent."[6] Mark Twain was strongly drawn to the cultural construct of the American Adam, utilizing it repeatedly in his fiction. Twain reveled in the notion that one might be "emancipated from history," as Huck appears to be when lighting out for the territory at the end of *Adventures of Huckleberry Finn.* Indeed even in Twain's quasi-autobiographical writings like *Roughing It* and *Life on the Mississippi,* he often depicts himself as the romantic, "self-reliant and self-propelling" American Adam. This view of the American Adam can be expanded to include other features of what has been variously called the American myth, the American Dream, and Yankee ingenuity. The story of the genesis of the American myth has been told frequently, perhaps most famously by the so-called "cold war critics" of the 1950s and '60s, a group that included (besides Lewis) critics like Henry Nash Smith, Perry Miller, and Leo Marx. Their versions of American myth included features that have become the keynotes of discussion about the very idea of America: the idea of progress, the self-reliance of the American individual, the power of the natural landscape, and the pastoral mode.

To summarize, American myth presented a highly romantic version of the American pioneer spirit, and Twain often participated in its construction. Twain's affinities with the sentimental myth of the American Adam are noticeable in many of his works. Stanley Brodwin once called *The Adventures of Tom Sawyer* (1876) an "Edenic, hymnal fairy tale . . . another version of the natural in the world of youth clinging to and playing out its instincts and need for adventure." Brodwin described the naturalness of its two main characters, Tom and Huck, as "profoundly Adamic." According to Brodwin, for Twain, youth is aligned with nature and an Edenic state of grace; yet the "state of grace that is youth cannot endure" because Tom and Huck will eventually succumb to the influence of civilization and become adults.[7] In this sense, civilization and adulthood are equated with man's fall from grace. (Brodwin seemed to miss the novel's large doses of murder, mayhem, darkness, thunder, lightning, ghosts, and outlaws that make this "Edenic" novel a profoundly dark novel as well). Numerous other critics have seen in much of Twain's more nostalgic and sentimentalized renditions of his childhood close connections with the Adamic stories of the book of

Genesis. As Kenneth Lynn noted, Twain almost idolized "the pleasant valley of childhood," the "Happy Valley of unspoiled youth and crystal-clear impressions which so captured the imagination of the post-Civil War generation." Twain once wrote, for instance, that remembering Hannibal was like "bathing in the Fountain of Youth."[8]

In Twain's mind (and more importantly in American culture) there was sufficient power inherent in this positive version of Adam to create what I would like to call an overarching "Adam ideology." This ideology essentially combined all of these positive features of the American Adam—typified by innocence and newness, as Lewis described it, but also including numerous other features of the regnant American myth—to form a powerful symbolic association. This Adam ideology became for Mark Twain a shorthand metonymy for the dominant religious position of the post–Civil War period with regard to the nature of man. This view consisted of a romantic position in its mildest form called Arminianism, and in its most extreme form, known in theological terms as Pelagianism.[9] The Adam ideology, rapidly becoming the mainstream view of the American church, signifies a romantic vision of mankind as inherently good and ultimately perfectible—an Arminianism at the heart of Social Christianity and the Social Gospel movements. Adam provided Twain with a powerful trope through which he could reinterpret his attitudes about God, good and evil, belief and skepticism, and indeed the theological nature of humor inherent in the very idea of a fallen world. Adam also helped Twain proclaim, examine, and reinterpret his culture's dualistic attitudes toward mankind in general. Twain's obsession with Adam can also be understood generally as his obsession with the darkness and sinfulness of humanity. Specifically, his use of Adam constituted an engagement in the religious controversy between classic Calvinism and an emergent Arminianism/Pelagianism, a controversy that spanned the entire century and beyond.

William Pellowe's analysis of Mark Twain's long engagement with issues related to theology and ecclesiology still provides refreshing insight nearly sixty years after its first publication. Pellowe notes for example Twain's "insistence within him for some solution to the problem of physical suffering and moral evil." In his search for evidence regarding this view, Pellowe contacted many of the surviving acquaintances and family members for their anecdotes or memories. He received a response from Mrs. Charles Ives (Joe and Harmony Twichell's daughter) dated October 13, 1945:

> I don't feel he was an atheist—how could he have got so enraged at the Deity if he thought there was nothing there! . . . the other day [my sister] reminded me of his saying or writing to my father at the time of Jean's death, "What have I lost! What has Jean gained!"—an illuminating sentence. . . . I feel that Mark Twain was a very sensitive, tenderhearted man who could not solve the problem of Pain in the world—none of us can—and who couldn't reconcile it with the idea of a loving Father in Heaven, and couldn't or wouldn't brace his faith for it. As I remember, this is the burden of his later letters to my father.[10]

These reminiscences invoke what many philosophers and theologians consider to be the single most difficult apologetic issue that must be addressed by any thinking person with regard to the Christian religion: the "problem of Pain." It is the attempt to answer the question of why there is evil, injustice, and intense pain in a world that is supposedly created and managed by a benevolent God. If there is a God, how can we explain chronic illness and premature death; the abuse and murder of innocent children; the seemingly random violence of so-called acts of God such as tornadoes, volcanoes, and earthquakes; or the systematic brutalization of entire people groups such as the harassment of African Americans under Jim Crow or the mass murder of Jews under the Nazi regime? The Bible includes many sustained meditations on the problem of pain, such as the Old Testament books of Job and Ecclesiastes; the various considerations of suffering, captivity, and estrangement recorded by the Old Testament prophets; the New Testament's vast coverage of the passion sequence of Christ; the several theological discussions in such letters as those of Paul and James; and the vision of the persecuted church in Revelation. Indeed pain and suffering can be said to constitute the heart of the biblical account of human life.

We might compare Mrs. Ives's comments above (he "was a very sensitive, tenderhearted man who could not solve the problem of Pain in the world") with those her father, the Reverend Joseph Twichell, made at the memorial service for Twain at Carnegie Hall: "[Mark Twain] was ever profoundly affected with the feeling of the pathos of life. Contemplating its heritage of inevitable pain and tears, he would question if to any one it was a good gift. 'Would you,' he demanded of me once—'would you, as a kind-hearted man, start the human race? Would you now?' "[11] Twichell here is remembering Twain's remarks during his prolonged period of grief in the final decade of his life, when his beloved daughter Susy, and then his wife Livy, passed away. The grief was compounded by financial failure, his own ill health, and numerous other sources of irritation (such as the Roosevelt administration).

Twain's final years are often remembered as a time of great pain, of course, but rarely is this pain considered from a theological position. But the problem of pain constitutes arguably the most devastating critique of Christianity as a system of thought, and Twain was a familiar of it in both theory and practice. The problem of pain also bears an intriguing connection with a much later observation by one of the strongest critics of American realism, Amy Kaplan, who has stated that "realistic novels have trouble ending because they pose problems they cannot solve, problems that stem from their attempt to imagine and contain social change."[12] The connection comes in the common awareness of the inability of writers like Mark Twain to solve certain problems—including the notoriously difficult problem of pain. In this sense, perhaps Kaplan's idea might be slightly altered to say that realistic lives (like Twain's) have trouble ending as well. The problem of pain becomes insoluble, without supernatural assistance. In addition, Pellowe has discussed another aspect of the problem of pain that has particular relevance for the study of nineteenth-century theology and the Social Gospel. The Christian liberalism that flowered to unprecedented degrees after the Civil War should be associated broadly with a liberation of mind and an embrace of new and different ideas. Perhaps the most important new idea had to do with the nature of mankind itself. The nineteenth century saw a radical move from the more pessimistic view of Calvinism to a much more romantic view associated broadly with the human-centered theology of liberal Christianity. However, as theologians from Horace Bushnell onward focused on God's love as opposed to justice, the problem of pain becomes increasingly intolerable.[13] That is, when we see God more and more as primarily a being of love and mercy, pain and suffering become less and less acceptable or logically supportable. The love element in the teaching of the Social Gospel, including that of the preachers closest to Twain, such as Joe Twichell and Thomas Beecher, emphasized the father heart of God and the true brotherhood of man. But a romanticized version of mankind's inherent goodness leads to all kinds of devastating disappointments when the sad details of ethical reality are brought into the equation. In this context, the problem of pain is greatly aggravated. More theologically speaking, liberalism tended heavily toward a Pelagian view of humanity, with its emphasis on man's freedom and natural tendency toward altruistic and ethical action. The name derives from Pelagius, the fourth-century monk who denied original sin and claimed perfect freedom for human beings. Instead of focusing on man's sinful nature due to the Fall, as traditional Calvinists might, liberal theologians blamed faulty child-rearing, poor ethical and moral training, or lack of social reform as the fundamental causes of human error. They argued for the autonomous and nearly godlike nature of the human spirit.

The most obvious outgrowth of this theological shift, and the most important religious movement of the second half of the nineteenth century in America, emerged when Protestant and Catholic leaders began to take seriously both the traumatic aftermath of the Civil War's immense violence and the severe problems arising within urban communities of the 1870s and '80s, including urban decay in slum areas, the rising tensions between labor and capital, rising crime rates, alcoholism, prostitution, and homelessness. Leaders of the Social Christianity movement responded by asserting the possibility that through diligent moral effort, Christians might help reform American political and economic institutions for the betterment of all, especially the oppressed. Adherents to the Social Gospel, believing the Kingdom of God to be at work within human communities through believers, strove for perfection through a compassionate and just service to those in need. As such, the Social Gospel can be understood, to some extent, as an outgrowth of the emerging Pelagian movement of Christian belief and ethics. Views of the nature of mankind turned from the realism of Calvin to the more sentimentalized romanticism associated in an earlier period with the likes of Emerson and the Transcendentalists. Among the many key figures of this movement were Henry Ward Beecher, Josiah Strong, and Phillips Brooks—all of whom, more or less, preached visions of a Christianized America of abundance, progress, civil religion, and vaguely social Darwinistic theories of race and the superiority of Anglo-Saxons and the American nation. It is this array of mythic ideals, religious in their most pristine versions, that form the core of what I am calling the Adam ideology—and all of these, roughly speaking, can be associated with the broad theological category of Pelagianism, insofar as they reject negative portrayals of human nature in favor of mankind's purity, goodness, and godlikeness. To say the least, this dramatic new vision of the human species flew in the face of a more traditional, deterministic Calvinism. The inner core of the rising American Adam ideology reflected a profound shift within Christian belief of the period, a decisive break with the view of Calvinistic depravity in favor of a Pelagian perfectionism. Clearly the demythologization of the biblical Adam, in combination with the Darwinian notion of the progress of animal species, greatly helped to undercut the possibility of belief in an act of original sin, except in only the most ethereal and symbolic ways.

Mark Twain was aware of and interested in the oppositional relationship between the biblical Adam and the American Adam. Joe Twichell was a well-read source of information on the theological issues involved, as were the many other members of the Monday Evening Club in Hartford. Twain noted and frequently commented on the tension between the newly emerging romantic view of mankind, characterized by the Adam ideology and the religious Pelagianism of the Social Gospel, and his growing conviction about what he more and more frequently referred to as the "damned human race." During the period in which he proposed the Adam monument, he began writing fiction employing characters from the Genesis account, including the first appearance of Adam as protagonist in "Adam's Expulsion" (1877), and he also referred to the biblical hero in speeches, as in his "On Adam" (1883). Among other things, Twain commonly associated the biblical Adam with both hope and memory, perfection and fallenness. Thus Adam is a figure of profound ambivalence, signaling Twain's unwillingness to assign him merely romantic interpretations: "to him we owe the two things which are most precious—life, and death. Life, which the young, the hopeful, the undefeated hold above all wealth and all honors; and death, the refuge, the solace, the best and kindliest and most prized friend and benefactor of the erring."[14]

It seems clear, then, that Twain's use of Adam involved him in the cultural discussion about these crucial theological issues. As stated earlier, Twain often found himself mildly defending a Pelagian view of man's nature, especially insofar as the myth of American progress is concerned. And yet Twain also frequently made brutal assaults on just such romantic ideologies. This tension became increasingly evident as he got older. While Huck may appear "emancipated" at the end of *Adventures of Huckleberry Finn,* American ideology as embodied in Tom is quite belligerently opposed to another important emancipation—that of the slaves, as incarnated in Jim. In *Life on the Mississippi,* the wiser the cub pilot gets, the more he realizes that he is far from self-propelling: in fact, he is very much dependent on the great brown river god to be transported, a powerful force he is unable to control or even understand. And in *A Connecticut Yankee in King Arthur's Court,* Twain questions the premises of American progress, including the Social Gospel's engagement with human misery and oppression, as deeply flawed due to the inherently evil nature of mankind. Many readers often understand *Connecticut Yankee* as a satire of English romanticism and Victorianism, class systems, and religious resistance to social progress. But *Connecticut Yankee* can also serve as a parable against the dangers of sustaining an inflated romantic view of mankind and thus again places Twain in the cultural conversations of mankind's theological nature. Those conversations interrogated the enterprise of American imperialism, debates that involved deeply held religious views of everything from America's sense of mission to the understanding of and sympathy for "uncivilized" peoples. Twain's involvement with anti-imperialism was a major theme for thirty years prior to the official founding of the Anti-Imperialist League in 1898, at which time his strong sentiments issued in severe political blasts excoriating what he called the "silent colossal National Lie" of American myth and ideology.[15] Ultimately, as Twain entered the final years of his life in the newly arrived twentieth century, his overall vision of mankind became little more than a bitter denunciation of humanity's ignorance, selfishness, and violence.

While some are content to label this as evidence of a deeply antireligious frame of mind, it is noteworthy that Joseph Twichell chided his good friend's obsession with this theme. Twichell considered these blasts against humanity to be nothing less than Twain's return to his roots in Calvinism, especially his emphasis on the total depravity of man.

Perhaps now it is appropriate to return to R. W. B. Lewis's description, as outlined in his volume (and drawing upon Emerson), of a model of cultural dialogue as an opposition between parties of "memory" and "hope."[16] Such a theoretical dualism can easily be applied to the religious debates between Calvinism and Pelagianism/Arminianism. According to such a model, memory would be associated with Calvinism, while hope would be paired with Pelagianism. This opposition appears problematic when we try to locate Twain as a member of one party or the other, since he certainly evinced contradictory attitudes toward America's regnant religious ideologies regarding humankind. At various times, Mark Twain both reveres and denigrates the progressive and idealistic ideology of the American Adam that I am associating with Pelagianism and the Social Gospel; similarly, he at times greatly extols and at other times irreverently chuckles at, if not openly condemns, the idea of a historical, biblical Adam representing the depravity of classical Calvinism. This inner tension is reflective of, and was indeed fostered by, the culture's own divided response to the spiritual crisis of the era.

Twain's engagement with these issues is evident almost every time he invokes Adam. For instance, in a piece published in the *New York Times* in 1883, Twain argued that Adam "ought to have a monument—for Evolution is steadily and surely abolishing him; and we must get up a monument, and be quick about it, or our children's children will grow up ignorant that there ever was an Adam."[17] While the comments are clearly written to be entertaining and ironic, a note of sadness is present in the fear that our grandchildren would end up "ignorant" of Adam and all that he represents. However, it is obvious that Twain did not merely have in mind the posterity of a singular biblical figure. Instead, his use of Adam progressed far beyond the mere character, becoming a significant metaphor in Twain's literary achievement. This metaphor stood for an important system of belief that was in danger of being lost. Mark Twain's reliance on Adam, and his clear championing of the biblical Adam as worthy of a place in America's national pantheon of heroes, would seem to constitute his suspicion of a Pelagian view of mankind. In calling for a renewed emphasis on the biblical Adam, Twain implied a critical rejection of or at least a deep ambivalence toward America's Adam ideology. Ironically the "demythologization of Adam," as illustrated in so many of Twain's works and typified in the biblical criticism and Darwinist science of the period, encompassed far more than the mere historicity of the biblical character. This demythologization of Adam quickly became a demythologization of the Adam ideology and thus challenged the very idea of America itself. (Demythologization itself would become a major theme of modern biblical studies, perhaps most famously in the work of Rudolph Bultmann.[18]) Conversely, Twain's frequent sentimentalization of the biblical Adam reminds us of our need to remember our own intrinsic limitations as a race—in short, it reminds us of our profound need for humility.

On the surface, Twain's view on this set of issues is confused and difficult to ascertain. A sense of double-mindedness regarding the Adam ideology is evident in a telling passage from *Life on the Mississippi,* in which Twain comments on the preponderance of goatees among the Missourians he encounters: "It was odd to come upon this thick crop of an obsolete and uncomely fashion; it was like running suddenly across a forgotten acquaintance whom you had supposed dead for a generation. The goatee extends over a wide extent of country; and is accompanied by an iron-clad belief in Adam and the biblical history of creation, which has not suffered from the assaults of the scientists."[19] In this passage, the goatee and the "iron-clad belief in Adam" are clearly metaphors invoking both obsolescence and a critical stance toward scientific progress. The herd mentality evinced here is like the "corn-pone opinions" that Twain frequently denounced—many if not most of the country folks' opinions derive from cultural conditioning and are "iron-clad." It is striking that initially Twain appears to be attacking the old-fashioned views of faith in both goatees and Adam. And yet the tone of nostalgia is also rather hard to miss: goatees and Adam are both cast in the role of the oppressed, "suffering" from the "assaults of science." This reading would agree with Thomas Werge's understanding of Twain's use of Adam "to caricature, not to accept, the excesses of scientific methods."[20] In any event, the passage demonstrates Twain's proclivities toward utilizing Adam (and goatees!) as a trope of far-ranging and multiplied levels of signification. As such, Adam can often stand simultaneously for both Calvinistic religion and for progressive American civil religion, for stasis and uniformity or for idealism in the face of an emergent realism.

Over the years, Adam became a figure of growing importance in Twain's literary production. Essentially Twain's engagement with Adam, in such works as *The Innocents Abroad* (especially in the "Tomb of Adam" episode), "Extracts from Adam's Diary," and *Captain Stormfield's Visit to Heaven,* as well as in his participation in the Adam monument project, is basically ironic and humorous. Yet just beneath the surface these works comprise a critical attack on the historic and symbolic depictions of the biblical hero. Through these humorous moments, Twain desired to mock and ridicule those Americans who literally believed in a historic Adam and by extension the ramifications of the Adam ideology. This attack, then, has obvious affinities with the simultaneous attacks of the higher critics of the Bible. Moreover, the tone of Twain's humorous allusions to Adam reminds the reader of his frequent ridicule of the many religious sites he endured on his own "pilgrim ship" to the Continent and the Middle East in *The Innocents Abroad.* In the passage quoted earlier, one is struck by the obvious satirical tone in Twain's suggestions that the Adam monument should become a sort of tourist trap, so famous that "every tourist would kodak it."[21] The mood of mechanical, canned response to respectable, pre-selected sites typified the Quaker City excursion. This mood had motivated Twain's own ennui of culture and religion and had become a major target of the satire in his first best-seller, *The Innocents Abroad.* Thus, at least on the surface, Twain's use of Adam is irreverent and ironic.

Despite all of this, a remarkable feature of Twain's writing is a sympathetic and even admiring use of the biblical patriarch, as seen for example in the recurring motif of Adam as forlorn and underappreciated forebear of the "damned human race." It is notable that Mark Twain's written works mention Adam more often by far than they do any other biblical person—almost twice as many times as the runner-up (and the far more crucial anti-type), Jesus. Additionally, Genesis is far ahead of any other biblical book.[22] The sheer amount of attention indicates Twain's near obsessions with beginnings and the primal biblical father, Adam, a character needing to be recognized as, above all else, our "benefactor," as Twain reminds us over and over: "What has Adam done for us? Everything. He gave us life, he gave us death, he gave us heaven, he gave us hell. . . . Whoever has lived long enough to find out what life is, knows how deep a debt of gratitude we owe to Adam, the first great benefactor of our race. . . . Let us be thankful to Adam our benefactor."[23] Here we note that Adam is responsible for much more than just the biological genesis of the human race. Significantly, in *Captain Stormfield's Visit to Heaven,* Adam is the figure who, among all the Bible heroes, receives the most adulation.

Although Twain's stance toward Adam is often ironic and even satirical of traditional forms of belief, one can hardly miss the obvious transcendental longing for a system of faith, a longing for something that may be slipping away. The "death of Adam" motif had by Twain's time become a trope for the loss of faith and the scientific questioning of the historicity of the Scriptures.[24] But with scientific progress came a certain sadness about the loss of innocent faith and a longing to recover it. This longing, divided as it surely is, becomes evident in the passage from *Innocents Abroad* that became one of Twain's most memorable episodes from his early work: the celebrated fit of weeping at the Tomb of Adam. Although this scene includes on one level an irreverent burlesque of the somber respect that characterized most trips to the Holy Land, the passage also raises more general questions regarding the act of reverence itself:

> How touching it was, here in a land of strangers, far away from home, and friends, and all who cared for me, thus to discover the grave of a blood relation. True, a distant one, but still a relation. . . . The fountain of my filial devotion was stirred to its profoundest depth, and I gave way to tumultuous emotion. I leaned upon a pillar and burst into tears. I deem it no shame to have wept over the grave of my poor dead relative. Let him who would sneer at my emotion close this volume here, for he will find little to his taste in my journeyings through Holy Land. Noble old man—he did not live to see me—he did not live to see his child. And I—I—alas, I did not live to see him. . . . Let us take comfort in the thought that his loss is our eternal gain.[25]

As Louis J. Budd has claimed, this passage exemplifies the irreverent quality of much of Twain's achievement—in Budd's view, the "dominant quality" of Twain's work.[26] The episode's notoriety during Twain's lifetime is well illustrated in the numerous graphic depictions that drew humorous attention to it.[27] This irreverence was hardly limited to a deconstruction of the biblical account of Adam: it simultaneously challenged the status quo, struck at the foundations of society, and enacted a social drama of protest and repentance, thus becoming in effect a rhetorical reenactment of the exemplary American act of declaring independence.[28]

Typically, similar "declarations of independence" have been associated with the motif of the American Adam throughout much of American literature. Strikingly, however, Twain's burlesque of Adam, and more generally his burlesque of Americans' veneration of the Holy Land, enacts this drama.[29] One key theme of *Innocents Abroad* is the crass commodification of the cultural and religious sites being visited (especially those valorized by the Roman Catholic church). Twain's contradictory style toward these sites reflects the pervasive ambivalence to be found throughout the ideological structures that most affected Twain's work, particularly that which was religious in nature. And yet both of his early best-sellers, despite their obviously satirical approach to institutional vision and religious dogmatism, also (and importantly) contain moments of strong sentimentality: exemplified in *Innocents,* for instance, that one dark evening in Palestine mentioned earlier, when Twain sings the praises of Jesus Christ, or in *Roughing It,* when the pastoral beauty of the landscape is described. As a result, and despite the critical consensus that has developed regarding these two volumes, *The Innocents Abroad* and *Roughing It* must be understood as highly contested works that simultaneously revere the Adam ideology even as they deconstruct it. Much of this cultural work is achieved through humor. As a result, some serious attention must be given to what humor is and how it functions—especially as a site for hope and apocalypse.

On his last visit to Hannibal in 1902, Mark Twain virtually preached a sermon on incarnational faith: "Our words and our acts are not for ourselves, but for others. . . . We are preaching all the time, even if we do not know it. . . . See that your preaching, when alive, be of the character that, when you are dead, others may reap the secondary effort of what you did."[30] These challenging words can be compared with Twain's story of St. Francis, who reminds his novice that "we have preached. . . . We have been happy in the love of God and the glory of His sunlight—that is our sermon for the day."[31] Both speeches emphasize the fact that we are always preaching, that we unconsciously incarnate our truest beliefs all day long. And both of these passages come from speeches Twain gave during the same, sentimental trip of 1902, his final visit to Missouri. Twain confirms this approach in another essay written late in life, where he provided what turned out to be one of the most profound and explicit explanations of his main profession in life, that of a humorist: "Humor must not professedly teach, and it must not professedly preach, but it must do both if it would live forever. By forever, I mean 30 years [after which the topics become passe or commonplace]. . . . I have always preached. That is the reason I have lasted thirty years."[32]

Of course, in these postmodern days, it is no longer conventional to analyze humor in general, let alone Mark Twain's humor, as a religious or theological phenomenon, but historically that has not been the case. As with a variety of other social phenomena, theological approaches have tended to fade with the advent of Marx, Freud, and the twentieth century. This is certainly the case with theories of humor. For instance, perhaps the most important attempt to theorize Twain's use of humor in recent years has been Bruce Michelson's study *Mark Twain on the Loose.* Michelson's approach focuses on the anarchic aspect of Mark Twain: "Is it possible that this 'self' that Mark Twain seems to exemplify . . . defines itself by how it refuses and evades, rather than by how and what it affirms? . . . I have heresies to suggest about Mark Twain as personage, as text, and as myth: that all these Mark Twains . . . might be more broadly and absolutely heretical than commentary about them has usually granted."[33] Michelson's analysis is important in its desire to refresh our understanding of the subversive and inexpressible quality of Twain's humor: its resistance to closure and conclusion, its rebellion against form and orthodoxy, which seems to mean for Michelson finally its amorality. But Michelson claims that for Twain, "rebellion against soul-confining consistency forms an eminently consistent quality," and the "threat, in other words, grew to be whatever seemed rigid and regulating to mind and identity: any confining orthodoxy, whether political, religious, aesthetic, imaginative, or even biological." This description rings true, but interestingly all of these passages also ring true to a more theological approach to Twain's humor. These quotes might easily be applied to the great Transcendentalist Emerson or, even more audaciously, to Jesus Christ himself. Michelson is also quite cagey in noting, for instance, the problem with identifying Twain's work within the confines of "realism," since the so-called "real world" itself is seen "to be saturated with delusion, pretense and fantasy. . . . The task of the realist in such straits may call not for box-cameras, but rather for dynamite."[34] Again Emerson in American history and Jesus in world history are good examples of philosophers who were experts with cultural dynamite. Finally Michelson notes the way that a categorization of Twain's humor, such as in James Cox's influential volume *Mark Twain: The Fate of Humor,* is useful but ultimately a sort of "domestication," since "these various motives, if motives they can even be called, will not keep separate, and turmoil generated by their interaction is no mere side effect of the humor. It is the humor in its essence."[35] But it seems that even what we might call Michelson's "anticategorization" is itself a form of categorization. For example, the phrase "if motives they can even be called" questions the entire moral underpinning that Michelson has seemingly set up. Wasn't the motive liberation and the dynamiting of tradition, pretense, and confinement? Michelson's approach is intriguing, but its underlying narrative seems to require a moral or ethical foundation, and so once more this approach only provides one part of the story.

As Twain himself said, "To my mind, a discriminating irreverence is the creator and protector of human liberty—even as the other thing [that is, solemnity and respect] is the creator and protector of all forms of human slavery, bodily and mental."[36] Here is at least one account (of many) where Twain provides a concrete expression of motivation. There are numerous other examples. For instance, Mark Twain was greatly interested in William Thackeray's essay on Jonathan Swift. In his copy of Thackeray's essay, Twain underlined the following: "The humorous writer professes to awaken and direct your love, your pity, your kindness —your scorn for untruth, pretension, imposture—your tenderness for the weak, the poor, the oppressed, the unhappy. . . . He comments on all the ordinary actions and passions of life almost. He takes upon himself to be the week-day preacher."[37] Elsewhere Twain compared himself to some of the other platform humorists with whom he competed for historical fame: "I succeeded in the long run, where Shillaber, Doesticks, and Billings failed, because they never had an ideal higher than that of merely being funny."[38] These quotes suggest Mark Twain's vision of his writerly task and office. First Twain desired to contribute to movements both "humanitarian and uplifting," ones that aim at "betterment and social improvement." Then, in his work as a writer, Twain conceived of two competing goals: the desire to "awaken and direct" the reader's love, pity, and kindness and thereby to foster "tenderness for the weak, the poor, the oppressed, the unhappy." At the same time, Twain wanted to trigger the reader's "scorn for untruth, pretension, imposture." This latter goal has certainly received the predominance of attention in terms of Mark Twain's rhetorical project and indeed in terms of his use of humor in general. But it need not be divorced from a theological approach centered on the needs of "the poor, the oppressed." Finally, it is notable that according to Twain himself, his own sustained historical reputation and legacy were achieved due to his preoccupation with an "ideal higher than that of merely being funny." This statement consciously subordinates Twain's humor to his role as ethicist.

As a result, if we stop with Michelson's analysis and content ourselves with calling Twain a master of the antinarrative, or of anarchy, let alone label him as simply a misanthrope, we are missing deeper motivations. On the other hand, there is so much to like about Michelson's account that I believe it leads naturally to another literary genre that has remained unexplored among Mark Twain scholars: the apocalyptic mode. Michelson's many fine descriptions of Twain's style and mode of humor almost define the means and ends of apocalyptic in itself—despite Michelson never mentioning the word or acknowledging awareness of its congeniality with his account. But in fact the apocalyptic mode very often appears anarchic and freewheeling, although an ethical effect is always just beneath the surface—as in the book of Revelation, a book so confusing and intimidating that both Martin Luther and John Calvin felt it was beyond their interpretive abilities. Later American prophets, including Emily Dickinson and Flannery O'Connor, considered the book of Revelation among their greatest resources for maintaining a fiery imagination, precisely due to its apocalyptic flavor.

Michelson's statement that "the task of the realist . . . may call not for box-cameras, but rather for dynamite" is particularly apt for understanding the apocalyptic mode and the way humor contributes to it (Dickinson and O'Connor were both, like Twain, experts in the deployment of imaginatively humorous dynamite). David Dark's recent exploration of the apocalyptic mode provides a blueprint for understanding how it works:

> apocalyptic expression is a radical declaration concerning the meaning of human experience. . . . By announcing a new world of unrealized possibility, apocalyptic serves to invest the details of the everyday with cosmic significance while awakening its audience to the presence of marginalizing forces otherwise unnamed and unchallenged. . . . It creates an unrest within our minds, and it can only be overcome by imagining differently, by giving in to its aesthetic authority, by letting it invigorate the lazy conscience. . . . apocalyptic has a way of curing deafness and educating the mind. . . . [it] will accommodate (indeed, insist upon) a socially disruptive newness. . . . [it] is the place where the future pushes into the present. It's the breaking in of another dimension, a new wine for which our old wineskins are unprepared.[39]

Ironically the Christian church, which is ostensibly called to be precisely this voice of the apocalypse within society at large, has frequently failed to maintain faithfulness to this calling. In part this is clearly something that Mark Twain (and, not coincidentally, his Hartford pastor Joe Twichell) repudiated: a lazy, status-quo church unable or unwilling to sustain the prophetic edge and act out its role as cultural dynamite. As Dark notes, "Few could have predicted that biblical language would become so tied up in social hierarchies that religion would become the object of critique rather than the acknowledged source of the critique itself. . . . A political-economic order has nothing to fear from a sentimental, fully 'spiritualized' faith."[40] The impotent prophetic voice of the church is of no relevance to the culture at large and is a complete contrast to the symbolic essence of the crucifixion of Jesus, described by theologian John Milbank as "the rejection by the political-economic order of a completely new sort of social imagination."[41] The apocalyptic mode seeks to challenge the existing order and as such its deployment is a major duty of the church. Indeed one of the reasons that a fine critic like Bruce Michelson can offer such an astute analysis of Twain's humor without recourse to the apocalyptic suggests that many intellectuals have bought into the belief that the power of Christian social and political thought in America has been nearly eviscerated, beginning in earnest in the aftermath of the Civil War.

Thus, despite his many rants against the organized religions, Mark

Twain simultaneously can be understood as an apocalyptic voice and as such a profoundly hopeful writer of fiction and political nonfiction. The moral aspect of his writings hinges upon both a desire for and an unshakable faith in the possibility that things might change for the better and that his work might become an agent for such change. One of the most overlooked keys to the religious and ultimately Christian nature of his achievement is what we might call Mark Twain's eschatology—meaning, his vision for how things might ultimately turn out, or the object of his hope. Twain frequently wrote from a modern sensibility that life might actually be going somewhere and that his work might contribute to the achievement of justice and peace—the achievement of shalom. Indeed Mark Twain was often and deeply moved by expressions of human hope, and much of his claim to literary greatness rests upon his endearing ability to foster human hope and aspiration. To the extent that Mark Twain utilized the apocalyptic mode whose goal is the achievement of a more humane and just civilization, his work is part of one of the great strains of the American project, itself deeply tied to the Christian prophetic traditions. As such, we can take him at his word—that he actually believed, as he said in 1902 during his final visit to Hannibal, that we are "preaching all the time, even if we do not know it."[42] This description transforms the office of humorist into that of preacher—both of whom share an interest in fostering hope. These theoretical insights can be applied to the works of Mark Twain, especially in the context of his humor. They also provide a framework for offering a needed balance to an understanding of Mark Twain's humor as merely anarchic and unmotivated—although it surely appears so at times. This approach suggests simply the eschatological directions of humor and the way that humor can be understood as participating in the prophetic office of apocalypse.

Stanley Brodwin has observed that humor is made possible through sympathy, by which he means close identification. Our alikeness, what we might call our "Adamness," allows humor its eschatological effect. According to Brodwin, "Mark Twain's Adamic Diaries reveal his understanding that his profound comic sense had theological roots; that it was a manifestation of man's fallen state and a dread cure for it that few men knew how to use; and that his 'kinship' with Adam gave him a universal relationship through which his deepest theological insights into the humor of the absurd could be illuminated."[43] Here Brodwin asserts a theological framework for understanding Twain's comic work, one premised on a certain view of humanity in general as being ultimately fallen and imperfect. One function of humor, that is, seems to be a constant reminder that humanity is not perfectible, as the Pelagian view might have it; humanity is finally both hideous in its errors and amusing in its sameness.

Brodwin's explanation can be compared to British commentator Malcolm Muggeridge's observations about the purpose of gargoyles on church steeples. According to Muggeridge, these gargoyles confront humans with their own frailties, to serve as a constant reminder of the laughable nature of all human achievement, this side of paradise. Muggeridge states that the gargoyle is "laughing at the inadequacy of man, the pretensions of man, the absolute preposterous gap—disparity—between his aspirations and his performance, which is the eternal comedy of human life."[44] Oddly enough, these gargoyles are not only humorous, they are brimming with hope, because it is within the context of our common humanity that our greatest hope is to be discovered. Furthermore, a cosmic and transcendent hope is not primarily located within humankind alone, but must somehow be aided by a benevolent God for its successful prosecution. The gargoyle, thus, is laughing at our shared fallenness and neediness. His laughter is carnivalesque in a manner similar to that described by the Russian theorist Mikhail Bakhtin: "Carnival laughter is the laughter of all the people. . . . It is directed at all and everyone. . . . The entire world is seen in its droll aspect. . . . It buries and revives. . . . It is also directed at those who laugh. The people do not exclude themselves from the wholeness of the world. They, too, are incomplete, they also die and are revived and renewed."[45] Bakhtin's analysis participates in a religious vocabulary here by noting how the carnival allows the celebrants to be revived; laughter somehow completes them. This sort of laughter acts as a revivifying agent, allowing all participants to enjoy momentary relief from all of the pressures and the responsibilities of their lives as workers, spouses, partners, parents, children, parishioners, and so forth. During carnival, all such responsibilities are laid aside; all forms of conscience are laid waste. The carnival is thus an enactment of the office of gargoyle: a celebration of our common humanity, our alikeness, and as such is able to revive us and sustain us for the next leg of the journey.

Obviously a complete survey of Mark Twain's humor would be a vast undertaking, but a few examples will help us begin. In the business and political realms, we might consider, for instance, the "Open Letter to Commodore Vanderbilt" that appeared in *Packard's Monthly* (March 1869). Vanderbilt, who had achieved great wealth by that time, seemed to Twain to symbolize a particularly immoral and selfish version of the American tycoon. In his scathing "Open Letter," Twain chastises Vanderbilt for his amoral activities: "All I wish to urge upon you now is, that you crush out your native instincts and go and do something worthy of praise—go and do something you need not blush to see in print—do something that may rouse one solitary good impulse in the breasts of your horde of worshippers . . . shine as one solitary grain of pure gold upon the heaped rubbish of your life."[46] In such pieces as "The Revised Catechism," a brief satirical essay that appeared in the *New York Tribune* of September 27, 1871, Twain excoriates the underlying lust for money at any cost as becoming essentially the reigning religious paradigm of the nation after the Civil War. This brief piece takes the form of a question-and-answer session in the field of "Moral Philosophy":

> Who is God?
> A. Money is God. Gold and greenbacks and stock—father, son, and the ghost of the same . . . these are the true and only God . . . and William Tweed is his prophet. . . . [47]

Obviously a critique of wealth was a preoccupation of the ministry of Jesus Christ as well as the Old Testament prophets, but perhaps more surprising is the relative silence on this topic by the American church throughout its history. Indeed the opposite view has often been perpetrated from the pulpits: that wealth itself is a blessing of God given in response to His favor and grace. But Douglas Frank has described how the growth of American wealth after the Civil War had detrimental effects for the church, including greatly neutralizing the radical and subversive aspects of American theology, in particular its view of God.[48] After the full separation of the church from state support, churches were forced to find funding from other sources, leading inevitably to the conception of churches as modern enterprises not unlike businesses, requiring advertising and promotion.

The invention of modern advertising has been attributed by many to the likes of P. T. Barnum, whose *Struggles and Triumphs* (1855; 1869) was one of the biggest self-promotional best-sellers in American history. Barnum's exploits, although Twain admired them, can nonetheless be included among those industries that greatly fostered the rise of the greedy Gilded Age economy Twain scorned in much of his best work. Advertising and self-promotion become doubly damnable when applied to the ministry. Barnum became the object of burlesque in Twain's piece "Barnum's First Speech to Congress" (1867), where Barnum's nonsensical speech takes the form of the classic jeremiad:

> "O, spirit of Washington! Forgotten in these evil times, thou art banished to the dusty corridors of memory. . . . O, shade of Jackson! O, ghost of gallant Lafayette! Ye live only in museums, and the sublime lessons of your lives are no longer heeded by the slumbering nation! Woe is me!
>
> "Rouse ye, my people, rouse ye! Rouse ye! Rouse ye! Shake off the fatal stupor that is upon ye, and hurl the usurping tyrant from his throne! Impeach! Impeach! Impeach!—Down with the dread boss monkey! O, snake the seditious miscreant out of the national feed-tub and reconstruct the Happy Family!"[49]

Twain's burlesque of Barnum takes on many of the central themes of American myth. The style of the language itself echoes King James English. Many of America's most mythic heroes are invoked, and the references to "usurping tyrants" recall America's great mythic genesis, the Declaration of Independence. Barnum also alludes to the eschatological American project—the achievement of the "Happy Family." Thus does Barnum's speech, given in the U.S. Capitol, invoke America's great civil religious themes. But the joke is in the realization that the speech serves as little more than an expression of Barnum's own interests and as mainly an advertisement for himself. We would miss the apocalyptic element if we forget that we are not just laughing at Barnum, but as in the Carnival, we are laughing at ourselves and our own proclivities toward pretentious self-boasting and empty allusions to past heroism.

Two famous examples will illustrate further the concept of apocalyptic humor: "The Facts Concerning the Recent Carnival of Crime in Connecticut" (1876) and "The Man That Corrupted Hadleyburg" (1899), both of which powerfully illustrate the theological contexts discussed in detail already. Both stories also show the major features outlined here briefly from critics like Brodwin, Muggeridge, and Bakhtin—humor's reliance on sympathy, its focus on the massive gap between human aspirations and performance, and its redemptive and reviving powers.

One of Twain's most fully developed comic tales related to all of these matters is "The Facts Concerning the Recent Carnival of Crime in Connecticut." Here is the story of a typical man, neither truly good nor bad, who is suddenly confronted by his conscience in a living form: "a shriveled, shabby dwarf . . . a vague, general, evenly-blended, nicely adjusted deformity."[50] (We might even say that the tale's conscience looks not unlike a gargoyle we might encounter on a church edifice.) Through an extended dialogue, it becomes clear that the man is considered the "slave" of the conscience and is ever driven to "repent" for his actions. But here the term "repent" is used in a less biblical sense, rejecting the possibility of a definitive turning point in life and focusing instead on a repetitive plea for forgiveness without substantial and permanent moral growth. That is, the story seems to burlesque the concept of repentance, focusing on the endless and repetitive sequence of repenting over and over again. The conscience says, "In your anxiety to get all the juice you can out of a sin, you make a man repent of it in three or four different ways." This torment is depicted in the narrator's indecisiveness about giving alms at church: "My first impulse was to give three hundred and fifty dollars; I repented of that and reduced it a hundred; repented of that and reduced it another hundred, repented of that. . . . when the plate came around at last, I repented once more and contributed ten cents." As the conscience says at one point, "It is my business—and my joy—to make you repent of everything you do."[51] In this sense, it is obvious why the narrator at first mistakes his conscience for Satan, the accuser of the brethren.

The story can only move forward when the narrator can attack the weakened conscience and destroy it, an act that results in the titular "Carnival" of crime. Ironically the conscience is weakened when the narrator's Aunt Mary, his "boyhood idol" and Christian mentor, implores him to give up smoking and to live a better life: "throw off this hateful slavery to tobacco! . . . Oh, hear me, hear me, and be saved! See, I plead with you on my very knees! . . . Oh, promise, or you are lost! Promise, and be redeemed! Promise! Promise, and live!"[52] At this moment the conscience falls fast asleep, allowing the narrator to begin his carnival. The choice of the term "carnival" is fortunate enough, anticipating as it does Bakhtin's theory of the carnivalesque and in this case also suggesting the need to "turn off" our social consciences temporarily once in a while. It may seem surprising that the conscience is disarmed at the height of Aunt Mary's revivalistic rhetoric. But it highlights the temporary nature of religious "conversions." In other words, perhaps we are only kidding ourselves by believing that we can actually kill off our consciences and assuage our massive guilt in life by saying a simple prayer of conversion at a revival meeting.

More generally the story illustrates the very real struggles that all of us have in wrestling with our consciences, like Jacob with his angel. Furthermore, the story underlines the legalistic excess of a religion without true grace. If Christianity becomes simply a set of rules without forgiveness, power, and grace, then of course Christians will find themselves enslaved by its dictates. The conscience is no longer empowering and righteous, but tyrannical and oppressive. Although this was written as a comic tale and delivered as such to the Monday Evening Club, January 24, 1876, Joe Twichell recognized immediately that it amounted to more than just a few laughs. In his journal after the club meeting he described it as "an interview between himself and his conscience—very finely written—serious in its intent though mostly funny and splendidly, brilliantly read."[53] Curiously Twichell identifies the narrator with Twain himself—an indication of Twain's lifelong struggles with guilt and shame, about which Twichell was quite familiar as pastor and advisor. It is also worth noting that Twain chose to deliver the tale initially at the Monday Evening Club, the literary and cultural discussion group featuring the Hartford elite, all of whom were immersed in the religious ethos of the period. Twain was confident that he could read the story to his genteel, liberally Christian audience. It is a fitting tribute to the intelligent faith of that time that Joe Twichell saw that the humor was thoroughly "serious in intent."

A much longer and even more detailed story with apocalyptic undertones is "The Man That Corrupted Hadleyburg." Here Mark Twain invents a simple town of regular folks whose lives are utterly disrupted by the arrival of a stranger. Not unlike the conscience in the "Recent Carnival of Crime," this mysterious man becomes in effect the accuser of the brethren—a Satan-like character. And what nice brethren they are—or appear to be. The story begins with the announcement that Hadleyburg "was the most honest and upright town in all the region. . . . in reality an incorruptible town."[54] The stranger, who has somehow been offended by one of the town's citizens, decides that "I will corrupt the town." Again, as mentioned earlier, as Twain aged he had an ongoing fascination with images of corruption and decay. The stranger offers a large cash reward for the town citizen who helped him with some advice many years earlier. The money will go to whoever reveals the mysterious advice once given. And because the Associated Press office was open late when the story of the fantastic monetary offer was made public, by breakfast the next day the "name Hadleyburg the Incorruptible was on every lip in America."[55] But a big part of the joke is the gradual revelation that the town is already corrupt at the core and that the seeming honesty and virtue are mere shams. Indeed the fact that the town is already corrupt is what makes it "in reality an incorruptible town." It cannot be corrupted, because it already is.

The essence of the joke is communicated in the mysterious slogan that everyone in town is trying to discover so that they can recover the loot. The remark, which turns out to be a hoax conjured by the stranger, is this: "You are far from being a bad man: Go, and reform." But as with the notion of the town's incorruptibility, this saying strikes at the heart of the issues related to the ongoing theological and philosophical attempts to define human nature. First, it draws upon the soft Pelagianism of Social Christianity in affirming that at the core, mankind is not evil but good. Nevertheless, humans must reform. A sort of double jeopardy is involved here. The story's magic formula consists of a nonsensical combination of attributes seemingly at odds with each other. Is humanity basically good or bad? This statement claims simultaneously both and neither. It is similar to calling the town incorruptible: the motto is an example of the shallow and pious church talk that was at the center of nineteenth-century uplift testimonies. In addition, it is the sort of ethical cliché that anyone might come up with; not only can virtually any of the townsfolk pretend to have been the wise person who said it to the stranger, but many of them actually remember having said it. Thus the generic nature of the saying allows everyone to imagine themselves as having been the sayer and thus the rightful claimant of the reward. Finally, the motto foregrounds a major motif of the story, the importance of and need for temptation. The story emphasizes the need for reformation and repentance in a town that was ostensibly not in need of it. Several times throughout the story, characters allude to (or sometimes overtly pray) the Lord's Prayer, in which Jesus beseeches the Father to "lead us not into temptation, but deliver us from evil" (Matthew 6:13). However, this prayer has been extrapolated by some of Hadleyburg's citizens to suggest that Christians can live a life without testing and suffering—a feature of what has come to be called in the twentieth century a therapeutic denial of pain and suffering. As a result the town has felt proud and blessed to have never suffered temptations—or so they thought. But the townspeople had actually suffered because they had never been truly tested, as all humans must be. In fact, Hadleyburg had made a habit of avoiding temptation, and "temptations were kept out of the way of the young people." But the stranger points out in his final written comments that Hadleyburg was "easy game" because "you had an old and lofty reputation for honesty; and naturally you were proud of it—it was your treasure of treasures, and the very apple of your eye. As soon as I found out that you carefully and vigilantly keep yourselves and your children out of temptation, I knew how to proceed. Why, you simple creatures, the weakest of all weak things is a virtue which has not been tested in the fire."[56] Ironically, the test brings true repentance to the town. The story ends with the line, "It is an honest town once more, and the man will have to rise early that catches it napping again." But the town's honesty consists precisely in its revived awareness of its own dishonesty, its own corruption. Further, the motto of the town has now become, "Lead Us Into Temptation."[57] The saying reflects the fact that the test of the stranger has fulfilled its apocalyptic purpose: to explode the town's mythic claim of being honest and righteous, and to invite the townsfolk (and the reader) to come face to face with their deepest and most hideous secrets about themselves. The title of the story, "The Man That Corrupted Hadleyburg," is an inaccurate description of what actually happens: the stranger does not really corrupt the town, but he does initiate the process by which the town realizes that it is already corrupt. The stranger's hoax, in effect, reveals the Adamic curse at the heart of Hadleyburg; it serves as a smirking gargoyle confronting the holy pilgrims on their climb to the top of the steeple called Hadleyburg.

"The Man That Corrupted Hadleyburg," like the other comic tales mentioned, relies on the reader's willingness to call into question a prevailing myth. The iconic American small town, with the church and its Sunday school squarely at its center, had by then become reified in the minds of many as an abstract symbol of all things good, pure, and right about their society. Children of the second half of the nineteenth century had been indoctrinated with such a view of midwestern civilization through texts like the McGuffey school readers. But this veneer was in need of an apocalyptic breakthrough, one that finally issued in an entire movement called the "Revolt from the Village" of which Mark Twain's many comic tales of small town America are some of the founding documents. As Michelson puts it, "The task of the realist in such straits may call not for box-cameras, but rather for dynamite."[58] In considering the mode of apocalypse, we have seen how this sort of dynamite can be powerful and invigorating. When apocalyptic dynamite exposes the gargoyled nature of all those Adams around us, somehow we are empowered by laughter to gather strength and take the next step in life's aggravating and marvelous journey. Apocalyptic dynamite can even provide us with the hope we need to carry on. As such, apocalypse and humor share much more than they might appear to at first glance: they share an inherent ability to give hope to the hearer and healing to the bones. Perhaps even more importantly, they share the burden of remaking the world into a more just and peaceable kingdom. Apocalypse and humor thus aim at similar ends—particularly in their desire to foster hope in a future world of shalom.

7

Mark Twain's Grief

The Final Years

With the completion of his around-the-world tour of 1895–96, Mark Twain was extremely fatigued but rather giddy with excitement at the prospect of finally seeing the return of his financial fortunes. He had taken up the arduous task of this journey primarily as a means of paying back his many debtors; by the summer of 1896 he could see the light at the end of the tunnel (even though, in fact, the trip was not nearly as profitable as he had hoped, and as it turned out, financial fortune was still a few years down the road). Throughout the journey, he longed to return to Hartford, his flamboyant home on Farmington Avenue, and the regularity of his home life there. He paid a visit to the house just before the beginning of the journey, after which he wrote to Livy of the experience and of his great desire to reunite his family in the beloved home: "[I]t seemed as if I had burst awake out of a hellish dream, and had never been away, and that you would come drifting down out of those dainty upper regions with the little children tagging after you. . . . I was seized with a furious desire to have us all in this house again and right away, and never go outside the grounds any more forever—certainly never again to Europe."[1] The "furious desire" of Twain's letter is underscored by the fact that during the world tour, he even began calling his platform program "At Home." It became his heart's greatest desire and the reason for all the hard work of paying off his extensive debts: he would return to Hartford to live out the rest of his years, surrounded by a dear and loving family.

While resting in Great Britain at the journey's end, he anticipated the arrival of his two daughters, Susy and Jean, from America, neither of whom had accompanied him on the year-long journey. But then in early August, around the time when they would be preparing to sail for England, a telegram brought Twain the news that Susy was ill. According to a later message, however, she apparently would recover given enough time. Thus did Twain decide to stay in England and send his wife Livy across the sea to nurse Susy back to health—one of the many decisions he would bitterly regret for the rest of his life. Sadly Twain would later discover that after many days of fitful delirium, fever, and even blindness, Susy died of spinal meningitis on August 18, 1896, while Livy was aboard ship in the mid-Atlantic. Susy was the favored daughter, their most prized production. Indeed it may not be too much to say that Mark Twain and Livy idolized their beautiful and highly intelligent oldest daughter. And so her death would have profound and lifelong effects on the Clemens household (figure 9).

Initially Twain and his wife took Susy's death very hard. Twain's refuge from the grief was obsessively working on *Following the Equator* or other manuscripts, endless hours of billiards or card games, or simply sitting and listening to music. One friend remembered her many visits with Twain while his family was still in America:

> It was just after the death of his favourite daughter, Susie [sic]. He was alone in London, and he used to come and see me quite often. I felt he was very unhappy and very restless. He used to talk very bitterly and often distressed me by his attitude. He would walk up and down the room and say: "If I was God, I would be ashamed to treat my children so. Don't talk to me about a Heavenly Father; no human father would behave as God does." Nothing that I could do was of any use, but I believe the fact that he could talk out what he felt was a relief, and I suppose I showed the intense sympathy I had with his great and bitter grief.[2]

One reporter in June 1897 described him this way: "there was a difference in his physiognomy: it was more lined and thinner than when I saw

9. Susy Clemens, 1892. Courtesy of the Mark Twain Project, Bancroft Library, University of California, Berkeley.

him last. . . . there was a species of hopeless resignation in his bearing, in painful contrast to his one-time easygoing carelessness. . . . [he appeared] so disturbed by mental worries that the report of his failing condition was practically well founded."[3] He showed wild swings of emotions. In August 1897 he wrote to a friend, "I am submerged in work again—9 hours a day, 7 days per week—& am well content. I have begun four books; & by shifting from one to another of them according to the impulse of the day, I shall expect them to keep me entertained & recreated for the next three or four years." None of those books, apparently, ever were published in his lifetime. But less than a month later he wrote the same friend, "I do not know, now, what I wrote you; but whatever it is, be charitable—for there was no August day in which I was in my right mind—& there will never be an August day, perhaps, in which I shall be sane. It is our terrible month. It is a whole month of awful anniversaries. . . . August is gone now, & we are adjusting ourselves again, & resuming our sanities, I hope."[4]

The fear of losing one's mind, along with the other physical and psychological traits listed here, are common symptoms of intensive parental bereavement. But grief is also a profoundly spiritual or religious experience as well, often wreaking havoc upon a person's worldview. Indeed, of all the crises in Twain's personal life, the death of Susy appears to be the culmination, even beyond the horror and darkness of Livy's death in 1904. On one level, Susy's death constituted the sudden and irrecoverable loss of hope's most tangible expression. This insight suggests that Susy's death became the crucial event of the final fourteen years of Twain's life, both as a parent, an author, and a public persona, and the key to unlocking the mental and emotional states of those years. This assertion is supported by an analysis of recent grief theory, much of which characterizes parental bereavement as resulting in the most horrific spiritual and emotional crisis that an adult can face in life. In addition, this research agrees "that bonds [with the dead] can be continued without the detrimental effects [that] were originally claimed and [that continued bonds with the dead] play a role in . . . the 'resolution' of grief."[5] As such, today's leading grief theorists focus on a constructivist model of bereavement, clearly rejecting much contained in the modern theories of grief of the early and middle twentieth century, especially insofar as these models label extended and grueling patterns of mourning as "pathological."[6]

Modern theories of grief sprang from Sigmund Freud's distinction between "mourning," which is the normal reaction to the loss of a loved one, and "melancholia," which is essentially a form of illness, or "pathology."[7] According to Freud, the goal of any mourner's attempt at resolution is to break free from the deceased, let go of the past, and reassert the autonomy of the individual by forging ahead and charting a new course for life. Freud also utterly rejected a belief in an afterlife and any potential for reunion with the dead, and thus his theory must be understood as profoundly anti-Christian in spirit. Freud's modernist approach might best be understood as a stern rejection of Victorian codes of grieving that foregrounded dependence on the deceased. But today Freud's influence is undergoing a stern critique of its own. In questioning and finally rejecting much of the critical spirit notable in modern versions of grief theory, almost all of which has been dominated by Freud, today's grief theorists are positing what has been called a "postmodern" version that has derived from the extensive findings of scientific and clinical studies on these subjects.[8]

In particular, research has consistently indicated that lengthy if not lifelong grief is normative rather than problematic in cases of the loss of close family members, especially children, and thus is not pathological at all. The loss of a child is commonly spoken of as the most traumatic event that one can experience; in research studies, this commonplace is routinely shown to be accurate. Parental grief is severe, long-lasting, extremely complicated, and indeed is often lifelong. Parental bereavement generally initiates a severe crisis of meaning that challenges held worldviews.[9] Specifically, it challenges previous assumptions about the purpose and meaning of life, often precipitating a total collapse of that structure.[10] The consequent loss of meaning or collapse of worldview commonly can lead to despair, which is quickly followed by a profound sense of hopelessness and apathy. Research indicates that the pain may even intensify as time goes on, especially in the third year after the loss.[11] And although there has been a strong assumption that mothers are somehow more emotionally vulnerable to the deaths of their children than fathers, some research has found no differences between fathers and mothers in terms of their changes in worldview and views of the meaning and purpose of life.[12] Finally, today's researchers recognize the importance of calling for the continuing bonds with the deceased, particularly in the case of parental loss of children.

Despite the abundance of evidence documenting the devastation of parents by the loss of children, the vast majority of literary scholarship on Twain's expressions of grief has been condescending for a long time. One example is Hamlin Hill's coverage of these matters in his influential work on Twain's final years, in which he castigates Twain's composition of a poem in 1902 in response to Livy's continuing illness and his own despair over Susy's death. Hill betrays in his comments an unwillingness or inability to tap into his subject's profound grief:

> Perhaps we can understand the mawkishness and banality of the "our Dark Day" brand of sentimentality; the funereal mode was an immensely compelling one for Mark Twain, and in serious moments he almost always descended into the lachrymose voice that he mocked when Emmeline Grangerford used it. But it is difficult to explain the parents' ghoulish attraction to Susy's memory. . . . The annual day of remorse on August 18, the public parading of grief which lost its effectiveness by its clockwork regularity, the saving of the "pressed plant from Susy's grave" . . . are less than mature reactions and responses to death, even by Victorian standards.[13]

Hill's remarks are insensitive to the kind of horror and despair that these two grieving parents were unable to dispel. But others have echoed his views: one describes Twain's grief over Susy's death as "patently contrived, false, and melodramatic"; another describes a "pattern of repressed grief and pathological mourning, [which] instilled a deep-seated, elemental incapacity to acknowledge the permanence of death, and thereby, to put his dead to rest."[14] These analyses of Twain's "pathology" derive plainly from the outdated (and unsympathetic) Freudian model. It is time to admit that all of this armchair psychoanalysis based on Freudian models more than fifty years out of date is very troubling—especially in its willingness to approach the tender subject of the death of a child with such ruthlessly cold logic.

Instead of combing through the documents and letters for traces of "pathology" in a condescending manner, we should investigate Twain's expressions of grief with a more compassionate and merciful spirit. The works that have been dismissively referred to as "graveyard poetry" amount to far more than the "trite utterance" or the "less than mature reactions" of a man bound by Victorian convention.[15] Rather, these pathos-ridden expressions are some of the most powerful and authentic literary achievements of Twain's lifetime, rooted as they clearly are in the most traumatic of life's events. If, as one theologian has stated, children "are incarnate hopes for a fulfilled life. . . . [and] embodiments of God's hopes for us," then the loss of a child severely undermines the very possibility of hope.[16] Thus it is plausible to argue that the death of Susy was the climactic moment of Mark Twain's personal spiritual crisis—a moment that bore both positive and negative fruit.

Obviously, as research indicates, the death of a child can have a highly negative effect on the spiritual lives of the parents. Additionally, however, the relationship with a deceased child frequently can also have a positive, even energizing, effect on the work and spiritual life of a surviving parent. Among other things, traumatic pain of this nature can produce within the subject a much more thorough awareness of the suffering of humanity and thus can engender sympathy. Indeed, Twain's "continuing bond" with Susy was a major motivating factor in his positive achievements for the remainder of his writing and public career—and perhaps even the central factor—insofar as those achievements issued from his profound sympathy for the "damned human race."

As a result, attention should be given to the literary productions that derived specifically from Susy's death. Examples of these are *What Is Man?* (1906), *A Horse's Tale* (1906), "A Dog's Tale" (1903), and *Christian Science* (1907), along with the so-called *Mysterious Stranger Manuscripts* (published posthumously in 1969). There is also a connection between Susy's death, the enhancement of Twain's sympathy for the downtrodden, and the resulting growth in his social justice agenda in the years after 1896. I would also connect the many dream narratives, such as *Which Was the Dream?*, "The Great Dark," and *Which Was It?*, along with many of the pieces included in the posthumous collection *Fables of Man* (1972), with Twain's mourning for Susy. The Mark Twain Papers hold a number of other similarly dark and depressing manuscripts, all started but many never completed by Twain during the years after Susy's death, some of which have still never been published. Finally, Twain's drive to dictate his autobiography can be associated with both Susy's and Livy's deaths. While there are numerous examples of work that Twain either explicitly or implicitly connected with Susy's death, we should consider specifically the formal elegies that Twain composed in her memory—the first, called "In Memoriam," composed in 1897 precisely one year after her death, and the second, "Broken Idols," exactly one year later.

The sarcastic dismissal of graveyard poetry, of course, was undertaken by Twain himself, as in the discussions of the lugubrious Emmeline Grangerford in chapter 17 of *Huckleberry Finn.* Emmeline, dead at the age of fifteen, and described as being dressed in black and wearing a black "scoop-shovel bonnet with a black veil" was given to writing "tributes" to the deceased. She searched the pages of the *Presbyterian Observer* for tales of obituaries, accidents, or the suffering of patients. Her finest work, which Huck calls "very good poetry," was an ode to a boy who drowned named Stephen Dowling Bots:

And did young Stephen sicken,
    And did young Stephen die?. . . .
O no. Then list with tearful eye,
    Whilst I his fate do tell.
His soul did from this cold world fly,
    By falling down a well.[17]

One could simply take the burlesque of the likes of Emmeline Grangerford as the final word on Twain's view of the sentimental mode. However, one of the insights of a postmodern theory of grief, and certainly one of the great accomplishments of much gender theory of recent decades in literary studies, is the recovery of the power of such sentimental works. While it seems rather foolish to hear of the demise of Stephen Dowling Bots, for instance, drownings were no laughing matter in Twain's childhood: they were fairly common, and once, when a friend of young Sam drowned in the river while the boys swam together, Sam had nightmares for weeks afterward. Despite his sarcasm in *Huckleberry Finn,* and on many other occasions, Twain was strongly attracted to platform renditions of funereal poetry, especially by the likes of James Whitcomb Riley, whom he considered one of the greatest live performers of the era and with whom he became friends in the 1890s.[18] Evidence of Twain's quick attempt to copy Riley's use of graveyard poetry came shortly after their first encounter at the American Copyright readings in New York in 1887. As early as January 21, 1889, Twain recited a poem by Riley at a reading at Smith College in Massachusetts. The poem, "The Absence of Little Wesley," a melodramatic lament grieving the death of a beloved grandson, first appeared in the *Century* magazine in May 1888.[19] The poem is typically Rileyesque: its performance would involve "absorbing" the persona of the grandfather and drawling out the lines written in misspelled Hoosier vernacular:

Sence little Wesley went, the place seems all so strange and still—
W'y, I miss his yell o' "Gran-pap!" as I'd miss the whipperwill!
And to think I ust to scold him fer his everlastin' noise,
When I on'y rickollect him as the best o' little boys![20]

The fact that Twain recited Riley's sentimental poem in numerous public performances indicates his awareness of the power of such works. Perhaps we might even say that Twain was sensitive to how these elegies carried out important ideological and religious work for their composers and listeners. As a result, when Twain faced the most traumatic event of his life in the death of Susy, it is not surprising that the record of his own spiritual crisis would be made most explicit in his two formal elegies.

Research shows that it is possible to discern patterns in how a parent processes the trauma in terms of his or her worldview.[21] Of these patterns, one in particular captures Twain's highly ambivalent, polarized, and twofold pattern of response to Susy's death: "When the symbols of affiliation of the parents' worldview are not useful, some live in a divided world. They maintain a *bond with the transcendent* that is linked to their children. In other parts of their lives, however, they feel cut off from the God in whom they still believe."[22] The link with Susy helped Twain "maintain a bond with the transcendent" to the extent that she continued as a sort of moral role model for him, providing him with not only the necessary motivation but even, at least in his own mind, some fairly specific guidance in his final period. (After Livy died in 1904, she served a similar role: such linkages are not limited to children.) These claims are in keeping with abundant research indicating that images of the deceased "serve a positive function guiding the bereaved as role models and in decision-making."[23] This sort of positive response seems most clearly represented in the first of the two elegies. The opposite response of being "cut off from God" corresponds to the second work, "Broken Idols." Thus do these two poems, composed exactly one year apart, document the divided and highly contested response to Susy's death—and thus do they represent the warring factions of Twain's religious and metaphysical universe for the final fourteen years of his life. Generally the theme of Twain being "cut off from God" has been emphasized far more than the theme of Twain's "continuing bonds with the transcendent."

The first of these elegies, "In Memoriam," published in *Harper's Monthly* of November 1897, presents Susy as a lovely temple that is not truly understood or valued by those who see it:

> In a fair valley—oh, how long ago, how long ago!—
> Where all the broad expanse was clothed in vines

And fruitful fields and meadows starred with flowers,
And clear streams wandered at their idle will,
And still lakes slept, their burnished surfaces
A dream of painted clouds, and soft airs
Went whispering with odorous breath,
And all was peace—in that fair vale,
Shut from the troubled world, a nameless hamlet drowsed.

    Hard by, apart, a temple stood;
And strangers from the outer world
Passing, noted it with tired eyes,
And seeing, saw it not:
A glimpse of its fair form—an answering momentary thrill—
    And they passed on, careless and unaware.[24]

While the general passersby are unable to receive the full revelation of this temple, some do truly understand its beauty and graces:

Only the dwellers of the hamlet knew:
. . . They knew
That in the temple's inmost place a spirit dwelt,
Made all of light!

A Christian metaphysic is invoked in Twain's statement that in the "inmost place a spirit dwelt." The citizens of the hamlet, then, are able to bear witness to much of the magnificence of the temple. The poem concludes with two important themes. The first is the strong sense that the death of Susy took place a very long time ago (although the poem was written just one year after her demise): "All this was long ago—so long ago!"[25]

The second key theme is Twain's powerful urge to admit the possibility, even the certainty, of a reunion in the hereafter:

The stricken ones that served it day and night,
Adoring it, abiding in the healing of its peace:
They stand, yet, where erst they stood
Speechless in that dim morning long ago;

And still they gaze, as then they gazed,
And murmur, "It will come again;
It knows our pain—it knows—it knows—
Ah, surely it will come again.[26]

Just prior to the composition of his own "In Memoriam," Twain and Livy had been reading and rereading Alfred Lord Tennyson's "In Memoriam," which had been given to Livy by J. Y. W. MacAlister. These facts are apparent from a letter Twain wrote to MacAlister from Weggis, Switzerland, dated July 20, 1897—the month before the one-year anniversary of Susy's death: "I have read part of In Memoriam again. It *is* a noble poem. Mrs. Clemens reads it persistently, & thanks you all the time for the healing it brings her."[27] Tennyson's poem consists of a long and profound meditation on loss and grief. Thematically, by its insistence on the maintenance of lifelong bonds with the dead, Tennyson favors an approach to grief opposed to the tendencies of a modernistic, pathological reading of continuing bonds as described by the Freudian school:

Let Love clasp Grief lest both be drown'd,
    Let darkness keep her raven gloss.
    Ah, sweeter to be drunk with loss,
To dance with Death, to beat the ground,
Than that the victor Hours should scorn
    The long result of love, and boast,
    "Behold the man that loved and lost,
But all he was is overworn."[28]

Twain's admiration for Tennyson's long elegy went back several decades. As early as a letter to Livy written from London on December 22, 1873, Twain comments that he went with some acquaintances to a friend's house in Harley Street. This detail is relevant to Tennyson's poem, as Twain points out: it is the "'Long, unlovely street' of Tennyson's In Memoriam."[29] The stanza from which the detail derives provides powerful images of romantic grief:

Dark house, by which once more I stand
    Here in the long unlovely street,

Doors, where my heart was used to beat
So quickly, waiting for a hand,
A hand that can be clasp'd no more.[30]

The resonance for Twain of these particular lines is worth noting. In particular, the image of the darkened house is both reminiscent of the temple imagery of his own poem and indicative of Twain's obsessive association of his nostalgia for family with the actual dwelling place—the Hartford home. Moreover, the passage describes the kinds of physical symptoms that plague the bereaved and that certainly were major aspects of Twain's own experience after the loss of Susy: feeling like a "guilty thing," and the persistent sleeplessness.

The ending of Twain's "In Memoriam" laments the fact that most have already forgotten the great temple being described. But not the priests—specifically, Mark and Livy—who are indeed expecting the return at any moment:

[They] gaze, as then they gazed,
And murmur, "It will come again;
It knows our pain—it knows—it knows
Ah, surely it will come again.

Twain's ending echoes similar expectations in Tennyson's poem. For example, in a passage from section 14, the narrator receives a report that the deceased has been spotted by a mutual friend and so goes to investigate:

And if along with these should come
The man I held as half-divine,
Should strike a sudden hand in mine,
And ask a thousand things of home; . . .

And I perceived no touch of change,
No hint of death in all his frame
But found him all in all the same,
I should not feel it to be strange.[31]

An important bridge between the Tennyson and Twain poems is the sense that the bond continues, the person remains the same, and the relationship transcends the death experience. Certainly this is clearly stated in Tennyson's version; for Twain, the expectation is more muted: "They stand, yet, where erst they stood"—and "surely" the reunion will occur. The temple continues to "know" the lookers' pain.

One critic has gone so far as to claim that Twain "had no questions whatsoever about the non-existence of an afterlife."[32] However, an abundance of evidence indicates that, even to the end of his life, Twain clung at least to the possibility that ultimately he would be reunited with his beloved Susy and Livy. For example, in a letter to Livy dated May 8, 1893, he wrote: "Livy darling, it broke my heart—what you wrote to Sue about immortality. Let us believe in it! I will believe in it *with* you. It has been the belief of the wise + thoughtful of many countries for three thousand years; let us accept their verdict; we cannot frame one that is more reasonable or probable. I will try never to doubt it again."[33] His biographer Albert Paine remembered this statement from Twain: "As to a hereafter, we have not the slightest evidence that there is any—*no* evidence that appeals to logic and reason. I have never seen what to me seemed an atom of proof that there is a future life. . . . And yet—I am strongly inclined to expect one."[34] In his unpublished and largely sarcastic review of George Warder's *The Cities of the Sun* (1901), a theological exposition of the vision of Heaven in the book of Revelation, Twain ridicules Warder's Americanized version of Heaven, a recurring theme of some of Twain's other writings, most notably *Captain Stormfield's Visit to Heaven.* As in the Stormfield material, Twain takes great exception to Warder's weak attempts to theorize, and thus to somehow domesticate, what he considers to be such a massive and sublime topic of concern—assuming, of course, that a Heaven actually does exist! Nevertheless, Twain still betrays a yearning for the concept of the hereafter, despite the sarcasm:

> It makes one's mouth water. It would be a wonderful experience to stand there in those enchanted surroundings and hear Shakespeare and Milton and Bunyon read from their noble works. And it might be that they would like to hear me read some of my things. No, it could never be;

> they would not care for me. They would not know me, they would not understand me, and they would say they had an engagement. But if I could only be there I should not mind disappointments; if I could only be there, and walk about, and look, and listen, I should be satisfied and not make a noise. My life is fading to its close, and some day I shall know.[35]

Twain and Livy experimented with several spiritualists in 1900–1901 in an attempt to communicate with Susy.[36] Additionally, Twain often theorized about the dream self during the period when he wrote "Broken Idols" (about 1898), including the dream self's relation to the hereafter: "we have a spiritualized self which can detach itself and go wandering off upon affairs of its own. . . . I do actually make immense excursions in my spiritualized person; when my physical body dies, my dream-body will doubtless continue its excursions and activities without change, forever."[37] His childhood girlfriend Laura Hawkins Frazer (the model for Becky Thatcher) wrote in 1923: "the last time I saw him [at Stormfield], he told me goodbye twice, came back the third time and said, 'We will meet in Heaven, Laura,' pointing upward."[38] When his daughter Jean died in 1909, Twain wrote in a letter to Twichell, "What have I lost! What has Jean gained!"[39] Likewise, Katy Leary, the faithful household servant, recalled Twain saying to her, " 'Oh, Katy! [Jean's] in heaven with her mother.' " Leary went on to state, "Oh, I think—I am sure he believed in the hereafter."[40] And consider his haunting last words to Clara: "Goodbye dear, if we meet. . . . "[41] All of this evidence suggests that even if Twain did not embrace wholeheartedly a Christian version of the afterlife, his hope in one lingered on, possibly even to the very end.

Compared with the sacred and hushed tone of "In Memoriam," Twain's dramatic poem "Broken Idols" is filled with throbbing pain and near delirium. This poem takes the form of a dramatic dialogue between two people. The main speaker of "Broken Idols" is a woman, very much patterned after Livy. The inconsolable mother is being interviewed by a narrator, ungendered, who has never known such grief and thus is not Twain himself. Since it is aimed at readers not familiar with parental grief, "Broken Idols" can be understood as a confessional exposition that tries to communicate the sheer horror of the experience to the uninitiated. As a result, this lengthy poem contains some of the most poignant material Twain ever composed on the topic of loss. In particular, "Broken Idols" bears strong autobiographical witness to the pathos of Twain's experience of parental loss. The poem conveys the powerful sense of grief that his wife Livy endured and his deep compassion for (and, indeed, participation in) her bitter experience:

Experience is age—not years. Your face
Is ignorantly smooth, and ignorantly pink;
You have lived long, and nothing suffered.
You try to pity me, I see the good intent,
I know it is your best: but how shall you
Pay out in cash what yet lies bedded in your ores?
The fires of grief! *They* lap the heart in flame,
They smelt the red gold free! It is the bleeding heart
That pays the due of woe in minted coin,
Not kindly-meaning paper
Drawn upon an unexploited treasure
Findable some day in case by malice of the fates
Misfortune shall so order it.[42]

The primary image here is one from Twain's prospecting years: smelting metals in the "fires of grief." These terrible experiences "lap the heart in flame," and they are such that the uninitiated cannot possibly fathom them. Twain's emphasis on fire and flame here suggests his continual use in the years after Susy's death of the metaphor of a burning or vacant, fallen house as emblematic of all that has been lost.[43] Related to this is the horrific nature of her illness, according to which, as one critic notes, Susy "had died of a brain-fever during an August heat-wave, had almost literally burned up in the Hartford house."[44] Curiously, another figure of this passage equates the daughter with a form of wealth. Losing the child has made a pauper out of the parent—a fact that speaks autobiographically of the contiguous tragedies of Twain's life in the 1890s of financial disaster and traumatic parental bereavement:

you cannot know how long that seems to me,
Whose heart was once so filled with wealth
And now so empty stands."[45]

Just as the poem's main character borders on madness, so did Livy for an extended period of time. Perhaps today a diagnosis of severe depression would apply to both the poem's protagonist and Livy Clemens during much of this period. Livy's sister Susan Crane described her this way in September 1896:

> You will be able to believe when I tell you that that beloved face was the most grief stricken face I ever looked upon, when she received this heaviest blow that has fallen upon her.
>
> As the days passed until she + Clara sailed, she grieved in power to look her sorrow + disappointment in the face—But it was all unspeakably hard, + at times she did not care to go on.[46]

Their household maid Katy put it this way: "The anguish of her heart was terrible. . . . I didn't think Mrs. Clemens could live then. Her heart almost broke in front of our eyes. . . . I don't think Mrs. Clemens ever stopped grieving for Susy. . . . She never really got over losing Susy."[47] Their daughter Clara describes "the violence of Father's grief. His unflinching self-condemnation brought him to the state of a crucified martyr. . . . without doubt Father's deep-seated pessimism of after-years had its birth in the tragedy of Susy's death. For not only had he to bear his own sorrow but the moving sight of Mother's grief."[48]

Thus, it seems clear that Livy's hallucinatory grief was the source of the protagonist rendered so powerfully in "Broken Idols." Other details bespeak the autobiographical nature of the poem. The four versions of the lost daughter—the baby girl playing the bear game; the ten-year-old girl being punished; the sixteen-year-old girl performing in a play of her own writing; and the older young lady who is the actual age of the deceased daughter—might each be taken as a version of Susy Clemens, even down to the details of the dress and mannerisms. The two years of the poem measure exactly the distance of time since Susy's death:

> Two years ago she died. Two years! To you
> The world is pleasant; it has not stung you
> In your heart: you cannot know how long that seems to me,
> Whose heart was once so filled with wealth
> And now so empty stands.[49]

The relationship of mother with daughter, verging on the closeness of "lovers," is also a curious aspect of much of the extant correspondence and diaristic record of Livy's relationship with Susy:

> I lived in her, and she in me.
> We were as one. And it was little like the common tie
> That binds the mother and the child, but like that
> Which binds two lovers.[50]

And in the mother's lament that she was "not by" the dying girl, especially when at the moment of death the mother's name was the final whisper, we recall Livy's desperation in not being there when Susy died:

> Struck down unwarned! . . .
>
> And I not by!
> Not by when the shadows fell, the night of death closed down,
> The sun that lit my life went out. Not by to answer
> When the latest whispers passed the lips
> That were so dear to me—my name!
> Far from my post![51]

Moreover, this passage recalls the sad detail that Susy's final death throe involved blindly stroking the housemaid Katy's face and crying, "Mamma!"[52] It becomes clear in the poem's final passages that the mother has apparently gone mad or else is on the brink of madness. She has lost her favored daughter but imagines that in fact she has lost four daughters: "Poor lady, she is mad. She is bereft of four, she thinks. / *There was but one.*"[53] Thus, as the poem comes to its conclusion, the reader understands that the "four" that have been lost are four chronological versions of the same angelic daughter. The traumatic experience of parental grief has distorted the mother's sense of the past and of her daughter's chronological development.

Even though this poem is about the mother, and thus centered on Mark Twain's observations of Livy, its stark and utterly remorseless picture of the mental states of the bereaved is not unlike those that Twain himself experienced for many years. Another major theme of the poem that coincided with one of Twain's emerging preoccupations of the 1890s and beyond is the connection of personal grief for the dead and a pathetic nostalgia for times past. This connection is a major theme of sentimental literature as a whole and is emphasized in the powerful concluding stanza:

> We who are old—we comprehend! Even we
> That are not mad: whose grown-up scions
> Still abide with us, their tale complete.
> Their earlier selves we glimpse at intervals
> Far in the dimming past,
> And whilst we ache to take them to our hearts
> They fade from sight. We know them lost to us—
> Forever lost; we cannot have them back;
> We miss them as we miss the dead,
> We mourn them as we mourn the dead.[54]

This passage joins the mourning process for the dead child with the process of grieving for the long lost past. In a sense, every single person we have known in the past is no longer the same person, and neither are we—and so we must mourn the "deaths" of these past subjectivities. Mark Twain would never again really "know" Hartford, or Joe Twichell, or Howells, or other friends as he knew them in the first dawning days of acquaintance. Even his "grown-up scions" Clara and Jean cannot be experienced as he once knew them in the "dimming past."

The aching melancholy of these observations became a major mode of the final years of Twain's life, when his grief often took the form of "immersion in the past . . . With each diminishment of his circle, Clemens reacted by turning inward and retracing his beginnings."[55] Another elegiac piece of this same period, "Early Days," represented "an ideal which existed only in Mark Twain's memories as he attempted to restore balance to his own life after the trauma of Susy's death."[56] Much of Twain's personal writing after 1896 pulsates with similar sensibilities, as he wrote on February 11, 1902, to Francis H. Skrine, while commenting on Skrine's biography of Sir William Wilson Hunter: "The passage where he went back alone to the humble early home in India + found it empty + falling to decay—that is a moving picture, eloquent of what success costs us, the pathos of it only realizable to the full when we stand where the march began—and think! I have had that experience, + know the deeps of it. The book stirs every emotion + throbs with every interest that human beings feel."[57] It is striking that out of Skrine's entire lengthy book, Twain is most moved to comment on the sketch of the famed man returning to his lost past and on its connection with the grief of personal loss. Similarly, some of Twain's more powerful expressions of sentimentality are in letters to Joe Twichell describing his responses to the deaths of close Hartford friends. In a letter of 1898 responding to news of the death of Ned Bunce, Twain states, "I will not try to talk about it, it breaks my heart. Ned Bunce was very very near + dear to me, + to all this home-circle of mine; + he was always that, from the beginning. They have begun to fall! The charm is broken, the others will follow, now."[58]

And in a letter of 1900 about the death of Henry Robinson, Twain laments,

> [his] death is a sharp wound to me, + it goes very deep. I had a strong affection for him, + I think he had for me. Every Friday, three-fourths of the year for 16 years he was at the billiard party in our house. When we come home, how shall we have billiard-nights again—with no Ned Bunce + no Henry Robinson. . . . Susy is gone . . . the friends are passing, one by one; our house, where such warm blood + such dear blood flowed so freely, is become a cemetery.[59]

Twain speaks here, as late as 1900, of returning to live in the Hartford home as if it were a real possibility, but both he and Twichell must have understood that by then it was just a charade of emotion.

The nostalgic reminiscences of old friends passing away, along with his elegiac poems, exploit the "poetics of sentimentality" described by Mary Kete, especially insofar as they attempt to "reattach symbolic connections that have been severed by the contingencies of human existence."[60] As Kete demonstrates, the theme runs through much of Twain's greatest fiction as well: for example, in the Mississippi fictions, which can be read as enactments "of a kind of mourning for the world that preceded" the post–Civil War era of industrialization and frenzied growth.[61] This mode signifies "the cultural expression of the desire for union. . . .

a manifestation of the belief in or yearning for consonance—or even unity—of principle or purpose."[62] In this sense, Twain's elegies for Susy are comparable to numerous longer works like "Old Times on the Mississippi" and *The Adventures of Tom Sawyer:* they can all be seen as spiritual works insofar as they participate in the cultural work of sentimentalism that seeks to conserve bonds with the transcendent and unite diverse human beings.

Thus recent theories of sentimentalism suggest another side to Twain's frequent chastisement of all manner of sentimental and funereal verse in such passages as the Emmeline Grangerford episode of *Huckleberry Finn.* Surprisingly, Twain may have been most powerful and authentic, and finally perhaps most convincing, at the two moments when his work derived overtly from his most devastating personal loss, the death of Susy. Although Twain's antisentimental stance is far better known, one might just as easily focus on his dependence on the pathos and emotional depth in these sentimental pieces. Indeed, as both "In Memoriam" and "Broken Idols" demonstrate, Twain worked effectively, and at times even powerfully, within this mode. As "acts of conservation" filled with "utopian promise that wielded great ideological effect,"[63] these works by Twain show that the skepticism and nihilism so prevalent in much of his other late work must be tempered by the hope and visionary longing for attachment and union that also remained—attitudes which, perhaps consciously or unconsciously, were the true results of his continuing bond with his beloved Susy.

Although both elegies are largely sentimental, their contrasting tones and elements are symptomatic of the spiritual crisis that raged in the mind of their author. Again the ideological battle is a common response among parents who have lost children: "some live in a divided world. They maintain a *bond with the transcendent* that is linked to their children. In other parts of their lives, however, they feel cut off from the God in whom they still believe."[64] These two trends are illustrated in much of the writing that Mark Twain either began or published during the remainder of his life. First we will consider this feeling of being "cut off" from God. Afterward we will present the far less obvious theme: the manner in which Twain maintained a bond with the transcendent.

It is a commonplace to point out that the bad times for Mark Twain and his family actually began a long time prior to Susy's death. The fairly lengthy halcyon days during which he wrote his greatest fiction featured Twain with his family in their resplendent Hartford home from the early 1870s through the mid to late 1880s. But things began turning sour near the end of their residence there. In a sense, the family's time together at 351 Farmington Avenue in Hartford was generally the best of times for Mark Twain, but only if one ignores the messiness of the last two years. The departure from that house in the summer of 1891 may have been the symbolic conclusion to the happy days associated with the house, and that departure certainly ushered in a long and steady decline of fortunes and health for virtually every member of the inner circle. But serious troubles began to surface prior to the move away. For example, in the final two years of the residence in the Hartford home, numerous unfortunate events conspired together to assure that the generally pleasant circumstances of the Clemens family would never be the same. In 1889, the Paige typesetter, in which Twain was heavily invested, continually had technical problems; brother-in-law Theodore Crane died; and Livy experienced chronic health issues. Meanwhile Twain completed and published *Connecticut Yankee,* which featured one of the darkest endings up to that time in the annals of American fiction. In 1890, the financial failure of the Paige typesetter became a constant source of stress; Twain was involved in litigation regarding the profits from the dramatization of *The Prince and the Pauper;* daughter Susy was sent off to Bryn Mawr College, signaling the end of her childhood; Twain's mother, Jane, suffered a stroke in Illinois and then died in October; Livy's mother died a month later; and daughter Jean suffered epileptic seizures. In 1891, Twain's publishing company spiraled deeper into debt; the Paige typesetter finally appeared to Twain to be a black hole of financial ruin, and he cut off any future investment in it and began regarding his previous investments lost; Charles Webster, despised former head of Twain's publishing company, who got most of the blame for its failures, died; Susy, homesick and possibly becoming romantically obsessed with her friend Louise Brownell, left college (or was forced out by her confused and concerned parents)[65]; Twain himself suffered chronic pain from rheumatism in his arm while Livy experienced increased problems with her heart; and the family as a whole closed the Hartford home (permanently, as it turned out) and relocated to Europe for most of the next nine years.

All of these events, along with numerous other deaths, discouragements, and disappointments, took their toll on Mark Twain and Livy, to be sure. But Susy's death in 1896 marked the absolute low point of the period of time when Mark Twain, as Michelson puts it, "sails into choppier waters."[66] The sailing metaphor here is particularly apt, since during these years Twain compulsively wrote tales of sea journeys, many of which end with ships trapped and unable to move, such as in the notorious "Devil's Race-Track" region of the ocean where vessels go round and round endlessly, never escaping. There they might end up as mere "derelicts"—a term that Mark Twain used in reference to himself on many occasions, most famously in the story of the "Refuge of the Derelicts." In a letter marked by discussion of their common grief experience (Howells had also lost a daughter, Winnifred, in 1889), Twain tells Howells, "for we *are* a pair of old derelicts drifting around, now, with some of our passengers gone & the sunniness of the others in (total) eclipse."[67] The tales of seafaring derelicts—including "The Great Dark," "The Enchanted Sea-Wilderness," "Indiantown," "Which Was the Dream?" and "Which Was It?"—feature overwhelming disorientation and annoying repetition, patterns that the protagonists are simply powerless to change or even understand. These nightmarish enactments dramatized the gist of a phrase that Twain began using occasionally in his writings of this period (as in "Hadleyburg," for instance): "And so on, and so on." It was a feature picked up later by one of Twain's truest literary protégés of the twentieth century, Kurt Vonnegut, to signify the apparent futility of human existence. Twain's occasional reliance on this little phrase is symptomatic of a deepening emotional ennui with life and a resignation to what Friedrich Nietzsche called, at about the same time, "eternal recurrence."[68] Mark Twain's encounter with Nietzsche's work was brief but suggestive, especially given their agreement on certain important ideas such as a sense of life as a cyclical process going nowhere: "And so on, and so on . . . "

Much of the expression of bitterness and nihilism in Mark Twain's final years should be connected with his debilitating experience of grief, beginning with Susy, but there were obviously many other contributing factors—some dating to childhood. Ron Powers has provided the most thorough account of the many gruesome experiences of violence, death, drowning, corpses, murder, and mayhem to which Sammy Clemens was privy in his youth. Among the most often discussed is the death of his father, John. But just as traumatic, if not more so, was the sudden death of his younger brother Henry. Injured mortally in the explosion of the steamboat *Pennsylvania* on June 13, 1858, Henry died in his sleep about a week later, with young Sam nearby. Twain's grief was unspeakable, and the guilt over Henry's death seemed to multiply over time. Over forty years later, Twain recalled that it was at his insistence that Henry had been given a "vast quantity" of morphine by a young physician "hardly out of college." Thus did the horror of the death of Henry implicate him as well: "if only Sam had not insisted on that morphine."[69] After Twain's path led him east and he married Livy, the Clemenses suffered the loss in 1872 of their firstborn son, Langdon, named after Livy's late father. Twain implicated himself in that tragedy as well, insisting that taking young Langdon for a carriage ride on a chilly spring day, and not diphtheria, had caused his son to die. By the time of the financial disasters and then Susy's death, Mark Twain was clearly well acquainted with grief—along with a feeling of guilt in somehow contributing to the deaths of his loved ones.

Given these traumatic events, Twain's nihilistic tirades are hardly unusual and certainly not pathological. Nor is it fair to consider these final fourteen years as representative of Mark Twain's view of religion over a long and full lifetime. Not only does traumatic grief tend to initiate a crisis in one's worldview, it also can bring about a profound collapse of one's ideological system. Thus conclusions drawn about Mark Twain's true religious beliefs based on his rants and screeds against the Almighty from this particular period are dubious. Nevertheless, these dark writings exist and must be accounted for. Indeed the vision of the alienated, grief-ridden curmudgeon shaking his fist at God has become the standard reading of the final period of Twain's life. As Hamlin Hill once memorably put it,

> Until 1900 Mark Twain managed to retain control over his universe, over his despair, pessimism, frustration, and insensitivity, by his artistic capacity. . . . [but after 1900] the bitterness which permeated *What Is Man?*, "Letters from the Earth," the "Mysterious Stranger" fragments, much of the autobiography, and most of the shorter political writings was a rage at the obscenity of life.[70]

Typical of this is a short piece entitled "In My Bitterness," written in 1897 at Weggis, Switzerland. It begins, "In my bitterness I said, blaspheming," and goes on to incorporate some of the most stinging and pointed remarks Twain ever wrote about the death of Susy and, by extension, the problem of pain:

> there you lie, poor abused slave, set free from the unspeakable insult of life. . . . you have not been freed out of pity for you, but to drive one more knife into my heart. . . . He never does a kindness. When He seems to do one it is a trap which He is setting; you will walk into it some day, then you will understand. . . . He gives you a wife and children whom you adore, only that through the spectacle of the wanton shames and miseries which He will inflict upon them He may tear the palpitating heart out of your breast and slap you in the face with it.[71]

This mood of despair is perhaps best captured in the rather startling denunciations of biblical Christianity contained in the autobiographical dictations of June 1906.[72]

Much of Twain's embrace of nihilism registered his increasingly cynical view of humans' status as moral free agents. His spiritual struggles are informed by the theological and ethical debates of the same period. Andrew Hoffman has briefly discussed the paradoxical nature of Mark Twain's musings upon human nature. Hoffman argues that Twain's relative absence from public life after his return to America in 1900 "had as much to do with an internal conflict as with his health or his desire for quieter company. He engaged himself in crusade after crusade in part to solidify the image of Mark Twain as a cultural and moral force, but that effort contradicted his belief in the utter absence of free will, which he had developed in his 'gospel,' *What is Man?*"[73] This internal conflict was a continuation of the nineteenth-century struggle to resolve the optimism and romance of Social Christianity's populist brand of Pelagianism with the problem of pain and the fallenness of man emphasized by Calvinists. But like the larger cultural debate, Twain was unable to find a solution, and his musings on the subject were often riddled with contradiction. These musings included lengthy exchanges with Twichell, often in letters debating complicated theological matters. Scholars have typically emphasized the polarizing differences between Twain and

Twichell, but Peter Messent's account usefully analyzes their "dialogic relationship." Messent brilliantly shows how Twichell was "peculiarly twinned with Twain" in a symbiotic relationship in these latter years not unlike the characters Angelo and Luigi in "Those Extraordinary Twins" of 1894.[74] These two characters, whose names echo "angel" and "Lucifer," are spiritual opposites: Angelo is a Methodist, Luigi a freethinker; Angelo reads Richard Allestree's devotional piece *The Whole Duty of Man,* while Luigi reads Tom Paine's *Age of Reason.*[75] Ironically they take turns having control over their shared body.

Messent's intriguing observation suggests that Twain and Twichell also shared much more than is commonly acknowledged and that they each needed and embraced the theological balance that the other provided. Like Angelo and Luigi, their arguments and counterarguments were also inseparable, joined at the hip, so to speak. For example, Joe Twichell understood better than anyone that there was an internal inconsistency in Twain's personal view, and more generally in American religious culture, both of which seemed to argue that man is responsible for the mess he is in, yet somehow is *not* responsible for it. Twichell occasionally pointed this out to Twain, or to Livy, as in a letter describing "Mark's eulogy of the Human Race" dated December 9, 1901: it was "like the strain of an Aeolian harp; such was my affection for the speaker. Of course, I didn't believe a word of it—any more than he did—but I was a charmed listener, and would like to hear it again."[76] This metaphor is stunning in its comparison of Mark Twain's vile denunciations of mankind with the "the strain of an Aeolian harp"—an image used by the Romantic poets to convey the transcendental music that one hears upon encountering the sublime. The phrase suggests not only Twichell's great affection for Mark Twain but also the sublime truth of Twain's denunciations. Twichell was fairly orthodox in his faith, knew well the biblical doctrine of the fallenness of man as depicted in both Genesis 3 and Romans 3, and agreed with the fundamentals of standard Christian faith, including its insistence on total depravity—even though his Social Christian sentiments tended toward a more liberal position. Twichell himself would have assented to the Calvinist doctrine of the fall, at least on some level. But he would also have embraced a mystical balance between fate and freedom. Twichell may be giving us a bit of a stretcher here in suggesting that Mark Twain "didn't believe a word of it." But both Twichell and Twain understood the theological complexities inherent in the issue itself—an issue long considered one of the great unsolvable paradoxes of the Christian faith, pitting free will against fate, Arminianism against Calvinism.

Twain and Twichell were not only conversant in the technical ideas and language of the theological issue, but they also discussed it in their letters on numerous occasions. Perhaps the most celebrated of these exchanges was initiated in 1902, when Twichell gave Twain a copy of Jonathan Edwards's *Freedom of the Will* to read on the train ride home after a visit to Hartford. A few days later, Twichell received a funny letter from Twain, calling Edwards a lunatic who wants to blame mankind even after proving that mankind's actions come from motivations beyond his control. But the letter is more than just a sarcastic swipe at Edwards; in fact, it shows Twain's keen theological interests at this late date and his desire to hash through difficult issues with an orthodox and highly educated expositor of the Bible:

> From Bridgeport to New York, thence to home, & continuously until near midnight I wallowed & reeked with Jonathan in his insane debauch; rose immensely refreshed & fine at ten this morning, but with a strange & haunting sense of having been on a three days' tear with a drunken lunatic. It is years since I have known these sensations. All through the book is the glare of a resplendent intellect gone mad—a marvelous spectacle. No, not all through the book—the drunk does not come on till the last third, where what I take to be Calvinism & its God begins to show up & shine red & hideous in the glow from the fires of hell, their only right and proper adornment.
>
> Jonathan seems to hold (as against the Arminian position) that the man (or his soul or his will) never creates an impulse itself, but is moved to action by an impulse back of it. That's sound!
>
> Also, that of two or more things offered it, it infallibly chooses the one which for the moment is most pleasing to ITSELF. Perfectly correct! An immense admission for a man not otherwise sane.
>
> Up to that point he could have written Chapters III & IV of my suppressed Gospel. But there we seem to separate. He seems to concede the indisputable & unshaken dominion of Motive & Necessity (call them what he may, these are exterior forces & not under the man's authority,

> guidance, or even suggestion); then he suddenly flies the logical track & (to all seeming) makes the man & not those exterior forces responsible to God for the man's thoughts, words, & acts. It is frank insanity.
>
> I think that when he concedes the autocratic dominion of Motive and Necessity he grants a third position of mine—that a man's mind is a mere machine—an automatic machine—which is handled entirely from the outside, the man himself furnishing it absolutely nothing; not an ounce of its fuel, & not so much as a bare suggestion to that exterior engineer as to what the machine shall do nor how it shall do it nor when.
>
> After that concession it was time for him to get alarmed & shirk—for he was pointed straight for the only rational & possible next station on that piece of road—the irresponsibility of man to God.
>
> And so he shirked. Shirked, and arrived at this handsome result: Man is commanded to do so & so. It has been ordained from the beginning of time that some men sha'n't & others can't. These are to blame: let them be damned.[77]

Twain's elaborate critique indicates that his powerful theological sensibilities are capable of making careful and complicated distinctions. It even indicates his sophisticated knowledge of and comfort with technical terms, including Arminianism, and with theological style, as in the distinction of "the man (or his soul or his will)." His general argument boils down to his resistance to two seemingly contradictory notions of Edwards: 1) that mankind "never creates an impulse itself, but is moved to action by an impulse back of it"; and 2) "Man is commanded to do so & so." It is a sophisticated attack against mankind's responsibility for any of his own actions—yet it comes from a man whose key contributions to American culture were often ethical in nature and thus premised on human responsibility. Furthermore these thoughts come from a man notoriously unable to deal with his own sense of personal guilt.

In the spirit of the insoluble nature of the debate, Twichell responded to Twain's charges in the following manner:

> Your report of your impressions of Edwards on The Will was vastly entertaining. I read it to Dean Sage when I was with him at Cornell University in May—'twas the last time I ever saw him—and he pronounced it sound i.e. as a criticism. While, of course, I do not believe—as you do—

> that we live move and have our being as moral creatures in a profound immitigable all encompassing element of Inveracity, I do think there's a deal of truth in what you say of Edwards. As a matter of fact he has always by many been held to be a flat necessitarian in spite of his disclaimers, and his flop to break the [meshes] of his own argument.[78]

Twichell here is generous in his response. He refers to human existence as that state in which we "live move and have our being," a biblical allusion to Acts 17:28 that is highly elevating and suggestive of a powerful moral agency. He follows by strongly disagreeing with Twain's position, which characterizes human existence as marked by a "profound immitigable all encompassing element of Inveracity." This may be a reference to something Twain said at some point of conversation. But in effect it is a strong yet accurate version of Twain's screed, and its humorous tone underlines Twain's extreme position. Again the casual manner in which Twichell describes Edwards as a "necessitarian" indicates the rigor of Twain's theological knowledge. He tells Twain that in fact "there's a deal of truth" in his critique of Edwards, suggesting that he also finds real problems in Edwards's analysis—not surprising, given the radical embrace of free will in nineteenth-century American liberal theology. Edwards, as Twain has complained, is "a flat necessitarian," meaning that he rejects flatly human free will. Despite his "disclaimers," says Twichell, Twain is right—Edwards cannot have it both ways. Twichell disagrees with Twain, however, in his rather one-dimensional understanding of the issue at stake. Twichell recognized that it is not simply an either/or proposition and that Edwards was attempting to show that in fact human acts can be simultaneously voluntary and necessary. Twain was unable to see this, perhaps because his extreme deism over the years had disallowed a mystical and supernatural angle of vision on the debate. Unable to embrace the paradoxical nature of this controversy, Twain was left to maintain a "flat necessitarianism" and accept the moral implications of that position: that ultimately mankind is not responsible for his sins, so God must be. Still he often suffered utter despair in the face of what he perceived to be his own guilt. For example, after the death of Susy, he wrote to Livy, "I pitied you in this awful trouble that my mistakes have brought upon you. You forgive me, I know, but I shall never forgive myself while the life is in me."[79] Somehow it escaped him that if he were a mere machine, forgiveness would be irrelevant.

Elsewhere, evidence shows that Twain frequently had second thoughts about his grand theory of mankind as machinery caught up in a mechanistic determinism—what Twichell called his "flat necessitarianism." For instance, in a dictation on November 4, 1904, Twain acknowledges these implications after a long rant on the nature of humans as mere machines:

> I wish I could learn to remember that it is unjust + dishonorable to put blame upon the human race for any of its acts. For it did not make itself, it did not make its nature, it is merely a machine, it is moved wholly by outside influences, it has no hand in creating the outside influences nor in choosing which of them it will welcome or reject, its performance is wholly automatic, it has no more mastership nor authority over its mind than it has over its stomach. . . . I wish I could learn to pity the human race instead of censuring it and laughing at it; + I could if the outside influence of old habit were not so strong upon my machine. It vexes me to catch myself praising the clean private citizen Roosevelt + blaming the soiled President Roosevelt, when I know that neither praise nor blame is due to him for any thought or word or deed of his, he being merely a helpless + irresponsible coffee-mill ground by the hand of God.[80]

Twain would have much more to say regarding President Roosevelt, as in this excerpt from June 1905:

> I am not laughing at Theodore, but only at the funny *results* of his make. I keep it clearly in mind all the time—try to, anyway—that he had nothing to do with building any part of himself + is not in any way to blame for the resulting conduct. . . . It is *handiest* to name the *man*—+ and it is habit, too, old lifelong silly habit, + now ineradicable—but understand me I always *mean* the coffee-mill.[81]

The problem is, as much as Twain would like to chastise and critique the man, Roosevelt is ultimately not to blame according to Twain's own gospel of mankind. One cannot read passages like these, however, without realizing that Mark Twain really was unable to embrace fully the gospel of his own making. Finally, without humanity being required to stand trial and answer for its failure to achieve shalom, humor, critical commentary, and art itself appear pointless and futile. And human hope simply disappears.

And yet the diatribe against Roosevelt is instructive in its apparent sympathies for its subject: "I know that neither praise nor blame is due to him for any thought or word or deed of his, he being merely a helpless + irresponsible coffee-mill ground by the hand of God." As Joe Twichell had put it, such venting involves not just a rage against the pain of life, but also a "device of his charity." Whether we can accept Twichell's optimistic opinion or not, it seems clear that Twain remained stumped by these notoriously difficult theological debates. Perhaps he should be forgiven if he simply threw up his hands and invoked the image of human existence as merely a "coffee-mill ground by the hand of God." It would be unfair to Mark Twain to overemphasize the blasts from the pain-ridden final years and to extrapolate from them in order to draw conclusions about the theological vision of the entire career. Such a method denies the hope that was inherent both in his humor and in the many forms in which he expressed his social critique. Despite his many claims in such late works as *What is Man?,* Twain was in fact no "flat necessitarian." Rather, Mark Twain was by and large a writer of hope, a visionary who hoped for a better world more fully modeled after shalom, the way things ought to be.

But as with many aging warriors, hope diminishes. By the time of his harshest words, he was more than seventy years old and plagued by chronic health problems brought on by incessant cigar smoking, severe personal and financial stress, and devastating loss. As one account has it, Twain did not arrive at his final view on these matters until 1906: "he had reached the conclusion that in establishing basic human temperament, and hence people's reactions to all 'circumstances' they might meet, God was fundamentally to blame for all the sufferings, shams, hypocrisies, and pretenses of the human race."[82] As he wrote in a letter to his daughter Jean, dated June 1907: "God Almighty alone is responsible for your temperament, your malady and all your troubles and sorrows. I cannot blame you for them and I do not."[83] One of the most blatant fictional treatments of this view is "Little Bessie," an extended dialogue between a three-and-a-half-year-old girl and her staunchly orthodox Christian mother on matters of ethics, responsibility, judgment, and virginity. The effect of having such a young protagonist, who typically gets the best of her mother's vapid and predictably programmed apologetic responses, is to show how even a very young intellect can see the stupidity of much Christian belief. Here Mark Twain trashes standard Christian explanations of pain and suffering as works of God's loving discipline and judgment. He also sketches a third character, an enlightened older man, the "irreligious" Hollister, who leads the young Bessie on her path to fuller understanding. Hollister invokes the image of Frankenstein and his monster, and compares this relationship with that of God and his monster, mankind: "Frankenstein was horrified and in despair, and said, I made him, without asking his consent, and it makes me responsible for every crime he commits. . . . God is responsible for everything man does, all the same; He can't get around that fact. There is only one Criminal, and it is not man."[84]

"Little Bessie" is Mark Twain at his "flat necessitarian" best. In his latter years, Twain delighted in playing a role not unlike that of Hollister. He took great pride in announcing to the world that human beings were themselves grotesque creations of a mad scientist like Frankenstein: they are mere "coffee mills" being cranked by the hand of a sinister God. He often felt giddy with pleasure that he might be remembered as the founder of a new and mystical revelation about the human condition. Regarding his "gospel," published after his death as *What Is Man?,* he once smirked, "whenever I read the small book myself to a person of good intelligence . . . I always capture a disciple. Generally against the disciple's will."[85] (Oddly, again, that statement contradicts his theory of the will, if you unpack it.) Somehow he was under the impression that these were new and daring ideas, although even in theological circles they certainly were not. And yet it is true that many of the themes that he focused on in these last decades presaged the modern temperaments of alienation, existential dread, a savage critique of bourgeois mentality, and even the hegemony of discursive fields that Michel Foucault and others have described as crucial insights of postmodernism.

Perhaps for these reasons, critics have tended to gravitate toward these elements in his writing, thus casting Twain as a sort of proto-postmodernist—although by doing so, they have only told part of the story. Twain critics have generally concluded that the last years illustrate a steady decline into nihilism, and there is much evidence to support this view. But a focus on the nihilism of the later writings is no more legitimate, on its own, than a strict focus on the ethical and moral dimensions of work from the same period. Both themes are there and act as counterbalances to one another. Both are necessary to illustrate the battles going on in the mind of Mark Twain and the battles going on within American and European culture at the turn of the century. These competing themes are like Angelo and Luigi, fighting for control over their joined body in "Those Extraordinary Twins."

But ultimately which side won those battles? Louis J. Budd has concluded, despite the strong evidence suggesting a turn to nihilism and deterministic pessimism in the latter years, that Twain "took active part in his city, nation-state, and world-state. My reading of our situation today calls for making this the final emphasis. In continuing to debate Twain's writing, some of us try to learn from his commitment to human responsibility."[86] This claim is particularly powerful because in his final fourteen years, Twain increasingly insisted that mankind has no responsibility. How is it then—if Twain truly believed during those dark years that humans have no responsibility—that the dean of today's Twain scholars can look to him and learn from his "commitment to human responsibility"? This conclusion can make sense if it is plausible that Twain maintained some semblance of an old-fashioned concept of a God-ordained moral universe. If this is true, then it is also plausible that Twain never could overcome the transcendental leanings of his mind and sensibility, nor the implications of the apocalyptic dynamite of his humor.

As a result, Twain's work, even in the so-called dark period after 1896, continued to be informed by and based on an eschatological vision of hope—despite the excruciating realities of the pain and suffering of the world, not to mention his and Livy's personal pain and grief. This hopefulness is illustrated in a wonderful story told by Adele le Bourgeois Chapin. Chapin narrates an episode that occurred presumably in late 1896, after Susy's death. In a visit with Twain, Chapin was struck by his tragic loneliness, especially with his wife Livy having returned to the States, and she sensed his need to get back out among the people.

Chapin asked him to accompany her during one of her regular visits to the London Hospital and tell funny stories to the sick men there, many of whom were dying of cancer and other untreatable illnesses. Twain agreed to go finally, and as many patients as possible crammed into the ward for his visit.

> One felt, listening to him, as one feels sitting in the sun—that the warmth of it sinks in and in; so his words gave one a feeling of mirth and warmth. . . . As we drove away in a hansom, he said to me: "I have never had such an appreciative audience," and spoke with great enthusiasm and wonderful words; alas! I cannot remember them now, but his eyes and mine were filled with tears.[87]

This is a remarkable act of courage and mercy, especially given the fact that the story begins in the throes of bitter and inconsolable grief for Susy. One senses the broken heart of the father here, who puts aside his personal horror and goes to these men in their own dying days to minister to them. Most importantly, one is struck by the hopeful spirit in the midst of crushing personal despair.

Twain's hopeful spirit is also reflected in his dealings with Rose Lathrop, daughter of Nathaniel Hawthorne, who later became Sister Alphonsa, the founder of the Servants for Relief of Incurable Cancer. In 1901, she asked Twain to write an essay for her publication *Christ's Poor,* believing his endorsement might bring it notoriety and perhaps increase its support. Twain did not agree to write for the publication, but in a letter to Lathrop he stated his willingness not only to support her work but to enlist his acquaintances for support:

> among the needs of your noble charity is money, and I know some people who have it and who have not been reluctant to spend it on good causes. And certainly if there is an unassailably good cause in the world, it is this one undertaken by the Dominican Sisters, of housing, nourishing, and nursing the most pathetically unfortunate of all the afflicted among us—men and women sentenced to a painful and lingering death by incurable disease.
>
> I have known about this lofty work of yours since long ago—indeed, from the day you began it; I have known of its steady growth and prog-

> ress, step by step, to its present generous development, and assured position among those benefactions to which the reverent homage of all creeds and colors is due; I have seen it rise from seedling to tree with no endowment but the voluntary aid which your patient labor and faith have drawn from the purses of grateful and compassionate men; and I am glad in the prosperous issue of your work, and glad to know that this prosperity will continue, and be permanent—a thing which I do know, for that endowment is banked where it cannot fail until pity fails in the hearts of men, and that will never be.[88]

The luminous quality of this passage indicates that even during his last decade, Mark Twain still entertained stirring emotions regarding the sublime "bank" of all human sympathy.

The sheer hopefulness of these episodes is often overlooked in descriptions of Twain's final years. But several years before Susy's death, as Twain grew more despondent about the freedom of individuals in the mid-1890s, he personified this hope in what he considered his masterpiece—a novelization of one of Europe's great individuals. Surely one of the most interesting phenomena during these years, especially in revealing both the father's tender heart for his daughter and his tendency toward moral freedom, was the extensive work and unusually focused and sustained level of attention that he put into his last published novel, *Personal Recollections of Joan of Arc* (1896). This historical novel, written in Italy and France between 1893 and 1895, was produced at a time of extreme financial despair and personal disappointment. Although it seems odd in retrospect, both Twain and Howells considered *Personal Recollections of Joan of Arc* to be of very high quality—perhaps, even, his literary masterpiece. Their high regard for this novel can be partially explained in view of certain cultural and religious contexts of the time. First, as often noted, Twain's great idolization of innocent young women, and particularly of his virgin daughter Susy, is reflected in this work.[89] In a sense, as one critic puts it, "Joan resembled the innumerable dying children of Victorian novels—descendants of Little Eva and Little Nell. All died young and undefiled, their innocence preserved forever." Tributes to the likes of Joan of Arc offered Twain, perhaps, "a vicarious escape from adult moral and sexual anxieties."[90] Secondly, the novel can be understood as a direct statement about Twain's long engagements with issues of gender and social reform, especially as supported by such organizations as the Women's Christian Temperance Union (WCTU). One critic writes, "Clemens's *Joan of Arc* espouses all the 'pet' causes of the WCTU: she is an adamant defender of children's rights, animal rights, dress reform, and temperance."[91] Finally, the novel should be considered in relation to Twain's ongoing interest in the American civil religion. Twain's connection of Joan with a strongly pro-American ideology that weds the Christian ethics of the Sermon on the Mount with a zealous patriotism constitutes a classic expression of the American jeremiad. Here, for example, are the rhetorically powerful concluding remarks of the book:

> I have finished my story of Joan of Arc, that wonderful child, that sublime personality, that spirit which in one regard has had no peer and will have none—this: its purity from all alloy of self-seeking, self-interest, personal ambition. In it no trace of these motives can be found, search as you may, and this cannot be said of any other person whose name appears in profane history.
>
> With Joan of Arc love of country was more than a sentiment—it was a passion. She was the Genius of Patriotism—she was Patriotism embodied, concreted, made flesh, and palpable to the touch and visible to the eye. . . . a slender girl in her first young bloom, with the martyr's crown upon her head, and in her hand the sword that severed her country's bonds—shall not this, and no other, stand for PATRIOTISM through all the ages until time shall end?[92]

Again Twain emphasizes an incarnational vision of patriotism: "she was Patriotism embodied, concreted, made flesh, palpable to the touch and visible to the eye." Finally, the novel celebrates home and hearth, and the composition process reflects that element. As he wrote to a friend, "[*Joan of Arc*] is private & not for print, it's written for love and not for lucre, & to entertain the family with, around the lamp by the fire."[93] For Twain, the nightly reading from the work was keenly associated with the warmth and love of his hearth and home; more broadly, Twain regarded the book as a sort of ameliorative relief from fallen and futile existence. As one critic put it, "There was that in Mark Twain's nature which recoiled from the darkness and cried out for affirmation of man's higher nature."[94]

Joan of Arc can also be read as a plainspoken hagiography of Susy. Since it is clear that *Joan of Arc* was at least partially modeled after Susy, these stylized musings show how much emotional and mental adoration Twain invested in his daughter. Susy and her sisters also represented the next generations beyond his own children and his legacy as forebear to future Clemenses. He makes clear his need to have descendants, as well as his sincere enjoyment of and devotion to the young, in the poignant dictation of April 17, 1908, which is filled with the grief of missing the little children. Here is a compelling account of Mark Twain's deep desire to have children around him, to hug and hold, and the poignant confession that "What I needed was grandchildren."[95] These emotions are the simplest and certainly the most satisfying explanation for the group of young girls called the "Aquarium" that gave Twain endless joy in his final years.[96] For Mark Twain and Livy, their children (and after Livy's death, the pseudo-children of the Aquarium) were the most tangible expression of hope remaining in their lives.

Sometimes critics have dismissed or even criticized Twain's close connections with the many young girls of the Aquarium with whom he became familiar in the last years. Some have even suggested that Twain eroticized these relationships. Another way to understand Twain's compulsive attention to young girls, however, is to see it as a symptom of what Erik Erikson has called "generativity." By generativity, Erikson refers to the complex choice middle-aged and older adults must face between stagnation in life and a creative means of affecting positively the younger generations that will follow. Erikson argues for the renewal of middle to late adulthood through a reconception of identity that focuses on two related aspects. First, generativity suggests creativity. Parker Palmer describes this as "the ongoing possibility that no matter our age, we can help co-create the world." Second, generativity suggests the perpetual emergence of generations behind each of us, implying the need for the elders to help guide the generations that will follow them. Palmer notes that when these two elements are brought together, generativity becomes "creativity in the service of the young—a way in which the elders serve not only the young but also their own well-being."[97]

Rather than dismiss *Personal Recollections of Joan of Arc*, or ridicule

Twain's seemingly abnormal attraction to the young girls of the Aquarium, one might read both as signals of Mark Twain's yearning for concrete outlets for his generative spirit, outlets for giving back to the younger generation. Perhaps we should regard *Joan of Arc* as a particularly clear confession of Twain's continued spiritual sensibility—a frank affirmation of the better angels of humanity's nature, or at least of his desire to continue striving after them. These better angels, manifested quite often in the form of Twain's moral outrage toward social injustice, became increasingly a regular feature of his late career. For example, one of the clearest expressions of Twain's desire for generativity comes in the remaining fragment of an essay or speech he composed some time after Susy's death called "The Divine Spark":

> My young friend, why do we say *the* divine spark? It is because we thus wish to recognize a certain imposing & impressive fact: That there is one quality which is peculiarly & especially, & almost entirely & exclusively, God's possession: of all his attributes the one which sheds the chiefest glory upon his name; in the flood of whose brightness His other attributes show faint & dim, like stars at noonday, drowned in the white splendors of the sun.
>
> Yes. With Him this attribute is as it were a blinding light which fills the wide heavens, inundates all space, while what we, poor humble creatures, possess of it & are so proud of & so grateful for, is so little, so modest, that we reduce it to microscopic measurement & call it a *spark*. We claim of this all-pervading effulgence no more than this; yet how rich it makes us! It lifts us far above the other creatures, & confers upon us kinship with God. Remote—yes, infinitely remote—but kinship nevertheless. What a noble possession, what an imperial possession, it is: the divine spark! *The* divine spark! Think of it—it is ours!—*ours*! Without it, we're poverty; with it, who can estimate our wealth![98]

This passage's opening words, addressing the essay to a "young friend," indicate that they were presumably to be part of a speech composed from a generative perspective—composed, that is, for the purpose of sowing hope into a younger generation of listeners. A later section of this document refers to "Howells's latest" fiction, *The Landlord at Lion's-*

Head (1897), so we can be rather certain about its date. This passage suggests Twain maintained a theistic outlook regarding his generative duties and that he still considered how a belief in God might influence the way we understand our world and our social functions. More importantly, it provides some theoretical/theological basis upon which Twain could ground his benevolent acts of Social Christianity. Specifically, by attributing to all humans a "divine spark," an "all-pervading effulgence" that puts us in the company of the divine, Twain becomes almost dumbfounded in a breathless consideration of the mystical aspect of humanity: "What a noble possession, what an imperial possession, it is: the divine spark! *The* divine spark! Think of it—it is ours!—*ours*! Without it, we're poverty; with it, who can estimate our wealth!" This view helps explain the metaphysical basis upon which he undertook his many charitable and Christian activities for over four decades: Twain's sympathy for mankind was founded, we might say, on the hunch that perhaps, after all, humankind had been created in the image of God, the master artisan. It places Twain's charitable words and deeds in an important context: the moral economy of New England Social Christianity, as modeled by Joe Twichell and the Asylum Hill Church. Within this frame, we might say, Twain's acts can be interrogated as profoundly Christian, insofar as they all assert the immeasurable value and beauty of each individual, who have been "endowed by their Creator," as the Declaration of Independence has it, with certain rights. Of course, along with this high praise we must always recall the pessimism just behind it: as Twain once put it, "All that I care to know is that a man is a human being—that is enough for me; he can't be worse."[99] But then again, this can also be contextualized into the religious ethos by its insistence on man's fallenness—perhaps the crucial doctrine of strict Calvinism, a topic at the heart of Twain's humor. One might even say that a harsh opposition to the concept of a divine spark against hellish corruption is the crucial insight of prophetic Christian faith—as posited by the later "Christian realism" championed by Reinhold Niebuhr and put to pragmatic effect by Martin Luther King Jr.[100]

For a world-famous author who had supposedly abandoned human responsibility much earlier, Twain certainly maintained and acted upon profoundly moral imperatives suggestive of a "divine spark" during his final decades. His long private criticism of Czarist Russia became public in 1905, for example, with the appearance of "The Czar's Soliloquy." His attacks on Western imperialism in such far-flung locales as South Africa, China, Cuba, the Congo, and the Philippines are illustrated in such pieces as "To the Person Sitting in Darkness" and "King Leopold's Soliloquy"; he equates imperialist motives more specifically with the work of the church in his "To My Missionary Critics." In 1901, Twain was so appalled by the injustices of the lynching of African Americans that he pledged to write a book on it. The result, "The United States of Lyncherdom," though it is one of his most powerful rhetorical *tours de force,* was unfortunately not published until after his death. Twain addressed anti-Semiticism in such works as "Stirring Times in Austria" and "Concerning the Jews"; he also wrote to President Cleveland in 1885–86 to protest the abuse of Native Americans in the Western lands.[101]

In addition, traces of a purely religious fervor still appeared from time to time. Much of the late work is narrated through religious figures such as Adam and Eve, Methuseleh, and Satan. John Tuckey, on this basis, has challenged Hamlin Hill's standard account by asserting that "this notion of a sustained despair is beginning to look like a disposable myth of Mark Twain's criticism."[102] Here, for instance, is a telltale statement from the Old Man's gospel in *What Is Man?*: humans should follow their "ideals upward and still upward toward a summit where you will find your chiefest pleasure in conduct which, while contenting you, will be sure to confer benefits upon your neighbor and community." Even in the work he considered to be his most blatant exposition of his so-called "gospel," Twain occasionally recognized his inability to live with the sheer implications of determinism and preached a doctrine of social uplift.[103] We can compare this with the angry passage (that is yet somehow riddled with sympathy) that closes what would be the final essay published in his lifetime, "The Turning Point of My Life":

> Necessarily the scene of the real turning-point of my life (and of yours) was the Garden of Eden. . . . Adam's temperament was the first command the Deity ever issued to a human being on this planet. And it was the only command Adam would never be able to disobey. It said, "Be weak, be water, be characterless, be cheaply persuadable. . . . For the tem-

> perament is the man . . . I cannot help feeling disappointed in Adam and Eve. That is, in their temperaments. Not in them, poor helpless young creatures."[104]

Fittingly Twain's last published piece focuses on a religious examination of his own life—and in the form of Adam and Eve, of all humankind. On a certain level, it sounds like the dying gasp of a man, as the stereotype has it, shaking his fist at God. But "The Turning Point of My Life" can also be read as Mark Twain extending a warm embrace to his fellow human beings, his "relations."

Thus did some of the old twinkle and optimism still remain—a legacy, perhaps, of the continuing bonds with the dead. The bitter screeds against humanity's machinelike nature contrast sharply with much of Twain's best writing in his final decade: his passages of literary domesticity in the various versions of his autobiography. Chief among all of these works may be his commemoration of the last great loss of his life: his daughter Jean, on Christmas Eve of 1909. Her story adds even more pain and guilt, and must be read as the final stroke of torment. Jean had been diagnosed many years before with epilepsy, a disease that during Twain's lifetime highly stigmatized its victims as potentially violent and irrational. For many years Jean had been shuttled from rest cures to sanitaria—especially in the years after her mother's death. Perhaps Mark Twain believed that as a man he was insufficiently equipped to care for Jean's needs. However, much of the blame for her abandonment must go to the manipulative efforts of Isabel Lyon, Twain's close aide and household manager for a number of years. Lyon apparently had designs on marrying the aging writer, whom she teased and fondly called "the King," and her attempts to keep Jean out of the picture were certainly part of that scheme. Later, when Twain finally caught on to Lyon's subterfuge and wasteful spending and terminated her, he recalled Jean to his home and began the long road toward reconciliation.[105] With the marriage and relocation of his only other child, Clara, in the fall of 1909, Jean became for all practical purposes the only family member that Mark Twain had left. For several months there was in fact a real renaissance in their mutual admiration, and they probably became closer than they had ever been. But on the morning of Christmas Eve in 1909, Jean apparently suffered an intense seizure while bathing, and drowned as a result. The illness that had separated her for so long had finally made that separation permanent.

Mark Twain sat alone in his huge mansion that day and the next, Christmas 1909. He refused to attend the funeral or to accompany the body to Elmira, where Jean would be buried with her mother and sister. The essay he composed during those lonely days, "The Death of Jean," was one of the last pieces he ever wrote and in many ways one of the most revealing. Michael Kiskis has observed that there is "no piece so likely to destroy conventional notions of Mark Twain. . . . it does not conform to established, comfortable ideas of Twain as misanthropic social philosopher."[106] The piece is solemn and moving, but not melodramatic. Twain recalls the "little things that have been always happening every day, and were always so unimportant and easily forgettable before—but now! Now, how different! How precious they are, how dear, how unforgettable, how pathetic, how sacred, how clothed with dignity!" As on the other occasions of his most severe grief, Twain stated that he turned to the pen for consolation: "I sit here—writing, busying myself, to keep my heart from breaking." His new house now seems a great irony: "Why did I build this house, two years ago? To shelter this vast emptiness?" Even the weather seems perverse: "How dazzling the sunshine is flooding the hills around! It is like a mockery." Alone in the vast house as the service begins, Twain imagines the scene: "It is the time appointed. The funeral has begun. Four hundred miles away, but I can see it all, just as if I were there. The scene is the library, in the Langdon homestead. Jean's coffin stands where her mother and I stood, forty years ago, and were married; and where Susy's coffin stood thirteen years ago; where her mother's stood, five years and a half ago; and where mine will stand, after a little time."[107]

Twain was correct in his prediction. Four months later his heart finally gave out, and his own coffin stood in that same location, in the farmhouse on a hilltop outside of Elmira. Fittingly Mark Twain called "The Death of Jean" "the final chapter of my autobiography."[108] It records two key religious sentiments that were crucial to his response to the spiritual crisis of his era and of his own life. The first is the search for home, and the second is the pain created by our difficulties in finding one—sentiments at the heart of the biblical mythos, as in the story of the Garden of Eden. Jürgen Moltmann has reminded us that Ernst

Bloch ended his magisterial study of the nature of hope with these words: "something comes into the world which shines out to all of us in childhood, and where no one has as yet ever been: home." The search for shalom, the object of human hope, is in the final analysis a search for a home, or homeland (*heimat* in German). Thus is it natural, in a sense, to "worship" the idea of home, as many Victorians did. As Moltmann puts it, home represents "the longed-for goal of hope in its totality. . . . [and] hope is the promised land of the fulfilled divine promise."[109] Jean's death was the final blow, assuring Twain that he would never regain, or even hope to see, such a home as he had once known.

After Livy died, Twain had written "Eve's Diary." There he has the forlorn Adam standing at the grave of his beloved, where he says, "Wheresoever she was, *there* was Eden."[110] Of course it was a poignant tribute to his late wife, written in the days after her "release." But one might say it was an appropriate summary for many other dearly beloved people as well, as in his first elegy for Susy:

> They knew
> That in the temple's inmost place a spirit dwelt,
> Made all of light![111]

And it was echoed in the composition of "The Death of Jean": "We were together; we were a family! The dream had come true. . . . "[112]

Adam's lament for the lost beloved was also the yearning for home illustrated by Twain's most memorable character, Huck Finn. But for Mark Twain, the dream of home and hearth, the yearning for some shadow of Eden, was elusive after all—at least in this life. Adam standing at the grave site symbolized the human condition. Eden would have to wait.

In 1897, Mark Twain agreed to sit for a bust by a well-known artist. A photograph of him posing in the Viennese atelier of the sculptress Theresa Fedorowna Ries survives as a memorial of this episode. But the photograph reminds us also that during these years, Mark Twain's image was becoming one of the most photographed, sketched, and otherwise manufactured human likenesses of his era (figure 10). Indeed one could argue that by the end of his life, Twain's likeness had become the most

10. Mark Twain, Theresa Fedorowna Ries, and bust of Twain. Courtesy of Kevin MacDonnell, Austin, Texas.

frequently reproduced of any person in all of human history up until that time.

In the photo, the bust rests between the subject and the sculptress, suggesting that between any observer and the subject of observation exists a semblance that is partly based on factual information and partly the creation of the viewer. Furthermore, the subject of the gaze, in this case Mark Twain, is fully aware that he is being observed, a fact that affects his posture. The bust is very close in detail to the subject, but obviously there are many differences, and nobody would mistake the one for the other. And the artist is deeply implicated in her quest to understand a complex subject. As arguably America's greatest cultural icon, we must always recognize that "Twain may be the consummate Rorschach test for anyone who sets out to understand the United States," as Shelley

Fisher Fishkin once put it. "The Twain we claim as our own reveals much about who we think we are—and who we want to be."[113]

In these curious ways, this fascinating photograph is symbolic of the hard work required in any attempt to remember Mark Twain—whether by an artist or by a biographer. Much can be determined as factual, and yet much is left up to the artist, the writer, or even the viewer of a statue, or the reader of a book like this one. In the beginning of this volume, I argued that critical discussions of Mark Twain had often ignored or underplayed the spiritual dimensions of both his literary work and his life and times. Now nearing the end of this version of Twain, I am reminded that some may respond to my claims in an opposite manner. Critics will possibly charge me with having too much emphasis on Twain's spiritual struggles, too much focus on his ostensibly spiritual nature, and too little regard for his dismissal and ridicule of the Christian religion. They may charge that this depiction is "too religious," and some may be particularly chagrined by what they perceive to be an attempt to "Christianize," and thereby to domesticate, this wild humorist from frontier Missouri and the Pacific slope.

But this version, as in Theresa Fedorowna Ries's bust of Twain, is merely an attempt to clarify and analyze one of the many faces of Mark Twain. Indeed my contention remains that the spiritual side has been perhaps the most overlooked in the cultural work of remembering this great figure. But as I also argued in my introduction, today even basic terminology about religion is fluid and to a large extent rather confusing. Americans of the early twenty-first century have widely divergent, and sometimes contradictory, understandings of words like *Christian* or *God*—even though polling data consistently show that the vast majority of all Americans self-identify as Christians and continue to believe in God. These data, by the way, betray a striking failure of the American church today, given the fact that these crucial terms cannot be effectively pinned down. Perhaps Harold Bloom's once controversial book, *The American Religion,* is correct in this regard: American Christianity has devolved into a completely subjective experience having more in common with ancient Gnosticism than with orthodoxy.[114] If Bloom is correct, then Christianity itself has become another cultural Rorschach test. And to whatever extent this is true, then serious analysis of religion is becoming harder and harder all the time. For starters, many of the keywords of Christianity seem to have lost their meanings. Thus definitive conclusions about Twain's particular *spirituality,* or *religion,* or *faith,* if we care to use any of those terms, or his understanding of American religion, remain difficult. As a result of the formidable confusion surrounding these terms today, I have worked hard to historicize them. And, despite all of these qualifications, some conclusions must be proposed.

Above all, we must remember that Mark Twain was neither systematic nor dogmatic about most theological issues. Furthermore, conclusions about Twain's faith have always been hotly debated. Even in the immediate aftermath of his demise, much confusion surrounded the issue of Twain's belief. For instance, until his dying days, Twain regularly read *The Truth Seeker,* the major journal of free thought espousing the views of the movement's founder, Robert G. Ingersoll, the famous freethinker and personal hero of the great American author. He even renewed his subscription to *The Truth Seeker* the month before he died.[115] The journal was founded by D. M. Bennett, "an outspoken atheist whose hatred of Christianity made the *Truth Seeker* the most vehemently anti-Christian of the free-thought periodicals."[116] It is also true that Twichell frequently threw away letters Twain sent him that contained "blasphemies or other indiscretions which Twichell did not want to survive because of the possibility of later misinterpretations."[117] Apparently Twichell, genuinely concerned about Twain's posthumous reputation, was unable to destroy all of those untoward documents of Twain's later period, since so many surviving letters burn with similar "indiscretions." Twichell understood that much of this material served more as "equilibrium restorer" for Twain than as purely sincere statements of belief. But much effort had also been expended to understanding the cosmos and its Creator. There is one claim that can be made without reservation. Mark Twain died as he had lived: as a truth seeker.

Beyond that, we should consider one of the oldest tricks in the trade—his doubleness, the classic expressions of which were the notorious Brooks-DeVoto debate and the title of Justin Kaplan's biography, *Mr. Clemens and Mark Twain.* Framed in religious terms, Leland Krauth's distinction between what he calls the "transgressive Twain" and the "bounded Twain" is relevant.[118] Krauth correctly points out the critical preoccupation with the transgressive Twain—to the regrettable exclusion of a full consideration of the bounded, or "proper" Mark Twain, a hole in Twain scholarship that Krauth has tried to fill. Strikingly, however, these categories obscure the fact that religious, and indeed Christian impulses (such as the act of repentance as rebellion or the rhetorical stylings of the jeremiad), played crucial roles in Twain's (and America's) transgressive mode. As a result, Krauth's work underplays the role of Christianity and gives almost no attention to Twain's liberal Protestant friends—and indeed the ways that they, by challenging the prevailing culture, operated according to the transgressive mode. Horace Bushnell, for example, was considered in his day a radically innovative theologian and social engineer whose theories flew in the face of more traditional thought. And it would be a monumental error to underestimate Christianity's fundamental powers of transgression, captured most memorably in the words and teachings of its founder, Jesus Christ. The Bible remains the greatest collection of social criticism in the history of the Western world.

Like the sculpting metaphor, memories of Mark Twain's faith depend a lot on who is doing the talking. Examples from Twain's obituaries verify that his contemporaries perceived the fallen celebrity in both Christian and agnostic terms. *The Truth Seeker,* Twain's favorite journal, described him this way: "We conclude that the religious views of Mark Twain, so far as they concerned the Christian system, were substantially those of Robert G. Ingersoll. We are told privately, by one having immediate knowledge of the fact, that Twain was less reverent than Ingersoll."[119] Conversely, Twain's childhood girlfriend Laura Hawkins Frazer (the model for Becky Thatcher) wrote in 1923: "the last time I saw him [at Stormfield], he told me goodbye twice, came back the third time and said, 'We will meet in Heaven, Laura,' pointing upward. He was a Christian."[120] Another boyhood friend, John L. Robards, did not agree with the inscription "His Religion was Humanity" on the Missouri state commemorative statue to Twain because "Mark Twain was not an Infidel but . . . the inscription made him out one."[121] Likewise, Katy Leary, the faithful household servant, recalled Twain saying to her, "Oh, Katy! [Jean's] in heaven with her mother. . . . Oh, I think—I am sure he believed in the hereafter. But he was pretty serious in arguing about religion."[122]

Some accounts of Mark Twain focused on his moral and ethical character. The obituary in the *London Times,* for example, was almost breathless in its admiration for Twain's financial integrity in paying back his many debtors and considered it his greatest achievement:

> [his] career was more notable for the nobility of the end at which he aimed than for the work he actually produced. . . . The parallel case of Sir Walter Scott at once comes naturally to mind as one contemplates the sturdy independence and unflinching commercial morality of this author who sat down at 60 to begin the world afresh. . . . It was in misfortune that the splendid qualities of the nature of "Mark Twain," recognized as they were by all who knew him well, became manifest to the world.[123]

Twain might have cringed momentarily in his grave at being compared to his old nemesis Scott; nevertheless the kind emphasis of the *Times* reflects a widespread awareness of Twain's moral character, the "splendid qualities" that he maintained despite the tragic nature of those final years. And Henry Van Dyke, friend and advisor for many years, remembered Twain this way:

> His honesty, his fidelity, his loving kindness to his neighbor, were fruits of faith—I will even say of Christian loyalty. No one who heard him speak with reverence of the simple faith of his dearly beloved wife (as he often spoke to me) could think of him as being indifferent to religion. His sense of humor made him keenly aware of its perversions and literal misinterpretations. . . . of genuine, simple Christian faith I never heard him speak without loving reverence.[124]

Perhaps it is best to go to the person who knew him best at his death and who could speak of him from the wide vantage place of many decades of friendship. Joe Twichell, often called upon to offer eulogies in his large urban church setting, usually made clear assertions about the Christian faith of the deceased.[125] Thus it is significant that he only indirectly made similar statements about Twain in any of his published remarks about him after his death. He certainly did comment on Twain's "character"—his gentleness, humility, and care for others, including surprisingly and memorably his tenderness toward animals.

However, on topics specific to Christian doctrine, Twichell maintained a public silence—probably because he knew firsthand of Twain's infidelity on key aspects of dogma; partly, perhaps, because of his desire not to add to the widely held opinion of Twain as a blasphemer or at least infidel. In any case, Twichell certainly never went on record defending Twain as an actual Christian believer. On the other hand, Twichell remained loyal and strongly attracted to the memory of the better angels of Mark Twain's character, framing him, like some of the others, as the "moralist in disguise" he most admired, and perhaps which Twain most aspired to be.

Twichell ended his eulogy with some remarkable insight into the pathos of those final years:

> His home life, as all who were observant of it will bear witness, was happy beyond measure. He was the most devoted of husbands, and fathers. His fireside was the dearest place to him in all the world. His desolation by successive domestic bereavements was pathetic in the extreme. With all his brilliant prosperities he had lived to be a lonely, weary-hearted man, and the thought of his departure hence was not unwelcome to him.[126]

These comments seem remarkable for several reasons—for the emphasis on the bereavements, the fond memories of Mark Twain as the quintessential Victorian family man, and especially for the final declaration that Twain was "not unwelcome" to his own dying. Without the warmth of that hearth, surrounded by the beloved, Twain simply tired of living and indeed could find nothing that made life worth living. Twichell paints a very sympathetic picture of his old friend, dying a lonely death, hurt beyond words by the grief of his life, "pathetic in the extreme."

Compare these remarks from the newspaper eulogy with Joe Twichell's spoken eulogy, delivered at the Carnegie Hall Memorial in 1910:

> it was not alone or chiefly his work judged simply as literature, or as humorous, that accounted for his so quickly accomplishing the conquest of the world. It was . . . the genial, kindly, friendly, human soul of him that was everywhere expressed in it, and made itself felt; it was, above all, of the general heart that he laid hold. His conquest was a spiritual one in

> that sense. He had, indeed, the keenest appreciation of the ignoble side of human nature. . . . Still and notwithstanding, his predominant mood toward humanity was that of sympathy. He commiserated it far more than he despised it. . . . The theory of character, as determined absolutely by the conditions to which the individual is subject, with the deduction of man's total moral irresponsibility which some of us had heard him maintain long before he came out with it, so inconsistent with those impeachments of mankind that have been referred to, was, I truly believe, a device of his charity.[127]

Mark Twain's pastor seemed to know the inner heart of the man better than anyone; here is one of the most incisive and clear analyses of Twain's theological view of mankind. Twichell suggests a startling theological device: perhaps Twain's insistence on man's machinelike determinism was merely a function of his charity. Perhaps Twain can embrace Adam, in all of his corruption and fallenness, by realizing that he ultimately has no moral responsibility for his sins.

Twichell's fond farewell shares similarities with Henry Van Dyke's. Both viewed Twain's religion as much more social and ethical than doctrinal. The same observation is made in Albert B. Paine's final analysis: "Twain's religion was a faith too wide for doctrines—a benevolence too limitless for creeds. . . . It was a religion identified with his daily life and his work."[128] Paine's sense of religion here reflects the influence of liberal Christianity and the Social Gospel. As such, it is different from the most common usage of *religion* among Americans today, who mainly associate it with specific doctrinal positions. But perhaps our conclusions about Twain's "religion" or "spirituality" are best formulated through a more intensive examination of the kind of moral and ethical life he tried to live.

As this version of the story has tried to show, the kind of social environment a person chooses to inhabit, and where one chooses to raise children, reveals much about one's values, beliefs, and ultimate concerns. A lot can be discerned in the kinds of people one chooses to spend time with, to invite along on holidays. Much can be detected in one's choice of music, or reading, or church life—the "habits of the heart" that make up the everyday lives that we lead. And finally, in terms of an overarching vision, we can learn much by studying the kind of world for which a person is hoping. The object of hope is a spiritual choice—and Mark Twain clearly yearned for a more beautiful expression of human society than the one in which he lived and moved and had his being. He was a seeker of shalom, the way things ought to be. His busy social justice agenda can only make sense if one believes in the possibility of hope for a better world. All of these things, as I have been suggesting, are religious to the core—although often we fail to see them that way, in our secularized and postmodern generation.

Mark Twain left us many legacies—not the least of which was a spiritual legacy. His spiritual presence affected immediately the family and friends who survived him. Twichell's fond farewell is all the more remarkable considering the extreme events during which he composed them. It was the most intensely traumatic week of Twichell's own life, as he superintended the funeral for his old friend even as his own angelic better half, Harmony, lay dying in Hartford. On Saturday, April 23, in Elmira, at about 2:00 p.m., "just before [Twain's funeral] began, Twichell received a telegram from Hartford telling him that his wife was very ill and saying that it was necessary that he return home immediately. He stayed for the service nevertheless, and then hurried to catch the first train for Hartford."[129] The brave manner in which Twichell stuck to the task of overseeing Mark Twain's funeral, even though he had been called home to his dying wife, says much about the character of Mark Twain's pastor. Twichell managed to complete the service, and then he took the four o'clock express, arriving at Hartford about 7:00 p.m. He talked with Harmony a bit at the house and then went with her to the hospital. Doctors operated around 11:30 p.m., and Harmony died April 24, 1910—just after midnight, the morning after Twain's funeral.

Tributes to Harmony called her the "ideal wife of a pastor." It was a devastating loss for Joe Twichell, greatly intensified by its proximity to the death of his oldest and dearest friend, Mark Twain. Finally, it seemed, Joe faced the utter devastation that he had seen his good friend suffer through for so long. His heart ached at the death of these two closest companions of his adulthood within days of each other. His son David made extensive notes about his father's behavior in the days following Harmony's death. David writes, "In regard to his own hope to future life, [Twichell] said, 'I am a miserable sinner and fear God's judgment, but I trust his mercy.' At another time he said, 'My strongest feeling about the Hereafter is one of curiosity, I feel as if I would say to myself if I were dying, "Now I will see for myself."' David slept with his father during this difficult time, and one night Joe had some memories of Mark Twain: "The first time he came to family prayers at our house, he went into the hall crying aloud. When he and I have been off together and sleeping in the same room, Uncle Mark always knelt with me in the evening when I prayed for the families and in the morning repeated the Lord's prayer with me. When it was time for our prayers he would say, 'Come on Joe.' "[130]

David Twichell noted one other detail. His father apparently had retrieved the letter that Mark Twain had sent to him when his own bride Livy had died: "Dad has read over many times and keeps in his hand Uncle Mark's letter written when Aunt Livy died. He has read it to many people here in the house." David supplies the contents of the letter, dated June 18, 1904, from Florence, Italy, sections of which read as follows:

> Dear Joe;
>
> It is 13 days. I am bewildered and must remain so for a time longer. It was so sudden, so unexpected . . . Some day I will tell you about it;—not now.[131]

The Asylum Hill Church gave Joe Twichell an extended leave of absence, and he went with his old friend Dr. Parker for what would be his final tour of Europe, from May through July of 1910. Just over a year later he wrote in a letter to a friend, "What you say of Mark's kindness to your wife goes to my heart. My wife, too, loved him dearly. She and I went to Clara's wedding, and there had our last visit with him. When the bad news came that he was gone, she was prostrate in a sickness that proved to be her last, and in a few days followed him into the other world, leaving me—but you know all about it."[132]

Mark Twain had left behind another legacy of his generative spirit, both to Joe Twichell, to Twichell's correspondent, and to us a century later. The legacy is symbolized by David's memory of his father holding on to the letter from his grief-ridden, and now dead, friend. According to David, the grieving Joe Twichell compulsively carried Mark Twain's letter about with him—an obsessive gesture, perhaps, that rings true to the obsessive acts of those in deep mourning. At the time of his own gravest spiritual crisis, Twichell held on tight to that letter from Mark Twain. It may be that Twain's letter seemed to say, "you can survive this rocky road, even with graciousness and kindness, for I have gone before you." Clutching that letter, Joe Twichell acknowledged his own continuing bond with his good friend who had suffered so much grief, and so much doubt and anger toward God. And yet, despite all the pain, Mark Twain still managed to leave a legacy of human hopefulness: hope for a world of shalom, the way things ought to be. His was a hope that somehow broke through the doctrinal particularities of any denomination or sect and reached for a living ethics that "preaches all the time." And it was a living hope that has survived long after Twain was dead and buried.

Like Joe Twichell, holding on for dear life to that letter, America and the world still look to Twain for hope, comfort, and courage in times of trouble. And when we do, we affirm the truly spiritual legacy of Mark Twain.

Acknowledgments

My acknowledgments begin with a confession. Like Mark Twain, much of my obsessive scribbling, as it turns out, has resulted from some fairly alarming personal pain and loss. This has certainly been the case with some other folks over the years—some of whom, like Ralph Waldo Emerson, Frederick Douglass, Harriet Beecher Stowe, Abraham Lincoln, William Dean Howells, and W. E. B. DuBois, appear in this book. (That is about all I have in common with that illustrious company.) In recognition of that common ground, and of what is truly most important about the past decade or so, this book is dedicated to the memory of Daniel Harrison Mitsunobu Bush (1993–99). Daniel was a fine boy and a funny one too, and we miss him terribly. There is still the strong sense of a "continuing bond," as those others listed above evidently had with their own lost children, and this book would have been impossible without that bond. Of course, without Hiroko there would have been, and there would be, no Daniel, so in a way this book, like the first one, is ultimately dedicated to her, too. And without God Almighty, I would have had neither Hiroko nor Daniel, nor the will or desire to complete this book. My enduring thanks to all of you—for making it doable and worthwhile.

Many other folks were important in keeping me honest and faithful along life's journey, a fairly minor part of which included the completion of this book. So many folks, in fact, that in making a list I will undoubtedly forget some, and potentially offend a few. Blanket statement: I thank the generous community of fellow travelers who have helped form the foundation of my career as a teacher and writer. More specifically: the Department of English at Saint Louis University has been a welcome and friendly academic home. Particular thanks go to the three chairs I have worked with here and who have been very supportive along the way: Tom Moisan, Georgia Johnston, and Sara van den Berg. I would also like to thank my research assistants over the years, who did so much for me on this project: Keith Wilhite, Aaron Belz, Aaron McClendon, and Melissa Mayus. Thanks to Dennis Klass for meeting with me, corresponding with me, and reading an early draft of the essay that became chapter 7; and Robert Hirst for his detailed comments on the original draft of my article in *Nineteenth-Century Literature,* especially his outstanding help editing the poem "Broken Idols" for publication.

Other heroic figures took the time to read all or parts of this book as it was being produced. I received from these readers many excellent suggestions, some of which I was humble enough to accept. David Nordloh is one of the finest academic editors I know, and he generously volunteered (under pressure) to read most of this book at various stages and provide painstaking advice, which he has been doing for my writing since about 1990. Shelley Fisher Fishkin was in a certain sense the fountainhead of the project. Who knew that our meeting way back in December of 1997 at the Toronto MLA would result in the long process culminating in the book you hold in your hands? I certainly did not. Roger Lundin has believed in my research for a pretty long time now, for reasons unbeknownst to me—thanks, Roger, for sticking with me. Malcolm Magee, Rich Keener, and David Stowe, all of whom are fellow workers at the Institute for the Study of Christianity and Culture at Michigan State University (www.christianityandculture.org), have been a great encouragement for many years. Among the other generous folks who read parts of the manuscript are Michael Kiskis, Robert Snyder, Bruce Michelson, Thomas Wortham, Laura Cerruti, Gary Scharnhorst, Steve Courtney, Peter Messent, Ralph Wood, and Terrell Dempsey, and the readers of the manuscript for the University of Alabama Press, David Sloane and Alan Gribben. Other long-term believers in this work deserve my thanks as well: my parents, Mary Lyon and Harold and Ione Bush, Ron and Karla Franko, Stan Herber, Ray Benoit, Donald and

Eleonore Stump, and many other individuals not listed here. A more general word of thanks must go out to all the members of the Mark Twain Forum (www.yorku.ca/twainweb), one of the best lists on the Web: ask that list almost anything about old Clemens and his world and within days if not hours you will know the answer. I certainly was never shy about asking.

I should also like to thank The College of Arts and Sciences at Saint Louis University and deans Shirley Dowdy, Joseph Weixlmann, Fr. Michael May, and Michael Sproule for the funding from the SLU 2000 Program that provided research leave, for various other travel monies that allowed much of my initial research to be completed, and for providing last-minute funding for illustrations. I have also had extensive support from the Mellon Grants here at Saint Louis University, along with excellent support from the Pius XII Memorial Library of Saint Louis University. I also thank the wonderful staffs at the Beinecke Rare Book and Manuscript Library at Yale University, the Connecticut State Library in Hartford, the Gannett-Tripp Library at Elmira College, and particularly the wonderful crew at the Mark Twain Project, the Bancroft Library, University of California at Berkeley. For help with illustrations and for permission to use their images, I thank Kevin Mac Donnell of Austin, Texas; Henry Sweets and the Mark Twain Boyhood Home and Museum of Hannibal, Missouri; Margaret Moore and the Mark Twain House and Museum of Hartford, Connecticut; the Lincoln Museum of Fort Wayne, Indiana; and Neda Salem and the Mark Twain Project, Bancroft Library, University of California at Berkeley.

Permission to quote previously unpublished words of Mark Twain was granted by the general editor of the Mark Twain Project. Various portions of this book have been adapted from my chapter, "'A Moralist in Disguise': Mark Twain and American Religion," by Harold K. Bush Jr., from *A Historical Guide to Mark Twain*, ed. Shelley Fisher Fishkin, copyright © 2002 by Oxford University Press Inc. Used by permission of Oxford University Press Inc. Some of the material in chapter 5 first appeared as "Mark Twain's Lincoln as Man of the Border: Freethinking and Epistemology after the Civil War," in *There Before Us: Religion and American Literature from Emerson to Eliot*, ed. Roger Lundin (Grand Rapids, MI: Eerdmans, 2006). An earlier version of chapter 6 first appeared as "Mark Twain's American Adam: Humor as Site for Hope and

Apocalypse," *Christianity & Literature,* vol. 53, spring 2004. Copyright 2004 by the Conference on Christianity and Literature. Reproduced by permission. Chapter 7 relies heavily on "'Broken Idols': Mark Twain's Elegies for Susy and a Critique of Freudian Grief Theory," *Nineteenth-Century Literature,* vol. 57, no. 2 (Sept. 2002): 237–68. Copyright 2002 by the University of California Press. I am grateful to the editors of these books and journals for permission to reprint.

Notes

Introduction

1. Quoted in Baetzhold, *Mark Twain and John Bull,* 138.

2. See Franchot, "Invisible Domain."

3. Burns, *Mark Twain.*

4. See, for example, Paul A. Carter, *The Spiritual Crisis of the Gilded Age.* Other important treatments of the late nineteenth-century spiritual crisis in the American church are Hutchison, *The Modernist Impulse in American Protestantism;* Turner, *Without God, Without Creed;* Delbanco, *The Death of Satan;* Kuklick, *Churchmen and Philosophers;* Menand, *The Metaphysical Club;* and Szasz, *The Divided Mind of Protestant America, 1880–1930.*

5. See Ahlstrom, *A Religious History of the American People,* 805–15.

6. See Frank, *Less Than Conquerors.*

7. For excellent analysis of Darwin's reception in America, see Roberts, *Darwinism and the Divine in America;* and Russett, *Darwin in America.* See also, for instance, Hutchison, *The Modernist Impulse in American Protestantism,* 88–90; Carter, *The Spiritual Crisis of the Gilded Age,* 21–62; and Ahlstrom, *A Religious History of the American People,* 767–72. For Twain's encounter with Darwin, see Cummings, *Mark Twain And Science,* 54–67 and 180–83.

8. Szasz, *The Divided Mind* 15.

9. Cummings, *Mark Twain and Science* and Hays, *Mark Twain and Religion* are both convincing on this point. See also my historical overview, " 'A Moralist in Disguise.' "

10. See Smith, "Force of Habit," 20. The classic contemporary expression of this viewpoint is Marsden, *The Outrageous Idea of Christian Scholarship;* for consideration of

this issue in the field of literary studies, see also Franchot, "Invisible Domain"; and Harold K. Bush Jr., "The Outrageous Idea of a Christian Literary Studies."

11. See for example Gordon, *Literary Atheism,* 85–94.

12. The ur-text for this account of Twain is Van Wyck Brooks, *The Ordeal of Mark Twain;* see also Hill, *Mark Twain: God's Fool;* Macnaughton, *Mark Twain's Last Years as a Writer;* Cardwell, *The Man Who Was Mark Twain;* and Boker, *The Grief Taboo in American Literature.*

13. Examples of this include the work of critics such as James D. Wilson, Stanley Brodwin, Lawrence Berkove, William Phipps, Joe B. Fulton, Gregg Camfield, Peter Messent, Sherwood Cummings, and Steve Courtney.

14. One critic has written "the religion of these preachers [including Twichell] was not evangelical." Andrews, *Nook Farm,* 51. But Twichell, as well as much less orthodox leaders like Horace Bushnell and Henry Ward Beecher, often self-identified as evangelical. Perhaps the quibble has to do with the meaning of *evangelical.* A succinct definition is in Noll, *The Scandal of the Evangelical Mind,* 7–10; and in Hunter, *American Evangelicalism,* 7–9. According to these definitions, I contend that Joe Twichell was evangelical in outlook. On the variety of uses of the term during Twain's lifetime, its fluid meanings, and its deployment by men like Bushnell and Beecher, see Brown, *The Word and the World,* 18–22.

15. Paine, *Mark Twain: A Biography,* 2:631.

16. Ibid., 632.

17. Ibid.

18. Joseph Twichell to Harmony Twichell, August, 10, 1878, JTP; the reference to one of these days as a Sunday indicates that that passage was written on August 11.

19. Quoted in Gribben, *Mark Twain's Library,* 1:218.

20. Twain to Twichell, September 9, 1878, attached to Twichell Journal 3.99, JTP.

21. *A Tramp Abroad,* 403.

22. See, for example, Wilton and Barringer, *American Sublime,* especially 11–18, and Veith, *Painters of Faith.*

23. *A Tramp Abroad,* 355–56, 408, 500, 503.

24. See Kuklick, *Churchmen and Philosophers,* 163–69.

25. *A Tramp Abroad,* 503.

26. Quoted in Pellowe, *Mark Twain, Pilgrim from Hannibal,* 155–56.

27. Paine, ed., *Mark Twain's Letters,* 719.

28. Quoted in Strong, *Joseph Hopkins Twichell,* 82.

29. Sixty-Seventh Birthday Speech, November 28, 1902. In Budd, ed., *Collected Tales, Sketches, Speeches, and Essays,* 458.

30. Andrews, *Nook Farm,* 71.

31. Holland, "Soul Butter and Hogwash," 14, 15.

32. Fuller, *Spiritual, But Not Religious.*

33. See Brown, *Spirituality and Liberation.*

34. Deming, *Rethinking Religion,* 14.

35. James, *The Varieties of Religious Experience,* 42.

36. From *Pragmatism,* quoted in Menand, *The Metaphysical Club,* 354.

37. Bellah et al., *Habits of the Heart,* 335.

38. Ibid., ix, 21.

39. Bercovitch, "The Problem of Ideology," 635.

40. Bellah et al., *Habits of the Heart,* 40.

41. E. Hudson Long, *Mark Twain Handbook,* 362.

42. Twain to Mary Fairbanks, November 26 and 27, 1868, in *Mark Twain's Letters Volume 2: 1867–68,* 284.

43. This insistence in recent theology has its roots in the incarnationalism of St. Augustine and is most clearly delineated in works by theologians as diverse as Stanley Hauerwas (an Anabaptist ethicist), Alisdair MacIntyre (a Roman Catholic philosopher), and Robert E. Webber (an evangelical-Episcopal theorist of worship). This approach is thus highly ecumenical in scope, and its influence is already widespread.

44. Stanley Hauerwas, *The Peaceable Kingdom,* 96, 99, 102.

45. Stanley Hauerwas, *Resident Aliens,* 81.

46. See MacIntyre, *After Virtue,* passim.

Chapter 1

1. Cummings, *Mark Twain and Science,* 6.

2. Wecter, *Sam Clemens of Hannibal,* 127.

3. "Jane Lampton Clemens," 84, 83, 82.

4. Camfield, *Sentimental Twain,* 34.

5. Elizabeth Barnes, "Affecting Relations," 597.

6. Moody, *Sentimental Confessions,* 9.

7. Ibid., 10.

8. Harriet Beecher Stowe, *Uncle Tom's Cabin,* 624.

9. "Hellfire Hotchkiss," 201–2. On Jane Clemens as model for Mrs. Carpenter, see Kiskis, *Samuel Clemens and Me,* 10–12.

10. Skandera-Trombley, *Mark Twain in the Company of Women,* 2.

11. Wecter, *Sam Clemens of Hannibal,* 86.

12. Howells, *My Mark Twain,* 125.

13. Cummings, *Mark Twain and Science,* 18; on Twain's familiarity with the Bible, see especially Ensor, *Mark Twain and the Bible.*

14. Cummings, *Mark Twain and Science,* 18.

15. *The Washoe Giant in San Francisco,* 134.

16. *The Adventures of Tom Sawyer,* 68.

17. Brooks quoted in Powers, *Dangerous Water,* 57.

18. Powers, *Dangerous Water,* 57.

19. *The Adventures of Tom Sawyer,* 60.

20. Ibid., 64.

21. *The Gilded Age,* 481–82.

22. Edward Eggleston, *The Hoosier School-Master,* 102.

23. Quoted in Wecter, *Sam Clemens of Hannibal,* 88.

24. Phipps, *Mark Twain's Religion,* 9.

25. See Schmidt, "Paine in the Lost and Found."

26. My account of these incidents is based on Fanning, *Mark Twain and Orion Clemens,* 12–20. Both quotes here are on p. 13.

27. Quetel, *History of Syphilis,* 3.

28. Fred Kaplan, *The Singular Mark Twain,* 33.

29. Quoted in Phipps, *Mark Twain's Religion,* 9.

30. Susan Jacoby, *Freethinkers,* 4.

31. Paine, *Mark Twain, A Biography,* 1445.

32. Both quotes in Cummings, *Mark Twain and Science,* 20–21.

33. *Mark Twain's Notebooks and Journals,* 33–4n36.

34. Quoted in Kaplan, *Singular Mark Twain,* 66.

35. See Coulombe, *Mark Twain and the American West* and Knoper, *Acting Naturally* on these lifestyles.

36. Budd, "Mark Twain Plays the Bachelor."

37. Hoffman, "Mark Twain and Homosexuality."

38. Fanning, *Mark Twain and Orion Clemens,* 16–17.

39. "Autobiography of a Damned Fool," 136.

40. Kaplan, *Singular Mark Twain,* 33.

41. Ibid., 32.

42. Fanning, *Mark Twain and Orion Clemens,* 20.

43. Twain, "Plymouth Rock and the Pilgrims," 163.

44. *A Connecticut Yankee in King Arthur's Court,* 50.

45. Powers, *Dangerous Water,* 71.

46. Kaplan, *Singular Mark Twain,* 17.

47. Shurr, *Rappacini's Children,* 30.

48. On the growing ideology of belief in God as immoral, see Turner, *Without God, Without Creed,* 203–25.

49. McLoughlin, *Revivals, Awakenings, and Reform,* 113.

50. Timothy L. Smith, "Righteousness and Hope," 44. See also McLoughlin, *Revivals, Awakenings, and Reform;* Perry Miller, *The Life of the Mind in America,* 49–58, 64–84; and Robert Handy, *A Christian America.*

51. Hatch, *The Democratization of American Christianity,* 22.

52. Dempsey, *Searching for Jim,* 23.

53. Hatch, *The Democratization of American Christianity,* 69–70 and 71.

54. Quoted in Phipps, *Mark Twain's Religion,* 31.

55. Ibid.

56. *Mark Twain's Letters Volume 1,* 72.

57. Kaplan, *Singular Mark Twain,* 66.

58. *Life on the Mississippi,* 18.

59. See Fulton, "Introduction," *Mark Twain's Ethical Realism,* on these distinctions. Quotes from Fulton and Bakhtin are on 14–15.

60. *Mark Twain—Howells Letters,* 1:245.
61. *Mark Twain's Letters Volume 1,* 88.
62. Bakhtin, *Rabelais and His World,* 11–12.
63. *Mark Twain's Letters Volume 1,* 87.
64. Wilson, *Bohemians,* 2–3.
65. Reynolds, *Walt Whitman's America,* 375, 377.
66. Wetzsteon, *Republic of Dreams,* 8.
67. Reynolds, *Walt Whitman's America,* 377; Terry Miller, *Greenwich Village and How It Got That Way,* 89.
68. Knoper, *Acting Naturally,* 42.
69. Reynolds, *Walt Whitman's America,* 378.
70. See Lears, *No Place of Grace,* esp. 22–37.
71. *Mark Twain's Letters Volume 1,* 324.
72. See both quotes in Gribben, *Mark Twain's Library,* 1:425–6.
73. Personal correspondence of Robert Hirst to the author.
74. Kaplan, *The Singular Mark Twain,* 127.
75. *Mark Twain's Letters Volume 1,* 77.
76. See Lowry, *"Littery Men",* esp. 16–65.
77. *Mark Twain's Letters Volume 1,* 322–23.
78. Ibid., 47.
79. Ibid., 29.
80. Budd, *Mark Twain: Social Philosopher,* 17.
81. Garrison, "Of Humor, Death, and Ministers," 199.
82. *Mark Twain's Letters Volume 1,* 272, 272–73.
83. *The Washoe Giant in San Francisco,* 63.
84. *Roughing It,* 309, 310, 314, 316–17.
85. Ibid., 317.
86. Leary, *Lifetime with Mark Twain,* 333–34.
87. *Mark Twain's Letters Volume 3,* 50.
88. *Mark Twain's Letters Volume 2,* 221.
89. *Mark Twain's Letters Volume 1,* 368.
90. Ibid.
91. Mott, *A History of American Magazines,* quoted in *Mark Twain's Letters Volume 1,* 369n4.
92. "Reflections on the Sabbath," 209.

Chapter 2

1. Twain to family, June 1, 1867, in *Mark Twain's Letters Volume 2,* 49.
2. Justin Kaplan, *Mr. Clemens and Mark Twain,* 39.
3. Pellowe, *Mark Twain, Pilgrim from Hannibal,* 105.
4. See Powers, *Dangerous Water,* 252–53, on this distinction.
5. Kaplan, *Mr. Clemens and Mark Twain,* 91.

6. Pellowe, *Mark Twain, Pilgrim from Hannibal,* 109.

7. *Mark Twain's Letters Volume 3,* 42.

8. Quoted in Hoffman, *Inventing Mark Twain,* 108.

9. *Mark Twain at the Buffalo Express,* 153–54.

10. Quoted in Steinbrink, *Getting to Be Mark Twain,* 12.

11. *Mark Twain's Letters Volume 2,* 295.

12. Twain to family, June 1, 1867, in *Mark Twain's Letters Volume 2,* 49.

13. Quoted in Wilson, "Religious and Esthetic Vision in Mark Twain's Early Career," 166.

14. Ensor, *Mark Twain and the Bible,* 39.

15. Harris, *The Courtship of Olivia Langdon and Mark Twain,* 70, 78, 79.

16. Wilson, "Religious and Esthetic Vision in Mark Twain's Early Career," 167, 168.

17. Wolterstorff, *Art in Action,* 86.

18. See especially Wilson, "Religious and Esthetic Vision in Mark Twain's Early Career," 155–57. Cummings, *Mark Twain and Science,* 23–28 is also enlightening on this.

19. Welter, "The Cult of True Womanhood."

20. See Krauth, *Proper Mark Twain,* 86.

21. Hoffman, *Inventing Mark Twain,* 148.

22. *Mark Twain's Letters Volume 2,* 289.

23. *Mark Twain's Letters Volume 3,* 61.

24. Hoffman, *Inventing Mark Twain,* 141, 148.

25. Kiskis, "Twain and the Tradition of Literary Domesticity," 15. See also Krauth, *Proper Mark Twain,* 78–102.

26. Gillian Brown, *Domestic Individualism,* 5.

27. Kiskis, "Twain and the Tradition of Literary Domesticity," 15.

28. Doyno, "Samuel Clemens as Family Man and Father," 35.

29. Quoted in Stahl, "'To His Preferred Friends,'" 57.

30. Quoted in Steinbrink, *Getting to Be Mark Twain,* 12.

31. Quoted in Doyno, "Samuel Clemens as Family Man and Father," 44–45.

32. Simpson, *German Aesthetic and Literary Criticism,* 161, 80.

33. Wolterstorff, *Art in Action,* 77.

34. Kiskis, "Twain and the Tradition of Literary Domesticity," 20.

35. Elizabeth Barnes, "Affecting Relations," quoted in Moody, *Sentimental Confessions,* 9.

36. Brodwin, "The Humor of the Absurd," 64.

37. See *William F. Buckley and Malcolm Muggeridge on Faith and Religious Institutions,* 40–43.

38. Trueblood, *The Humor of Christ;* see also Cormier, *The Humor of Jesus* and Palmer, *The Humor of Jesus.*

39. Plantinga, *Not the Way It's Supposed To Be,* 10.

40. Wolterstorff, *Art in Action,* 79. See also Wolterstorff, *Until Justice and Peace Embrace,* 69–72.

41. Eagleton, *After Theory,* 149.

42. Doyno, "Samuel Clemens as Family Man and Father," 44.

43. Goldman, *Melville's Protest Theism,* 131.

44. Moltmann, *Theology of Hope,* 21.

45. "About Smells," 365–6.

46. Quoted in Phipps, *Mark Twain's Religion,* 109.

47. "The Indignity Put Upon the Remains of George Holland by the Rev. Mr. Sabine," 517, 518, 518–19.

48. See David Hegeman, *Plowing in Hope,* esp. 28–29.

49. "The Indignity Put Upon the Remains of George Holland by the Rev. Mr. Sabine," 520–21.

50. Quoted in "Not Funny This Time."

51. Quoted in Shippey, *J. R. R. Tolkien,* 164. See Shippey's commentary on applicability, 164–74.

52. "Not Funny This Time."

53. *Mark Twain in Eruption,* 202.

54. On anti-Catholicism in *Innocents,* see Hays, *Mark Twain and Religion,* 44–47; in *Connecticut Yankee,* see Leo F. O'Connor, *Religion in the American Novel,* 225–30; on antebellum attitudes toward Catholicism see Franchot, *Roads to Rome* and Shea, *The Lion and the Lamb.*

55. *The Innocents Abroad,* 57.

56. Ibid., 209.

57. Forrest G. Robinson, "The Innocent at Large," 30.

58. Robinson, "The Innocent at Large," 33.

59. *Roughing It,* 123.

60. Ibid., 86.

61. Ibid., 107.

62. Budd, *Our Mark Twain,* 25.

63. *The Innocents Abroad,* 511.

64. Ibid., 513.

65. Krauth, *Proper Mark Twain,* 54, 61.

66. Robinson, "The Innocent at Large," 34.

67. Perry Miller, *Nature's Nation,* 23. In particular, see Miller's chapter "Declension in a Bible Commonwealth," 14–49. Further discussion of the jeremiad tradition in American culture can be found in Bercovitch, *The American Jeremiad;* and Bush, *American Declarations,* 1–11.

68. Holland, "Soul-Butter and Hogwash," 14, 15.

Chapter 3

1. Paine, *Mark Twain, A Biography,* 528.

2. Ibid.

3. Kaplan, *Mr. Clemens and Mark Twain,* 185.

4. Ibid.

5. Holmes, *Ralph Waldo Emerson,* 115.

6. Howells, *Literary Friends and Acquaintance,* 16.

7. Kaplan, *Mr. Clemens and Mark Twain,* 185.

8. Ibid., 184.

9. Quoted in Hoffman, *Inventing Mark Twain,* 227.

10. See Courtney, "To the Tower."

11. Quoted in Courtney, "To the Tower," 13.

12. Elie, *The Life You Save May Be Your Own,* x.

13. Twain's responses are in *Mental Photographs: An Album for Confessions of Tastes, Habits, and Convictions,* the Beinecke Rare Book and Manuscript Library.

14. Quote from Gribben, *Mark Twain's Library,* 91; see the entries in Gribben, *Mark Twain's Library,* 91–106, as well as Gribben's citations on p. 91.

15. Steinbrink, *Getting to Be Mark Twain,* passim.

16. *Mark Twain's Letters Volume 3,* 101.

17. Quotes from Steinbrink, *Getting to Be Mark Twain,* 31–32, 189.

18. Quoted in Wilson, "Religious and Aesthetic Vision in Mark Twain's Early Career," 156.

19. Quoted in Wilson, "Religious and Aesthetic Vision," 156.

20. For background on this movement see Hall, *Muscular Christianity: Embodying the Victorian Age;* Tony Ladd and James Mathieson, *Muscular Christianity: Evangelical Protestants;* and Clifford Putney, *Muscular Christianity: Manhood and Sports.* On the view of the church becoming effeminate during the Gilded Age period, see Douglas, *The Feminization of American Culture.*

21. See Ahlstrom, *A Religious History of the American People,* 765–804.

22. Ibid., 779–81. On Bushnell's influence in the literary culture see R. W. B. Lewis, *American Adam.*

23. Howard A. Barnes, *Horace Bushnell and the Virtuous Republic,* 17. On Bushnell's vision of a "virtuous republic" see 3–62.

24. Quoted in Pellowe, *Mark Twain, Pilgrim from Hannibal,* 131.

25. Quoted in Gamble, *The War for Righteousness,* 27.

26. For description and analysis of the Whittier Birthday Speech episode, and for consideration of Twain's and Howells's mixed feelings about Boston, see Bush, *American Declarations,* 124–46, and Lowry, *"Littery Men,"* 16–44.

27. Twichell Journal, dated July 17, 1877, Journal 3.4–7. JTP.

28. *Hartford Courant,* March 2, 1875.

29. Both in JTP.

30. Twichell to Twain, May 29, 1888, in JTP.

31. Twichell Journal 6.54. The attached news clipping has no date or page number.

32. Wilson, *A Pilgrim Adrift,* 98.

33. Twichell Journal 6.141.

34. Twichell Journal, June 13, 1875.

35. Dictation of Jan. 12, 1906, in MTP.

36. Quoted in an article, "Mark Twain Entertained," [no date, no page, no clear publisher, appended in Twichell Journal 7.145].

37. Mansfield, *The History of Asylum Hill Congregational Church,* 10.

38. Twain to Twichell, June 24, 1905 and January 19, 1897, in MTP.

39. Twichell Journal 3.7, July 17, 1877.

40. Twichell's eulogy, in *Hartford Courant,* April 23, 1910.

41. Appended to Twichell Journal 1.108–109.

42. Pellowe, *Mark Twain, Pilgrim from Hannibal,* 119.

43. Clipping attached in Twichell Journal 1.75.

44. Unidentified clipping attached to Scrapbook volume 2, JTP.

45. Unidentified clipping attached to Journal 5.166.

46. Unidentified clipping attached to Scrapbook volume 2.

47. Unidentified clipping in Memorabilia 3.6; no date, no publisher, JTP.

48. Unidentified clipping pasted into Twichell Journal 5.60.

49. Unidentified clipping pasted into Twichell Journal 7.70–1.

50. Twichell Journal 5.115.

51. *Hartford Courant* article pasted into Twichell Journal 5.117–8.

52. See Kaplan, *Mr. Clemens and Mark Twain,* 23–25; on Beecher's flamboyant style see Rourke, *Trumpets of Jubilee,* 127–28.

53. Budd, *Mark Twain: Social Philosopher,* 108.

54. *Selected Mark Twain-Howells Letters,* 1:435–36.

55. Budd, *Mark Twain: Social Philosopher,* 227n32.

56. Mansfield, *The History of Asylum Hill Congregational Church,* 15.

57. Budd, *Mark Twain: Social Philosopher,* 227n32.

58. "Mock Oration on the Dead Partisan," 852.

59. See *Mark Twain's Autobiography,* 2:6ff.

60. "The Character of Man," 857.

61. Willard, *Divine Conspiracy,* 191. Also see the entry by Kittay, "Hypocrisy," 1:582–87.

62. See *Mark Twain's Autobiography,* 23–26.

63. Noll, *The Scandal of the Evangelical Mind,* 1.

64. Besides Noll's *Scandal,* see also Marsden, *Fundamentalism and American Culture* and *The Soul of the American University.*

65. Lecky quoted in Baetzhold, *Mark Twain and John Bull,* 136.

66. Lecky quoted in Roger Salomon, *Twain and the Image of History,* 99. Salomon's excellent reading of *Connecticut Yankee* in the context of Lecky is in 95–132.

67. Lecky quoted in Baetzhold, *Mark Twain and John Bull,* 138; Baetzhold's reading of *Connecticut Yankee* in the context of Lecky is developed in full in 131–61.

68. *Innocents Abroad,* 209.

69. Louis Rubin discusses this illustration in *William Elliott Shoots a Bear,* 52.

70. An excellent overview of these ideas is in Sire, *Habits of the Mind.*

71. Quoted in Pellowe, *Mark Twain, Pilgrim from Hannibal,* 155–56.

72. Baetzhold, *Mark Twain and John Bull,* 59.

73. Phelps, *Autobiography, With Letters,* 64.

74. Quotes are from Krauth, *Proper Mark Twain,* 191–92. Krauth is citing here Holloway, *Victorian Sage;* Landow, *Elegant Jeremiahs;* and Lears, *No Place of Grace.* Krauth's entire discussion of the phenomenon of the Victorian Sage is enlightening; see 189–218.

75. See Cheney, *The List of Members of The Monday Evening Club,* copy in MTP.

76. Harris, *The Courtship of Olivia Langdon and Mark Twain,* 150.

77. See Robert Weir's discussion of this in "Mark Twain and Commerce," 98–99.

78. Gregg Camfield, *Oxford Companion to Mark Twain,* 630.

79. From typescript of autobiographical dictation, January 12, 1906, in MTP.

80. Twichell's tribute to Edwin Parker was published in the *Hartford Courant* of January 8, 1910.

81. Szasz, *The Divided Mind of Protestant America,* 17.

82. My coverage of modern biblical criticism is indebted to Szasz, *The Divided Mind of Protestant America,* 15–29; see Szasz, 19, for specific information on the Revised Version and for the quote from the *New York Times.*

83. Szasz, *The Divided Mind,* 21.

84. Harold Frederic, *The Damnation of Theron Ware,* 69.

85. *Life on the Mississippi,* 62, 68.

86. Ibid., 84, 87–88.

87. Ibid., 118–20.

88. Twain to Orion Clemens, quoted in Brodwin, "Mark Twain's Theology," 227.

89. For one reconstruction of the blurry details of the tale's composition, see Howard Baetzhold and Joseph McCullough, eds., *The Bible According to Mark Twain,* 129–38.

90. On romantic views of the afterlife, see Douglas, *Feminization of American Culture,* 220–226.

91. Ibid., 223.

92. Ibid., 224.

93. See Gribben, "When Other Amusements Fail," 177. See also Gribben, *Mark Twain's Library,* 741, and Rees, "*Captain Stormfield's Visit to Heaven* and *The Gates Ajar,*" for information that complicates the relation between these two works.

Chapter 4

1. Ensor, "A Clergyman Recalls Hearing Mark Twain," 6.

2. Decker, *Hartford Immigrants,* 46.

3. Ahlstrom, *Religious History,* 794–95.

4. Gladden, *Recollections,* 116, 90.

5. Budd, "The American Background," 33.

6. Quoted in Delbanco, *The Death of Satan,* 151.

7. Quoted in Budd, "The American Background," 39.

8. See Chura, *Vital Contact.*

9. Lathrop, "The Novel and its Future," 31.

10. Howells, *Criticism and Fiction,* 15. The quotation first appeared in an article published in *Harper's Magazine.*

11. Quoted in Decker, *Hartford Immigrants,* 48–49.

12. Ibid., see also Paine, *Mark Twain: A Biography,* 540–41.

13. Decker, *Hartford Immigrants,* 119; see also Andrews, *Nook Farm,* 130–31.

14. Quoted in Landfear, *Reminiscences of Father Hawley,* 68, 76, 77.

15. Quoted in Landfear, *Reminiscences of Father Hawley,* 83, 84, 85.

16. Douglass, *Narrative,* 153

17. Moody, *Sentimental Confessions,* 10.

18. Stowe, *Uncle Tom's Cabin,* 624.

19. Paine, *Mark Twain: A Biography,* 371.

20. Quoted in McWilliams, *Mark Twain in the St. Louis Post-Dispatch,* 212.

21. See especially Zwick, "Mark Twain and Imperialism," 227–56; Rowe, *Literary Culture and U.S. Imperialism,* 121–39; and Michael O'Connor, *Mark Twain and the Missionary.*

22. See Gamble, *The War for Righteousness.*

23. *Following the Equator,* 625–26.

24. Bridgman, *Traveling in Mark Twain,* 143–44.

25. Baetzhold, *Mark Twain and John Bull,* 138.

26. Wing, *My Life in China and America,* 211, 227–8.

27. Twichell Journal 4.59–62.

28. Letter attached to Twichell Journal 4.75.

29. Twichell Journal, March 25–28, 1881, J.4.76–78.

30. Twichell Journal, July 7–9, 1881, J.4.84–88.

31. Twain to Twichell, Aug. 12, 1900, MTP.

32. Quoted in Budd, *Mark Twain: Social Philosopher,* 32.

33. "To the Person Sitting in Darkness," 459.

34. Twain to Twichell, December 22, 1877 [?], quoted in Paine, *Mark Twain: A Biography,* 615.

35. Twichell Journal 1.11.

36. Mansfield, *The History of Asylum Hill Congregational Church,* 39–40.

37. Twichell's obituary for Fr. O'Hagan appeared in the *Hartford Courant,* Dec. 1878.

38. Parker, letter titled "Dr. Parker and the YMCA," in *Hartford Courant,* Jan. 20, 1894.

39. "Dr. Parker on Romanism," *Hartford Courant,* February 18, 1894.

40. Unidentified clipping in Twichell Journal 4.105.

41. Twichell to Twain, Nov. 8, 1897.

42. Cited in *Contributions to the Ecclesiastical History of Connecticut,* 2:274.

43. Mansfield, *History of Asylum Hill Congregational Church,* 39–40.

44. Twichell Journal 3.16.

45. Twichell Journal 5.34.

46. Leary, *A Lifetime with Mark Twain,* 213.

47. Paine, *Mark Twain: A Biography,* 1217–18.

48. *Mark Twain's Letters Volume* 5, 317n2.

49. Quoted in *Mark Twain's Letters Volume* 5, 316n2.

50. *Mark Twain's Letters Volume* 5, 315–16.

51. Quoted in Stowe, *How Sweet the Sound,* 97.

52. *Mark Twain's Autobiography,* 102.

53. Quoted in Stowe, *How Sweet the Sound,* 114.

54. W. E. B. DuBois, *Souls of Black Folk,* 13.

55. See Marshburne, "The NAACP and Mark Twain."

56. On Bushnell's theory of race, see Frederickson, *The Black Image in the White Mind,* 155–57.

57. See Luker, *The Social Gospel in Black and White,* esp. 1–6 for a historical overview of the critical work described in this paragraph. The sources of specific interest in Luker's account are Arthur Schlesinger, "A Critical Period in American Religion, 1875–1900," and Rayford W. Logan, *The Betrayal of the Negro.*

58. Luker, *The Social Gospel in Black and White,* 4.

59. Ibid., 2.

60. Among the more important documents of this ongoing debate in recent years, and the ones that were most helpful to my own account, are James Leonard et al., *Satire or Evasion?;* S. D. Kapoor, "Race and Mark Twain," in Leonard, *Making Mark Twain Work in the Classroom;* Jocelyn Chadwick-Joshua, *The Jim Dilemma;* Eric Sundquist, *To Wake the Nations;* Shelley Fisher Fishkin, *Was Huck Black?* and *Lighting Out for the Territory,* as well as her article "Mark Twain and Race" in Fishkin, *A Historical Guide to Mark Twain;* and David Lionel Smith, "Humor, Sentimentality, and Mark Twain's Black Characters," along with "Black Critics and Mark Twain"; the ur-text of all of this material is Ralph Ellison's *Shadow and Act.* Other sources related to Twain and the Civil War, Reconstruction, and Jim Crow come later in the story.

61. Bell, "Twain's 'Nigger' Jim," 128. On Twain's enjoyment of minstrelsy and its ramifications on his work, see also Woodard and MacCann, "Minstrel Shackles and Nineteenth-Century 'Liberality' in *Huckleberry Finn,*" 141–53; and Eric Lott, "Mr. Clemens and Jim Crow," 129–52. On *Tom Sawyer Abroad* see Woodard and MacCann, "Minstrel Shackles," 147–48. The quote is on p. 147.

62. Lott, "Mr. Clemens and Jim Crow," 143.

63. Excellent accounts of Twain's changing attitudes about race, with each emphasizing somewhat different factors, are in Chadwick-Joshua, *The Jim Dilemma;* Arthur Pettit, "Mark Twain in Our Times"; and Salomon, *Mark Twain and the Image of History,* 74–94.

64. *Adventures of Huckleberry Finn,* 196.

65. Bell, "Twain's 'Nigger' Jim," 135.

66. Chadwick-Joshua, *The Jim Dilemma,* 116.

67. Wallace, "The Case Against Huck Finn," 16. A sweeping and influential version of this critique is in Jonathan Arac, *Huckleberry Finn as Idol and Target.*

68. "A True Story," 578.

69. Chadwick-Joshua, *The Jim Dilemma,* 20.

70. Paine, *Mark Twain: A Biography,* 599–600.

71. Chadwick-Joshua, *The Jim Dilemma,* 23.

72. Phipps, *Mark Twain's Religion,* 166.

73. Quoted in Fishkin, *Was Huck Black?,* 124.

74. Guy Cardwell provides excellent analysis of this relationship in *Twins of Genius,* esp. 64–77.

75. *Life on the Mississippi,* 442–43.

76. Quotes from Cardwell, *Twins of Genius,* 64, 66, 67.

77. From "The South as a Field of Fiction," quoted in David Blight, *Race and Reunion,* 219.

78. Blight, *Race and Reunion,* 220.

79. Ibid.

80. Ibid.

81. Cowie, *The Rise of the American Novel,* 533.

82. See Sundquist, *To Wake the Nations,* chapter 3, "Mark Twain and Homer Plessy."

83. Gillman, *Dark Twins,* 88–89.

84. *Mark Twain Speaking,* 479.

85. Quoted in David L. Smith, "Black Critics and Mark Twain," 117. For a nuanced discussion of Twain's affinities with Washington, see Smith, 117–19.

Chapter 5

1. Extensive discussion of these tendencies is in Tuveson, *Redeemer Nation;* Bloch, *Visionary Republic;* and Hatch, *Sacred Cause of Liberty.*

2. Robert Bellah, "Civil Religion in America," 13.

3. Program attached to Twichell Journal 4.82.

4. Leon, *Mark Twain and West Point.*

5. Messent and Courtney, *Civil War Letters,* 92, 115, 126, 252.

6. Shattuck, *A Shield and Hiding Place,* 58.

7. Much of this material is available in Messent and Courtney, *Civil War Letters.*

8. Twichell to sister Jane, July 5, 1863, in JTP.

9. Both quotes in letters to Howells, in *Selected Mark Twain-Howells Letters,* 407, 380.

10. Twichell to Harry Hopkins, n.d., in box 11, Twichell Papers.

11. Quoted in Swanberg, *Sickles the Incredible,* 150.

12. Twichell Journal 6.83.

13. See, for example, McPherson, *What They Fought For;* Mitchell, *The Vacant Chair;* and Gardiner Shattuck, *A Shield and Hiding Place.*

14. "Hartford's Joseph Twichell," unidentified clipping, dated Dec. 31, 1905, Twichell Journal 8.

15. See *Mark Twain's Autobiography* 1:335–45 for Twain's account of meeting Sickles; the quote is from p. 338.

16. Twichell Journal 5.94.

17. *Hartford Evening Post,* July 17, 1888; in Twichell Journal 6.16.

18. James Cox, *Mark Twain: Fate of Humor,* 194.

19. Hoffman, *Inventing Mark Twain,* 281–82. Hoffman provides a thorough discussion of the Twain-Grant relationship in 323–29. See also Perry, *Grant and Twain.*

20. Hoffman, *Inventing Mark Twain,* 325.

21. Kaplan, *Mr. Clemens and Mark Twain,* 224.

22. Quoted in Lloyd Lewis, *Sherman,* 639.

23. Hoffman, *Inventing Mark Twain,* 326.

24. Jacoby, *Freethinkers,* 148. The previous quotation is an adaptation of the title of chapter 6 from this same book, 149.

25. Ingersoll, *Complete Lectures of Col. R. G. Ingersoll,* 131–32.

26. Ibid.

27. On this transition see Delbanco, *The Real American Dream.*

28. Kaplan, *Mr. Clemens and Mark Twain,* 226.

29. "The Babies," 727–28.

30. Ibid., 729.

31. *Mark Twain's Letters,* 372.

32. Twichell Journal 5.68.

33. Twichell Journal 5.68.

34. Quoted in program and news account of oration, attached to Twichell Journal 5.69ff.

35. *Mark Twain Speaking,* 137.

36. Quoted in Kaplan, *Mr. Clemens and Mark Twain,* 274.

37. See Cmiel, *Democratic Eloquence,* on this style of speech.

38. See Wilson, *Baptized in Blood,* 42.

39. Ibid., 62–63.

40. See Rolle, *The Lost Cause,* and Hanna and Hanna, *Confederate Exiles in Venezuela.*

41. Wilson, *Baptized in Blood,* 59. More extensive information on Ryan is in Wilson, *Baptized in Blood,* 58–61.

42. Wilson, *Baptized in Blood,* 60.

43. Noll, *The Civil War as a Theological Crisis.*

44. Miller, Stout, and Wilson, "Introduction," in *Religion and the American Civil War,* 3–4.

45. Wilson, *Baptized in Blood,* 13.

46. I have told part of this story in *American Declarations,* 101–6. See also Waldo Braden, *Building the Myth.*

47. Paludan, "Religion and the American Civil War," 35. See also Clebsch, "Christian Interpretations of the Civil War."

48. Quoted in Paludan, "Religion and the American Civil War," 28.

49. Historical accounts of the Lost Cause are numerous; most valuable for my work here have been Miller et al., *Religion and the American Civil War;* Wilson, *Baptized in*

Blood; Gallagher and Nolan, *The Myth of the Lost Cause and Civil War History;* Osterweis, *The Myth of the Lost Cause;* Woodward, *The Burden of Southern History;* Blight, *Race and Reunion;* and Connelly and Bellows, *God and General Longstreet.* The best overview of Twain's use of the Civil War is Schmitz, "Mark Twain's Civil War." See also Rubin, *William Elliot Shoots a Bear.*

50. Quoted in Blight, *Race and Reunion,* 32.

51. Pollard, *Southern History of the War,* 13.

52. Gallagher, "Introduction," in Gallagher and Nolan, *The Myth of the Lost Cause,* 1–2.

53. See Alan T. Nolan's exposition of the content of the myth in "The Anatomy of the Myth," 11–34.

54. Nolan, "The Anatomy of the Myth," 15.

55. Ibid., 15–16.

56. Ibid., 16.

57. Ibid.

58. Ibid.

59. Ibid., 17.

60. Ibid. The reference is to Foster, *Ghosts of the Confederacy.*

61. Ibid., 17–18.

62. Ibid., 18.

63. Ibid.

64. Geertz, *The Interpretation of Cultures,* 90.

65. For contemporary obsessions with Civil War memory, see Horwitz, *Confederates in the Attic.*

66. Blight, *Race and Reunion,* 221–22.

67. Nolan, "The Anatomy of the Myth," 27–28.

68. See Blight, *Race and Reunion,* passim.

69. Cox, "Introduction," 16.

70. Schmitz, "Mark Twain's Civil War," 79. Schmitz also includes in this grouping "A True Story," which appeared in 1874.

71. *Mark Twain's Letters,* 419.

72. *Life on the Mississippi,* 377.

73. "The Private History of a Campaign that Failed," 864. See Gerber, "Mark Twain's Private Campaign," 37–39, for the various manifestations of this tale; Gerber counts eight, including Absalom Grimes's account in his book published over sixty-five years after the war's inception.

74. *Mark Twain Speaking,* 229.

75. Dempsey, *Searching for Jim,* 259.

76. Gerber, "Twain's Private Campaign," 39n7.

77. Quoted in *Mark Twain Business Man,* 62.

78. Dempsey, *Searching for Jim,* 271.

79. "The Private History of a Campaign that Failed," 863.

80. *Mark Twain Speaking,* 231.

81. On Twain's critical treatment of Scott's novels, see Krause, *Mark Twain as Critic,* 148–89.

82. Connelly and Bellows, *God and General Longstreet,* 2.

83. *Life on the Mississippi,* 467.

84. *Life on the Mississippi,* 417, 468, 469.

85. See Landrum, "Sir Walter Scott and His Literary Rivals in the Old South"; and Orians, "Walter Scott, Mark Twain, and the Civil War."

86. *Life on the Mississippi,* 468.

87. Quotes from Pettit, *Mark Twain and the South,* 72; and Schmitz, "Mark Twain's Civil War," 86.

88. Quirk, *Coming to Grips With Huckleberry Finn,* 54.

89. Cox, *Mark Twain: The Fate of Humor,* 218.

90. Smith, "Mark Twain's Images of Hannibal, from St. Petersburg to Eseldorf," 15.

91. Pettit, *Mark Twain and the South,* 70.

92. Cox, *Mark Twain: Fate of Humor,* 197.

93. Mattson, "Mark Twain on War and Peace," 784.

94. Schmitz, "Mark Twain's Civil War," 80.

95. *Life on the Mississippi,* 242.

96. *Adventures of Huckleberry Finn,* 147.

97. Pettit, *Mark Twain and the South,* 91.

98. Mattson, "Mark Twain on War and Peace," 785.

99. "Private History," 880.

100. Mattson, "Mark Twain on War and Peace," 793.

101. "The War Prayer," 654.

102. Mattson, "Mark Twain on War and Peace," 794.

103. For an overview of the lengthy cultural debate over some of these issues, see Jocelyn Chadwick-Joshua, *The Jim Dilemma,* especially 3–27 and 115–35. Two of the early statements of this position are in Schmitz, "Mark Twain, *Huckleberry Finn,* and Reconstruction," and Charles H. Nilon, "The Ending of *Huckleberry Finn,*" 62–75.

104. Pettit, *Mark Twain and the South,* 70.

105. *Adventures of Huckleberry Finn,* 293.

106. *Adventures of Huckleberry Finn,* 322.

107. *Adventures of Huckleberry Finn,* 293.

108. Schmitz, "Mark Twain, *Huckleberry Finn,* and Reconstruction," 60.

109. Fishkin, "Mark Twain and Race," 145–46.

110. Ibid., 146.

111. DuBois, *The Souls of Black Folk,* 30, 139, 47.

112. Cox, *Fate of Humor,* 175.

113. *Adventures of Huckleberry Finn,* 343. For some amusing speculations about this episode, see Steinbrink, "Who Shot Tom Sawyer?"

114. Wert, "James Longstreet and the Lost Cause," 133.

115. Quoted in Fishkin, "Mark Twain and Race," 149.

116. Gribben, *Mark Twain's Library,* 410.

117. *Mark Twain Speaking,* 229–30, 230–31.

118. Quoted in Budd, *Mark Twain: Social Philosopher,* 109.

119. "A Lincoln Memorial: A Plea by Mark Twain for the Setting Apart of His Birthplace."

120. On these matters, see Menand, *The Metaphysical Club,* and Frederickson, *The Inner Civil War.*

121. Menand, *The Metaphysical Club,* 75.

122. On these three themes in Lincoln's work, see Noll, *America's God,* 426–32.

123. Jacoby, *Freethinkers,* 225.

124. Noll, *America's God,* 426, 425. My analysis of Lincoln draws heavily on Noll's work, 422–38.

125. Hawthorne, *The English Notebooks,* 432–33.

126. Guelzo, *Abraham Lincoln: Redeemer President,* 329, 446.

127. Ibid., 446.

128. Delbanco, *The Death of Satan,* 138.

129. Howells, *My Mark Twain,* 101.

130. West, *Democracy Matters,* 16.

Chapter 6

1. Jerome and Wisbey, *Mark Twain in Elmira,* 83.

2. Jerome and Wisbey, *Mark Twain in Elmira,* 84–85.

3. Quotes from Szasz, *The Divided Mind,* 5.

4. Szasz, *The Divided Mind,* 17.

5. Szasz, *The Divided Mind,* 38.

6. R. W. B. Lewis, *American Adam,* 5.

7. Brodwin, "Mark Twain's Theology," 225, 226.

8. Lynn, *Mark Twain and Southwestern Humor,* 186–87.

9. Throughout my discussion here I will be associating Arminianism with Pelagianism, generally favoring Pelagianism as a term and thus subsuming Arminianism. Either is useful as a broad descriptive term, meaning that whenever invoking either I am referring to an emergent romantic view of human nature. Veteran philosophers and theologians should proceed with an awareness of my decision to use these terms fluidly.

10. Quoted in Pellowe, *Mark Twain, Pilgrim from Hannibal,* 219–20.

11. Quoted in *Mark Twain's Fables of Man,* 133–34.

12. Amy Kaplan, *The Social Construction of American Realism,* 160.

13. Pellowe, *Mark Twain, Pilgrim from Hannibal,* 214–15.

14. *Mark Twain Speaking,* 180.

15. Brodwin, "Mark Twain and the Myth," 146. On anti-imperialism see Zwick, "Mark Twain and Imperialism."

16. See Lewis, *American Adam,* 6–10.

17. "Mark Twain Aggrieved."

18. See, for example, Bultmann, *Jesus Christ and Mythology.*

19. *Life on the Mississippi,* 248–49.

20. Werge, "Mark Twain and the Fall of Adam," 6.

21. Jerome and Wisbey, *Mark Twain in Elmira,* 84–85.

22. Ensor, *Mark Twain and the Bible,* 110n5 and 6.

23. "Mark Twain Aggrieved."

24. On the trope of the "Death of Adam" in the culture at large, see Robinson, *The Death of Adam;* and Greene, *The Death of Adam.*

25. *Innocents Abroad,* 567.

26. Budd, *Our Mark Twain,* 25.

27. See for example Budd, *Our Mark Twain,* 36–37.

28. Extensive discussion of the rhetorical mode of enactment and the many invocations of the declaration in American culture is available in Bush, *American Declarations.*

29. An excellent discussion of these matters is in Budd, *Our Mark Twain,* 19–47.

30. "Not Funny This Time," 3.

31. Ensor, "A Clergyman Recalls Hearing Mark Twain," 6.

32. *Mark Twain in Eruption,* 202.

33. Michelson, *Mark Twain on the Loose,* 2, 3.

34. Ibid., 7, 9.

35. Ibid., 7.

36. Twain, "The American Press," quoted in Salomon, *Twain and the Image of History,* 97.

37. Carter, "Mark Twain: 'Moralist in Disguise,'" 65.

38. Henderson, *Mark Twain,* 99.

39. Dark, *Everyday Apocalypse,* 11, 10, 12.

40. Dark, *Everyday Apocalypse,* 15.

41. Milbank, *Theology and Social Theory,* 171.

42. "Not Funny This Time."

43. Brodwin, "The Humor of the Absurd," 64.

44. See *William F. Buckley and Malcolm Muggeridge on Faith and Religious Institutions,* 40–43.

45. Bakhtin, *Rabelais and His World,* 11–12.

46. "Open Letter to Commodore Vanderbilt," 287.

47. "The Revised Catechism," 539.

48. See Frank, *Less Than Conquerors.*

49. "Barnum's First Speech to Congress," 212–13.

50. "The Facts Concerning the Recent Carnival of Crime in Connecticut," 645.

51. Ibid., 653, 654.

52. Ibid., 659.

53. Twichell Journal 2.7

54. "The Man That Corrupted Hadleyburg," 1–2.

55. Ibid., 21.

56. Ibid., 63.

57. Ibid., 83.

58. Michelson, *Mark Twain on the Loose,* 7.

Chapter 7

1. Quoted in Tuckey, "Introduction," x–xi.

2. Chapin, "*Their Trackless Way,*" 140–41.

3. "Mark Twain Interviewed in London," unidentified clipping in June 1897 file, MTP.

4. Twain to F. H. Skrine, Aug. 22, 1897, and Sept. 9 or 10, 1897, in MTP.

5. Stroebe, "Bereavement Research and Theory," 857.

6. See, for example, the collection of essays edited by Klass et al., entitled *Continuing Bonds: New Understandings of Grief;* Klass, *The Spiritual Lives of Bereaved Parents;* Stroebe, "Coping with Bereavement"; Paul Rosenblatt, *Bitter, Bitter Tears;* and Neimeyer, *Meaning Reconstruction and the Experience of Loss.* An expanded version of my argument here is in Bush, "'Broken Idols.'"

7. See especially Freud's essay "Mourning and Melancholia."

8. Among grief theorists themselves, the term "postmodern" has never really caught on. These new developments are generally incorporated under the broad terms of a "constructivist model" of grief. Sometimes this model is referred to as the "Continuing Bonds theory of grief," which alludes to Klass's and Silverman's influential volume.

9. Inese Wheeler, "The Role of Meaning and Purpose in Life in Bereaved Parents Associated with a Self-Help Group," 261.

10. Ibid., 262; see also Marriss, *Loss and Change.*

11. Pine and Brauer, "Parental Grief" 73–75; see also Rando, "An Investigation of Grief and Adaptation in Parents Whose Children Have Died from Cancer."

12. C. M. Parkes, "Research: Bereavement"; and Wheeler, "The Role of Meaning and Purpose in Life in Bereaved Parents," 269.

13. Hill, *Mark Twain: God's Fool,* 50–51.

14. Macnaughton, *Mark Twain's Last Years as a Writer,* 23; Boker, *The Grief Taboo in American Literature,* 105.

15. Anderson et al., *Selected Mark Twain-Howells Letters,* 316n1; Hill, *Mark Twain: God's Fool,* 50–51.

16. Moltmann, *In the End—The Beginning,* 16–17.

17. *Adventures of Huckleberry Finn,* 139.

18. On Twain's admiration for Riley, see Bush, "'Absorbing' the Character."

19. Boewe, "On Stage and Off with James Whitcomb Riley and Mark Twain."

20. Riley, "The Absence of Little Wesley," 414–15.

21. See Klass, *Spiritual Lives of Bereaved Parents,* 126–65.

22. Ibid., 142, emphasis mine.

23. Marwit and Klass, "Grief and the Role of the Inner Representation of the Deceased," 298.

24. "In Memoriam," 217.

25. Ibid., 217, 218.

26. Ibid., 218–19.

27. Quoted in Gribben, *Mark Twain's Library,* 2:693.

28. Buckley, *Poems of Tennyson,* 179.

29. Gribben, *Mark Twain's Library,* 2:693.

30. Buckley, *Poems of Tennyson,* 182.

31. Ibid., 186–87.

32. Camfield, *Oxford Companion to Mark Twain,* 22.

33. Quoted in Harnsberger, *Mark Twain's Views of Religion,* 47.

34. Quoted in Paine, *Mark Twain, A Biography,* 1431.

35. From "About Cities in the Sun," 19, in MTP.

36. Hill, *Mark Twain: God's Fool,* 33–4, Willis, *Mark and Livy,* 244–45.

37. Tuckey, "Mark Twain's Later Dialogue," 535.

38. Letter written by Laura Hawkins Frazer, dated Jan. 23, 1923, in JTP.

39. Quoted in Pellowe, *Mark Twain, Pilgrim from Hannibal,* 219–20.

40. Quoted in Jerome and Wisbey, *Mark Twain in Elmira,* 93.

41. Harnsberger, *Mark Twain's Views of Religion,* 47.

42. "Broken Idols," 262–63.

43. See Emerson, *Mark Twain: A Literary Life,* 218–32.

44. Tuckey, "Introduction," in *The Devil's Race Track,* xi.

45. "Broken Idols," 263.

46. Susan Crane to Harriet Whitmore, Sept. 9, 1896; copy in MTP.

47. Leary, *A Lifetime with Mark Twain,* 138–39, 140.

48. Clemens, *My Father, Mark Twain,* 176.

49. "Broken Idols," 263.

50. Ibid.

51. Ibid., 263–64.

52. Hoffman, *Inventing Mark Twain,* 413.

53. "Broken Idols," 267–68.

54. Ibid., 268.

55. Skandera-Trombley, *Mark Twain in the Company of Women,* 173.

56. Kiskis, "Susy Clemens as the Fire for Mark Twain's Autobiography," 45.

57. Mark Twain to F. H. Skrine, dated February 5, 7, 11, and 13, 1902, photocopy in MTP.

58. Twain to Twichell, December 2, 1898, from Vienna, in MTP.

59. Twain to Twichell, March 4, 1900, in MTP.

60. Kete, *Sentimental Collaborations,* 6.

61. Ibid., 146.

62. Barnes, "Affecting Relations," 597.

63. Kete, *Sentimental Collaborations,* 6.

64. Klass, *Spiritual Lives of Bereaved Parents,* 142, emphasis mine.

65. Opinions vary regarding the nature of Susy's relationship with Brownell; see Hoffman, *Inventing Mark Twain,* 367; Neider, "Introduction"; and Lystra, *Dangerous Intimacy,* 16 and 280n40.

66. Michelson, *Mark Twain on the Loose,* 173.

67. *Mark Twain—Howells Letters,* 318.

68. On Nietzsche and "eternal recurrence," see his *The Gay Science,* esp. 273–74; useful commentary on the specific term is in Bauckham and Hart, *Hope Against Hope,* 20–25. Interesting discussion of Twain's encounter with Nietzsche is in Jennifer L. Zaccara, "Mark Twain, Isabel Lyon, and the 'Talking Cure,'" 115–17 and 120.

69. Quotes from Powers, *Dangerous Water,* 287; an excellent account of this incident as the end of Twain's childhood is in *Dangerous Water,* 274–89.

70. See Hill, *Mark Twain: God's Fool,* 272, 274.

71. "In My Bitterness," in *Mark Twain's Fables of Man,* 131–32.

72. See in particular the autobiographical dictations of June 19, 20, 22, 23, and 25, 1906, all in MTP. These dictations were edited by Charles Neider and published as "Mark Twain: Reflections on Religion."

73. Hoffman, *Inventing Mark Twain,* 436–47.

74. Messent, "Mark Twain, Joseph Twichell, and Religion," 401, 398.

75. *The Tragedy of Pudd'nhead Wilson and the Comedy of Those Extraordinary Twins,* 329.

76. Twichell to Olivia Clemens, Dec. 9, 1901, in MTP.

77. *Mark Twain's Letters,* 719–21.

78. Twichell to Twain, Sept. 2, 1902, JTP.

79. Quoted in Willis, *Mark and Livy,* 237.

80. Autobiographical dictation of November 4, 1904, typescript in MTP.

81. Autobiographical dictation of June 24, 1905, typescript in MTP.

82. McCullough and Baetzhold, *The Bible According to Mark Twain,* 217.

83. Mark Twain to Jean Clemens, June 1907, MTP.

84. "Little Bessie," in *The Devil's Race-Track,* 7.

85. Quoted in Paul Baender, "Introduction," in *What is Man?,* 18.

86. Budd, *Mark Twain: The Ecstasy of Humor,* 22.

87. Chapin, *"Their Trackless Way": A Book of Memories,* 140–41.

88. Mark Twain to Rose Lathrop, Oct. 19, 1901, in MTP.

89. See Cooley, *Mark Twain's Aquarium,* xxiii, 282.

90. Lears, *No Place of Grace,* 151.

91. Skandera-Trombley, *Mark Twain in the Company of Women,* 160. For more on the WCTU and reform, see *Mark Twain in the Company of Women,* 65–154.

92. *Personal Recollections of Joan of Arc,* 461.

93. Quoted in Hays, *Mark Twain and Religion,* 172.

94. Frederick, *The Darkened Sky,* 166.

95. Cooley, *Mark Twain's Aquarium,* xix.

96. For excerpts of the dictation, see Cooley, *Mark Twain's Aquarium,* xix ff.

97. Palmer, *The Courage to Teach,* 48–9. For Erikson's discussions of generativity as the seventh stage in an eight-stage model of psychological development, several of his volumes are useful, including *Childhood and Society* and *Identity and the Life Cycle.*

98. Twain, "The Divine Spark," unpublished manuscript in MTP.

99. Quoted in Foner, *Mark Twain: Social Critic,* 237.

100. See Chappell, *A Stone of Hope.*

101. On these matters, see Budd, *Mark Twain: Social Philosopher;* and Foner, *Mark Twain: Social Critic.* On Twain and anti-Semiticism, see Dolmetsch, *"Our Famous Guest,"* 160–80. Regarding the protest to President Cleveland, see Foner, *Mark Twain: Social Critic,* 236–37.

102. Tuckey, "Mark Twain's Later Dialogue," 532.

103. Quoted in Hays, *Mark Twain and Religion,* 185; for Hays's unusually uplifting reading of *What Is Man?,* see 179–211.

104. "The Turning Point of My Life," 937.

105. This narrative is told in moving detail in Lystra, *Dangerous Intimacy.*

106. Kiskis, "Twain and the Tradition of Literary Domesticity," 20.

107. *Mark Twain's Own Autobiography,* 246, 247, 249, 247, 252.

108. Quoted in Kiskis, "Twain and the Tradition of Literary Domesticity," 20.

109. Moltmann, *In the End,* 15–16. Bloch is quoted from his work, *The Principle of Hope.*

110. "Eve's Diary," 709.

111. "In Memoriam," 218.

112. *Mark Twain's Own Autobiography,* 252.

113. Fishkin, *Lighting Out for the Territory,* 145, 11.

114. Bloom, *The American Religion.*

115. Schwartz, "Mark Twain and Robert Ingersoll," 191.

116. Ibid., 191n23.

117. Strong, *Joseph Hopkins Twichell,* 111.

118. See Krauth, *Proper Mark Twain,* passim but especially 1–6, for this distinction.

119. Quoted in Schwartz, "Mark Twain and Robert Ingersoll," 192–93.

120. Letter written by Laura Hawkins Frazier, Jan. 23, 1923, in JTP.

121. B. Q. Stevens to Willard Morse, Dec. 12, 1922, in JTP.

122. Quoted in Jerome and Wisbey, *Mark Twain in Elmira,* 93.

123. "Death of 'Mark Twain,'" *London Times,* April 22, 1910, 10.

124. Quoted in Cyril Clemens, *Mark Twain's Religion,* 11.

125. This is clear from his many published obituaries (most from the *Hartford Courant*) that Twichell kept and pasted into his journals.

126. Twichell, "Mark Twain," letter in *Hartford Courant,* April 22, 1910.

127. Unidentified news clipping, book 5 of Twichell Family Scrapbooks, JTP.

128. Paine, *Mark Twain, a Biography,* 1584.

129. Unidentified clipping attached to Twichell Journal 11.86.

130. David C. Twichell, "Memoranda on His Mother's Death," JTP, 1, 3.

131. David C. Twichell, "Memoranda on His Mother's Death," JTP, 8.

132. Twichell to Frank Fuller, Oct. 17, 1911, JTP.

Bibliography

List of Abbreviations

The following abbreviations for major works by Twichell and Twain are used in the endnotes.

JTP Joseph Twichell Papers, Beinecke Rare Book and Manuscript Library, Yale University

MTP Mark Twain Papers, Bancroft Library, University of California, Berkeley

Works by Mark Twain

Twain, Mark. "About Cities in the Sun." Manuscript. Mark Twain Papers. Bancroft Library, University of California, Berkeley.

———. "About Smells." In *Collected Tales, Sketches, Speeches, and Essays, 1852–1890*, ed. Louis J. Budd, 365–66. New York: Library of America, 1992.

———. *Adventures of Huckleberry Finn*. Ed. Walter Blair, Victor Fischer, and Lin Salamo. Berkeley: University of California Press, 2003.

———. *The Adventures of Tom Sawyer, Tom Sawyer Abroad, Tom Sawyer, Detective*. Ed. John C. Gerber, Paul Baender, and Terry Firkins. Berkeley: University of California Press, 1980.

———. Autobiographical Dictations. Mark Twain Papers. University of California, Berkeley.

———. "Autobiography of a Damned Fool." In *Mark Twain's Satires and Burlesques*, ed. Franklin B. Rogers, 136–61. Berkeley: University of California Press, 1968.

———. "The Babies: As They Comfort Us in Our Sorrows, Let Us Not Forget Them in

Our Festivities." In *Mark Twain: Collected Tales, Sketches, Speeches, and Essays, 1852–1890,* ed. Louis J. Budd, 727–29. New York: Library of America, 1992.

———. "Barnum's First Speech to Congress." In *Collected Tales, Sketches, Speeches, and Essays, 1852–1890,* ed. Louis J. Budd, 210–13. New York: Library of America, 1992.

———. *The Bible According to Mark Twain: Writings on Heaven, Eden, and the Flood.* Ed. Howard G. Baetzhold and Joseph B. McCullough. New York: Touchstone, 1996.

———. "Broken Idols." In "'Broken Idols': Mark Twain's Elegies for Susy and a Critique of Freudian Grief Theory," by Harold K. Bush Jr. *Nineteenth-Century Literature* 57 (2002): 327–368.

———. "Captain Stormfield's Visit to Heaven." In *The Bible According to Mark Twain: Writings on Heaven, Eden, and the Flood,* ed. Howard G. Baetzhold and Joseph B. McCullough, 129–88. New York: Touchstone, 1996.

———. "The Character of Man." In *Collected Tales, Sketches, Speeches, and Essays, 1852–1890,* ed. Louis J. Budd, 854–58. New York: Library of America, 1992.

———. *Collected Tales, Sketches, Speeches, and Essays, 1852–1890.* Ed. Louis J. Budd. New York: Library of America, 1992.

———. *Collected Tales, Sketches, Speeches, and Essays, 1891–1910.* Ed. Louis J. Budd. New York: Library of America, 1992.

———. *A Connecticut Yankee in King Arthur's Court.* Ed. Bernard L. Stein. Berkeley: University of California Press, 1983.

———. *The Devil's Race Track: The Best from Which Was the Dream? and Fables of Man.* Ed. John S. Tuckey. Berkeley: University of California Press, 1980.

———. "The Divine Spark." Manuscript. Mark Twain Papers. University of California, Berkeley.

———. Entries. *Mental Photographs: An Album for Confessions of Tastes, Habits, and Convictions.* Compiled by Charles J. Rosenbloom. New York: Leypodt and Jolt, 1869. Beinecke Rare Book and Manuscript Library, Yale University.

———. "Eve's Diary." In *Collected Tales, Sketches, Speeches, and Essays, 1891–1910,* ed. Louis J. Budd, 695–709. New York: Library of America, 1992.

———. "The Facts Concerning the Recent Carnival of Crime in Connecticut." In *Collected Tales, Sketches, Speeches, and Essays, 1852–1890,* ed. Louis J. Budd, 644–60. New York: Library of America, 1992.

———. *Following the Equator.* In *The Oxford Mark Twain,* ed. Shelley Fisher Fishkin. 29 vols. New York: Oxford University Press, 1996.

———. *The Gilded Age.* In *The Oxford Mark Twain,* ed. Shelley Fisher Fishkin. 29 vols. New York: Oxford University Press, 1996.

———. "The Great Dark." In *Mark Twain's Which Was the Dream?: and Other Symbolic Writings of the Later Years,* ed. John S. Tuckey, 102–50. Berkeley: University of California Press, 1968.

———. *Great Short Works of Mark Twain.* Ed. Justin Kaplan. New York: Harper & Row, 1967.

———. "Hellfire Hotchkiss." In *Mark Twain's Satires and Burlesques,* ed. Franklin B. Rogers, 175–203. Berkeley: University of California Press, 1967.

———. *Huck Finn and Tom Sawyer Among the Indians and Other Unfinished Stories.* Ed. Dahlia Armon and Walter Blair. Berkeley: University of California Press, 1989.

———. "The Indignity Put Upon the Remains of George Holland by the Rev. Mr. Sabine." In *Collected Tales, Sketches, Speeches, and Essays, 1852–1890,* ed. Louis J. Budd, 517–21. New York: Library of America, 1992.

———. "In Memoriam." In *Collected Tales, Sketches, Speeches, and Essays, 1891–1910,* ed. Louis Budd, 217–19. New York: Library of America, 1992.

———. *The Innocents Abroad.* In *The Oxford Mark Twain,* ed. Shelley Fisher Fishkin. 29 vols. New York: Oxford University Press, 1996.

———. "Jane Lampton Clemens." In *Huck Finn and Tom Sawyer Among the Indians and Other Unfinished Stories,* ed. Dahlia Armon and Walter Blair, 82–92. Berkeley: University of California Press, 1989.

———. "Letters From the Earth." In *The Bible According to Mark Twain: Writings on Heaven, Eden, and the Flood,* ed. Howard G. Baetzhold and Joseph B. McCullough, 213–60. New York: Touchstone, 1996.

———. *Life on the Mississippi.* In *The Oxford Mark Twain,* ed. Shelley Fisher Fishkin. 29 vols. New York: Oxford University Press, 1996.

———. "A Lincoln Memorial: A Plea by Mark Twain for the Setting Apart of His Birthplace." *New York Times,* January 13, 1907, 8.

———. "Little Bessie." In *The Devil's Race Track: The Best from Which Was the Dream? and Fables of Man,* ed. John S. Tuckey, 3–13. Berkeley: University of California Press, 1980.

———. "The Man That Corrupted Hadleyburg." In *The Man That Corrupted Hadleyburg and Other Stories and Essays, 1891–1910.* In *The Oxford Mark Twain,* ed. Shelley Fisher Fishkin, 1–83. 29 vols. New York: Oxford University Press, 1996.

———. "Mark Twain Aggrieved." *New York Times,* December 4, 1883.

———. *Mark Twain at the Buffalo Express: Articles and Sketches by America's Favorite Humorist.* Ed. Joseph B. McCullough and Janice McIntire-Strasburg. DeKalb: Northern Illinois University Press, 1999.

———. *Mark Twain, Business Man.* Ed. Samuel Charles Webster. Boston: Little, Brown and Company, 1946.

———. *Mark Twain–Howells Letters.* Ed. Henry Nash Smith and William M. Gibson. 2 vols. Cambridge: Harvard University Press, 1960.

———. *Mark Twain in Eruption.* Ed. Bernard DeVoto. New York: Capricorn, 1940.

———. *Mark Twain, the Letter Writer.* Ed. Cyril Clemens. Boston: Meador Publishing Company, 1932.

———. *Mark Twain Speaking.* Ed. Paul Fatout. Iowa City: U of Iowa P, 1976.

———. *Mark Twain's Autobiography.* Ed. Albert B. Paine. New York: Collier, 1924.

———. *Mark Twain's Fables of Man.* Ed. John S. Tuckey. Berkeley: University of California Press, 1972.

———. *Mark Twain's Letters.* Ed. Albert B. Paine. 2 vols. New York: Harper, 1917.

———. *Mark Twain's Letters Volume 1: 1856–66.* Ed. Edgar Marquess Branch et al. Berkeley: University of California Press, 1988.

———. *Mark Twain's Letters Volume 2: 1867–68*. Ed. Harriet Elinor Smith and Richard Bucci. Berkeley: University of California Press, 1990.

———. *Mark Twain's Letters Volume 3: 1869*. Ed. Victor Fisher and Michael B. Frank. Berkeley: University of California Press, 1992.

———. *Mark Twain's Letters Volume 4: 1870–71*. Ed. Victor Fisher and Michael B. Frank. Berkeley: University of California Press, 1995.

———. *Mark Twain's Letters Volume 5: 1872–73*. Ed. Lin Salamo and Harriet Elinor Smith. Berkeley: University of California Press, 1997.

———. *Mark Twain's Letters Volume 6: 1874–75*. Ed. Michael B. Frank and Harriet Elinor Smith. Berkeley: University of California Press, 2002.

———. *Mark Twain's Mysterious Stranger Manuscripts*. Ed. William M. Gibson. Berkeley: University of California Press, 1969.

———. *Mark Twain's Notebooks and Journals, Volume 1 (1855–73)*. Ed. Frederick Anderson, Michael B. Frank, and Kenneth M. Sanderson. Berkeley: University of California Press, 1975.

———. *Mark Twain's Own Autobiography: The Chapters from the North American Review*. Ed. Michael J. Kiskis. Madison: University of Wisconsin Press, 1990.

———. *Mark Twain's Satires and Burlesques*. Ed. Franklin R. Rogers. Berkeley: University of California Press, 1967.

———. "Mock Oration on the Dead Partisan." In *Collected Tales, Sketches, Speeches, and Essays, 1852–1890*, ed. Louis J. Budd, 852–53. New York: Library of America, 1992.

———. "Not Funny This Time." *St. Louis Globe-Democrat*, June 2, 1902, 3.

———. "Open Letter to Commodore Vanderbilt." In *Collected Tales, Sketches, Speeches, and Essays, 1852–1890*, ed. Louis J. Budd, 285–90. New York: Library of America, 1992.

———. *The Oxford Mark Twain*. Ed. Shelley Fisher Fishkin. 29 vols. New York: Oxford University Press, 1996.

———. *Personal Recollections of Joan of Arc*. In *The Oxford Mark Twain*, ed. Shelley Fisher Fishkin. 29 vols. New York: Oxford University Press, 1996.

———. "Plymouth Rock and the Pilgrims." In *Mark Twain Speaking*, ed. Paul Fatout, 44–55. Iowa City: University of Iowa Press, 1976.

———. "The Private History of a Campaign that Failed." In *Collected Tales, Sketches, Speeches, and Essays, 1852–1890*, ed. Louis J. Budd, 863–82. New York: Library of America, 1992.

———. "Reflections on the Sabbath." In *Collected Tales, Sketches, Speeches, and Essays, 1852–1890*, ed. Louis J. Budd, 208–9. New York: Library of America, 1992.

———. "The Revised Catechism." In *Collected Tales, Sketches, Speeches, and Essays, 1852–1890*, ed. Louis J. Budd, 539–40. New York: Library of America, 1992.

———. *Roughing It*. Ed. Harriet Elinor Smith and Edgar Marquess Branch. Berkeley: University of California Press, 1993.

———. "A Salutation Speech from the Nineteenth Century to the Twentieth." In *Mark Twain's Weapons of Satire: Anti-Imperialist Writings on the Philippine-American War*, ed. Jim Zwick. Syracuse, NY: Syracuse University Press, 1992.

———. *Tales, Speeches, Essays, and Sketches.* Ed. Tom Quirk. New York: Penguin Books, 1994.

———. "To the Person Sitting in Darkness." In *Collected Tales, Sketches, Speeches, and Essays, 1891–1910,* ed. Louis J. Budd, 457–73. New York: Library of America, 1992.

———. "To Walt Whitman." In *Collected Tales, Sketches, Speeches, and Essays, 1852–1890,* ed. Louis J. Budd, 940–41. New York: Library of America, 1992.

———. *The Tragedy of Pudd'nhead Wilson and the Comedy of Those Extraordinary Twins.* In *The Oxford Mark Twain,* ed. Shelley Fisher Fishkin. 29 vols. New York: Oxford University Press, 1996.

———. *A Tramp Abroad.* In *The Oxford Mark Twain,* ed. Shelley Fisher Fishkin. 29 vols. New York: Oxford University Press, 1996.

———. "A True Story." In *Collected Tales, Sketches, Speeches, and Essays, 1852–1890,* ed. Louis J. Budd, 578–82. New York: Library of America, 1992.

———. "The Turning Point of My Life." In *Collected Tales, Sketches, Speeches, and Essays, 1891–1910,* ed. Louis J. Budd, 929–38. New York: Library of America, 1992.

———. "The War Prayer." In *Collected Tales, Sketches, Speeches, and Essays,* ed. Louis J. Budd, 652–55. New York: Library of America, 1992.

———. *The Washoe Giant in San Francisco.* Ed. Franklin Walker. San Francisco: Fields, 1938.

———. *What Is Man? And Other Philosophical Writings.* Ed. Paul Baender. Berkeley: University of California Press, 1973.

———. "Which Was the Dream?" *Mark Twain's Which Was the Dream?: and Other Symbolic Writings of the Later Years.* Ed. John S. Tuckey, 33–73. Berkeley: University of California Press, 1968.

———. "Which Was It?" *Mark Twain's Which Was the Dream?: and Other Symbolic Writings of the Later Years.* Ed. John S. Tuckey, 179–429. Berkeley: University of California Press, 1968.

Secondary Works

Ahlstrom, Sydney E. *A Religious History of the American People.* New Haven: Yale University Press, 1972.

Anderson, Frederick, William M. Gibson, and Henry Nash Smith, eds. *Selected Mark Twain-Howells Letters, 1872–1910.* New York: Atheneum, 1967.

Andrews, Kenneth Richmond. *Nook Farm, Mark Twain's Hartford Circle.* Cambridge: Harvard University Press, 1950.

Arac, Jonathan. *Huckleberry Finn as Idol and Target.* Madison: University of Wisconsin Press, 1997.

Atherton, Lewis Eldon. *Main Street on the Middle Border.* Chicago: Quadrangle Books, 1966.

Baender, Paul. Introduction. In *What is Man? And Other Philosophical Writings,* 1–34. Berkeley: University of California Press, 1973.

Baetzhold, Howard G. *Mark Twain and John Bull: The British Connection.* Bloomington: Indiana University Press, 1970.

Bakhtin, M. M. *Rabelais and His World.* Trans. Hélène Iswolsky. Bloomington: Indiana University Press, 1984.

Baldwin, James. *The Fire Next Time.* New York: Dell, 1963.

Barnes, Elizabeth. "Affecting Relations: Pedagogy, Patriarchy, and the Politics of Sympathy." *American Literary History* 8 (1996): 597–614.

Barnes, Howard A. *Horace Bushnell and the Virtuous Republic.* Philadelphia: American Theological Library Association; Metuchen, NJ: Scarecrow Press, 1991.

Bauckham, Richard, and Trevor Hart. *Hope Against Hope: Christian Eschatology in Contemporary Context.* Grand Rapids, MI: Eerdmans, 1999.

Beecher, Rev. Thomas K. "To Joe Twichell." June 14, 1875. Joseph Twichell Journal 1.108–109. Joe Twichell Papers. Yale University.

Bell, Bernard. "Twain's 'Nigger' Jim." In *Satire or Evasion?: Black Perspectives on Huckleberry Finn,* ed. James S. Leonard, Thomas A. Tenney, and Thadious M. Davis. Durham: Duke University Press, 1992.

Bellah, Robert. "Civil Religion in America." *Daedalus* 96 (1967): 1–21.

Bellah, Robert N., et al. *Habits of the Heart: Individualism and Commitment in American Life.* Berkeley: University of California Press, 1985.

Bercovitch, Sacvan. *The American Jeremiad.* Madison: University of Wisconsin Press, 1978.

———. "The Problem of Ideology in American Literary History." *Critical Inquiry* 3 (1986): 631–53.

Blight, David W. *Race and Reunion: The Civil War in American Memory.* Cambridge: Belknap Press of Harvard University Press, 2001.

Bloch, Ernst. *The Principle of Hope.* Cambridge: MIT Press, 1986.

Bloch, Ruth. *Visionary Republic: Millennial Themes in American Thought, 1756–1800.* New York: Cambridge University Press, 1985.

Bloom, Harold. *The American Religion: The Emergence of the Post-Christian Nation.* New York: Simon and Schuster, 1992.

Boewe, Mary. "On Stage and Off with James Whitcomb Riley and Mark Twain." *Traces* 7 (1995).

Boker, Pamela. *The Grief Taboo in American Literature: Loss and Prolonged Adolescence in Twain, Melville, and Hemingway.* New York: New York University Press, 1996.

Boudreau, Kristin. *Sympathy in American Literature: American Sentiments from Jefferson to the Jameses.* Gainesville: University Press of Florida, 2002.

Braden, Waldo, ed. *Building the Myth: Selected Speeches Memorializing Abraham Lincoln.* Urbana: University of Illinois Press, 1990.

Bridgman, Richard. *Traveling in Mark Twain.* Berkeley: University of California Press, 1987.

Broadhead, Richard. "Literature and Culture." In *The Columbia Literary History of the United States,* ed. Emory Elliot et al., 467–81. New York: Columbia University Press, 1988.

Brodwin, Stanley. "Extracts from Adam's Diary." In *The Mark Twain Encyclopedia,* ed. J. R. LeMaster and James D. Wilson, 273–75. New York: Garland, 1993.

———. "The Humor of the Absurd: Mark Twain's Adamic Diaries." *Criticism: A Quarterly for Literature and the Arts* 14 (1972): 49–64.

———. "Mark Twain and the Myth of the Daring Jest." In *The Mythologizing of Mark Twain,* ed. Sara deSaussure Davis and Philip D. Beidler, 136–57. Tuscaloosa: University of Alabama Press, 1984.

———. "Mark Twain's Theology: The Gods of a Brevet Presbyterian." In *The Cambridge Companion to Mark Twain,* ed. Forrest G. Robinson, 220–48. Cambridge: Cambridge University Press, 1995.

Brooks, Van Wyck. *The Ordeal of Mark Twain.* New York: Dutton, 1920.

Brown, Candy Gunther. *The Word in the World: Evangelical Writing, Publishing, and Reading in America, 1789–1880.* Chapel Hill: University of North Carolina Press, 2004.

Brown, Gillian. *Domestic Individualism: Imagining Self in Nineteenth-Century America.* Berkeley: University of California Press, 1990.

Brown, Robert McAfee. *Spirituality and Liberation: Overcoming the Great Fallacy.* Philadelphia: Westminster, 1988.

Buckley, Jerome H., ed. *Poems of Tennyson.* Boston: Houghton Mifflin, 1958.

Budd, Louis J. "The American Background." In *The Cambridge Companion to American Realism and Naturalism,* ed. Donald Pizer, 21–46. New York: Cambridge University Press, 1995.

———. *Mark Twain: The Ecstasy of Humor.* Elmira: Quarry Farms Papers, 1995.

———. "Mark Twain Plays the Bachelor." *Western Humanities Review* 9 (Spring): 157–67.

———. *Mark Twain: Social Philosopher.* 1962. Columbia: University of Missouri Press, 2001.

———. *Our Mark Twain: The Making of His Public Personality.* Philadelphia: University of Pennsylvania Press, 1983.

Bultmann, Rudolph. *Jesus Christ and Mythology.* New York: Scribner's, 1958.

Burns, Ken, dir. *Mark Twain.* Burbank: Warner Home Video, 2001. Florentine Films.

Bush, Harold K., Jr. "Absorbing the Character: James Whitcomb Riley and Mark Twain's Theory of Performance." *American Literary Realism* 31 (1999): 31–47.

———. *American Declarations: Rebellion and Repentance in American Cultural History.* Urbana: University of Illinois Press, 1999.

———. "'Broken Idols': Mark Twain's Elegies for Susy and a Critique of Freudian Grief Theory." *Nineteenth-Century Literature* 57 (2002): 327–68.

———. "'A Moralist in Disguise': Mark Twain and American Religion." In *A Historical Guide to Mark Twain,* ed. Shelley Fisher Fishkin, 55–94. New York: Oxford University Press, 2002.

———. "The Outrageous Idea of a Christian Literary Theory." *Christianity and Literature* 51.1 (2001): 79–103.

Bushnell, Horace. *Christian Nurture.* New York: Scribner, 1860.

———. *The Vicarious Sacrifice, Grounded in Principles of Universal Obligation.* London: A. Strahan, 1866.

Camfield, Gregg, ed. *The Oxford Companion to Mark Twain.* New York: Oxford University Press, 2003.

———. "A Republican Artisan in the Court of King Capital: Mark Twain and Commerce." In *A Historical Guide to Mark Twain,* ed. Shelley Fisher Fishkin, 95–126. New York: Oxford University Press, 2002.

———. *Sentimental Twain: Samuel Clemens in the Maze of Moral Philosophy.* Philadelphia: University of Pennsylvania Press, 1994.

Cardwell, Guy. *The Man Who Was Mark Twain.* New Haven: Yale University Press, 1991.

———. *Twins of Genius.* Michigan: Michigan State College Press, 1953.

Carter, Paul. "Mark Twain: 'Moralist in Disguise.'" *University of Colorado Studies* 6 (Jan. 1957): 65–78.

Carter, Paul A. *The Spiritual Crisis of the Gilded Age.* DeKalb: Northern Illinois University Press, 1971.

Carter, Stephen L. *The Culture of Disbelief: How American Law and Politics Trivialize Religious Devotion.* New York: Basic Books, 1993.

Castronovo, Russ. *Necro Citizenship: Death, Eroticism, and the Public Sphere in the Nineteenth-Century United States.* Durham: Duke University Press, 2001.

Chadwick-Joshua, Joceyln. *The Jim Dilemma: Reading Race in Huckleberry Finn.* Jackson: University Press of Mississippi, 1998.

Chapman, Mary, and Glenn Hendler, eds. *Sentimental Men: Masculinity and the Politics of Affect in American Culture.* Berkeley: University of California Press, 1999.

Chapin, Adèle Le Bourgeois. *"Their Trackless Way": A Book of Memories.* New York: Henry Holt and Company, 1932.

Chappell, David L. *A Stone of Hope: Prophetic Religion and the Death of Jim Crow.* Chapel Hill: University of North Carolina Press, 2004.

Cheney, Howell. *The List of Members of The Monday Evening Club, Together with the Record of Papers Read at Their Meetings, 1869–1954.* Hartford: privately printed, 1954. Mark Twain Papers. University of California, Berkeley.

Cheng, Anne Anlin. *The Melancholy of Race.* New York: Oxford University Press, 2000.

Chura, Patrick. *Vital Contact: Downclassing Journeys in American Literature from Herman Melville to Richard Wright.* New York: Routledge, 2005.

Clebsch, William. "Christian Interpretations of the Civil War." *Church History* 30 (1961): 212–22.

Clemens, Clara. *My Father, Mark Twain.* New York: Harper & Brothers, 1931.

Clemens, Cyril. *Mark Twain's Religion.* Webster Groves, MO: Centenary, 1935.

Cmiel, Kenneth. *Democratic Eloquence: The Fight Over Popular Speech in Nineteenth-Century America.* New York: Morrow, 1990.

Connelly, Thomas L., and Barbara L. Bellows. *God and General Longstreet: The Lost Cause and the Southern Mind.* Baton Rouge: Louisiana State University Press, 1982.

Contributions to the Ecclesiastical History of Connecticut. Vol. 2. 1860–1967. Connecticut State Library.

Cooley, John, ed. *Mark Twain's Aquarium: The Samuel Clemens Angelfish Correspondence, 1905–1910.* Athens: University of Georgia Press, 1991.

Cormier, Henri. *The Humor of Jesus.* New York: Alba House, 1977.

Coulombe, Joseph L. *Mark Twain and the American West.* Columbia: University of Missouri Press, 2003.

Courtney, Steve. "To the Tower." Asylum Hill Congregational Church Web site. http://www.ahcc.org/TWAIN/ToTheTower.htm.

Cowie, Alexander. *The Rise of the American Novel.* New York: American Book, 1951.

Cox, James M. Introduction. In *Life on the Mississippi,* 9–24. New York: Penguin, 1984.

———. *Mark Twain: The Fate of Humor.* 1966. Columbia: University of Missouri Press, 2002.

Crane, Susan. "To Harriet Whitmore." September 9, 1896. Mark Twain Papers. University of California, Berkeley.

Cummings, Sherwood. *Mark Twain and Science: Adventures of a Mind.* Baton Rouge: Louisiana State University Press, 1988.

Dark, David. *Everyday Apocalypse: The Sacred Revealed in Radiohead, the Simpsons, and Other Pop Culture Icons.* Grand Rapids, MI: Brazos Press, 2002.

Davis, Rebecca Harding. *Bits of Gossip.* Boston: Houghton Mifflin, 1904.

"Death of 'Mark Twain,'" *London Times,* April 22, 1910, 10.

Decker, Robert Owen. *Hartford Immigrants: A History of the Christian Activities Council (Congregational), 1850–1980.* New York: United Church Press, 1987.

Delbanco, Andrew. *The Death of Satan: How Americans Have Lost the Sense of Evil.* New York: Farrar, Straus and Giroux, 1995.

———. *The Real American Dream: A Meditation on Hope.* Cambridge: Harvard University Press, 1999.

Deming, Will. *Rethinking Religion: A Concise Introduction.* New York: Oxford University Press, 2005.

Dempsey, Terrell. *Searching for Jim: Slavery in Sam Clemens's World.* Columbia: University of Missouri Press, 2003.

Dolmetsch, Carl. *"Our Famous Guest": Mark Twain in Austria.* Athens: University of Georgia Press, 1992.

Douglas, Ann. *The Feminization of American Culture.* New York: Knopf, 1977.

Douglass, Frederick. *Narrative of the Life of Frederick Douglass, an American Slave.* New York: Penguin, 1982.

Doyno, Victor. "Samuel Clemens as Family Man and Father." In Kiskis and Skandera-Trombley, *Constructing Mark Twain,* 28–49.

DuBois, W. E. B. *The Souls of Black Folk.* New York: Penguin, 1989.

Eagleton, Terry. *After Theory.* New York: Basic, 2003.

Eckenrode, Hamilton James. "Sir Walter Scott and the South." *North American Review* 206 (1917): 595–603.

Eggleston, Edward. *The Hoosier School-Master.* 1871. Bloomington: Indiana University Press, 1984.

Elie, Paul. *The Life You Save May Be Your Own: An American Pilgrimage.* New York: Farrar, Straus and Giroux, 2003.

Ellison, Ralph. *Shadow and Act.* New York: Random House, 1964.

Emerson, Everett. *Mark Twain: A Literary Life.* Philadelphia: University of Pennsylvania Press, 2000.

Ensor, Allison. "A Clergyman Recalls Hearing Mark Twain." *Mark Twain Journal* 15 (1970): 6.

———. *Mark Twain and the Bible.* Lexington: University of Kentucky Press, 1969.

Erikson, Erik H. *Childhood and Society.* New York: Norton, 1950.

———. *Identity and the Life Cycle: Selected Papers.* New York: International University Press, 1959.

Fanning, Philip. *Mark Twain and Orion Clemens: Brothers, Partners, Strangers.* Tuscaloosa: University of Alabama Press, 2003.

Fiddes, Paul S. *The Promised End: Eschatology in Theology and Literature.* Malden, MA: Blackwell, 2000.

Fishkin, Shelley Fisher, ed. *A Historical Guide to Mark Twain.* New York: Oxford University Press, 2002.

———. *Lighting Out for the Territory: Reflections on Mark Twain and American Culture.* New York: Oxford University Press, 1996.

———. "Mark Twain and Race." In *A Historical Guide to Mark Twain,* ed. Shelley Fisher Fishkin, 127–62. New York: Oxford University Press, 2002.

———. *Was Huck Black?: Mark Twain and African-American Voices.* New York: Oxford University Press, 1993.

Florian, Victor. "Meaning and Purpose in the Life of Bereaved Parents Whose Son Fell During Active Military Service." *Omega* 17 (1989): 91–102.

Foner, Philip S. *Mark Twain: Social Critic.* New York: International Publishers, 1958.

Foster, Gaines. *Ghosts of the Confederacy: Defeat, the Lost Cause, and the Emergence of the New South, 1865–1913.* New York: Oxford University Press, 1987.

Franchot, Jenny. "Invisible Domain: Religion and American Literary Studies." *American Literature* 67 (1995): 833–42.

———. *Roads to Rome: The Antebellum Protestant Encounter with Catholicism.* Berkeley: University of California Press, 1994.

Frank, Douglas. *Less Than Conquerors: How Evangelicals Entered the Twentieth Century.* Grand Rapids, MI: W. B. Eerdmans, 1986.

Frankl, Victor. *Man's Search for Meaning: An Introduction to Logotherapy.* New York: Simon and Schuster, 1984.

Frazer, Laura Hawkins. "To Joseph Twichell." January 23, 1923. Joseph Twichell Papers. Yale University.

Frederic, Harold. *The Damnation of Theron Ware; or Illumination.* New York: Penguin, 1985.

Frederick, John T. *The Darkened Sky: Nineteenth-Century American Novelists and Religion.* Notre Dame, IN: University of Notre Dame Press, 1969.

Frederickson, George M. *The Black Image in the White Mind.* New York: Harper and Row, 1971.

———. *The Inner Civil War: Northern Intellectuals and the Crisis of the Union.* New York: Harper and Row, 1965.

Freud, Sigmund. "Mourning and Melancholia." In *The Standard Edition of the Complete Psychological Works of Sigmund Freud,* ed. James Strachey, 239–58. Vol. 14. London: Hogarth Press, 1966–74.

Fuller, Robert C. *Spiritual, But Not Religious: Understanding Unchurched America.* New York: Oxford University Press, 2001.

Fulton, Joe B. *Mark Twain's Ethical Realism: The Aesthetics of Race, Class, and Gender.* Columbia: University of Missouri Press, 1997.

Gage, Rev. William L. "The Hartford Minister's Meeting." *Hartford Courant* March 2, 1875.

Gallagher, Gary W. Introduction. In *The Myth of the Lost Cause and Civil War History,* ed. Gary W. Gallagher and Alan T. Nolan, 1–10. Bloomington: Indiana University Press, 2000.

———. "Jubal A. Early, the Lost Cause, and Civil War History: A Persistent Legacy." In *The Myth of the Lost Cause and Civil War History,* ed. Gary W. Gallagher and Alan T. Nolan, 35–59. Bloomington: Indiana University Press, 2000.

Gamble, Richard M. *The War for Righteousness: Progressive Christianity, the Great War, and the Rise of the Messianic Nation.* Wilmington: ISI Books, 2003.

Garrison, Charles. "Of Humor, Death, and Ministers: The Comstock of Mark Twain." *Nevada Historical Society Quarterly* 38.3 (Fall 1995): 189–202.

Geertz, Clifford. *The Interpretation of Cultures: Selected Essays.* New York: Basic Books, 1973.

General Association of Connecticut. *Contributions to the Ecclesiastical History of Connecticut.* Ed. Leonard Bacon, S. W. S. Dutton, and E. W. Robinson. Vol. 2. New Haven: W. L. Kingsley, 1861.

Gerber, John. "Mark Twain's Private Campaign." *Civil War History* 1.1 (1955): 37–60.

Gill, Gillian. *Mary Baker Eddy.* Reading, MA: Perseus, 1998.

Gillman, Susan. *Dark Twins: Imposture and Identity in Mark Twain's America.* Chicago: University of Chicago Press, 1989.

Gittleman, Edward. "Jefferson's Slave Narrative: The Declaration of Independence as Literary Text." *Early American Literature* 8 (1974): 239–56.

Gladden, Washington. *Recollections.* Boston: Houghton Mifflin Company, 1909.

Goldman, Stan. *Melville's Protest Theism: The Hidden and Silent God in* Clarel. DeKalb: Northern Illinois University Press, 1993.

Gordon, David J. *Literary Atheism.* New York: Peter Lang, 2002.

Greene, John C. *The Death of Adam: Evolution and Its Impact on Western Thought.* Ames, IA: Iowa State University Press, 1959.

Gribben, Alan. *Mark Twain's Library: A Reconstruction.* 2 vols. Boston: G. K. Hall, 1980.

———. "When Other Amusements Fail: Mark Twain and the Occult." In *The Haunted Dusk: American Supernatural Fiction, 1820–1920,* ed. Howard Kerr et al. Athens: University of Georgia Press, 1983.

Guelzo, Allen C. *Abraham Lincoln: Redeemer President.* Grand Rapids: Eerdmans, 1999.

Hall, Donald E., ed. *Muscular Christianity: Embodying the Victorian Age.* New York: Cambridge University Press, 1994.

Handy, Robert. *A Christian America: Protestant Hopes and Historical Realities.* New York: Oxford University Press, 1971.

Hanna, Alfred Jackson, and Kathryn Abbey Hanna. *Confederate Exiles in Venezuela.* Tuscaloosa, AL: Confederate Publishing Company, 1960.

Harnsberger, Caroline. *Mark Twain's Views of Religion.* Evanston, IL: Schori Press, 1961.

Harris, Susan K. *The Courtship of Olivia Langdon and Mark Twain.* Cambridge: Cambridge University Press, 1996.

"Hartford's Joseph Twichell." December 31, 1905. Joseph Twichell Journal 8. Joseph Twichell Papers. Yale University.

Hatch, Nathan. *The Democratization of American Christianity.* New Haven: Yale University Press, 1989.

———. *The Sacred Cause of Liberty: Republican Thought and the Millennium in Revolutionary New England.* New Haven: Yale University Press, 1977.

Hauerwas, Stanley, and William H. Willimon. *The Peaceable Kingdom: A Primer in Christian Ethics.* Notre Dame, IN: Notre Dame University Press, 1983.

———. *Resident Aliens: Life in the Christian Colony.* Nashville: Abingdon Press, 1989.

Hawthorne, Nathaniel. *The English Notebooks.* Ed. Randall Stewart. New York: Modern Language Association of America, 1941.

Hays, John Q. *Mark Twain and Religion.* New York: Peter Lang, 1989.

Hegeman, David. *Plowing in Hope: Toward a Biblical Theology of Culture.* Moscow, ID: Canon, 1999.

Henderson, Archibald. *Mark Twain.* New York: Stokes, 1912.

Hendler, Glenn. *Public Sentiments: Structures of Feeling in Nineteenth-Century American Literature.* Chapel Hill: University of North Carolina Press, 2001.

Hill, Hamlin Lewis. *Mark Twain: God's Fool.* New York: Harper & Row, 1973.

Hoffman, Andrew Jay. *Inventing Mark Twain: The Lives of Samuel Langhorne Clemens.* New York: William Morrow and Co., 1997.

———. "Mark Twain and Homosexuality." *American Literature* 67.1 (March 1995): 23–49.

Holland, Jeffrey R. "Soul-Butter and Hog Wash: Mark Twain and Frontier Religion." In *"Soul-Butter and Hog Wash" and Other Essays on the American West,* ed. Thomas G. Alexander. Provo, UT: Brigham Young University Press, 1978.

Holloway, John. *Victorian Sage: Studies in Argument.* Hamden, CT: Archon, 1962.

Holmes, Oliver Wendell. *Ralph Waldo Emerson.* Boston: Houghton Mifflin, 1884.

Horwitz, Tony. *Confederates in the Attic: Dispatches from America's Unfinished Civil War.* New York: Pantheon Books, 1998.

Howells, William Dean. *Criticism and Fiction.* New York: Harper, 1892.

———. *Literary Friends and Acquaintance.* New York: Harper, 1902.

———. *My Mark Twain: Reminiscences and Criticisms.* Harper, 1910.

Hubbell, Jay B. *The South in American Literature, 1607–1900.* Durham: Duke University Press, 1954.

Hunter, James Davison. *American Evangelicalism: Conservative Religion and the Quandary of Modernity.* New Brunswick, NJ: Rutgers University Press, 1983.

Hutchison, William R. *The Modernist Impulse in American Protestantism.* Durham: Duke University Press, 1992.

Ingersoll, Robert G. *Complete Lectures of Col. R. G. Ingersoll.* Chicago: Regan, 1930.

Jackson, E. N. *Understanding Grief: Its Roots, Dynamics, and Treatment.* New York: Abingdon Press, 1957.

Jacoby, Susan. *Freethinkers: A History of American Secularism.* New York: Metropolitan, 2004.

James, William. *The Varieties of Religious Experience.* New York: Touchstone, 1997.

Jerome, Robert D., and Herbert A. Wisbey Jr., eds. *Mark Twain in Elmira.* Elmira, NY: Mark Twain Society, 1977.

Kaplan, Amy. *The Social Construction of American Realism.* Chicago: University of Chicago Press, 1989.

Kaplan, Fred. *The Singular Mark Twain.* New York: Doubleday, 2003.

Kaplan, Justin. *Mr. Clemens and Mark Twain: A Biography.* New York: Simon and Schuster, 1966.

Kerr, Howard. *Mediums, Spirit-Rappers, and Roaring Radicals: Spiritualism in American Literature, 1850–1900.* Urbana: University of Illinois Press, 1972.

Kete, Mary. *Sentimental Collaborations: Mourning and Middle-Class Identity in Nineteenth-Century America.* Durham: Duke University Press, 2000.

Kiskis, Michael. *Samuel Clemens and Me: Class, Mother, and the Trauma of Loss.* Elmira, IL: Quarry Farm Papers, 2001.

———. "Susy Clemens as the Fire for Mark Twain's Autobiography." *Mid-Hudson Language Studies* 10 (1987): 43–50.

———. "Twain and the Tradition of Literary Domesticity." In Kiskis and Skandera-Trombley, *Constructing Mark Twain,* 13–27.

Kiskis, Michael, and Laura Skandera-Trombley, eds. *Constructing Mark Twain: New Directions in Scholarship.* Columbia: University of Missouri Press, 2001.

Kittay, Eva F. "Hypocrisy." In *Encyclopedia of Ethics,* ed. Lawrence C. Becker and Charlotte B. Becker. 2nd ed. Vol. 1. New York: Routledge, 2001.

Klass, Dennis et al., eds. *Continuing Bonds: New Understanding of Grief.* Washington, DC: Taylor & Francis, 1996.

———. *The Spiritual Lives of Bereaved Parents.* Philadelphia: Brunner/Mazel, 1999.

Knapp, R. J. *Beyond Endurance: When a Child Dies.* New York: Schocken, 1986.

Knoper, Randall. *Acting Naturally: Mark Twain in the Culture of Performance.* Berkeley: University of California Press, 1995.

Krause, Sydney J. *Mark Twain as Critic.* Baltimore: Johns Hopkins University Press, 1967.

Krauth, Leland. *Proper Mark Twain.* Athens: University of Georgia Press, 1999.

Kuklick, Bruce. *Churchmen and Philosophers: From Jonathan Edwards to John Dewey.* New Haven: Yale University Press, 1985.

Ladd, Tony, and James A. Mathison. *Muscular Christianity: Evangelical Protestants and the Development of American Sport.* Grand Rapids, MI: Baker, 1999.

Landfear, N. Maria, ed. *Reminiscences of Father Hawley.* Hartford: Case, Lockwood and Brainerd Co., 1877.

Landow, George P. *Elegant Jeremiahs: The Sage from Carlyle to Mailer.* Ithaca, NY: Cornell University Press, 1986.

Landrum, Grace Warren. "Sir Walter Scott and His Literary Revivals in the Old South." *American Literature* 2 (1930): 256–76.

Lathrop, George Parsons. "The Novel and Its Future." In *Documents of American Realism and Naturalism,* ed. Donald Pizer, 18–32. Carbondale: Southern Illinois University Press, 1998.

Lears, T. Jackson. *No Place of Grace: Antimodernism and the Transformation of American Culture, 1880–1920.* Chicago: University of Chicago Press, 1981.

Leary, Katy. *A Lifetime with Mark Twain.* New York: Harcourt Brace, 1925.

Leon, Philip W. *Mark Twain and West Point.* Toronto: ECW Press, 1996.

Leonard, James S., ed. *Making Mark Twain Work in the Classroom.* Durham: Duke University Press, 1999.

Leonard, James S., Thomas A. Tenney, and Thadious M. Davis, eds. *Satire or Evasion?: Black Perspectives on Huckleberry Finn.* Durham: Duke University Press, 1992.

Lewis, C. S. *A Grief Observed.* San Francisco: HarperCollins, 1994.

Lewis, Lloyd. *Sherman, Fighting Prophet.* New York: Harcourt Brace, 1958.

Lewis, R. W. B. *The American Adam: Innocence, Tragedy, and Tradition in the Nineteenth Century.* Chicago: University of Chicago Press, 1955.

Logan, Rayford Whittingham. *The Betrayal of the Negro: From Rutherford B. Hayes to Woodrow Wilson.* New York: Collier, 1969.

Long, E. Hudson. *Mark Twain Handbook.* New York: Hendricks House, 1958.

Long, Lisa A. *Rehabilitating Bodies: Health, History, and the American Civil War.* Philadelphia: University of Pennsylvania Press, 2004.

Longfellow, Henry Wadsworth. "A Psalm of Life." In *The Norton Anthology of American Literature,* ed. Nina Baym et al, 1319–20. 2nd ed. New York: W. W. Norton & Co., 1985.

Lott, Eric. "Mr. Clemens and Jim Crow: Twain, Race, and Blackface." In *The Cambridge Companion to Mark Twain,* ed. Forrest G. Robinson, 129–52. Cambridge: Cambridge University Press, 1995.

Lowry, Richard S. *"Littery Man": Mark Twain and Modern Authorship.* New York: Oxford University Press, 1996.

Luker, Ralph. *The Social Gospel in Black and White: American Racial Reform, 1885–1912.* Chapel Hill: University of North Carolina Press, 1991.

Lynn, Kenneth S. *Mark Twain and Southwestern Humor.* Boston: Little, Brown, 1960.

Lystra, Karen. *Dangerous Intimacy: The Untold Story of Mark Twain's Final Years.* Berkeley: University of California Press, 2004.

MacIntyre, Alasdair C. *After Virtue: A Study in Moral Theory.* Notre Dame, IN: Notre Dame University Press, 1981.

Macnaughton, William. *Mark Twain's Last Years as a Writer.* Columbia: University of Missouri Press, 1979.

Mansfield, Lillian M. *The History of Asylum Hill Congregational Church.* Hartford, CT: Asylum Hill Congregational Church, 1965.

"Mark Twain Entertained." Joseph Twichell Journal 7.145. Joseph Twichell Papers. Yale University.

"Mark Twain Interviewed in London." Unidentified clipping, in June 1897 file, MTP.

Marriss, Peter. *Loss and Change.* New York: Pantheon Books, 1974.

Marsden, George M. *Fundamentalism and American Culture: The Shaping of Twentieth-Century Evangelicalism, 1870–1925.* Oxford: Oxford University Press, 1980.

———. *The Outrageous Idea of Christian Scholarship.* Oxford: Oxford University Press, 1997.

———. *The Soul of the American University: From Protestant Establishment to Established Nonbelief.* New York: Oxford University Press, 1994.

Marshburne, Larry. "The NAACP and Mark Twain." *Mark Twain Journal* 36 (Spring 1998): 2–7.

Marty, Martin E. *The Infidel.* Cleveland: Meridian Books, 1961.

Marwit, Samuel J., and Dennis Klass. "Grief and the Role of the Inner Representation of the Deceased." In *Continuing Bonds: New Understanding of Grief,* 297–310. Washington, DC: Taylor & Francis, 1996.

Marx, Leo. *The Pilot and the Passenger: Essays on Literature, Technology, and Culture in the United States.* New York: Oxford University Press, 1988.

Matthews, Donald G. "The Second Great Awakening as an Organizing Process, 1780–1830: An Hypothesis." *American Quarterly* 21.1 (1969): 23–43.

Mattson, J. Stanley. "Mark Twain on War and Peace: the Missouri Rebel and 'The Campaign that Failed.'" *American Quarterly* 20 (1968): 783–94.

McLoughlin, William. *Revivals, Awakenings, and Reform.* Chicago: University of Chicago Press, 1978.

McPherson, James M. *What They Fought For, 1861–1865.* Baton Rouge: Louisiana State University Press, 1993.

McWilliams, James. *Mark Twain in the St. Louis Post-Dispatch, 1874–1891.* Troy, NY: Whitson, 1997.

Menand, Louis. *The Metaphysical Club.* New York: Farrar, Straus & Giroux, 2001.

Mental Photographs: An Album for Confessions of Taste, Habits, and Convictions. Compiled by Charles J. Rosenbloom. New York: Leypodt and Jolt, 1869. Beinecke Library, Yale University.

Messent, Peter. "Mark Twain, Joseph Twichell, and Religion." *Nineteenth-Century Literature* 58.3 (Dec. 2003): 368–402.

Messent, Peter, and Steve Courtney, eds. *The Civil War Letters of Joseph Hopkins Twichell: A Chaplain's Story.* Athens: University of Georgia Press, 2006.

Michelson, Bruce. *Mark Twain on the Loose: A Comic Writer and the American Self.* Amherst: University of Massachusetts Press, 1995.

Milbank, John. *Theology and Social Theory: Beyond Secular Reason.* Cambridge, MA: B. Blackwell, 1991.

Miller, Perry. *Nature's Nation.* Cambridge, MA: Belknap Press, 1967.

———. *The Life of the Mind in America.* New York: Harcourt, Brace, 1965.

Miller, Randall M., Harry S. Stout, and Charles Reagan Wilson, eds. Introduction. In *Religion and the American Civil War,* 3–18. New York: Oxford University Press, 1998.

Miller, Terry. *Greenwich Village and How It Got That Way.* New York: Crown, 1990.

Mitchell, Reid. *The Vacant Chair: The Northern Soldier Leaves Home.* New York: Oxford University Press, 1993.

Moltmann, Jürgen. *The Coming of God: Christian Eschatology.* Trans. Margaret Kohl. Minneapolis: Fortress Press, 1996.

———. *In the End—The Beginning: The Life of Hope.* Minneapolis: Fortress Press, 2004.

———. *Theology of Hope; on the Ground and the Implications of a Christian Eschatology.* Trans. James W. Leitch. New York: Harper & Row, 1967.

Moody, Joycelyn. *Sentimental Confessions: Spiritual Narratives of Nineteenth-Century African American Women.* Athens: University of Georgia Press, 2001.

Mott, Frank Luther. *A History of American Magazines.* Cambridge: Harvard University Press, 1958–68.

Neider, Charles. Introduction. In *The Outrageous Mark Twain,* 1–29. New York: Doubleday, 1987.

Neider, Charles, ed. "Mark Twain: Reflections on Religion." *Hudson Review* 16 (1963): 329–52.

Neimeyer, Robert A., ed. *Meaning Reconstruction and the Experience of Loss.* Washington, DC: American Psychological Association, 2001.

Nelson, Dana D. *National Manhood: Capitalist Citizenship and the Imagined Fraternity of White Men.* Durham: Duke University Press, 1998.

Neuhaus, Richard John. *The Naked Public Square: Religion and Democracy in America.* Grand Rapids, MI: W. B. Eerdmans, 1984.

Nietzsche, Friedrich Wilhelm. *The Gay Science.* Trans. Walter Kaufmann. New York: Random House, 1974.

Nilon, Charles H. "The Ending of Huckleberry Finn: Freeing the Free Negro." In *Satire or Evasion? Black Perspectives on Huckleberry Finn,* ed. James S. Leonard et al. Durham: Duke University Press, 1992.

Nolan, Alan T. "The Anatomy of Myth." In *The Myth of the Lost Cause and Civil War History,* ed. Gary W. Gallagher and Alan T. Nolan, 11–34. Bloomington: Indiana University Press, 2000.

Noll, Mark A. *America's God: From Jonathan Edwards to Abraham Lincoln.* New York: Oxford University Press, 2002.

———. *The Civil War as a Theological Crisis.* Chapel Hill: University of North Carolina Press, 2006.

———. *The Scandal of the Evangelical Mind.* Grand Rapids, MI: W. B. Eerdmans, 1994.

"Not Funny This Time." *St. Louis Globe-Democrat,* June 2, 1902, 3.

Numbers, Ronald L. *Darwinism Comes to America.* Cambridge: Harvard University Press, 1998.

Obenzinger, Hilton. *American Palestine: Melville, Twain, and the Holy Land Mania.* Princeton: Princeton University Press, 1999.

O'Connor, Leo F. *Religion in the American Novel.* Lanham, MD: University Press of America, 1984.

O'Connor, Michael Levine. *Mark Twain and the Missionary.* PhD diss., University of Missouri, 1997.

Orians, G. Harrison. "Walter Scott, Mark Twain, and the Civil War." *South Atlantic Quarterly* (1941): 342–59.

Osterweis, Rollin G. *The Myth of the Lost Cause, 1865–1900.* Hamden, CT: Archon Books, 1973.

Paine, Albert Bigelow. *Mark Twain, a Biography; the Personal and Literary Life of Samuel Langhorne Clemens.* 2 vols. New York: Harper & Brothers, 1912.

Palmer, Earl F. *The Humor of Jesus: Sources of Laughter in the Bible.* Vancouver: Regent College, 2001.

Palmer, Parker. *The Courage to Teach: Exploring the Inner Landscape of a Teacher's Life.* San Francisco: Jossey-Bass, 1998.

Paludan, Phillip Shaw. "Religion and the American Civil War." In *Religion and the American Civil War,* ed. Randall M. Miller, Harry S. Stout, and Charles Reagan Wilson, 21–42. New York: Oxford University Press, 1998.

Parker, Edwin. "Dr. Parker on Romanticism." *Hartford Courant,* February 18, 1894.

———. "Dr. Parker and the YMCA." *Hartford Courant,* January 20, 1894.

Parkes, C. M. "Research: Bereavement." *Omega* 18 (1988): 365–77.

Pellowe, William Charles Smithson. *Mark Twain, Pilgrim from Hannibal.* New York: The Hobson Book Press, 1946.

Perry, Mark. *Grant and Twain: The Story of an American Friendship.* New York: Random House, 2004.

Pettit, Arthur G. *Mark Twain and the South.* Lexington: University Press of Kentucky, 1974.

———. "Mark Twain in Our Times." In *Huck Finn Among the Critics,* ed. M. Thomas Inge. Frederick, MD: University Publications of America, 1985.

Phelps, William Lyon. *Autobiography, with Letters.* New York: Oxford University Press, 1939.

Phipps, William E. *Mark Twain's Religion.* Macon: Mercer University Press, 2003.

Pine, Vanderlyn R., and Carolyn Brauer. "Parental Grief: A Synthesis of Theory, Research and Intervention." In *Parental Loss of a Child,* ed. Therese A. Rando, 59–96. Champaign, IL: Research Press, 1986.

Pizer, Donald, ed. *Documents of American Realism and Naturalism.* Carbondale: Southern Illinois University Press, 1998.

Plantinga, Cornelius. *Not the Way It's Supposed To Be: A Breviary of Sin.* Grand Rapids, MI: Eerdmans, 1995.

Pollard, Edward Alfred. *The Lost Cause: A New Southern History of the War of the Confederates.* New York: E. B. Treat, 1866.

———. *Southern History of the War.* New York: C. B. Richardson, 1866.

Powers, Ron. *Dangerous Water: A Biography of the Boy Who Became Mark Twain.* New York: Basic Books, 1999.

——. *Mark Twain: A Life.* New York: Free Press, 2005.

Prime, William Cowper. *Tent Life in the Holy Land.* New York: Harper & Brothers, 1858.

Putney, Clifford. *Muscular Christianity: Manhood and Sports in Protestant America, 1880–1920.* Cambridge: Harvard University Press, 2001.

Quetel, Claude. *History of Syphilis.* Baltimore: Johns Hopkins University Press, 1990.

Quirk, Tom. *Coming to Grips With Huckleberry Finn: Essays on a Book, a Boy, and a Man.* Columbia: University of Missouri Press, 1993.

Rando, Therese A. "An Investigation of Grief and Adaptation in Parents Whose Children Have Died from Cancer." *Journal of Pediatric Psychology*" 8 (1983): 3–20.

Reynolds, David. *Walt Whitman's America: A Cultural Biography.* New York: Knopf, 1995.

Riley, James Whitcomb. "The Absence of Little Wesley." In *The Complete Poetical Works of James Whitcomb Riley,* 414–15. Bloomington: Indiana University Press, 1993.

Roberts, Jon H. *Darwinism and the Divine in America: Protestant Intellectuals and Organic Evolution, 1859–1900.* Madison: University of Wisconsin Press, 1988.

Robinson, Forrest G. "The Innocent at Large: Mark Twain's Travel Writing." In *The Cambridge Companion to Mark Twain,* ed. Forrest G. Robinson, 27–51. Cambridge: Cambridge University Press, 1995.

Robinson, Marilynne. *The Death of Adam: Essays on Modern Thought.* Boston: Houghton Mifflin, 1998.

Rolle, Andrew F. *The Lost Cause: The Confederate Exodus to Mexico.* Norman: University of Oklahoma Press, 1965.

Rosenblatt, Paul C. *Bitter, Bitter Tears: Nineteenth-Century Diarists and Twentieth-Century Grief Theories.* Minneapolis: University of Minnesota Press, 1983.

Rourke, Constance. *Trumpets of Jubilee.* New York: Harcourt, Brace, 1963.

Rowe, John Carlos. *Literary Culture and U.S. Imperialism: From the Revolution to World War II.* New York: Oxford University Press, 2000.

Rubin, Louis D. *William Elliot Shoots a Bear: Essays on the Southern Literary Imagination.* Baton Rouge: Louisiana State University Press, 1975.

Russett, Cynthia Eagle. *Darwin in America: The Intellectual Response, 1865–1912.* San Francisco: W. H. Freeman, 1976.

Salomon, Roger B. *Twain and the Image of History.* New Haven: Yale University Press, 1961.

Schlesinger, Arthur. "A Critical Period in American Religion, 1875-1900." Massachusetts Historical Society Proceedings 64 (1932): 523–47.

Schmidt, Barbara. "Paine in the Lost and Found." *Mark Twain Journal* 31.2 (1993): 32.

Schmitz, Neil. "Mark Twain's Civil War: Humor's Reconstructive Writing." In *The Cambridge Companion to Mark Twain,* ed. Forrest G. Robinson, 74–92. Cambridge: Cambridge University Press, 1995.

——. "Mark Twain, *Huckleberry Finn,* and Reconstruction." *American Studies* 12: 59–72.

Schwartz, Thomas D. "Mark Twain and Robert Ingersoll: The Freethought Connection." *American Literature* 48 (1976): 183–93.

Shattuck, Gardiner. *A Shield and Hiding Place: The Religious Life of the Civil War Armies.* Macon: Mercer University Press, 1987.

Shea, William M. *The Lion and the Lamb: Evangelicals and Catholics in America.* New York: Oxford University Press, 2004.

Shippey, Tom. *J. R. R. Tolkien: Author of the Century.* Boston: Houghton Mifflin, 2000.

Shurr, William. *Rappacini's Children: American Writers in a Calvinist World.* Lexington: University of Kentucky Press, 1981.

Silverman, Phyllis R., and Steven L. Nickman. "Concluding Thoughts." In *Continuing Bonds: New Understanding of Grief,* 349–56. Washington, DC: Taylor & Francis, 1996.

———. "Introduction: What's the Problem?" In *Continuing Bonds: New Understanding of Grief,* 3–30. Washington, DC: Taylor & Francis, 1996.

Simpson, David, ed. *German Aesthetic and Literary Criticism.* New York: Cambridge University Press, 1984.

Sire, James W. *Habits of the Mind: Intellectual Life as a Christian Calling.* Downers Grove, IL: InterVarsity Press, 2000.

Skandera-Trombley, Laura E. *Mark Twain in the Company of Women.* Philadelphia: University of Pennsylvania Press, 1994.

Smith, Christian. "Force of Habit." *Books and Culture,* Sept.–Oct. 2002.

Smith, David Lionel. "Black Critics and Mark Twain." In *The Cambridge Companion to Mark Twain,* ed. Forrest G. Robinson, 116–28. Cambridge: Cambridge University Press, 1995.

———. "Humor, Sentimentality, and Mark Twain's Black Characters." In *Constructing Mark Twain: New Directions in Scholarship,* ed. Laura E. Skandera-Trombley and Michael J. Kiskis, 151–68. Columbia: University of Missouri Press, 2001.

Smith, Henry Nash. "Mark Twain's Images of Hannibal, from St. Petersbury to Eseldorf." *University of Texas Studies in English* 37 (1958).

Smith, Timothy L. "Righteousness and Hope: Christian Holiness and the Millennial vision of America, 1800–1900." *American Quarterly* 31 (Spring 1979): 21–45.

Stahl, J. D. "'To His Preferred Friends He Revealed His True Character': Mary Mason Fairbanks's Disguised Debate with Sam Clemens." In Kiskis and Skandera-Trombley, eds., *Constructing Mark Twain,* 50–71.

Steinbrink, Jeffrey. *Getting to Be Mark Twain.* Berkeley: University of California Press, 1991.

———. "Who Shot Tom Sawyer?" *American Literary Realism* 35.1: 29–38.

Stevens, B. Q. "To Willard Morse." December 12, 1922. Joseph Twichell Papers.

Stowe, David W. *How Sweet the Sound: Music in the Spiritual Lives of Americans.* Cambridge: Harvard University Press, 2004.

Stowe, Harriet Beecher. *Uncle Tom's Cabin.* New York: Penguin, 1986.

Stroebe, Margaret. "Bereavement Research and Theory: Retrospective and Prospective." *American Behavioral Scientist* 44.5 (2001): 854–65.

———. "Coping with Bereavement: A Review of the Grief Work Hypothesis." *Omega* 26 (1992–93): 19–42.

Strong, Leah A. *Joseph Hopkins Twichell, Mark Twain's Friend and Pastor.* Athens: University of Georgia Press, 1966.

Sundquist, Eric J. *To Wake the Nations: Race in the Making of American Literature.* Cambridge: Bellknap Press of Harvard University Press, 1993.

Swanberg, W. A. *Sickles the Incredible.* New York: Scribner's, 1956.

Szasz, Ferenc Morton. *The Divided Mind of Protestant America, 1880–1930.* Tuscaloosa: University of Alabama Press, 1982.

Trueblood, Elton. *The Humor of Christ.* New York: Harper & Row, 1964.

Tuckey, John S. Introduction. In *The Devil's Race-Track: Mark Twain's Great Dark Writings: The Best from Which was the Dream? And Fables of Man,* ix–xx. Berkeley: University of California Press, 1980.

———. *Mark Twain's Fables of Man.* Berkeley: University of California Press, 1972.

———. "Mark Twain's Later Dialogue: The 'Me' and the Machine." *American Literature* 41 (1970): 532–42.

Turner, James. *Without God, Without Creed: The Origins of Unbelief in America.* Baltimore: Johns Hopkins University Press, 1985.

Tuveson, Ernest Lee. *Redeemer Nation; The Idea of America's Millennial Role.* Chicago: University of Chicago Press, 1968.

Twichell, David. "Memoranda on His Mother's Death." Typescript. Joseph Twichell Papers. Beinecke Rare Book and Manuscript Library, Yale University.

Twichell, Joseph. Civil War Memorabilia. Joseph Twichell Papers. Beinecke Rare Book and Manuscript Library, Yale University.

———. Correspondence. Joseph Twichell Papers. Beinecke Rare Book and Manuscript Library, Yale University.

———. Journals. Joseph Twichell Papers. Beinecke Rare Book and Manuscript Library, Yale University.

———. "Mark Twain." Letter published in *Hartford Courant,* April 22, 1910.

Veith, Gene E. *Painters of Faith: The Spiritual Landscape in Nineteenth-Century America.* Washington, DC: Regnery, 2001.

Wallace, John. "The Case Against Huck Finn." In James Leonard et al., *Satire or Evasion?,* 16–24.

Wecter, Dixon. *Sam Clemens of Hannibal.* Boston: Houghton Mifflin; Cambridge, MA: Riverside Press, 1952.

Weir, Robert. "Mark Twain and Social Class." In *A Historical Guide to Mark Twain,* ed. Shelley Fisher Fishkin, 195–226. New York: Oxford University Press, 2002.

Wells, David F. *God in the Wasteland: The Reality of Truth in a World of Fading Dreams.* Grand Rapids, MI: W. B. Eerdmans, 1994.

Welter, Barbara. "The Cult of True Womanhood: 1820–1860." *American Quarterly* 18 (1966): 151–74.

Werge, Thomas. "Mark Twain and the Fall of Adam." *Mark Twain Journal* 15.2 (1970): 5–13.

Wert, Jeffry D. "James Longstreet and the Lost Cause." In *The Myth of the Lost Cause and Civil War History,* ed. Gary W. Gallagher and Alan T. Nolan, 127–46. Bloomington: Indiana University Press, 2000.

West, Cornel. *Democracy Matters: Winning the Fight Against Imperialism.* New York: Penguin, 2004.

Wetzsteon, Ross. *Republic of Dreams: Greenwich Village, the American Bohemia, 1910–1960.* New York: Simon and Schuster, 2002.

Wheeler, Inese. "The Role of Meaning and Purpose in Life in Bereaved Parents Associated with a Self-Help Group: Compassionate Friends." *Omega* 28 (1993–94): 261–71.

Willard, Dallas. *The Divine Conspiracy: Rediscovering Our Hidden Life in God.* San Francisco: HarperSanFrancisco, 1998.

William F. Buckley & Malcolm Muggeridge on Faith and Religious Institutions. New York: National Committee of Catholic Laymen, 1981.

Willis, Resa. *Mark and Livy: The Love Story of Mark Twain and the Woman Who (Almost) Tamed Him.* New York: TV Books, 1992.

Wilmer, Richard H. *The Recent Past from a Southern Standpoint: Reminiscences of a Grandfather.* New York: T. Whitaker, 1887.

Wilson, Charles Reagan. *Baptized in Blood: The Religion of the Lost Cause, 1865–1920.* Athens: University of Georgia Press, 1980.

Wilson, Elizabeth. *Bohemians: The Glamorous Outcasts.* New Brunswick, NJ: Rutgers University Press, 2000.

Wilson, James D. *A Pilgrim Adrift: Mark Twain and Religion.* Unpublished manuscript. Copy in author's possession.

———. "Religious and Esthetic Vision in Mark Twain's Early Career." *Canadian Review of American Studies* 17 (Summer 1986): 155–72.

Wilton, Andrew, and Tim Barringer. *American Sublime: Landscape Painting in the United States, 1820–1880.* Princeton: Princeton University Press, 2002.

Wing, Yung. *My Life in China and America.* New York: Arno, 1978.

———. "To Joe Twichell." Journal 4.75. Joseph Twichell Papers. Yale University.

Wolterstorff, Nicholas. *Art in Action: Towards a Christian Aesthetic.* Grand Rapids, MI: Eerdmans, 1980.

———. *Until Justice and Peace Embrace.* Grand Rapids, MI: Eerdmans, 1983.

Woodard, Fredrick, and Donnarae MacCann. "Minstrel Shackles and Nineteenth-Century 'Liberality' in *Huckleberry Finn.*" In James Leonard et al., *Satire or Evasion?*, 141–53.

Woodward, C. Vann. *The Burden of Southern History.* Baton Rouge: Louisiana State University Press, 1968.

Youngs, William T. *The Congregationalists.* New York: Greenwood, 1990.

Zaccara, Jennifer L. "Mark Twain, Isabel Lyon, and the 'Talking Cure': Negotiating Nostalgia and Nihilism in the Autobiography." In Kiskis and Skandera-Trombley, *Constructing Mark Twain,* 101–121. Columbia: University of Missouri Press, 2001.

Zwick, Jim. "Mark Twain and Imperialism." In *A Historical Guide to Mark Twain,* ed. Shelley Fisher Fishkin, 227–56. New York: Oxford University Press, 2002.

Index